HEAVEN BORN MERIDA AND ITS DESTINY

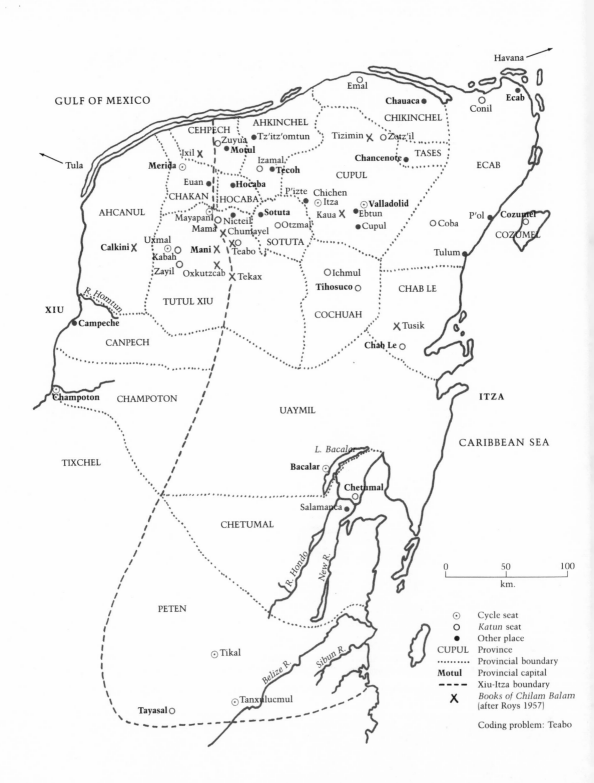

The Ordered Country: Mayan Yucatan. After Roys 1943.

HEAVEN BORN MERIDA AND ITS DESTINY

The Book of Chilam Balam of Chumayel

Translated and annotated by
Munro S. Edmonson

UNIVERSITY OF TEXAS PRESS
AUSTIN

The Texas Pan American Series

*The Texas Pan American Series is pub-
lished with the assistance of a revolving
publication fund established by the Pan
American Sulphur Company.*
The publication of this volume was as-
sisted in part by a grant from the National Endowment for the Humanities,
an independent federal agency whose
mission is to award grants to support
education, scholarship, media program-
ming, libraries, and museums in order to
bring the results of cultural activities to
the general public. Preparation was made
possible in part by a grant from the
Translations Program of the endowment.

The illustrations from the original manuscript are reproduced here by permission
of Princeton University Library.

First edition, 1986

Requests for permission to reproduce ma-
terial from this work should be sent to
Permissions, University of Texas Press,
Box 7819, Austin, Texas 78713.

Library of Congress Cataloging-in-Publication Data

Chilam Balam de Chumayel (Manuscript). English
& Mayan.
  Heaven born Merida and its destiny.
  (The Texas Pan American series)
  Text of Chilam Balam de Chumayel in English
and Mayan; notes and other materials in English.
  Includes index.
  Bibliography: p.
  1. Mayas—History. 2. Indians of Mexico—
Yucatán (State)—History. 3. Mayas—Religion and
mythology. 4. Indians of Mexico—Yucatán
(State)—Religion and mythology. 5. Mayan lan-
guage—Texts. I. Edmonson, Munro S. II. Title. III.
Series.
F1435.C5613 1986   972'.65   85-17886
ISBN 0-292-73027-6

Contents

ILLUSTRATIONS

The following illustrations from the original manuscript are reproduced courtesy of Princeton University Library.

Acknowledgments

My sincere thanks are due to a number of people for divers reasons. Victoria R. Bricker read the entire manuscript and offered me more and better advice than I have found it possible to incorporate into the work. If errors remain in the Mayan text, they are certainly not her fault, and any errors in the interpretation of it are far more likely to be mine. I shall always be grateful for her attitude of generous collegiality and for a collaboration which in this instance verges at times on coauthorship. The anonymous readers of the manuscript for the University of Texas Press have also been more than ordinarily helpful, and I have tried hard to pay proper attention to their suggestions. If I have failed in that attempt, both the fault and the loss are mine.

I am grateful to Tulane University for my sabbatical leave in 1980, and to the National Endowment for the Humanities I owe additional thanks for making it a full year and enabling me to get a lot more done—faster. This was my first leave of absence from teaching after thirty years, and I can readily understand now how sabbaticals could become habit-forming. I am deeply indebted to the late Roger T. and to Doris Z. Stone for providing me with a *pied-à-terre* outside New Orleans and for their friendship and encouragement before, during, and after my sabbatical year.

I owe my life (and the chance to finish this project) to the physicians who saw me through the anthropological nightmare of appendicitis at Chichen Itza: Orlando Orozco Herrera of Merida, Yucatan, and Charles S. Field and Edward S. Lindsey of New Orleans.

Harvey M. Bricker has been a good friend and a wise *ah kin* whose patience with my astronomical demands is deeply appreciated.

T u men in u atan
  U chilam ca nah.
T in tz'ocol in beel:
  Ma tz'ooc c et cuxtal.

Introduction

Manuscripts

The *Books of Chilam Balam* of Yucatan are so called because of the sermon (prophecy) texts that occur in some of them, which are identified as
the work of the Spokesman of the Jaguar (Chilam Balam), the official
prophet of the *katun* (twenty-year cycle). Conventionally, they are mainly
named after the towns in which they were found, and fourteen *Books*
have been so titled, even though only five contain the defining sermons
(chapters 7, 9, 10, 13, and 21 of the present volume). These are the Chumayel, Tizimin, Mani, Chan Cah, and Kaua. A sixth, the Tusik, contains
"The Language of Zuyua" (chapters 30 and 31) and is therefore germane to
this volume. The others are not: the Ixil because it is medicinal in character, the Tekax and Nah (of Teabo) because they are calendrical, and the
Hocaba, Nabula, Telchac, Tihosuco, and Tixkokob because they are lost.

Three other documents have sometimes been classified as *Books of
Chilam Balam* but should not be: the *Cuaderno de Teabo*, a medical text,
and the *Crónica de Oxkutzcab* (or *Crónica de los Xiu*) and *Crónica de
Calkiní*, purely historical works. These are certainly useful parts of general Mayan literature, as are the *Ritual of the Bacabs* and the *Títulos de
Ebtun*, but they have nothing to do with the Spokesman of the Jaguar. I
accept Barrera Vásquez' argument (1948: 39) that the *Teabo* is merely another name for the Tekax, and I accept as well his reclassification of the
Oxkutzcab.

In addition to the sermons already mentioned, the four central *Books* of
the Chilam Balam tradition—the Chumayel, Mani, Tizimin, and Kaua—
share a series of *katun* histories, and the first three of them have some
chronicles in common. Thanks to the translation of Roys (1967) in English (first edition, 1933) and those of Mediz Bolio (1930) and Barrera
(1948) in Spanish, the Chumayel has come to be the best known of all the
Books, but sections of the texts (especially the chronicles) have been
translated by a number of others. A concordance of the various manuscripts and translations will be found in appendix A.

The history of the manuscripts is ably summarized by Barrera (1948:
17ff.), updating previous treatments by Tozzer (1921) and Roys (1933). I do
not agree with Barrera and Roys that the manuscript of the Chumayel was
compiled as it stands by Juan Josef Hoil in 1782. It shares with the Tizimin and the Mani the tale of Antonio Martínez (chapter 46), which

clearly dates itself to 11 Ahau (1824–1848), and the Mani version of the
same text was copied by Juan Pío Pérez at Mani in 1837. The Chumayel
must therefore have been written between 1824 and 1837. The original
was in the hands of Audumaro Molina and then in those of the bishop of
Yucatan, Crescencio Carrillo y Ancona, by 1868. It was in Philadelphia in
1913, in Merida in 1916, in Boston in 1938, and in Durham, N.H., in
1945, was lost when Barrera wrote in 1948, and has only recently resur-
faced in the Princeton University Library (Edmonson 1970).

Unless otherwise noted, the documentation for the following assertions
is to be found in the present volume or in its predecessor, cited as the
Tizimin (Edmonson 1982). References to both works are cited by line or
note number, and both books are copiously indexed. On calendrical matters, see also Edmonson 1976.

Language

The language of the Chumayel is Yucatecan Maya, which, as the early
Franciscans noted with great relief, was and is a widespread and homoge-
neous tongue spoken in the Mexican states of Yucatan, Campeche, Quintana Roo, and Chiapas, in the Guatemalan department of Peten, and in
Belize (formerly British Honduras). Even the most deviant dialects (the
Lacandon of Chiapas and the Mopan and Itza of Belize and Guatemala)
offer only minor obstacles to intelligibility. In the peninsula of Yucatan it
is possible to differentiate between an eastern and a western dialect, the
former being identifiable with the Itza of Chichen (as opposed to those of
Peten), the latter with the Toltec Xiu. Following the usage in the
Chumayel, I have used Itza throughout to mean the Itza of Chichen unless otherwise specified. The Chichen Itza and the Toltec Xiu were the
two principal groups of elite lineages in post-Classic and colonial
Yucatan.

The town of Chumayel is close to the political and linguistic boundary
between the Itza and the Xiu, but its affiliations are clearly with the latter, and it identifies the Xiu and their language simply as Maya 'people of
the cycle'. The Tizimin, which comes from Itza territory, uses the term
Itza 'water witches' in a similar fashion and refers to the western Yucatecans as Tutul Xiu (Nahuatl 'Toltec grasses').

To the south of the Chichen Itza were the provinces of Uaymil and
Chetumal. It is my guess that they and Belize constituted a dialect area
ancestral to Mopan, but the conquest decimated their population, and the
original inhabitants were swamped by immigrants from eastern and western Yucatan.

To the southwest of Champoton, in the ancient provinces of Tixchel
and Acalan, lay the territory of the Chontal, but, while the ancestors of
both the Itza and the Xiu entered Yucatan from that direction, I find no
reason to believe that the Chontal had any particular cultural or linguistic
influence on either of them, Thompson (1970) notwithstanding. Still farther to the west, in southern Veracruz, was Nahuat country, speaking the
southern dialect of Nahuatl, and there is clear evidence of Nahuat influ-

ence on both the Itza and the Xiu, particularly the latter. Many Xiu had Nahuat names, and there is a thin scattering of Nahuat place-names: Mayapan, Zaciapan, Tzimentan, Zuyua, Pax Ueuet, P'en Cuyut, and Yucatan itself. It is perhaps surprising that there are not more, as there are in Chiapas and Guatemala. The Xiu were fond of characterizing the Itza as stupid, stuttering foreigners, but this is a political slur rather than a linguistic allegation, and it is clear that the Xiu were the more foreign (that is, Mexicanized) of the two.

The influence of Spanish on the language of the Chumayel is far greater than that of Nahuat. (And there are nearly three times as many Hispanicisms as in the Tizimin.) This corresponds to the fact that the Spanish penetration into Yucatan, like the Nahuat incursion, was primarily from the west, and the initial conversion and the linguistic as well as religious instruction occurred earlier and were more intensive at Merida and Mani than in the Itza towns. Furthermore, the Xiu saw prompt conversion as a way of making the Spanish their allies against the still pagan Itza, and the Xiu texts constantly exhort the stupid, stuttering Itza to convert and accept "our older brothers" the Spaniards.

It is congruent with this picture that the Chumayel contains a notable infusion of Latin, while the Tizimin contains none at all. To be sure, it isn't very good Latin, but it is clearly identifiable, even if not always easily deciphered. Much of the Latin appears in eighteenth-century texts, but nonetheless it seems to represent a survival of the effects of the intensive Franciscan missionary effort of the sixteenth century, especially at Merida, Mani, and Izamal.

Nearly half of the text of the Chumayel may be considered to be composed in Classical Yucatec (McQuown 1967). The latter half has undergone various degrees of modernization, but even the latest segments differ substantially from modern spoken Yucatec, and all of it presents problems of phonology, syntax, and vocabulary.

The orthography of the text is generally clear, but it is flawed at a number of points. The glottalized consonants (written *pp*, *th*, *ɔ*, *cħ*, and *k*) are not always reliably copied, and the glottal stop is not written at all. Vowel length is phonemic in Yucatec but is not always indicated. Vowel tone is also phonemic but is not marked at all. I have transcribed the text as it is written, except for changing *ɔ* to *tz'*, *cħ* to *ch'*, *pp* to *p'*, and the abbreviation *y* to *y etel* ('and, together with').

Many of the long-standing problems of Mayan lexicography have been solved by the publication of the *Diccionario Maya Cordemex*, under the direction of Alfredo Barrera Vásquez (1980). Unfortunately, the present translation was completed before this invaluable resource became available. I prepared my own card file dictionary, incorporating Brasseur 1872; Pío Pérez 1866–67; Solís Alcalá 1949; Swadesh, Alvarez, and Bastarrachea 1970; Roys 1931; Blair and Vermont-Salas 1965–67; approximately one-third of the Motul dictionary (Ciudad Real 1600); and my own notes from work with informants, principally Eleuterio Poot Yah of Hocaba and Merida. This general dictionary contained some thirty to forty thousand cards and several times that many entries. I then condensed this into a root dictionary of about four thousand entries. I have translated primarily from these two instruments, consulting other dictionaries when necessary (see the bibliography in Barrera 1980).

The lexical problems of the *Books of Chilam Balam* are severe, and it would be foolhardy to claim to have solved them all. I am satisfied that I have solved some of them, and I believe that some of these solutions are consequential beyond the minutiae of specific etymologies. Four examples will illustrate this point.

1. *Ix.* In my notes this can be a particle meaning 'she who, little, too, shoo!'; a noun for 'scales', the day name 'jaguar', or something to do with 'chalk'; or a verb for 'spoil' or something like 'lie in'. Previous translators have opted for the first two alternatives, preferring to read *ix* as a feminine marker or, failing that, as a diminutive. I find that the form can much more frequently be sensibly read as 'and'. In the nineteenth-century dictionaries (e.g., Brasseur 1872), it is frequently reduced to *x* and often appears in compounds with sentence-initial elements (*baalx, macx, hex*, etc.). I read these as 'and what', 'and who', 'and that'.

This form first occurs in the Chumayel text in "The Third Chronicle" (tenth century): *la ix u katunil cimc i* 'and that was the *katun* count of the death' (lines 295–296). Then we read *yx ma pic tz'ul u kaba* 'and Foreigners without Skirts was their name' (line 309). Or again: *buluc ahau u katunil ti ix hop'i xp̄noil lae* '11 Ahau was also the *katun* period that began Christianity' (lines 360–362).

Ix is frequently encountered as an element in place-names, earliest (and still preconquest) at *t ix meuac* (line 910). I assume that the implication here is diminutive: no important town or city is so named.

It may or may not be significant that it is not until after the conquest that we encounter an *ix* that might mean 'she', and even then the usage is extremely rare. Of the seventeen goddesses listed by Barrera (1948: 83), I am prepared to concede one: Ix Tab, goddess of the hanged. I believe all the others to be phrases introduced by 'and'. I am also willing to grant the plausibility of Ix Chel, goddess of the rainbow, who didn't make Barrera's list for some reason, and there can be no doubt about the acceptability of *ix mehen* 'daughter' or *ix ahau* 'queen'.

2. *May.* This is an even more consequential lexical problem, since it goes to the heart of the whole organization and meaning of the *Books of Chilam Balam*. This noun may signify 'dust, hoof, mild, example, wink', but by far the most frequent implication is 'cycle', specifically the cycle of thirteen *katuns*. Previous translators have passed over the term because it does not seem to have made the dictionaries, but from the contexts in which it appears I believe its meaning to be unmistakable (Chumayel, line 5315; Tizimin, lines 2121, 2914, 2942, 4879, 5067).

Thus at differing dates Mayapan, Merida, Valladolid, and other cities are referred to as *may cu* 'seat of the cycle'. Landa (Tozzer 1941: 27) acknowledges the titles *ahau can may* 'rattlesnake of the cycle' and *ah kin may* 'sun priest of the cycle' as references to the highest priesthood in Yucatan but without understanding their significance. This is the priest more commonly called the Jaguar (*balam*) or the Rattlesnake (*ahau can*), since his formal robes included the skins of both animals. He was expected to hold office for a full *katun*, and it was competition for this position of power, prestige, and profit that the *katun* histories are all about. It is the Spokesman (*chilam*) of this priest who provides the name to the *Books of Chilam Balam*.

The importance of the seat of the cycle is underlined by a number of related usages. The city that had this honor was held to be sacred: born of heaven, *ziyan caan*, or, in the case of Merida, *caan zih*. It was regarded as the capital (*tan cah* 'front city' or *tan tun* 'front stone'), and its plaza was the Plaza (*zac lac tun* 'white flat stone'; see Tozzer 1941: 230) and the religious center of the country, along with its ceiba tree (*yax che* 'green or first tree' but by color symbolism 'center tree') and its cenote (*ch'een*). It is this last feature which explains the name Mayapan 'cycle water place', which would translate back into Maya as Chi Ch'een Maya 'well mouth of the (people of the) cycle'. When Valladolid became the seat of the cycle in 1752, it was called both Mayapan and Zaciapan 'well mouth of the white sparrow hawk' as well as 'heaven born'.

The Maya were clearly the people of the cycle in post-Classic and colonial times and had been for a very long time (Edmonson 1979). The 13-*katun* cycle based on the 360-day *tun*, the central and unique feature of the Mayan calendar, appears to have been the basis for dynastic politics in the Classic period. Mayanists have been accustomed to referring to this cycle as *u kahlay katunob* 'the account of the *katuns*', a barbarism popularized by Morley (1946), but that expression properly refers to the *katun* histories. The cycle itself was called the *may*, and it was still going strong in the nineteenth century.

3. *Cangel*. Previous translators have not really known what to do with this expression, and it *is* curious. It is also spelled *canhel* and in one case *congel*; see also the unusual rebus spelling *2n hel*, line 1366. The use of the letter *g*, which does not occur in Maya, strongly suggests a conscious syncretistic pun. The clear meaning of *can hel* is 'four changers', and the reference is to the yearbearers, both as gods and as priests. But *c angel* in colonial Maya could also mean 'our angels' and probably did mean that to the nativistic sun priests, who were trying to preserve the Mayan religion against the onslaught of "their" angels.

The yearbearers were the 4 days out of the sacred 20 that could begin the 365-day year (the *hab*). As directional gods and priests they were known collectively as *can tzicnal* 'the four honored ones' (*pace* Landa, who rarely gets his Maya altogether straight and offers this as the name of a single divinity). In the period from 1539 on, these days were Kan, Muluc, Ix, and Cauac in that order, Kan being the senior member of the four. Their directional associations rotated counterclockwise annually, beginning with Kan in the east and repeating after four years.

The days took numeral prefixes from 1 to 13 successively, so the calendar round cycle that began on 1 Kan repeated after 4 times 13 or 52 years. Such a cycle began in 1581. I believe this is the reference of the expression *kin tun y abil* 'day stone year period', which is paired in the Chumayel and Tizimin with *ma ya cimlal* 'no pain death'. Roys (1967: 138) and Barrera (1948: 65) interpret these expressions as referring to diseases, but from the contexts in which they occur I am convinced that they allude to the calendar round and its sacrifices (see below).

As gods, but again also as priests, the yearbearers are identified as Fathers of the Land (*ba cabob*) and as rain gods (*chacob*), and they may also be identical with the four Stone Giants (*pauah tun*), the four winds (*ikil*), and the four death gods (*tenel ahau*). They are also closely associated with the four Burners (*ah toc*). All these sets of deities, then, are in charge of time, rain, death, the sky, and fire, and they are conceived in various connections as bearing the burden of the sun and holding up the four corners of the sky.

Because of their directional associations, the yearbearer priests also appear to be given color titles: red, white, black, and yellow for east, north, west, and south, respectively. They may all be referred to by the suffixed title *chac* 'rain priest', but the prefixed title *chac* 'red' refers to the East priest. (*Chac* may also mean 'boil, fuzz, appear, trample, big' and is the name of a lineage and a village as well, so it is not always easy to determine which meaning is intended.) In some contexts a fifth priest is added to the basic four, identified with the color *yax* 'blue/green' and the direction of the center. Unlike Roys (1967: 139, notes), I regard this usage as a Mexican aberration.

The rain priests, who apparently wore ceremonial necklaces, are referred to as necklaced rain priests (*yuuan chac*). They were also identified by honorific kinship terms (father, mother's mother, and younger brother rain priest). The yearbearer ceremonies of 11 Ahau are described in detail in chapter 15.

4. *Kin tun y abil* 'day stone year period' and *ma ya cimlal* 'no pain death, Maya death'. These two expressions have commonly been interpreted on the basis of colonial dictionaries as 'drought' and 'pestilence', respectively. I believe that this interpretation is usually (though perhaps not always) wrong as a reading of the *Chumayel* text. The phrases occur as a couplet in lines 5039–5040 (and in the Tizimin, lines 319–320, 2615–2616). *Kin tun y abil* occurs alone in lines 1247, 5158, 5224, and 6178; and *ma ya cimlal* occurs in lines 112, 338, 2643, 4922, 5325, and 6283 (also in the Tizimin, lines 675, 722, 2770, 2920, 3646, 3932, 4090, 4537, 4637, 4771, and 5269). I read them as 'calendar round' and 'no pain death', respectively, and I consider the latter expression as a euphemism for sacrifice, perhaps specifically for calendar round sacrifices.

If the calendar round in the Mayapan calendar (see below) began on 1 Kan, as I believe it did, there are eight such beginnings in the twenty *katuns* between 1441 and 1848. If the calendar round began on 1 Ik, as I believe it did in the Tikal calendar (see below), there are eight such beginnings in the same time span, but they land in different *katuns*. Four *katuns* of the twenty do not correspond to the beginning of a calendar round in either system.

Six of the eight calendar round beginnings in the Tikal calendar correspond to *katuns* in which either *kin tun y abil* or *ma ya cimlal* or both are mentioned in the Chumayel or the Tizimin. The calendar rounds beginning in 1710 and 1814 are missed. And six of the eight calendar round beginnings in the Mayapan calendar correspond to *katuns* in which either *kin tun y abil* or *ma ya cimlal* or both are mentioned in the Chumayel or the Tizimin. The calendar rounds beginning in 1477 and 1581 are missed. The texts for the remaining four *katuns* (those without calendar round beginnings in either system) include mention of *ma ya cimlal* once in each book (Chumayel, line 4922 and Tizimin, line 3932), both in relation to the same *katun* (beginning in 1638).

There are twenty-four occurrences of one or the other of the two expressions, separately or together, in the two *Books*, thirteen in the Tizimin and eleven in the Chumayel. In sixteen of the twenty-four cases the contexts are clearly calendrical; in the remaining cases they concern illness, famine, or warfare. I conclude that it is likely that the colonial Maya calculated the calendar round in both the Mayapan and the Tikal calendars and that they used the two expressions under discussion to refer both to the calendar round and its sacrifices and to drought and plague. But the commoner usage seems to have been the former.

Science

Mayan science was highly but differentially developed, and scientific aspects of Mayan culture receive distinctive treatment in the Chumayel. References to biology are numerous (agriculture, animals, plants, food, medicine; see the index), though less full than in other sources, such as the Kaua or the *Ritual of the Bacabs* (Roys 1965). The physical sciences receive very short shrift. Chemistry is largely a matter of cuisine. Physics and geology scarcely appear. Geography is largely ritual, focusing upon meteorology and ceremonially important places (caves, cenotes, the sea, the directions, wells, roads, cities, towns, villages, ports, and Yucatan's meager hills; see the index and appendix B). Psychology is implied here and there by assumptions about perception and motivation.

But the highest development of Mayan science occurred in mathematics and astronomy, and both are correspondingly prominent in the Chumayel, two chapters of which (32 and 39) are entirely concerned with calendrical and astronomical matters. The Maya were extraordinarily fond of measuring and counting things. This is reflected in the language itself, which has several hundred numeral classifiers. They counted things by the pack, by the pile, by the stack, by the mound, heap, bend, pinch, fragment, fold, bunch, bundle, piece, cup, cask, bowl, plate, fistful, handful, armload, netload, and so on and on. They found out that there were 11,200 Itza and 6,050 pyramids in Yucatan. They measured value in cacao beans and quetzal feathers. They measured linear distance by the thumb joint, the thumb, the palm, the span, the foot, the forearm, the pace, the armspan, a man's length, the shot (the distance a man can shoot an arrow, perhaps a hundred meters), the shout (the distance a man's voice carries, perhaps a kilometer), the rest or stop (the distance a man can carry a load before resting, perhaps four kilometers), and the sleep (a day's travel). They used a measuring stick (*p'iz te*) to survey land in "paces" analogous to the

Spanish *vara* (but presumably shorter, as the Maya themselves are). And above all they measured time.

Not all the above units appear in the Chumayel, but a number of them are used metaphorically in relation to the calendar (particularly the fold, cup, bowl, plate, cask, foot, pace, shot, shout, and rest), and all these are frequently mentioned. The fundamental units in the counting of time were the *kin* 'days, suns'.

The Maya had no clocks, and their conceptions of the divisions of day and night were gestural indications of the movements of the sun and stars. They were correspondingly imprecise—nothing like Greek geometry developed in Mayan mathematics. But Mayan arithmetic was sophisticated and precise, and the Mayan calendar was a marvel of both mathematical and astronomical accuracy.

The number series is named in Maya in decimal fashion, with separate roots for each numeral from 1 through 10 and compounds for the numerals from 11 through 19. However, the word for '20' is simply the word for 'man' (*uinic*), and most higher numbers are counted vigesimally in units metaphorically equated with 20 and its multiples (*kal* 'armload' = 20, *bak* 'coil' = 400, *pic* '?knuckle' = 8,000, and *chil* '?occasions' = 3,200,000). Linguistically it was a decimal system, but conceptually it was a vigesimal one.

The *Tzol Kin*.   The basic unit of the calendar was a period of 20 named days, the *uinal* (see appendix C). The names of the days are evocative, archaic, and broadly similar in meaning in the various calendar systems of nuclear Middle America, though many of them cannot be clearly translated, particularly not in Yucatec. The myth of the origin of the *uinal* is given in chapter 20 together with folk etymologies for the meanings of the day names. They are almost always puns. In effect, the *uinal* is a second and sacred number system, and it is entirely vigesimal.

Along with the cycle of the day names was the cycle of the 13 sacred day numbers, the *xoc kin*. These were counted permutatively and concurrently with the day names: 1 Imix, 2 Ik, 3 Akbal, 4 Kan, 5 Chicchan, etc. The number count from 1 to 13 and then from 1 to 7 completes the *uinal*, which the Maya noted tersely: "13 and 7 make 1." Thus the numerals 1 and 7 came to represent the concepts of alpha and omega, the beginning and the end, and the unity of the divine.

If a given *uinal* begins with 1, its successors will follow a 13-*uinal* sequence running 1, 8, 2, 9, 3, 10, 4, 11, 5, 12, 6, 13, 7. It then starts over. Thus in this cycle, too, 1 is the beginning and 7 is the end. The completed cycle of 13 *uinals* constitutes a *tzol kin* or 'count of days'. This cycle of 260 days was the intertribal calendar of Middle America from Costa Rica to Michoacan. Because 20 has the factors 4 and 5, the Maya were impressed with the one-fifth *tzol kin* ($4 \times 13 = 52 \times 5 = 260$ days) and the one-quarter *tzol kin* ($5 \times 13 = 65 \times 4 = 260$ days) and used those cycles in ritual and divination along with the complete *tzol kin* of 260 days.

The *Tun*.   Because the Maya counted vigesimally, it is likely that they originally counted *uinals* by twenties as well as by thirteens (as the Cakchiquel of the seventeenth century still did), thus reaching a cycle of 400 days. However, they became persuaded at an early date that a cycle which more closely approximated the solar year would be more convenient, and they settled on a cycle of 18 *uinals*, or 360 days, which they called the *tun* 'stone'. All the *uinals* of the *tun* began with the day Imix and ended with the day Ahau, and their numeral coefficients followed the same sequence as the *tzol kin*: 1, 8, 2, 9, 3, 10, etc. This cycle is neither named nor exploited in any other Middle American calendar, though it is implicit in the cycle of the 365-day year.

From long before the birth of Christ down to the middle of the eighteenth century, the Maya counted time in *tuns*. As with the *uinals*, they counted them by both thirteens and twenties. The 13-*tun* cycle simply started over, and it seems to have remained unnamed, but the 20-*tun* cycle was numerologically more interesting. Called the *katun* 'pile of stones', it became the basis of the Long Count Mayan calendar. As in the *tun*, all *uinals* within the *katun* began with the day Imix and ended with the day Ahau, at least before 1539—after 1539 they began with Ahau. Whether they are last or first, the numerical coefficients of these Ahau days yield a cycle of 260 *tuns* or 13 *katuns*.

The period of the *katun* (7,200 days) divided by 13 gives 553 cycles of 13 and a remainder of 11. Thus the sequence of the coefficients of the Ahau days that ended (or, later, began) the *katun* followed the order 13, 11, 9, 7, 5, 3, 1, 12, 10, 8, 6, 4, 2. This cycle of 13 *katuns* was called the *may*, a cycle of 260 years minus 1,300 days, 160 days short of 256 years of 365 days each. It was the basis of the longest calendar count in general use in post-Classic and colonial times, and it is fundamental to the religion and politics of the Chumayel.

There was continuing disagreement over the correct counting of this cycle. The Xiu and the Peten Itza followed the Classic Mayan cycle and counted the *may* as beginning with 6 Ahau and ending on 8 Ahau. The Chichen Itza counted it as beginning with 11 Ahau and ending on 13 Ahau. (Aberrant cycles beginning with 1, 4, 5, and 13 Ahau also appear to be alluded to in the Chumayel, though these may be late or even non-Mayan speculations.) It is convenient to identify the 6 to 8 cycle as Xiu and the 11 to 13 cycle as (Chichen) Itza.

Like *uinals* and *tuns*, *katuns* were counted by twenties as well as by thirteens, 20 *katuns* making up a *baktun* '400 stones'. The Maya wrote Long Count dates on their Classic monuments and in their books using this unit and a convention of place value enumeration. A bar was 5, a dot was 1, and the symbol for zero was ⬭. There were glyphs for the *baktun*, *katun*, *tun*, *uinal*, and *kin*. Thus a typical Long Count date may be transcribed as 11.17.0.0.0 (11 *baktuns*, 17 *katuns*, no *tuns*, no *uinals*, no *kins*). All these units were counted vigesimally from 0 to 19 except for the *uinals*, which were counted from 0 to 17, thus totaling 18. (Zero in Maya is *m ix baal* 'no little thing' or *ma hun* 'not one'.) The Maya stopped carving Long Count dates on their monuments in the *katun* ending 10.6.0.0.0 (948), but they did not stop using them. Contrary to what has usually been supposed, Long Count dates are explicitly mentioned in the Chumayel; the latest one known is the one cited above, 11.17.0.0.0, corresponding to 1559, the beginning of *katun* 9 Ahau. There is clear evidence that the Maya were still counting them at 12.0.0.0.0 (1618).

The *Hab*.   The use of the *tun*, *katun*, and *baktun* was unique to the Yucatecan Maya, but they shared with the other cultures of nuclear Middle America the 260-day *tzol kin* and the 365-day *hab* or "vague year." They reached this cycle by counting 18 *uinals* of 20 days each and adding another *uinal* of 5 days. The *uinals* of the *hab* are different from those of the *tun* because of these extra 5 days, so they were distinguished by being given names, and their days were numbered serially from 0 to 19 (or, in the last *uinal*, from 0 to 4; see appendix C).

Also because of the extra 5 days, the *tzol kin* count operated differently within the *hab* from the way it worked in the *tun*. The first day of the year advanced by 5 day names each year, and, since 5 goes into 20 4 times, only 4 of the 20 sacred days (every fifth one) could begin the year. These were the yearbearers (*ah cuch hab*) or the four changers (*can hel*). The yearbearer that began the first *uinal* of a given year also began all the others.

Different calendars used different yearbearers. The Olmecs, for example, used their equivalents of Type I (Imix, Cimi, Chuen, Cib). The Quiche, Cakchiquel, Ixil, and Classic Maya used Type II (Ik, Manik, Eb, Caban). The Aztecs, Tzotzil, and Tzeltal used Type III (Akbal, Lamat, Ben, Etz'nab). The colonial Maya used Type IV (Kan, Muluc, Ix, Cauac). The Type V set (Chicchan, Oc, Men, Ahau) is the focus of the Yucatecan Burner cycle of fire ceremonies, which is completed once in each quarter *tzol kin* (65 days). Each of the yearbearer sets is ranked; Kan, for example, is the senior yearbearer in the colonial Mayan system (see appendix C).

Since 13 goes into 365 28 times with a remainder of 1, the numeral coefficient of the first day of the year advanced by 1 each year, thus producing a cycle of 13 years, each such cycle being associated with a direction. The cycle beginning with 1 Kan was east, 1 Muluc was north, 1 Ix west, and 1 Cauac south. The same day appeared with the same coefficient only after all four cycles had been completed, producing the *kin tun y abil* or calendar round of 52 years. In the colonial calendar, the calendar round began on 1 Kan in 1581, for example.

The yearbearer for each year was also associated with a direction, the yearbearer for the current year always being seated in the east. At the beginning of the 5 dreaded days of the final *uinal*, Uayeb 'specter steps', the year's end ceremonies were initiated. These 5 were called nameless days (*x ma kaba kin*), although they were numbered and named normally both in the *tzol kin* count and in the *hab* count. The yearbearers were then rotated counterclockwise and the new year ceremonies were held, the yearbearer for the new year taking his seat in the east.

The general relationship among these various cycles was well understood by the Maya. They realized that 73 *tzol kins* equaled 52 *habs* (52 × 365 = 73 × 260). They knew that 72 *habs* equaled 73 *tuns* (72 × 365 = 73 × 360). And they calculated that 9 × 65 = 13 × 45 = 585, just a day more than the Venus year of 584 days! They concluded that they were right in thinking 9 and 13 to be important.

On the Classic Mayan monuments, formal dates are recorded in all three of the major cycles that have been described. Such a date is preceded by an initial series glyph to warn of its coming. Then follow the Long Count, *tzol kin*, and *hab* dates, for example, 11.16.0.0.0   13 Ahau 8 Xul, which was November 13, 1539 (Gregorian). This was the last day of the Tikal calendar.

The Tikal Calendar. From the earliest known dates of cycle 7 (353 B.C.) to 1539, the Maya used the classical calendar, first identified at Tikal. From 1539 to 1752 they used the colonial calendar, inaugurated at Mayapan, and from 1752 to 1848 (and perhaps later), they used a second colonial calendar inaugurated at Valladolid. Certain aberrant inscriptions suggest a fourth calendar, largely found in the Usumacinta Valley, but that does not affect the dating of the Chumayel (Edmonson 1976).

The Tikal calendar used Type II yearbearers, numbered the days of the *uinals* of the *hab* from 0 to 19, and counted *katuns* terminally. It used the Xiu cycle (the *may*), ending in 8 Ahau. Its last *katun*, 13 Ahau, ended on 11.16.0.0.0 (1539).

The Mayapan Calendar. In or shortly before 1539, a calendrical congress was held to resolve the Xiu-Itza dispute over the cycle. This resulted in the promulgation of a new calendar which both groups accepted, inaugurated first by the Itza in 1539 at Mayapan and then slightly later in the year at Merida by the Xiu. The Xiu compromised by accepting 11 Ahau as the beginning of a new cycle. The Itza compromised by accepting initial dating of the *katun*. They both compromised by agreeing to disagree: the Itza seated the new cycle at Mayapan, the Xiu at Merida. The date chosen was dictated by calendrical considerations—the conjunction of the cycles was unusually favorable to the change contemplated.

The Mayapan calendar was inaugurated by the Itza on 11 Ahau, 80 days before the end of *katun* 13 Ahau on 11.16.0.0.0. It differed from the calendar of Tikal by adopting Type IV yearbearers, numbering the days of the *uinal* from 1 to 20, and naming the *katuns* from their initial days rather than their final ones. It did not alter the Long Count. The change was literally epochal. As with B.C. and A.D. centuries, Mayan dates for the *may* and the *katun* before 1539 are counted backward from their endings, and those afterward are counted forward from their beginnings.

The Valladolid Calendar. As dated in the Mayapan calendar, *katun* 4 Ahau began in 1737. Five years before it ended, a new calendar was promulgated at Valladolid. By calendrical coincidence, in 1752 the name day of the *katun* (4 Ahau) fell on the second day of the Mayan year. The Itza sun priests, who were due to be obsolete in 1797 (the end of 13 Ahau), figured out that by redesigning the *katun* as a period of 24 *habs* instead of 20 *tuns* the initiation of future *katuns* would always fall on the second day of the year. But, if they also converted the *may* into a cycle of 24 new "*katuns*" of 24 years each, they (or their descendants) could remain in office until 2088! They therefore inaugurated *katun* 4 Ahau in Valladolid on the 24-*hab* basis, ending it in 1776.

All dates in the Tizimin and Chumayel subsequent to 1752 are given in the Valladolid calendar. In the Chumayel, however, it occurred to some clever and overzealous copyist to apply the system retroactively, thus making rather a hash of various post-Classic and early colonial dates. Fortunately, it is a hash that can be unscrambled.

During the relevant period, the discrepancies between the Valladolid (V) and Mayapan (M) calendars were as follows.

	V	M	Difference
8 Ahau began	1392	1441	49 years
6 Ahau began	1416	1461	45 years
4 Ahau began	1440	1480	40 years
2 Ahau began	1464	1500	36 years
13 Ahau began	1488	1520	32 years
11 Ahau began	1512	1539	27 years
9 Ahau began	1536	1559	23 years

Thus our scribe refers to 8 Ahau as beginning 151 years before 1543 (line 2722: 49 years off); he dates Francisco de Montejo's landing at Ecab in 1526 to 11 Ahau (line 2676: 32 years off) and Montejo the Nephew's landing at Campeche in 1540 to 1513 (line 2705: 27 years off); and he places the coming of Christianity in 1546 at 1519 (lines 365, 2722: 27 years off). Even his mistakes are systematic. Somehow getting the impression that he was in 9 Ahau and expressing the correct Mayapan date of 1518, he applies the 23-year correction for 9 Ahau but applies it backward—landing 23 years off in 1541 (line 2743)! Well, nobody's perfect.

The *Año.* The Maya thought it very clever of the Spanish to have their own year. They learned it rapidly and found it child's play. By the time Landa got around to asking them (in 1553) when their year began, they were able to give him a deceptively simple but absolutely correct answer: Sunday, July 16. The 365-day cycle was nothing new to them, of course, and they figured out how to handle leap years by reckoning them separately.

Every Christian leap year day fell in a Mayan year with the yearbearer Ix, and the day 1 Ix initiated the second half of the calendar round in 1555. In the only really direct correlational statement in the Chumayel, written in 1556, it is clear that the July 16 date is pegged to the year 10 Ix, 1551. The true Christian date for any one particular year can thus be reached by adding to July 16 one day for each of the intervening Ix years for dates before 1551 or subtracting them for dates thereafter. The Maya did that in their heads, but they simplified matters by clinging permanently to the July 16 correlation of 1551. It was not until the present century that the Europeans generally accepted the Goodman-Martínez-Thompson (GMT) correlation and acknowledged that the Maya were correct (Edmonson 1976).

The only direct correlational statement in the Tizimin, in a text written around 1618 to 1623, also dates the beginning of the Mayan year to July 16 but pegs this not to 1 Ix, the middle of the calendar round, but to 1 Kan, its beginning. This was 1581. But the priest who wrote this must surely have been aware that the true correlational date was half a calendar round (26 years) earlier, including 7 Ix years (from 1 Ix in 1555 to 12 Ix in

1579 inclusive). All references to the Christian year in the *Books* are tied
to the July 16 date for 1 Pop, the first day of the colonial Mayan year. And
that was true only for 1548 to 1551.

The sophistication of Mayan chronology and the reliability of their histories can be appraised by a parallel sequence of events, reported by the
Chumayel and by Landa (Tozzer 1941: 42) as follows.

Chumayel	Landa
1. 1441 Beginning of 8 Ahau	1. 1441 Fall of Mayapan
2. 1451 Fall of Mayapan (Mani)	
3. 1484 Sacrifices	
4. 1500 Fire	2. 1464 Hurricane and fire
5. 1516 Plague	3. 1480 Plague
6. 1536 Murder of Pot Xiu	4. 1496 War
	5. 1516 Plague
	6. 1566 Landa's *Relación*

The Chumayel dates events 3, 4, and 5 only to the nearest *katun*, though
it dates event 6 to the day. Landa dates backward from the year in which
he was writing—in Spain in 1566. Thus he estimates event 5 at 50 years
earlier than 6, 4 at 20 years before that, 3 another 16, 2 yet another 16,
and 1 another 23 years before, totaling 125 years.

Accepting Landa's estimate that a plague occurred 50 years before he
wrote, we find confirmation in the Chumayel: there was a plague in 1516
or, at least, in 2 Ahau. Landa's second plague, his event 5, is simply an
illusion. The 20-year interval between the 1516 plague and war in 1536 is
confirmed by Chumayel event 6, as is the fire 16 years before the plague
there, which could have occurred in 1500, the first year of 2 Ahau. The
Chumayel doesn't mention the hurricane. Chumayel event 3 has been included because other translators have considered *ma ya cimlal* to be a
plague. I don't think so (*vide supra*), and in any case it is out of order. The
exact year of Chumayel event 2 actually comes from the Mani. Landa's
event 1 can only be construed as an estimate of the beginning of 8 Ahau:
right *katun*, wrong year for the fall of Mayapan. Landa's total of 125 years
is fundamentally correct, and so are most of his intervals, but I conclude
that, while Mayan sources are sometimes less precise, they are more
credible.

The Julian Calendar.   All the European dates in the Chumayel are in the
Julian calendar. Despite the promulgation of the Gregorian calendar by
the pope in 1582, the Maya clung to the Julian one throughout. In the sixteenth and seventeenth centuries, the Gregorian calendar added 10 days
to Julian dates (in the eighteenth it added 11, and in the twentieth 12). It
was only in some late marginal notes of the middle nineteenth century
that the Maya began using Gregorian dates. Since the Gregorian reform
was accepted immediately in the Spanish world (as opposed to the later
eighteenth century in the English one), this is an interesting documentation of the autonomy of Mayan calendrical thought.

The *Semana*.   The Mayan reaction to the 7-day week merits special comment. They realized promptly that the days of the Spanish week acted as
yearbearers, constituting (leap years ignored) a 7-year cycle. (That is, the

365-day year contains 52 weeks plus 1 day.) Eventually they figured out that because of leap year these Christian "yearbearers" occur in cycles of 4, and it takes 28 years before any particular 4-year set will be repeated. The numbers 4 and 7 were already important in Mayan numerology, so they comfortably added the weekdays and their planetary associations to the native cosmology and used them for divination.

The Arts

The Chumayel contains numerous direct allusions to dance, music, and architecture (see the index) and indirect references to painting and sculpture. Sometimes these allusions are quite graphic—particular artifacts are named; colors are specified; everyday objects are given metaphorical significance (loincloths, drums, lances, plates, ropes, et al.). While the primary emphasis is placed on literature, philosophy, and history, which are closely tied to religion, all the Mayan arts are intimately related to the calendar, from poetry to dress and from ideology to cuisine.

Cuisine.   Let us begin with the least verbal of the arts: cookery. Modern Yucatecan cuisine is regionally distinctive and delicious. It appears to have been no less so in the seventeenth century. Poultry (turkey, curassow, quail) was baked, steamed, roasted, broiled, and stewed. Various saltwater and freshwater fish, crab, conch, and turtle were cooked. There was plenty of game (deer, agouti, armadillo, peccary, paca, iguana), and it too was well prepared. (Scent glands were a problem with paca, armadillo, and agouti, but properly treated they are delicious fare, and roasted iguana tail was a delicacy.) Sauces, colorful and savory, were oriented to the four directions: red (add red chile or achiote), white (how about *pollo en atole?*), black (stew it with ground charred chile—an acquired taste), yellow (you can do marvelous things with fresh corn, which itself came in several colors), or even green ("greens" attained ceremonial significance on the basis of fresh green chiles and a number of local leafy vegetables). The Mayan dedication to bees and their honey led to a number of sweet sauces. They made underground ovens (*pib*) for true barbecuing, and *pollo pibil* is a standard modern result in the regional restaurants.

Mayan vegetables were a national treasure rather than a mere resource. Honeyed baked yams? Stuffed cabbage? Lima bean soup? Cassava? How do you want your squash—baked, stewed, roasted—or would you prefer fried squash flowers? Or (again this is on modern menus) how about *huevos motuleños*—a tortilla with tomatoes, cooked vegetables, refried beans, cheese, and a fried egg on top? Or *papadzules*—a hard-boiled egg wrapped in a soft tortilla with a delicate tomato sauce flavored with ground amaranth and pumpkin seeds? Baked fresh corn? Bean soup? Stewed pumpkin? And, if you are Aztec enough to want your food spicier, try *x ni pek* 'dog's nose', hot chiles in a fresh tomato sauce.

A variety of native fruits added to the menu: mamey, fig, nance, custard apple, melon. Well, have a cigar and another cup of mead or a gourd of chocolate. Most of these foodstuffs are referred to in the Chumayel, particularly in relation to the ceremonial examination of the lords, which took place in conjunction with a feast (see chapters 30 and 31 and the index).

Toponymy. In the welter of titles, gods, metaphors, personal names, puns, riddles, kennings, and ritual in the Chumayel, it is important to be able to identify a real place-name when one occurs. Many of the glamour names that color Mayan religion and literature also adorn the landscape of Yucatan. As in most systems of toponymy, Mayan place-names make use of a number of classifiers emphasizing location and the kinds of locations that are of particular interest. These include at (*chi, ti*), in (*ich*), front (*tan*), back (*pach*), right (*noh*), left (*tz'ic*), between (*xol*), inside (*t u y ol*), below (*hom*), above (*ok*), near (*nak*), east (*lakin*), north (*xaman*), west (*chikin*), south (*nohol*), and country (*peten*).

Among the natural features that are emphasized are water (*a, ha*), land (*luum*), hole (*hol*), hill (*uitz, puuc*), island (*oy*), cenote (*tz'onot, ch'een*), cave (*kop*), forest (*kax*), shore (*pay*), sea (*kaknab*), sand (*zuz*), swamp (*putun*), tree (*che*), stone (*tun*), spring (*ak, zayab*), and the names of an almost indefinite number of plants (e.g., *nicte* 'flower') and animals (e.g., *balam* 'jaguar'), as well as features of human origin: pyramid (*eb*), house (*na*), mound (*mul*), mask (*koh*), field (*col*), oven (*pib*), painting or writing (*tz'ib, bon*), settlement (*cah*), gate (*hol tun*), and wall (*paa, tulum*).

A more problematic usage in Yucatec is the incorporation of numerals into place-names: Hunuc Ma, Caucel, Ox Cum, Can Ul, Ti Ho, Uuc y Ab Nal, Uaxac Tun, Bolon Te Uitz, Lahun Chable, Oxlahun Zuyua. This usage seems to be confined to the first thirteen numerals and presumably had calendrical significance, but I don't know what it was. Larger numerals were occasionally used in place-names, apparently as metaphoric status claims (*kal, pic, bak*). A number of special usages distinguished the rank of cities of real importance, rather in the manner of the Spanish hierarchy (*rancho, ranchería, cantón, paraje, congregación, pueblo, villa, villa real, ciudad, capital, metrópoli,* etc.). The Spanish carried this sort of thing pretty far—and so did the Maya. Compare Nuestra muy Noble y muy Leal Ciudad de Santiago de los Caballeros de Antigua de Guatemala and Tan Tun, Tan Cah, ich Caan Ziy Ho, u Hetz' Katun, May Cu, Mayapan, Yax Che, Zac Lac Tun 'the first stone, the first town, in heaven born Five, seat of the *katun*, seat of the cycle, the cycle well, the first tree, the Plaza', which was Merida in Maya, at least for a time.

Names of small villages are commonly introduced by *ix* 'little', and sometimes a certain wry humor surfaces, as in Muxu P'ip' 'bursting at the seams', Zahab Balam 'spooked jaguar', or Tz'ooc 'the end'. There is a general preoccupation with water (*a, ha, ch'en, tz'onot, ak, zayab*) in the place-names, understandable enough in view of Yucatan's total lack of streams and the natural beauty of its underground water sources. The towns and villages are referred to poetically through their water sources as "the wells and springs," which were considered sacred. Only rarely and coincidentally are calendrical names applied to places. Time was of course on the roads, and places were merely way stations on the journey of the sun.

Yucatan was divided into eighteen provinces at the time of the Spanish conquest, though only some of them are mentioned in the Chumayel: Chakan, Chikin Ch'el, Cozumel, Ecab, Uaymil, Tutul Xiu, and Chable. It can hardly be coincidental that the number of provinces matches the number of *uinals* in the *tun*, but this fact does not appear to be particularly stressed. The Maya called Yucatan the Ordered Country, the Land of the Ceiba, or the Four-Part Country (the fifth part was the center). The expression Cycle Country (*mayab*), which occurs elsewhere, does not appear in the *Books*, nor does the expression Land of the Deer and Pheasant. If my surmise that there were 13 numeral prefixes for cities is correct, all the major cycles of the calendar (4, 5, 13, and 18) may have been projected onto Mayan geography. It is not clear how 7, 9, and 20 figured in, but they must have been involved somehow terrestrially as they were cosmologically. After all, Yucatan was the Ordered Country (*tzol peten*).

The place-names mentioned in the Chumayel are listed in the index, and a ritual gazetteer of 171 of them will be found in chapter 12 and appendix B.

Onomastics.   The Yucatecans do not appear to have used the naming system, based on the *uinal*, that was employed throughout Middle America to name individuals. They knew about it, of course, but the only example in the Chumayel is Nahuat: Five Flower. This appears in both Nahuat and Maya (Macuilxuchit, Ho Nicte), but Flower is not a day name in Maya. The naming of persons in Yucatan was almost entirely a matter of lineage.

A proper name in Maya was always binary: it was composed of a maternal patronymic and a paternal one, in that order. Thus Yax Chuen's mother's father was a Yax and his father was a Chuen. Patrilineages were the basic units of Mayan society, and they were rigidly exogamous. If Yax Chuen's wife were Ek Balam, their children would be named Balam Chuen. They would be eligible to marry someone named Yax Ek or Ek Yax, including their first cross-cousins, but they could not marry a Chuen or a Balam. Sometimes the name was preceded by the word Na 'mother', as in Na Tzin Yabun, but that was not mandatory. It may indicate cases in which the maternal patrilineage had higher status.

Having all one's siblings running around with the same name presented obvious problems. These were solved by adding titles, usually prefixed, and nicknames, usually suffixed, as in Ah Kin Na Ahau Pech Chan 'the sun priest (mother) lord tick the younger' (the example is a hypothetical composite) or Uayom Ch'ich' Chich 'sleeping bird the strong' (lines 695–696). Sometimes the order of elements was inverted, as in Kin Ich Kak Mo 'sun face fire macaw' or Kukul Can Ah Nacxit 'quetzal snake priest of Four Leg'. Proper names were sometimes inflected, particularly the maternal patronymic, taking the suffix -Vl or -*il*, as in Yaxal Chac, Kukul Can, or Ulil Ahau. This may have been primarily for euphony and clarity of enunciation.

A number of the 150 to 200 recorded lineage names were common to the Xiu and the Itza: Ahau, Amayte, Ay, Chac, Coc, Itzam, Kak, Kau, Mo, Puc, Zac. Others were not. The Xiu frequently had Nahuat names:

Cacalli, Cinti, Etzti, Huehuet, Ihuit, Nahuat, Panti, Tecome, Temit, Teut, Tlaxti, Tutul, Tzonti, Xiu, Xupan. The Itza did not. A number of the lineage names were calendrical—general: Ahau, Yax, Zac; Itza: Balam, Can, Ceh, Chuen, Hun, Ik, Kin, Lahun, Mac, Tun, Uac, Uuc, Zip; Xiu: Acat, Callan, Cuat, Ho, Itzti, Thul, Xuchit. Animals and plants figure prominently. In addition to those already named, we find Buzzard (*kuch*), Puma (*coh*), Quetzal (*kuk*), Squirrel (*cuc*), Possum (*och*), Snail (*ul*), Corn Ear (*nal*), Yam (*iz*), Annona (*op*), Bird (*ch'ich'*), and many others. Body parts also occur: Ich 'eye', Chi 'mouth', Ol 'heart', Mex 'whisker', Chan 'molar'.

With the Spanish conquest the baptized Indians received Christian names: Antonio, Lorenzo, Martín, etc. Few of these are cited in the Chumayel, which is after all dedicated to the preservation of the Mayan tradition. By the early eighteenth century, the naming system and the associated matrimonial rules of the preconquest Maya had become more or less dead letters. But many, perhaps even most, of the traditional lineage names have survived into modern times.

It is of interest to note that the Maya did not apply their own naming system to the gods. A few gods received binary names—Muzen Cab, Kak Mo, and Itzam Na, and perhaps Tenel Ahau, Kukul Can, Cab Ain, and Ahau Can, and just *maybe* Ix Chel, Ix Tab, and Ah Puch'. The Maya may have been skeptical about the gods' ability to abide by the rules of exogamy, or they may have had other reasons, but they do not appear to have worked out the genealogy of the gods. They knew where they and the gods were in time, and that was enough.

The Maya identified themselves the way they identified everything else: in couplets. A profound dualism is intrinsic to Mayan discourse, both formal and informal, but it becomes coercive in formal speech. A Mayan noble "born and engendered" who knew his ancestry on both sides of the family was eligible to become a *hal ach uinic*, a 'true virile man', a ruler. There is a dialectic to procreation. The Maya felt it keenly, and they expressed this awareness not only in their identification of themselves but in the poetry of their formal speech and writing. Like *all* other expressions of the Mayan soul, the Chumayel is entirely composed in couplets.

Poetry. The couplets of Mayan formal discourse and poetry are primarily semantic. In some cases they are emphasized by syntactic parallelism. A frequently repeated couplet is:

Hulom kuk	Come is the quetzal;
Ulom yaxum	Come is the blue bird. (lines 425–426)

Here the root verbs *huul* and *ul* are synonyms for 'arrive', identically inflected and followed by two nouns of closely similar meaning. This is not, however, a poetic rule:

Çi uinal	The month was born
Çihci kin u kaba	And the day name was born. (lines 2041–2042)

A perfectly strong couplet may be made without any syntactic
parallelism:

Yax coc ay mut	The center priest Coc Ay the Crier
U u ich ti y ahaulil	Was the face in the lordship.
	(lines 1769–1770)

Often the scansion of a weak couplet appears to be coerced by surround-
ing strong ones:

T u nohochil	For the great,
T u chanchanil	For the very small.
Minan to nohoch can	There may be no great teacher
Ti u hach çatal	Who can really forgive
Caan	Heaven
Y etel luum ti ob i	And earth for them. (lines
	2541–2546)

As in the last line here, the deictic particles *e* and *i* are phrase or sentence
terminals and are often helpful in tracing syntax and hence scansion. That
the problematic middle couplet in this passage is correctly scanned is
confirmed by the parallelism of *nohoch* 'great' and *hach* 'really, very'
(both nouns in Maya), and it may be that there is more of a relationship
between 'teach' and 'forgive' than my translation suggests.

The opening lines of "The First Chronicle" present a similar case:

U kahlay	The account
U xocan katunob uchc i	Of the counted *katuns*
U chictahal u chi ch'een ytza	Of the appearance of the Chichen Itza
U chi lae	Says this. (lines 1–4)

The first couplet is strong and obvious. The second is something of a pun
on *chi* 'mouth', which is poetically related to 'face' and hence to appearance. It is thus both formally linked to the 'mouth of the well of the Itza'
and semantically aligned with the preceding verb.

There are strong couplets and weak couplets, but I do not believe that
any part of the Chumayel is composed in "prose." Scansion problems are
often produced by copyists' errors and omissions. I have tried to indicate
these and, sometimes, to supply the latter. I remain uncertain about the
proper scansion of vocatives ("O Fathers") or direct discourse ("he said"),
and I have tried to fit my treatment of them to the context, with resulting
inconsistencies. Note also the problem of "Zuyua" in chapter 30.

Scansion of Mayan poetry is totally dependent upon semantics, and,
while other linguistic clues may be provided, they do not have to be (see
Burns 1980). The linkage between the lines is dependent upon a degree
of synonymy or antinomy between two or more key words, but they
may even be different parts of speech, provided that they are linked by
meaning:

Thirteen folds of *katuns* they resided
   At Champoton. (lines 29–30)

Here a locational verb is keyed to a locational noun. Or again:

They were removed there
   At Babylonia. (lines 1417–1418)

The keys are a locational particle and a locational noun.

    When the key to a couplet is a pun, it obviously cannot be translated satisfactorily. Couplets of this sort are explained in the notes when I understood them. A similar problem is presented by kennings, more or less esoteric symbolic meanings superimposed on everyday words. A number of these are explained in the two chapters on riddles (30 and 31). Many more can be decoded by context. I have largely kept to a literal translation, so the reader will just have to learn that sun means beginning and moon means end, that monkeys : peasants, older brothers : nobles or Spaniards depending on the context, sprinkle : baptize, stalk : lineage, mat : authority, red : east, green : center, and the bearer of land : its owner. A partial dictionary is provided in the index under "kennings."

    Key words of the couplets are frequently kennings, and thus when combined they may imply a third meaning quite different from the literal meaning of the elements. Thus wells and springs means settlements, sticks and stones or rope and cord : war, born and engendered : noble, fatherless and motherless : poor peasants, older and younger brothers : everybody, gourdroot and breadnut : famine, food and water : fate, shot and shout : soon, pants and sandals : religion. A partial list of these is also provided in the index under "couplets."

    The Chumayel makes extensive use of all manner of poetical and rhetorical devices, from the metaphor conceiving Yucatan as a bird with one wingtip in Campeche and the other in Valladolid to the humorous riddle likening the church to a leaky cenote because it's always dripping on people. It makes extensive use of puns and riddles (see "pun," "riddle," "metaphor" in the index). It is fond of euphemisms, referring to sacrifice as "painless death" and to Spaniards by a whole series of circumlocutory expressions: foreigners, bearded ones, conquerors, annona slurpers, older brothers, oppressors, people of the eastern land, sons of the sun, white people, red beards. The Chumayel uses hyperbole: "Indeed the Itza could come here three times over for one occurrence of (Spaniards)" (lines 2899–2900). And it is capable of ironic meiosis, referring to the climactic *katun* 8 Ahau as "tiny little 8 Ahau" (line 1234).

    Our text asks rhetorical questions: "Who will be the prophet, who will be the sun priest who will correctly interpret the word of these glyphs?" (lines 625–628; the clearly implied answer is, "I shall"). It uses personification: "Here I am, I, *katun* 3 Ahau, who have seated my city, Heaven Born Merida!" (lines 2951–2954). Many of the tropes are standardized, and some of them descend to being clichés, as in the obligatory reference to "the lying earth," at least in Christianized contexts. Lies and insanity are a standard accusation against enemies.

There is a strong polarization by rank and favor in these texts. Insults abound—since the text is Xiu, the Itza are often characterized as lying, stupid, stuttering orphans and insane fly-by-night (two-day and three-day) lords, drunken buzzards, monkeys and dogs, oversexed, lustful, and addicted to sodomy. The Itza of course reciprocate in kind. When they are really aroused, the Maya produce slang curses that sound almost like GI Joe: "This asshole boils war!" Correspondingly, the language of deference is considerably elaborated, and there are many standard honorifics: father, older brother, honorable, remote or holy, heaven born, glorious (sun face), great (seventh, ninth, thirteenth), or tremendous (*chac*).

Even more poetic effects are found occasionally, as in the anaphoric repetition and climax of the following:

There appeared the moon;
  The moon left.
It returned,
  And the moon of the moon occurred. (lines 669–672)

There is sometimes a deft use of chiasmus:

Shaped by the juice of heaven:
  By dew of heaven shaped. (lines 1703–1704)

Allegory is also to be found, as in the myth of the origin of the Xiu as a consequence of Hummingbird's sipping the nectar of the flowers, alluded to following line 3324.

Although the entire text of the Chumayel is poetic, it appears to be specifically lyric in only a few passages: "The Song of the Itza" in chapter 42 and the elegant introit to "The Count of the *Katuns*" in chapter 17. Sections of the myth "The Birth of the *Uinal*" in chapter 20 attain a similar lyricism. At least the first two of these fully qualify as poems.

Drama.   Drama is fundamental to our text. There is a great deal of preoccupation with ritual throughout the work—with the Christian sacraments (baptism, marriage, burial) and rites (absolution, benediction, kneeling, repentance, mourning, sermons, prayer, praise, anointing with oil, the sign of the cross) as well as Mayan ceremonials (of the *uinal*, the *tzol kin*, the *tun*, the *hab*, the *katun*, the *may*, the *baktun*) and ceremonies (sacrifice, divination, curing, examination, request, pacing and seating of land, commemoration). It is curious that there is no specific reference to the eucharist among the Christian rites or to confession, which is prominent in both Catholic and Mayan religions. Perhaps the emphasis on the rite of forgiveness is intended to refer to the latter.

The ceremonials of the Maya are largely tied to the cycles of the calendar. The principal *tzol kin* ceremonies were those of the Burner (*ah toc*) cycle of the quarter *tzol kin*. These were held on certain occurrences of the days Chicchan, Oc, Men, and Ahau, and they survive as the *tup' kak* 'quenching fire' ceremonies described by Villa Rojas (1945: 79, 116). In each quarter *tzol kin* there was a cycle of fire ceremonies; thus on 3 Chicchan the Burner "took his fire," on 10 Chicchan he lit it, on 4 Chicchan his fire "dawned," and on 11 Chicchan it was extinguished. The cycle was then repeated for the other Burner days. The Tizimin account is fuller than that of the Chumayel, but neither describes the actual ritual. Since they are pegged to the *tzol kin*, these ceremonies are movable feasts in relation to those of the *hab*.

Uinal ceremonies are not described in the Chumayel, though there are scattered references to the major gods in whose honor such ceremonies were held. By implication, these allusions fairly well blanket the eighteen *uinals* of the *tun* (see table 3 below).

Tun ceremonies are primarily linked to those of the *katun*. They are not described in the Chumayel either, though there are some references to them, particularly to the *ho tun* (quarter *katun*), *lahun tun* (half *katun*), and *ho lahun tun* (three-quarter *katun*) ceremonies. The half *katun* is particularly emphasized. It is identified with 11 Ch'ab Tan, the installation of the Jaguar designate, and the notion of the "remainder" of the *katun*.

All ritual has some elements of the dramatic, but the complex rituals of the *katun*, the *may*, and the *baktun* incorporated numerologically significant ceremonies (thirteen for the *katun* and the *may*, twenty for the *baktun*), and some of these escape the confines of ritual to become true drama. All the *katun* histories (chapters 4, 5, 6, 8, 11, 16, 18, 19, 22, 25, 26, 28, 33, 35, 36, 38, 40, 45) contain allusions to the *katun* ritual, and, despite the fact that their content is historical, the references to music, incense, ceremonial insignia, fire, riddling, penance, masks, costume, and the like make it clear that this is ritual drama.

Four of the chapters of the Chumayel give more or less detailed descriptions of major Mayan ceremonials: the ceremonial of the *may* (chapters 12 and 46), the ceremonial of the *baktun* (chapter 29), and the ceremonial of the *hab* (chapter 15). That these are in fact ceremonials and in spots ceremonial drama is demonstrated by the distinction drawn between the characters portrayed and the actors portraying them (e.g., line 3389), by stage directions and explanations of symbolism (e.g., lines 3120–3121), by details of costuming, paraphernalia, props, masks, music, and sometimes directly quoted dialogue (lines 6391 ff.). There is reference to the impersonation of the gods (line 3150) as well as of historical figures (lines 1179–1180).

The choice of historical and mythological elements was no doubt dictated at least in part by calendrical considerations, but the fact that there was a choice separates many of the Mayan ceremonies from the mechanical repetition of ritual acts. Historical and mythological events were reenacted and comedies were performed.

The ceremonial of the *katun* is mentioned frequently but is nowhere directly described. It appears to have been patterned rather strictly on the ceremonial of the *may* (chapter 12), a drama in thirteen acts, and all of the eighteen *katun* histories refer to anywhere from two to twelve of these acts in more or less recognizable form and always in the same order. For reasons that will become clear below, I prefer to number the acts from 8 to 20 rather than from 1 to 13. They may be reconstructed as follows.

Act 8. Ceremonial Circuit. This seems to be implied in various other passages but is not mentioned in the *katun* histories. It may have ended in a balche ceremony.

Act 9. Seating of the *Katun*. This is the main point of the ritual. The new Jaguar Priest, dressed in robes of jaguar and rattlesnake skin and with his face tied (i.e., masked), having been ceremonially designated ten years before, took his place on the throne and mat of the *katun* in the cycle seat (Merida for the Xiu, Mayapan for the Itza).

Act 10. Seating of the Yearbearers. These were local priests; each city had its own set of four, each identified with and by a direction color. They were probably thought to represent not only the years but also the gods of death, wind, sun, rain, and fire. The "high fan" may have been part of their paraphernalia.

Act 11. Pacing of the *Katun*. This was a ceremonial procession of seven priests, the Pacers (*uuc taz cab*), with a surveying stick (*p'iz te*), who ritually confirmed land titles. The corresponding references in the *katun* histories are to settling, tying, bearing, dividing, and measuring the land, as well as to payment of tribute.

Act 12. Dawn. This was the moment for the counting (ranking) of the mats (of the lords) and for accepting "requests," that is, applications for future offices. This was in many respects the most political moment of the drama, since what was at stake were not only the priesthoods but also the positions of governor (*hal ach uinic*) and "fathers of the rope" (*ba tabob*) of the subject towns and cities. A declaration of candidacy in this ceremonial context was like the ritual of nomination at a national convention in the United States, and the ceremonial recognition mattered.

Act 13. Sacrifice. In the *katun* histories the references to sacrifice are euphemistic and elliptical. They are a little more explicit elsewhere. The heart sacrifice ("painless death"), the arrow sacrifice, hanging, burning, and drowning were the principal forms, but often the only reference is to the accompanying music: the drum and rattle of the *katun*.

Act 14. Examination. The examination ceremony was always accompanied by a feast at which aspirants to lordship were tested by ritual riddles (chapters 30 and 31). Naturally most of these concerned food, but examinations are also referred to in the *katun* histories in more or less riddle form: the food and water of the *katun*, its speech, judgment, and "face."

Act 15. The Word. The general character and fate of the *katun* are always given in the *katun* histories, usually in a terse riddle, metaphor, kenning, or keyed couplet: shield and arrow, lying and crazy, quetzal and blue bird, gods, sticks and stones, hanging, church, war, full swollen, locust, cord and rope, feast and famine. This was presumably announced by the new Spokesman of the Jaguar.

Act 16. Penance. References in the *katun* prophecies to work, hunger, poverty, sins, burning, need, and lamentation normally follow the imagery of act 15. There is also reference to the gourd, bowl, and cup of the *katun*. I believe that all this refers to the continence, fasting, and bloodletting expected of the lords and that this was the point at which they collected their own blood in bowls and offered it to the gods. The yearbearers were certainly involved, but I think the rest of the higher priesthood was, too, including the Jaguar.

Act 17. Commemoration (*natabal*). In Classic times this was certainly the moment for the erection and/or unveiling of a carved stone monument. There are fleeting suggestions that a wooden pole may have been substituted in post-Classic and colonial times. Eventually the substitute was the cross. In the ritual drama, a substantive bit of history was introduced, evoking calendrically significant bits of past history. There are references in the *katun* histories to writing, dating stones, and origin myths at this point.

Act 18. Counting. All the *katun* histories down to 12 Ahau (1658) refer explicitly to the counting of the *katun*. Only two put this reference into what appears to be the correct order of the *katun* ceremony. The others mention it at the outset.

Act 19. Farce. Comic relief was offered in the penultimate act of the ceremonial. This took the form of a morality play focused upon such characters as Desire and Suffering, Thief and Official, Sin and Blame, Lust, or even contemporary characters like those representing the military orders (Fox and Earth Lion). The suggestion is strong from other passages that the humor of these farces was broad. The characters were deformed, with "bent necks"; they drooled; they burlesqued the sins they represented.

Act 20. Sermon. The sermon of the *katun* was normally delivered by a prophet (*ah bobat*), but the official prophet of the *katun* was the Spokesman of the Jaguar. Sermons of the *katun* constitute chapters 7, 9, 10, 13, 21, 34, and 46, and two more are incorporated into chapters 19 and 29. All the *katun* histories from 8 Ahau to 10 Ahau (1441–1677) include at least references to the content of the sermon: war, Christianity, God, etc.

It appears that the acts of the ceremonial of the *katun* did not have equal weight to the Maya and that the most important were act 9 (seating), act 15 (the word), and act 20 (the sermon).

The ceremonial of the *hab*, a ten-day program of activities that began on the first day of Uayeb and extended five days into the new year, is the subject of chapter 15. This is an interesting ritual text clearly organized around the four directions, though it appears to be somewhat garbled here and there. It lists the circuit of the directions counterclockwise six times, associating the directions with (1) a lineage and a lineage head, (2) ten kinds of ritual insignia, (3) a stopping place, (4) four counselors, (5) three more insignia, and (6) a *katun* keeper. Each direction is also associated with a color. The structure of the ritual is given in table 1.

It is of interest to note that the items of insignia total thirteen and that the total number of associations is eighteen. Various symbolic substitutions in them are reminiscent of the ritual riddles. The lists of insignia are apparently both incomplete and out of order, as though this text were being dictated or composed by memory from oral tradition. The whole passage is explicitly dated to 11 Ahau (1539).

The ceremonial of the *kin tun y abil* was held at fifty-two-year intervals to mark the completion and reinauguration of the calendar round. It was

Table 1. The Ceremonial of the *Hab*

Association	East (Red)	North (White)	West (Black)	South (Yellow)
1. Lineage	?	Uaxim	Yaxum	Puch
Lineage head	Can Ul	Culux Chacah	Cau Ich	Kan Tacay
2. Stone	flint	flint	flint	flint
Honey	harvest	harvest		honey water (?)
Arbor	alligator ceiba	alligator ceiba	alligator ceiba	alligator ceiba
Tree	bullet tree			bullet tree
Beans			black beans	yellowbacks
Greens	?	lima beans	black-as-nights	corn ear
Turkey	yellow-breast	whitebreast	roadrunner	bullet tree roadrunner
Corn	annona	corn	conch	
Yam			stem yam	bullet tree
Lima beans	sapote		lima beans	
3. Stopping place	P'iz Te	Chac Te	Xiu Tic	Miz Tic
4. Counselors	Noh Uc	Ba Tun	I Ban	Ah Puch
	Tocoy Mo	Ah Puch	Ah Chab	Cau Ich
	Paua Hel	Balam Na	Tuc Uch	Co Uoh
	Ah Mis	Ake	Yam Az	Ah Puc
5. Bees	honeybees	honeybees	honeybees	honeybees
Cup	blossoms	flowers	blossoms	blossoms
Flower	flowers	whiteback buds	laurel flowers	yellowbell flowers
6. *Katun* keeper	Hul Neb	Cusamil	Ac Chinab	Kak Mo

known as Oc Na 'entering the house', and some version of it may also have been performed to mark the quarter and halfway points (each thirteen years). As with the ceremonial of the *katun*, which appears to have been modeled on that of the *may*, the Oc Na was probably an expanded version of the annual ceremonial of the *hab*. Landa (Tozzer 1941: 161) says in fact that it was held annually, but I believe that to be a mistake. (A half–calendar round ceremony was due in 1555.) In its full form it was supposed to involve the rebuilding of the temple in which it was held, and it is always mentioned in connection with sacrifices. We have no explicit description of it.

It would be logical to present the ceremonial of the *may* next. As a matter of exposition, however, I believe I can make the matter clearer if I move on to the ceremonial of the *baktun* and then return to the *may*.

The ceremonial of the *baktun*, chapter 29 of the Chumayel, is a detailed description of the *katun* ceremonies at Merida at the beginning of 3 Ahau in 1618. But, because eighty days after the beginning of this *katun* was the end of an even *baktun*, 12.0.0.0.0 (the end of 5 Ahau in the Tikal calendar), the occasion was celebrated with a ritual extravaganza: a ceremonial drama in twenty acts. (The *baktun* has twenty *katuns*.) The previous performance of such a drama occurred in 1224; the one before that

was in 830; the next one is not scheduled until the twenty-first century.
The occasion provides us with a kind of ritual key to the whole meaning
of the *Books of Chilam Balam* and to the theology and mysticism they
reflect and reproduce. The component ceremonies were as follows.

Act 1. Mead. The balche ceremony, involving at least three days for the
preparation of the mead, made from cooked and fermented honey and the
bark of the balche tree, has been described by Redfield and Villa Rojas
(1934) and by Tozzer (1907) among the Lacandon.

Act 2. Tying. The bee god ties the faces of (i.e., masks) the 13 gods. The
identity of the impersonators of these gods was supposed to be secret,
so this may have been done in private. According to the Tizimin they
were named Puzlum Pach 'hunchback', Thuchlum Ich 'squatface',
Naclah Muyal 'rising storm', Naclah Uitz 'rising mountain', Chuclum
Tz'iitz' 'sooty hoof', Hubul Hub 'sinking snail', Cotz' y Ol Ch'elem 'rolling
agave heart', Etz'el Etz' 'placing fakes', Ox Tz'alab u Nak Yax Che 'three
squeezed in the belly of the ceiba', Cuchlahom y Al Max 'carrying baby
monkey', Ox Ch'uilah Xotem 'thrice hanged', Pan Tzintzin 'old bugger',
and Ban Hob 'many guts'.

Act 3. Cycle Ending. The 9 Gods fight with, conquer, and sacrifice the
13 Gods, thus symbolizing the end of the thirteen-*katun* cycle: night con-
quers day. The Tizimin gives the names of the 9 Gods: Hau Nab 'slice
point', Hutz' Nab 'split point', Kuk Nab 'quetzal point', Oyal Nicte 'island flower', Ninich Cacau 'wormy cacao', Chabi Tok 'digging knife', Ma-
cuilxochit 'five flower', Hobon y Ol Nicte 'colored flower heart', and Kouol
y Ol Nicte 'pouched flower heart'. The Chumayel lists the 9 Gods among
the 18 Flower lords under slightly different names.

Act 4. Yearbearer. The 4 Yearbearers appear in the guise of the 4 Burners
soot heads'. Some kind of fire ritual may be implied.

Act 5. Bird. Quetzal and Hummingbird appear, representing the ancestry of the Itza and the Xiu, respectively. They bring offerings.

Act 6. Heart. There is a procession, followed by the heart sacrifice on
the pyramid. In this instance the sacrifice is symbolic: hearts of plants are
substituted for human ones.

Act 7. Rain. The 4 Yearbearers reappear, this time with, or in the guise
of, the 4 Chacs. (They are also called Ba Cabs here.) They produce a rainstorm. There may be an implication that this symbolizes baptism, which
has conquered the country and is the path of the future.

Act 8. Circuit. There is then a ritual circuit to the four directions, each
of the yearbearers carrying an alligator (Imix) tree of the appropriate directional color. This procession is said to symbolize the subjugation of the
lands in all directions. A fifth priest, presumably the Center priest, carries
his green tree to the center of the plaza. The procession was probably
more complex than advertised. It almost certainly included the retiring
Jaguar Priest and his Spokesman, the Jaguar designate and his Spokesman,
the previously mentioned characters of the drama (the bee god, the 9
Gods, Quetzal, and Hummingbird), and probably other important lords,
priests, and officials.

Act 9. Seating of the *Katun*. The retiring Jaguar now divests himself of his regalia—his mask, robe, staff, crown, fan, cask, cup, bowl, plate, burden, and probably other paraphernalia as well—and the new Jaguar is seated, suitably accoutred, on his mat and throne. (The throne must certainly have been a stone bench, and the mat on it was a necessity for comfort. Quiche lords got pillows, too.) Presumably the Jaguar's Spokesman was similarly invested, but nowhere is there any indication of how he was dressed or equipped.

Act 10. Yearbearer Seating. Since this ceremony was held in 1618, the senior yearbearer was 11 Kan, here identified with the Red Noble. The East and North priests were "leaders of the foot"; those of the west and south were "leaders of the hand," a detail not mentioned elsewhere. The yearbearer-seating ceremony is said to "establish the town," and presumably everybody else could now sit down, but in the strictest order of rank.

Act 11. Pacing. The 7 Pacers (uuc taz cab) now parade, their surveying stick (p'iz te) borne on the back of the alligator god. The pacers are elsewhere identified as the Surveyor (ah p'iz te), the Marker (ah lub te), the Scrubber (ah xuk, who was the Jaguar himself), the Sweeper (ah miz), the Remover (cit ahau), the Wakener (ahel cab), and the Renewer (tumte ahau). At the end of a katun, all titles to lands and offices were canceled and renewed. This is the ceremony that did it. The ex officio participation of the Jaguar is thus highly significant. The alligator god, who has the power to destroy the world by earthquakes, demonstrated his beneficence by bringing light, in what must have been an impressive candlelight procession. (Yucatan is outside the earthquake zone in any case.)

Act 12. Dawn. The 9 Gods sacrifice the 7 Pacers and count (and rank) the mats. This had the same significance for titles to office that the preceding act had for titles to land. What was involved was an initial (ceremonial) lineup of the candidates for investiture for the coming katun, subject to their satisfactory (ceremonial) demonstration of legitimacy in act 14. No wonder this taxing job was delegated to the impersonators of the gods of the underworld. No wonder either that haggling and trading and envy were involved.

Act 13. Sacrifice. The 4 Yearbearers reappear, this time in the guise of the four death gods. Some (symbolic?) sacrifice was doubtless made, but it is discreetly omitted from the text. Human sacrifice was still going on in Yucatan at this date, but in Merida!?

Act 14. Examination. The examination ceremony was always accompanied by a feast. Chapters 30 and 31 provide a pony for the questions and answers expected in "The Language of Zuyua." Itza or Xiu, every aspirant to nobility had to know the right answers, whatever scandal may have surrounded his birth. The ritual riddles largely concern the feast—and one may well imagine that it was usually memorable, even apart from the spice added by the examination, which must in any case have been largely pro forma.

Act 15. The Word. This is also referred to as the news (mut) of the katun. The 9 Gods announce the fate of the katun, phrased as a matter of its food. As usual, the news in this case was bad.

Act 16. Penance. The yearbearers then perform the bloodletting rite, drawing blood from their tongues, earlobes, or penises. Perhaps other lords did so too, but the text doesn't say so.

Act 17. Commemoration (*natabal*). This is the point at which in former times a *katun* monument would have been erected or unveiled as a memorial to the ancestors. Elsewhere there are suggestions of the possible erection of wooden poles or crosses, as seems to be suggested here. This was accompanied by a play within a play, a dramatization of mythology or history or both. In this instance the performance was "The Birth of the Flowers," a reenactment of the origin myth of the Xiu (Flower) lineages. The characters include the 4 Yearbearers (here for some reason called the *hoch kom* 'empty pits'), the 13 Gods, and Flower (*nicte*), the mother of the Flowers. Together these make up the 18 Flowers, symbolizing the *uinals* of the *tun*. The nineteenth character is Hummingbird (*tz'unun*), who is thus in the structural position of Uayeb. This completes the symbolization of the year and the calendar round (4 × 13 × 365) as well as the *tun*. At the same time, the drama reenacts the myth in which Hummingbird engenders the Xiu by descending to suck the nectar of the Flowers. The 9 Gods made up half the Flowers and, together with the 4 Yearbearers, symbolized the 13 Gods.

Act 18. Counting. Flower is then seated and, in the counting ceremony, explicates the calendrical structure just described.

Act 19. Farce. Another play within a play was performed at this juncture, a morality play concerning envy and spite. Lahun Chan acts the part of Envy's wife, and the whole play is one of comic relief: they act crazy, dizzy, furtive, bad, and ignorant. The 9 Gods are also involved.

Act 20. Sermon. The lordship has been passed, and what follows is a sermon by the Spokesman of the Jaguar, prophesying the fate of 3 Ahau. It accuses the Itza of being commoners and predicts that one of these *tuns* they will see the light. God will triumph and, by flood and storm, will bring about redemption through Jesus Christ for all, even the stupid Itza.

The ceremonial of the *may* held in Merida in 1539 is the subject of chapter 12, celebrating the beginning of 11 Ahau. The ritual structure of the ceremonial is entirely parallel in detail to that of the *baktun* drama, except that the first seven acts are omitted. The 9 Gods, the 13 Gods, and the 18 Flowers are missing, but the 4 Yearbearers are here together with the 7 Pacers, the Jaguars and their Spokesmen, and eighteen characters of the time of "The Fall of Mayapan," the historical drama which appears in act 17 in place of "The Birth of the Flowers." Chapter 12 begins, in fact, with a synopsis of this drama. Then follow the thirteen acts of the ceremonial of the *may*.

Act 8. Circuit. The text outlines a double counterclockwise circuit of the geography of Yucatan, listing 171 cities, towns, and villages, starting from P'ool on the east coast and winding up in Merida. If, as I suspect, representatives of a substantial number of these were on hand for the folding of the cycle in 11 Ahau, the seating arrangements must have been a pain even for the rank-happy Maya.

Act 9. Seating of the *Katun*. It appears that seven lords may have been seated: Mutecpul (as Jaguar), Can Ul, Uayom Ch'ich', Nunil, Chable, Hol Tun Balam, and Yaxum. (At least three of these are characters in "The Fall of Mayapan": Can Ul, Uayom Ch'ich', and Chable.)

Act 10. Seating the Yearbearers. Five lords are named: Hol Tun Ake, Zabac Na, Hol Tun Balam, Pochek Ix Tz'oy (a Xiu from Copo, presumably the Spokesman), and Chac Te. If Pochek Ix Tz'oy was the Spokesman, the other four were presumably the Ba Cabs.

Act 11. Pacing. The 7 Pacers appear and survey and seat the lands.

Act 12. Dawn. The text doesn't say so, but presumably the mats (lordships) were counted; then tribute was collected.

Act 13. Sacrifice. This is acted out as a scene from "The Fall of Mayapan," the victim being cast as Mex Cuc, who was thrown into the cenote of Chichen Itza by Hunac Ceel in 8 Ahau (1451). Cau Ich apparently replaced Mex Cuc as governor of Mayapan at that time.

Act 14. Examination. No feast is mentioned but presumably there was one. The examination is rather obliquely referred to, and there is reference to another scene from "The Fall of Mayapan," apparently relating to the birth of Mex Cuc.

Act 15. The Word. The word of the *katun* is announced by the impersonator of Mex Cuc, presumably as a Jaguar of 8 Ahau.

Act 16. Penance. There is only a fleeting allusion to suffering, but it comes at the right point and presumably represents the penance of the yearbearers, here played as Mex Cuc, Cau Ich, Hunac Ceel, and the sun priest of Coba, all of them real people of 8 Ahau.

Act 17. Commemoration. What are commemorated are not only the fall of Mayapan but also the beginning of the calendar round in 1529 (which would have been the time for the induction of the Jaguar designate for the 1539 ceremonial being described here) and an eclipse.

Act 18. Counting. The text alludes briefly to the writing of the *katun* history for 13 Ahau, now ended.

Act 19. Farce. In this case the farce is called "Centipedes and Gnats," presumably a burlesque of the pesky military orders.

Act 20. Sermon. The text peters out in the midst of dire predictions of war and bloodshed.

The ceremonial of the *may* in chapter 12 is that for 11 Ahau in 1539. Another version is given in more fragmentary form in chapter 46 for the 11 Ahau of 1824. Five of the thirteen acts are omitted. The circuit (act 8) is probably taken for granted. The seating of the yearbearers (act 10) may be omitted in honor of the impending calendar round celebration, which fell in 1841, later in the same *katun*. (This is referred to in line 6284.) The pacing (act 11) may have been deferred because land titles were still under negotiation (line 6462). The counting (act 18), like the circuit, is often taken for granted. It is possible that the farce (act 19) is referred to, but out of order (line 6287). The remaining eight acts are alluded to in order as indicated in the translation. The commemoration (act 17) enacts the story of Antonio Martínez, a latter-day prophet who identifies himself with Jesus Christ and promises the defeat of the French and the king of Havana and the suspension of tribute payments, all this to be achieved in a great sea battle. Aside from the Chumayel, Tizimin, and Mani, Martínez is unknown to history. There are anachronistic references to him in the *katun* histories for 1 Ahau (1638), and his prophecies seem to be based on even Christian centuries rather than on even cycles of Mayan time.

The thirteen-act ceremonials of the *may* and the *katun* seem to provide the model for such fragments of Mayan ritual as have survived into the twentieth century (table 3). These include (8) the *balche* 'mead' ceremony (Redfield and Villa Rojas 1934: 129), (9) the *hetz' mek* 'seated embrace' ceremony (Redfield and Villa 1934: 188), (10) the cuch 'burden' ceremony (Redfield and Villa 1934: 154), (11) the uklic (or *hanlil*) col 'dinner of the cornfield' ceremony (Redfield and Villa 1934: 134), (12) the *kaan* 'hammock' ceremony against the winds (informant), (13) the *cub p'ol* 'seating the head' ceremony (Redfield and Villa 1934: 157), (14) the *hol che* 'finish the young' firstfruits ceremony (Redfield and Villa 1934: 143), (15) the *tup' kak* 'quenching fire' ceremony (Villa 1945: 79, 116), (16) the *x pa' pul* 'little breaking divination' ceremony (informant), (17) the *zip* 'deer' demon (Redfield and Villa 1934: 117), (18) the *xtabay* 'hanging woman' demon (Redfield and Villa 1934: 122), (19) the *ch'a chaac* 'bring rain' ceremony (Redfield and Villa 1934: 138; Andrews 1961: 79–164), and (20) the *ch'uyenil na* 'hanging the house' ceremony (Redfield and Villa 1934: 146).

A number of the modern Catholic rituals parallel the Mayan structure in a somewhat overlapping fashion. These analogies may be suggested: (8) *procesión*, (9) *novena*, (10) *día del santo*, (11) *candelaria*, (12) *velorio*, (13) *viernes santo*, (14) *bautizo*, (15) *amonestaciones*, (16) *cuaresma*, (17) *todos santos*, (18) *navidad*, (19) *carnaval*, and (20) *cruz*.

It is clear that the ceremonial of the *katun* and that of the *may* are abbreviated thirteen-act versions of the twenty-act ceremonial of the *baktun*. But it is not quite accurate to say that the former simply omit the first seven acts of the latter. It is more likely that the first seven were assimilated into the next seven. Thus the balche ceremony crops up in the circuit (line 803), the tying of masks was presumably incorporated into the *katun*-seating ceremony, cycle ending was probably symbolized in some way in conjunction with the seating of the yearbearers. The offerings of act 4 could be moved to act 11 (line 2946), those of act 5 to act 12 (line 426), those of act 6 to act 13, and those of act 7 to act 14 (line 2254). In the reconstructed *katun* ceremonial there is more than a suggestion that this is in fact what happened.

Narrative. The Chumayel contains no narrative tales comparable to "The Maiden Theodora" of the Kaua and the Mani. Its narrative is therefore confined to myth and history. Two of the chapters are myths (chapters 20 and 41). Seven are chronicles (1, 2, 3, 14, 24, 27, and 37). One is a collection of brief annalistic notes (44). Eighteen are *katun* histories (4, 5, 6, 8, 11, 16, 18, 19, 22, 25, 26, 28, 33, 35, 36, 38, 40, and 45). It is a mistake to call these prophecies (as I have occasionally done myself). They are called *kahlay* 'account, relation' in Maya and *historia* in Spanish, and that is what they are.

All these materials are profoundly interwoven with the mystique and ritual of the calendar. They are dated by *katuns* and are preoccupied with *katun* ritual, referring frequently to the various acts of the *katun* ceremonial drama as outlined above. All the *katun* histories, for example, mention seating (act 9) and the word of the *katun* (act 15), and most of them give at least a précis of the sermon (act 20). All the earlier *katun* histories refer to at least four and as many as eight of the thirteen acts of the ceremonial of the *katun*. This structure disappears rapidly after 1677. None of the histories appears to refer to the first seven acts of the *baktun* ceremonial. In almost all cases, allusions to the ritual follow the order of the acts in the original *may* ceremonial of 11 Ahau in 1539.

The *katun* histories may be precisely characterized, then, as ritual history. They are considerably constrained by the expectation that they will convert the real history of each twenty-year period into the language and ritual order of the *katun* ceremonial. And that they do—often with remarkable economy and elegance. By the same token, this is intentionally esoteric history, and, while the Mayan sun priests had an intensive education in it, we latter-day scribes are forced to educate ourselves, inevitably somewhat imperfectly. Like our Mayan forebears, we worry a lot about philosophy, specifically about the cosmology and theology that shaped, and were shaped by, the mystique of the *katun*, the *may*, and the *baktun*.

Myth.   Mayan cosmology formally begins with a characteristic ending: 13.0.0.0.0   4 Ahau 8 Cumku (August 15, 3115 B.C.). The morning after that date was the beginning of the pseudohistorical Mayan calendar. It was also zero. Nothing existed—not even God, according to some accounts. There is reason to suppose that this date was the end of the third or possibly even the fourth *baktun* cycle of 5,200 *tuns*, implying an even earlier starting date around 20,000 B.C., but even that was merely a moment in a cycle that is bound to repeat itself. The first beginning of everything was time itself.

This mystery is beautifully expressed in the creation myth "The Birth of the Uinal," which constitutes chapter 20 of the Chumayel. This delicate allegory likens the birth of time to the origin of man, a man traveling like the heavenly bodies on the road of days, time, sun, and fate (*kin*), carrying his burden of sin and shame to its inevitable and self-regenerative end.

Did man come before woman? No, it was four female relatives of his who discovered time. So much for the rib of Adam. This may be an exquisite recognition that women counted time more precisely by the moon (*u*), as most American Indians did, for a long time before it could be paced (*oc*) by the sun priest. And for very good reasons: women were naturally more concerned with the approximately lunar cycle of menstruation and with the period of gestation, which seems to have given rise to the (again approximate) cycle of the 260-day *tzol kin*. What the women discovered in the footprints of Time was sex: the footprint of *lah ca oc* '12 Oc, twelve foot, or all of two feet'. After that, men and women traveled together. No wonder the cycles were self-regenerative.

From 12 Oc we move by an impossible calendrical leap to 13 Oc, but Time and his four forbidden female relatives matched their footsteps and traveled together, and "the month was born and the day name was born, and the sky was born and the earth, the pyramid of water and land, stone and tree." This act of generation was incestuous but effective. It produced and named the twenty sacred days of the *uinal* and the thirteen sacred numbers to count them with, and on the thirteenth day, 13 Night (Akbal) "took water and moistened the earth and shaped it and made man."

The world pyramid of the Mayan universe had thirteen levels of heaven and nine levels of the underworld. The upper world had six levels going up and six coming down, so the seventh level was the highest. The underworld had four steps going down and four coming back up, so the fifth level was the lowest. After counting thirteen days, our father who is God counted the remaining seven and announced, "13 heaps and 7 heaps make 1." One *uinal* or one *uinic* ('man, twenty'), it comes to the same thing.

As in the *Popol Vuh* and the Bible, the mechanism of creation was the Word. "Everything there was not was then spoken in heaven." And, having invented speech, God endowed man with it. And men took each other by the hand and stood in the middle of the country and divided it into four parts, designating a god for each. And (line 180) Four-Part Country (*can tzucul cab*) was what they named it.

The God of this creation was our father *Dios citbil*, God the remote, the holy. He is clearly here (and is elsewhere called) the creator (*ah ch'ab*). He appears anachronistically under his Spanish name in a number of passages that otherwise seem to antedate the Spanish conquest, so his appearance here in a text that almost surely dates to 9 Ahau (1559) is not surprising. Like the triune god of the Spaniards, he unites all other gods in his person, and hence he is referred to as *hunab ku* 'the unified god'. Religious controversy led to his being called also the True God (*hahal ku*), irrespective of the fact that conceptions of his divinity (*diosil, kuil*) are subject to variation even when he is being called true.

The Mayan concept of divinity was clearly plural as well as singular, and one finds explicit references to *kuob* 'gods'. Even in reference to the 13 Gods of heaven and the 9 Gods of the underworld, however, a certain linguistic ambiguity is maintained: *oxlahun ti ku* is literally 'the 13 who are god'.

The basic set of Mayan gods was a set of twenty associated with the twenty days of the *uinal* and seemingly, like them, thought of in year-bearer sets (table 2). One of the gods in each yearbearer set was thought of as quadripartite. These are italicized in the table. Some of the implied associations of the gods with the days are reasonably clear and explicit. Others are pure guesswork. The matter is complicated by the existence of more than one name for a particular god and more than one way of fitting him into the sacred numerology. All the gods listed in the table are at least mentioned in the Chumayel, with the exception of the corn god and Hummingbird.

Table 2. Gods of the *Uinal*

Alligator	*Death*	Monkey	Rainbow
Wind	Deer	Bee	Buzzard
Sun	Rope	(Corn)	Flower
Rattlesnake	(Hummingbird)	Jaguar	Rain
Fire	Dog	Bird	Lord

1. The alligator god is Itzam Cab Ain, clearly associated with the day Imix and thought of as living in the underworld in the water and causing earthquakes.

2. There were four wind gods, Ikil, clearly associated with the day Ik, with the Type II yearbearers, and with the four directions. This is Kukul Can as Ehecatl.

3. There were four Sun Giants, Pauah Tun, who were thought to hold up the corners of the sky, and there was a sun god, Ku Kin. My relating them to Akbal is a guess, which would associate them with the Type III yearbearers. I believe this is also Kukul Can as Venus.

4. The rattlesnake god, Ahau Can, should perhaps be associated with Chicchan, but I think he got displaced by the fire gods and by his association with rain (Kukul Can as Tlaloc, Mayan Chac). There were four rain gods, Chacob, who were also the yearbearers after 1539; the senior one is identified with the day Kan.

5. There were four fire gods called the Burners, Ah Toc, who were associated with the Type V yearbearers, of which Chicchan is the senior member. The god of this day is Kak Mo 'fire macaw'.

6. The death god, Ah Puch', is mentioned in the Tizimin and is clearly associated with the day Cimi. This is Kukul Can as Mictlantecuhtli. In the Chumayel there are four death gods, Tenel Ahau, associated with the four directions and with Type I yearbearers.

7. The deer god, Zuhuy Zip, was probably associated with the day Manik, which corresponds to 'deer' in Nahuatl and Quiche. He was also associated with the third *uinal* of the year, which is also Zip. In modern times he has become a plural set of spirits of the forest, but he is not quadripartite.

8. The rope goddess, Ix Tab, was seemingly the goddess of the hanged. Her association with Lamat is a guess. The similar goddess Ix Q'anil fits here in the Quiche calendar.

9. I do not find a deity for Muluc, but the ceremonial of the *may* clearly places Hummingbird, Tz'unun, here. He is mentioned in the Chumayel only by euphemisms, as Yax Um. Instead of being multiplied by four, he is multiplied by nine to become the 9 Gods of the underworld.

10. The dog god, Pek, was probably associated with Oc, which corresponds to the day 'dog' in Nahuatl and Quiche, but so is Nacxit 'four leg', the fire guise of Kukul Can.

11. The monkey god, Maax, is clearly associated with the day Chuen.

12. The bee god, Muzen Cab, is associated with Eb only by guess.

13. The corn god may belong with Ben, which is the day 'corn' in Quiche. He does not appear as such in the Chumayel or the Tizimin but

instead is multiplied by thirteen to become the 13 Gods of heaven. This is probably the Yum Kax of modern times.

14. The jaguar god, Balam, is clearly associated with the day Ix.

15. The bird god, Ch'ich', probably belongs with Men, which is the day 'bird' in Quiche and 'eagle' in Nahuatl.

16. The rainbow goddess, Ix Chel, may belong with Cib, but that is a guess. She is also called Ix Kalem 'brilliant lady' in the Tizimin.

17. The buzzard god, Ah Kuch, may be associated with Caban, which corresponds to the day 'buzzard' in Nahuatl and 'owl' in Quiche.

18. The Flower goddess, Nicte, Xuchit, may belong with Etz'nab despite her association with the twentieth day in Nahuatl.

19. There was a rain god, Chac, and four rain gods (see number 4). The association with Cauac and with Type IV yearbearers is clear.

20. There was one lord god, the father of the gods, Itzam Na, associated with the day Ahau.

Twenty gods are a satisfactory roster for a cycle of four hundred days, but, when the *tun* was invented, the twenty gods had to be squeezed somehow into eighteen *uinals*. The Nahuatl solution was to assign two of the *uinals* two gods each. Another solution appears to have been to multiply the Flower goddess by eighteen, producing eighteen Flower gods. Yet another may be to omit two gods, as the Chumayel appears to have done with the hummingbird god and the corn god.

The Tizimin lists the names of the 13 Gods and the 9 Gods, and the Chumayel lists the names for the 7 Gods who are known collectively as the pacers. As has been mentioned, there are five sets of four gods each who are closely related to each other and to the direction gods (*ba cabob*). Finally, there are the 2 Gods. The Yucatecans do not emphasize Mother and Father or Grandmother and Grandfather, nor do they double up the gods of the underworld as the Quiche and Nahua do. Dualism is represented rather by Quetzal and Hummingbird, associated respectively with the Itza and the Xiu and obviously cousins of the Mexican Quetzalcoatl and Huitzilopochtli. They probably also represent the morning and evening stars, and that brings us back to the unity of *hunab ku* and the Ordered Country.

The unity in diversity of the Mayan pantheon is governed, then, by the unity of the calendar. It is obscured by the welter of synonyms for particular deities, but, like the myriad names of the Virgin Mary, these may be regarded as merely aspects of divinity leading back to unity. The blue-green bird, an image which unifies the quetzal and the hummingbird, also refers to the fifth direction: the center, the crossroads of the other four, spatially symbolizing the unity of god. Whether Hummingbird or Quetzal is intended, it would appear that this conception may also have included a five-fold subdivision of Quetzalcoatl: as death god, as wind, as Venus (sun), as rain, and as fire (Nacxit), thus further unifying the five sets of directional gods, the Ba Cabs or Fathers of the Land.

We are now in a position to summarize and synthesize the calendrical, theological, and ceremonial aspects of Mayan religion as the Chumayel describes it during the first century after the Spanish conquest. The syn-

optic table (table 3) lists the twenty acts of the *baktun* ceremonial—
which includes the thirteen acts of the *may* and *katun* ceremonials, beginning at act 8. The days of the *uinal* (and the *tzol kin*) are listed next,
aligned with the ceremonies I believe to be related to them. Their associations are also given. Where possible these are translations, but many of
the day names cannot be translated. The yearbearers (*can hel*) and Ba Cabs
are capitalized in the table, together with the gods multiplied by nine,
thirteen, and eighteen. The days are followed in turn by the nineteen
"months" of the *hab*, together with their associations, also aligned with

Table 3. Mayan Myth and Ritual

Ceremonies (*Baktun*)	Days (*Uinal*)	Months (*Hab*)	Gods (*Tun*)	Today (*Katun*)
1. Mead	Chuen (monkey)	Pop (mat)	Monkey (Maax)	
2. Tying	Eb (step)	Uo (frog)	Bee (Muzen Cab)	
3. Cycle ending	Ben (corn)	Zip (deer)	(CORN) Quetzal	
4. Yearbearer	IX (jaguar)	Zotz' (bat)	Jaguar (Balam)	
5. Bird	Men (bird)	Tzec (skeleton)	Quetzal (Kuk)	
6. Heart	Cib (wax)	Xul (end)	Rainbow (Ix Chel)	
7. Rain	Caban (earth)	Yaxkin (green sun)	Buzzard (Ah Kuch)	
8. Circuit	Etz'nab (flint)	Mol (track)	FLOWER (Nicte)	*Balche* (mead)
9. *Katun* seating	CAUAC (rain)	Ch'en (well)	RAIN (Chac)	*Hetz' mek* (seating)
10. Yearbearer seating	Ahau (lord)	Yax (first)	Lord (Itzam Na)	*Cuch* (burden)
11. Pacing	Imix (alligator)	Zac (white)	Alligator (Itzam Cab Ain)	*Uklic col* (field feeding)
12. Dawn	Ik (wind)	Ceh (deer)	WIND (Ikil)	*Kaan* (hammock)
13. Sacrifice	Akbal (night)	Mac (cover)	SUN (Pauah Tun)	*Cub p'ol* (head seating)
14. Examination	KAN (yellow)	Kankin (yellow sun)	Rattlesnake (Ahau Can)	*Hol che* (first fruits)
15. The word	Chicchan (snake)	Muan (macaw)	FIRE (Ah Toc)	*Tup' kak* (quench fire)
16. Penance	Cimi (death)	Pax (break)	DEATH (Ah Puch')	*X pa' pul* (breaking)
17. Commemoration	Manik (deer)	Kayab (songs)	Deer (Zuhuy Zip)	*Zip* (deer demon)
18. Counting	Lamat (flood)	Cumku (dark god)	Rope (Ix Tab)	*Xtabay* (hanging woman)
19. Farce	MULUC (rainstorm)	Uayeb (specters)	(HUMMINGBIRD) (Tz'unun)	*Ch'a chaac* (rainmaking)
20. Sermon	Oc (foot)	(Oc Na) (enter house)	Dog (Nacxit)	*Ch'uyenil na* (housewarming)

what I perceive to be those of the days and ceremonies. Finally, there are
the eighteen gods of the *tun* (plus two to make twenty). Mayan ceremonies and beliefs that survived into the twentieth century are added in the
last column. They appear to be aligned with the *katun*.

Interwoven in the table are the significant cycles of 4, 5, 7, 9, 13, 18, 19,
and 20 that are fundamental to Mayan numerology. Note, for example,
that the "month" Kankin 'yellow sun' follows Yaxkin 'green sun' by exactly seven months. Note that five of the gods are quadripartite and that
thirteen are not. Remember that religiously 13 and 7 make 1, that 18 is
construed as 5 and 13, 13 as 6 and 7, and 9 as 4 and 5, and that 19 appears
only through mention of the unmentionable Uayeb. Note too that the
ninth god is multiplied by nine and the thirteenth god by thirteen. The
table is intended to suggest something of the richness and complexity of
Mayan religious metaphor. And the associations and interassociations
among the categories are ultimately metaphorical, not numerological or
calendric.

The preceding synopsis comes about as close as the Chumayel itself to
describing the theogony of the period of 9 Ahau (1559), when the myth
"The Birth of the *Uinal*" was composed. It was obviously somewhat
Spanish-influenced already, but only to a highly limited degree. A number
of other Mayan myths are referred to in the text, but without much exposition: "The Birth of the Flowers" and the origin of the Itza as descendants of Itzam Na. A sermon of 11 Ahau (chapter 19) presents a memorable picture of the coming of Jesus to Yucatan:

The man of the cycle city,
    Engendering himself all alone,
Is tried
    And put in irons.
He is tied up.
    When he is tied
Then he is beaten.
    Then next he is seated.
Then he speaks
    To the ear of his son.
He has his hat on his head
    And his sandals on his feet.
He has his sash tied around his waist,
    And thus perhaps is his coming. (lines 1977–1990)

Obviously he will have to do better than that to best the blue-green bird.

Eventually he did, and the Chumayel includes a highly syncretistic
creation myth, "The Sevenfold Creation" of chapter 41, dating to 2 Ahau
(1776). Composed in seven cycles of sevens, this mystical text mingles
Mayan cosmology with biblical citations; Spanish and frequently mangled
Latin are added to provide the right implication of secret knowledge. The
seven cycles of the myth are (I) 7 Creations, (II) 7 Angels, (III) 7 Winds, (IV)
7 Graces, (V) 7 Layers of Heaven, (VI) 7 Saints, and (VII) 7 Names of God.
These are indicated by roman numerals in the translation. Furthermore,

there are seven other names of God scattered through the text, and there are at least two cycles of seven names for Christ.

I and II. The 7 Creations and the 7 Angels. We begin with the first age, "the first *katun*," the first creation. Each creation is enumerated and provided with an angel: (1) Dominus, (2) Woman Born Baby, (3) Dawn of the Four Changers, (4) Child Two Knowing, (5) the Egyptian, (6) Child of a Thousand, and (7) Sustaining Grace.

III. The 7 Winds: (1) ?Rolling Moon, (2) Thomas Doubted, (3) Archangel, (4) Herodias, (5) Stained Wrap in Front, (6) Virtue, and (7) Jeremiah.

IV. The 7 Graces: (1) Jerome, (2) Bol Ay, (3) Jesus. The name Jesus does not occur in this text. In this cycle he is called by seven other names: Man (*xib*), Complete the Sky, Great Deeds, Hebron, Medicine Water, Brilliance of Heaven, and Child of Fruit Offering. The cycle of the Graces is then completed by the addition of the four winds, who are equated with the directions, the yearbearers, and the rain giants, thus covering three of the five manifestations of the Ba Cabs. There is also a somewhat confused effort to name them: (4) Corpinus, (5) Orale, (6) ?Trinity, and (7) ?Unity. This 3 plus 4 approach to making 7 is repeated in cycle VII.

V. The 7 Layers of Heaven: (1) Sirius, (2) Thou Wast Buried, (3) Praise Be to God, (4) Bol Ay, (5) Jaguar Cacao, (6) Exhale, and (7) Inhale.

VI. The 7 Saints: (1) Spirit (*Espíritu*), (2) Saint Edendeus, (3) Saint Elisha, (4) Enos, (5) Joseph, (6) Infinite, and (7) Thrice Tripled.

VII. The 7 Names of God: (1) Holy God (*Dios citbil*), (2) Joshua, (3) Jesus. This time he is called Master, Dei, Messiah, Christ, Immanuel, and Jeremiah, and he may also be called Jupiter (perhaps in confusion with Lucifer, whose fall is alluded to). Again the four winds are added. Their associations are (4) red, Saturn, (5) white, Jupiter, (6) black, Mars, and (7) yellow, Venus, Moses.

Running through the whole text is another set of seven names of God. In the order in which they appear, they are (1) Lord (*dominus*), (2) God (*ku*), (3) Sustaining Grace (*sustinal gracia*), (4) Holy God (*Dios citbil*), (5) Unity (*unidad*), (6) God Made Son (*Dios mehenbil*), and (7) God the Holy Ghost (*Dios Espíritu Santo*). He is also referred to as a father (*yum*), but he is not named that in this text, as in God the Father (*Dios yumbil*).

The author has achieved a quite remarkable synthesis of Mayan and Christian religion, incorporating the Trinity and the yearbearers, cosmological space and time, saints, angels, and Mayan (wind) spirits into a single numerologically elegant scheme, focusing on the number that symbolizes the highest level of the Mayan heaven. If his command of Latin and Spanish leaves much to be desired, there is nothing wrong with his mathematics. And you cannot avoid thinking that he had been exposed to Saint John's dream of the seven angels and seven plagues that end the world (Revelation 15).

Between the composition of the myths "The Birth of the *Uinal*" in 1559 and "The Sevenfold Creation" in 1776, there is a gradual accretion of Christian imagery and mythology: the Virgin of Izamal, patron saint of Yucatan, the concepts of the catechism, the commandments of God and the church. To some extent these new elements were numerologically assimilated into the preexisting system. Dualism is underlined by the images of Adam and Eve and the opposition of God and the devil, Kizin 'the Old Fart'. The number 3 attains special status through the introduction of the Trinity. But the seven-day week and other emphases on seven in Christianity had a special appeal to the Maya.

It remains possible that the emphasis on seven in "The Sevenfold Creation" is intended as a reference to the first seven *baktuns* of the Mayan era. The earliest date referred to in the Chumayel is in any case the following *baktun*, 8.0.0.0.0, which is cited as a more or less mythical reference date for the beginning of the building of the pyramids. This was A.D. 41. The next date given is 9.13.0.0.0 (8 Ahau), and it is specified that in a year 4 Muluc (674) Chichen Itza was destroyed. It must be significant that this *katun* brackets the starting date of the Aztec calendar in 682 (Graulich 1981).

In the following *katun* (6 Ahau or 711), the Chichen Itza appeared, claiming to be the divine descendants of the father of the gods, Itzam Na, and of Quetzalcoatl as well. Then 4 Ahau (731) is given as the date of the equally mythical birth of the Sun Giants (*pauah tun*). True to their view of the dating of the *may*, the Itza "ordered the mat" at the end of their thirteenth *katun* in 13 Ahau (771), and at the following 8 Ahau (948) Chichen Itza is said to have been destroyed again.

The arrival of the Xiu is not dated in the Chumayel, but the Tizimin puts it in the last year of 13 Ahau (770). The Mani places it at the end of 8 Ahau (692). They were, or claimed to be, Toltecs (*tutul xiu*) from Tula, the direct descendants of Hummingbird (*tz'unun, uitzitzillin*) and his consort Flower (*nicte, xuchit*). On the other hand, it is not clear just where they arrived at that date. Their chief was the East priest Bi Ton, but it is possible to construe this phrase (*chacnabiton*) in Nahuat as *chicnahuitan* 'nine country'; if so, their place of entry was probably outside of Yucatan altogether.

History

Tenth Century. Something like real history begins to emerge in the tenth century. After the destruction of Chichen Itza in 948, the "Chontal" took Champoton (in 987), and in 1059 Chichen is reported to have been destroyed again. Were these "Chontal" actually Xiu, who had merely come from Chontal country? In any case, the Itza seized Champoton in 948 and held it off and on against stiff opposition from somebody until 1204.

Thirteenth Century. A restless period followed. Conil is reported destroyed in the extreme northeast of Yucatan in 1224, and there appears to have been a Xiu incursion at Chichen in 1244. The Xiu established themselves at Uxmal in 1264 and thus became identified as Hill Lords (*uitzil*) as well as Flowers.

Fourteenth Century. It was 11.3.0.0.0 13 Ahau (1283) when the Xiu and the Itza settled their differences and established the League of Mayapan, which therefore was programmed to last until 1539. There was an incursion of naked cannibals (Caribs or Miskitos?) in 1362, and Izamal was reported destroyed, probably by Xiu. Chichen was destroyed again in 1382, Uxmal in 1401.

Fifteenth Century.   The League of Mayapan presupposed a Xiu hegemony in western Yucatan, centered at Uxmal, an Itza preeminence in the east, centered at Chichen, and joint rule in the walled city of Mayapan in the center, the seat of the cycle. As the terminal *katun* of the Xiu cycle approached (8 Ahau), tensions mounted. Otzmal had seated the *katun* in 12 Ahau (1401)—in Itza territory. (From this date until 1848, the *Books* chronicle the lordship of the *katuns*. A synopsis of the cities, Jaguars, and Spokesmen is given in appendix D.) Zizal and Coba disputed the seating of the *katun* in 10 Ahau—both also in Itza country. When Kan Cab A and Izamal (also Itza) claimed 8 Ahau (1441–1461), things were ripe for an explosion. The Peten Itza (who then called themselves the Xuluc 'the remnant of the Itza') saw the handwriting on the wall, and in 1448 they migrated south to the heart of the Guatemalan Peten and seated a new cycle and *katun* at Tan Xuluc Mul. They seem to have lived in and near Mayapan and were particularly exposed to the coming storm, which hit in 1451.

The Itza governor of Mayapan at the beginning of 8 Ahau was apparently Mex Cuc. The governor of Uxmal was probably Hunac Ceel. The governor of Izamal was Ul Ahau, the governor of Merida was Tzim Thul, and the governor of Chichen Itza was Xib Chac. Izamal was the primary seat of the *katun*, and the Jaguar of Izamal was ailing. A plot was hatched which involved the dynastic politics of Izamal and a number of other cities, including Champoton, whose governor may have been Kak Mo, closely linked to Izamal, and Chichen, whose Can lineage was also related to the Izamal dynasty.

8 Ahau was the terminal *katun* of the Xiu *may*. In anticipation of the start of a new cycle in 6 Ahau, new officials were supposed to be named at the mid-*katun* ceremonies of 8 Ahau in 1451. Merida got into the act by naming Tzim Thul as Jaguar and Uayom Ch'ich' the Strong as Spokesman, at the same time designating Merida as the new seat of the cycle as well as the *katun*. Can Ul was named counselor to the Jaguar, thus giving Xiu ceremonial backing to his claim to the governorship of Izamal.

When Ul Ahau died, his heirs in Izamal included Ahau Can, Hapay Can, Itzam Can, and Can Ul, all of them relatives of Kukul Can at Chichen, priest of Quetzalcoatl and next in line to the governorship of that city. Ahau Can had the best claim, and the Itza of Chichen were determined to support him. Before they could act, however, Hunac Ceel deposed the Itza governor of Mayapan, replacing him with Cau Ich, naming Chab Le as the Spokesman, and throwing Mex Cuc into the cenote at Chichen.

To counter or perhaps to forestall these moves (the dating of the events is uncertain), the Itza of Chichen sent an embassy to Izamal. It was made up of three of the four Ba Cabs of Chichen Itza: the East priest Xib Chac, the North priest Xib Chac, and the South priest Uoh Puc. Chichen was left in charge of Kukul Can, the priest of Nacxit and apparently West priest as well (the "father of the rain priests"). Apparently at the instigation of Hunac Ceel and Can Ul, the delegation was seized at Izamal and sacrificed. This appears to have been more or less simultaneous with the seizure of the walls of Mayapan and the expulsion of the Itza from there. The Chumayel lists the Ba Cabs of Mayapan as Co Uoh, Ah Ek, Zulim Chan, and Nahuat (reading from east to south). Presumably they were all Xiu.

The decision on the Izamal succession then went to Hapay Can, apparently a compromise candidate, but there was a considerable amount of confusion and local opposition. Finally, in 1458, Hapay Can was deposed by Can Ul, whose claim to the lordship of Izamal was almost certainly based on an incestuous union (see the Tizimin) but who was an ally of Hunac Ceel. Hapay Can was sent to Chem Chan, a village dependent on Uxmal, where he was sacrificed. Kukul Can became governor of Chichen Itza, Can Ul became governor of Izamal, and apparently both claimed the Jaguar priesthood. Cau Ich continued as governor of Mayapan, Uxmal Chac (another name for Hunac Ceel?) of Uxmal, Kak Mo of Champoton, and Tzim Thul of Merida, and apparently all of them claimed to seat the *katun.*

The fall of Mayapan definitively ended the religious and political unity of Yucatan. Subsequent prophets from the fifteenth to the nineteenth and twentieth centuries pled for unity, but the basis for it—agreement on the calendar—had been destroyed. Underlying personalities and the calculation of personal advantage was the argument between the Xiu and the Itza about the dating of the *may.* Mayapan fell on Xiu time (8 Ahau rather than 13 Ahau), and the Itza could neither forgive nor forget that fact. The interlude between the two dates, 1461 and 1539, was marked by increasing turmoil and disunion.

The victors of the conspiracy of Mayapan (Can Ul, Hunac Ceel, Cau Ich, and Kak Mo) were not victorious for long: they all disappeared from history in the following *katun.* Hunac Ceel claimed the right to seat 6 Ahau at Uxmal, but the *katun* was also claimed by Hunac Thi and Teabo and just about everybody else. Champoton was put out of business by Izamal. The Chumayel notes that the last (major?) pyramid was built in 1467. It does not say where.

The nobles were having plenty of trouble with each other. There were no less than seven claimants to the seating of 4 Ahau. But by that time they were having trouble with the peasants as well. A resurgent Kukul Can seated the *katun* at Chichen Itza and attacked the Xiu. There were plagues. And the peasantry took to the woods and formed guerrilla bands to defend themselves from the tribute and captive raids of the marauding nobles. Modeled after the military orders of the nobility, these companies were a prominent feature of the disturbances of the sixteenth and early seventeenth centuries. They are first mentioned in the prophecy of Ahau Pech in 4 Ahau: Ants, Many Skunks, Hanging Rabbits, Cowbirds, Magpies, Blackbirds, and Mice.

As sun priest and Spokesman, apparently at Teabo, Ahau Pech predicted the demise of these orders in 4 Ahau, but he must have got his glyphs shuffled. Atikuhe also seated this *katun*, and heart sacrifices are mentioned for 1485 in connection with the calendar round ceremonies (Oc Na) at Mayapan. Although Mayapan had already fallen, it was not until this *katun* that it was destroyed, according to the Tizimin.

Sixteenth Century.   *Katun* 2 Ahau opened in 1500 with a great hurricane and fire, and in 1516 there was a plague. The latter, tersely described as a fever (*kakil*), may have been a consequence of the first contacts with the Spaniards. The celebrated encounter between Columbus and a boatload of Maya on the high seas in the preceding *katun* is not mentioned in any of the *Books*. But Spanish *entradas* began in earnest in 2 Ahau: Aguilar in 1507, Valdivia in 1511, Ponce de León in 1513, Córdoba in 1517, Grijalva in 1518, and Cortés in 1519. The arrival of Ponce de León appears to be recognized and correctly dated in line 140. Other apparent references to dates in this *katun* are, however, erroneous because they are stated in the Valladolid calendar: when corrected they prove to be later. The *katun* was seated at Chacal Na and also at Cozumel. The sermon of the *katun* by its Spokesman, Puc Tun, is brief and vague, but dire.

The final *katun* in the Itza may, 13 Ahau, was a turbulent and eventful period. At least four towns (Cozumel, Kin Colah Peten, Euan, and Coba) tried to seat the *katun*, clear enough evidence of the continuing chaos left by the fall of Mayapan. The sermon of the Spokesman, Xopan Nahuat, predicts the imminent arrival of the Spaniards (no great trick, as they had already arrived) and attempts to relate it to the origin myth of the Xiu, "The Birth of the Flowers."

In 1526 Francisco de Montejo landed on the east coast with the intent of initiating the long, hard conquest of Yucatan. Three years later a new calendar round began, coinciding with the mid-*katun* ceremonies and further exacerbating the political troubles, since this was the moment for designating the Jaguar for the next *katun*.

Matters came to a head in 1536. Because of a drought in the province of Tutul Xiu (according to the Mani), the governor of Mani, Pot Xiu, decided to lead a water pilgrimage to Chichen Itza. He was accompanied by his lieutenant, Kin Chi, and eleven other lords from adjacent towns: Iban Can of Tekit, Pa Cab of Oxkutzcab, Kan Caba of Panabchen, Ku Pul of Sacalum, Nahuat of Teabo, Ul Uac Chan of Cauich, Zon Ceh of P'en Cuyut, Ahau Tuyu of Muna, Xulcum Che of Tipikal, Tu Cuch of Mama, and Zit Couat of Chumayel. As a water priest (*pul ha*) and as a pilgrim, Pot Xiu (and his companions) should have been secure enough, and he had been assured of a safe-conduct by Chi Cocom, governor of Otzmal. However, when they reached Otzmal, the whole party was seized and murdered. This was on February 2, 1536 (Craine and Reindorp 1979: 77, note 60). The Mayan date was a calculated insult. It fell on 9 Imix, the day after 8 Ahau, the traditional end of the Xiu cycle, and hence it was a direct assertion of the Itza intention of seating their own cycle, which they did, three years later.

It must be remembered too that the Spanish had reached Campeche the year before and that Pot Xiu's father, Tutul Xiu, was their first important convert. He had even headed a delegation of most of these same lords to meet Chi Cocom at Sotuta to try to persuade him to accept Spanish rule. Mani was all the more incensed at the governor's murder.

On August 27, 1537, another thirteen lords of Mani got together to plan their revenge. According to the Chumayel, they were Ah Mo, Chan Xiu, Ahau Ez, Ah Tz'iu of Chi Nab, Pot Cupul, Pot Che, Batun Itza, E Uan of Cocel, Chan Uc of Tz'ibil Kak, U Can of Ekob, Chi Uc of Kul Koh, Chan Motul, and Ahau Coy. Whether anything came of this planning does not appear, but the battle between the Xiu and the Itza was clearly joined, the Xiu siding with the Spanish against the pagan Itza.

The Xiu were sufficiently moved by the murder of Pot Xiu and his companions that they made heroes of all of them, using their portraits and names as the lords of the thirteen *katuns* in the Mani and Kaua (Craine and Reindorp 1979: 77 ff.).

But the most important event of 13 Ahau was its ending. This was scheduled to fall on 11.16.0.0.0 13 Ahau 8 Xul, November 3, 1539 (Julian), in the Tikal calendar. The Mayan year began on 11 Ix 1 Pop (July 21) in the new Mayapan calendar, which was formally inaugurated by the Itza at Mayapan on 11 Ahau 7 Uo (August 16). The Xiu started their ceremonies a month later in Merida on 3 Oc 17 Tzec (September 15), focusing on the terminal date of the old *katun*. In the new calendar this was 13 Ahau 8 Xul (November 3). Their ceremonial program went on until 1 Cimi 13 Ch'en (January 9, 1540), according to the Tizimin. The Xiu ceremonial of the *may* for the inauguration of 11 Ahau has already been described. It included the historical drama "The Fall of Mayapan." We do not possess a description of the Itza ceremonial.

The conquest of the Maya took a long time. In a sense it is still going on. But *katun* 11 Ahau was the *katun* of the conquest par excellence. It was nicknamed the Flower *katun* as a euphemism for the fact that it was a period of war. The Spanish reached Heaven Born Merida (which was now the seat of the *may* as well as of the *katun*) in 1540 and "founded" it as a Spanish city the following year. The founding of the cathedral in Merida is duly noted. Yax Chac was Jaguar at Merida, but Zulim Chan was the Itza Jaguar at Emal, and Colox Peten (Kin Colah Peten?) also claimed to seat the *katun*. The Spokesman at Merida at the beginning of 11 Ahau was Tzin Yabun the Younger, and his sermon (which is garbled and fragmentary in chapter 12) is given clearly in chapter 13: it is rotundly pro-Christian and antipagan.

According to the Chumayel, tribute and forced labor were established and the province of Chikin Ch'el was subdued in 1542, and this was confirmed in a treaty (*concierto*) of 1543. Baptisms began in 1544. What the Spanish perceived as the Great Mayan Revolt of 1545 to 1546 passes unnoticed in the Chumayel. Reference is made to the devastating conquest of Uaymil and Chetumal in 1546 and 1547 (line 2431).

The coming of the missionaries (the fathers of our souls) was correctly perceived by the Maya as an important event. The "arrival of Christianity" is usually placed in 1546, the date the Franciscans reached Campeche. They got to Mani in 1548, to Merida, Conkal, and Izamal in 1549 (line 2347), and to Valladolid in 1552. At least in Merida and Mani, the fathers almost immediately began to instruct the Maya in Spanish, Latin, and alphabetic literacy, and before the end of the *katun* (by 1556 in fact) their students were producing Mayan chronicles in Latin letters (see chapter 14). There can be no question but that hieroglyphic literacy and Long Count dating were still intact as the *katun* ended on 11.17.0.0.0: the text says so (line 2496).

Although the Maya recorded (if incompletely) their early brushes with the Christians in 2 Ahau, the genesis of pro- and anti-Christian polarization in 13 Ahau, and their first encounters with missionaries in 11 Ahau, they generally regarded 9 Ahau as the period of the "coming of Christianity." The *katun* was seated at Merida and Teabo in 1559. The Jaguar at Merida is named as Ul Uac in the Kaua and as Uac Nal in the Tizimin; his Spokesman was Kauil Ch'el, whose sermon (chapter 21) is a lament over Itza factionalism.

The Chumayel references are oblique, but they are almost certainly allusions to the actions of Diego de Landa, whose auto-da-fé in Mani in 1562 (the famous "Burning of the Books") appears to have made a deep impression on the Maya, even though it is not directly described in the Chumayel. The period is remembered as one of sprinklings and hangings (baptisms and inquisitional tortures: the victims were suspended by their armpits or feet to encourage confessions of heresy). When Francisco de Toral arrived as bishop of Yucatan in 1564 and suspended Landa's Inquisition, the Maya had good reason to remember him—and did so.

The coming of the Virgin of Izamal is recorded as July 11, 1568, in the middle of this *katun*. By that time, Landa was back in Spain writing his *Relación* and defending himself from charges of having exceeded his authority. He was exonerated and returned to Yucatan as bishop in 1573. The Chumayel does not record any of this, though it does note his death at the beginning of the following *katun*. An extremely important consequence of Landa's trial was the removal of the Indians from the jurisdiction of the Holy Inquisition.

Yax Chac of Merida seated 7 Ahau for the Xiu, and Chu Uah seated it at Mayapan for the Itza. The calendar round of 1581 passes unremarked. The *katun* was distinguished by the outbreak of the Bech' Kab war, a bitter civil struggle that seems to have dominated the period. No details are given. At some point during the *katun*, Yax Chac was replaced by Amayte Kauil. The peasant military companies were again active, particularly the Strong Skunks, Jaguar Possums, Jaguar Foxes, Deer, and Rabbits, according to the Tizimin. A congress of sages was held in Merida under Amayte Uitz. It was attended by both Xiu and Itza, but it appears to have been unable to bring peace (see the Tizimin).

5 Ahau was seated at Merida January 1, 1599 (Gregorian). Amayte Kauil continued as Jaguar. The Itza seated Puz Hom at Zotz'il, east of Tizimin. (He was later replaced by Kaua Hom.) And the war went on. The military companies (Possums, Foxes, Bedbugs, Suckers, Earth Lions) were active in both eastern and western Yucatan, as peasants and merchants united in their opposition to paying double tribute—to the Spanish and to the Mayan lords.

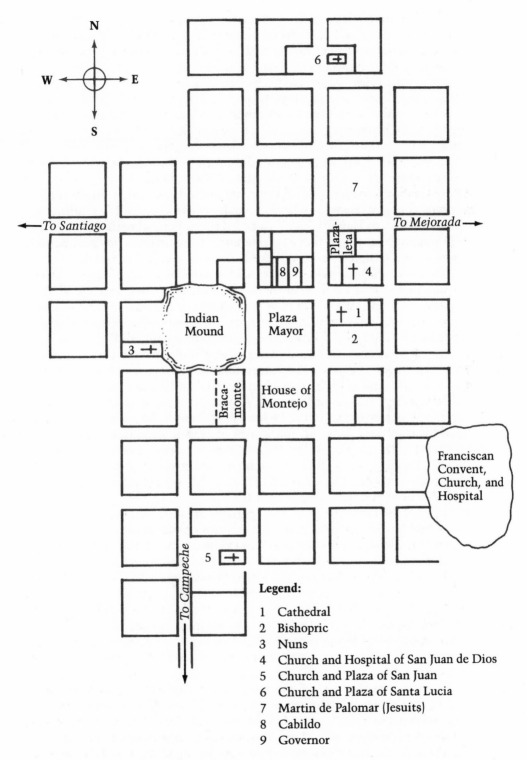

N

W — E

S

To Santiago →

To Mejorada →

6 ⊞

7

Plaza-leta

8 9

† 4

Indian Mound

Plaza Mayor

3 †

† 1

2

Braca-monte

House of Montejo

Franciscan Convent, Church, and Hospital

To Campeche

5 ⊞

Legend:

1 Cathedral
2 Bishopric
3 Nuns
4 Church and Hospital of San Juan de Dios
5 Church and Plaza of San Juan
6 Church and Plaza of Santa Lucia
7 Martin de Palomar (Jesuits)
8 Cabildo
9 Governor

Merida at the end of the sixteenth century. After Hunt 1974.

The Chumayel reports the completion of the cathedral of Merida in 1598 (line 5208) and takes the occasion to insert a chronicle (chapter 27) reviewing the history of the Spanish conquest and demanding an end to Spanish tribute in accordance with the treaty of 1543. The Spanish are blamed for tribute, hangings, plague, and the destruction of 13 cities—Valladolid, Coba, Chichen Itza, Uxmal, Cib, Kabah, Zayi, Pakam, Hom Tun, Ake, Ake Gate, Emal, and Izamal. The Itza are blamed for continuing to oppose Christianity, thus giving the Spanish a pretext for continuing to punish the innocent Xiu along with the guilty Itza. But, if the Itza are bad, the Spanish are worse: "Indeed the Itza could come here three times over for one occurrence of aliens" (lines 2899–2900).

Seventeenth Century.   Toward the end of the *katun* the military companies appear to have been brought under control, possibly by calling in assistance from Uaymil. Hol Och and Xaclam Pat and perhaps other leaders were captured, and there are references to sacrifice. They may actually have been sacrificed: the end of 5 Ahau was a splendid occasion.

The dawn of 3 Ahau in 1618 coincided with an even *baktun*: 12.0.0.0.0. It was therefore ushered in at Merida by the twenty-act ceremonial of the *baktun*, which is described in detail in chapter 29 (and has been summarized above). Competent hieroglyphic writing probably lasted this long (see line 5289), and the Long Count calendar certainly did.

Coc Ay was seated as the Xiu Jaguar in Merida, and another Coc Ay was the Itza Jaguar at Zuyua. The Xiu sermon of the *katun* predicts a flood and the conversion of the Itza, even though the Spokesman who presumably delivered it is identified as an Antichrist. The military companies were still active enough that the leaders of three of them (the Ants, Jaguars, and Locusts) were captured and sacrificed by nine rain priests—identified as Bol Ay, Pat Ay, Thul Caan, Bohol Caan, Ch'uhum Caan, Caan Il, Kuch Caan, Thel En, and Ceh Il—presumably impersonating the 9 Gods. The new calendar round began in 1633 (line 1247), overshadowed perhaps by the *baktun* ceremonial that began the *katun*.

Toward the end of the *katun* (or perhaps at the mid-*katun* ceremonies, as would have been more proper), a colorful character named Caesar Augustus registered his "request," his claim to the Jaguar priesthood of Merida in 1 Ahau, and Ol Zip of Emal announced the same intention for the Itza priesthood. Both encountered opposition.

1 Ahau was seated in 1638 at Merida by Amayte Kauil, according to the Mani, and by Puc Ol at Emal, according to the Chumayel. The Spokesman at Emal was Ual Ac (or Ual Icim in the Tizimin). Later, however, Ol Zip succeeded in becoming Jaguar at Emal—a politically significant development, as he had converted to Christianity in 1611. His Spokesman was apparently Ol Ha.

It was a disturbed *katun*, marked by war, plague (1652), and famine (1654–1658). Early in the period (1644?), Ol Zip was overthrown by Hun Pic, who in turn was replaced (1651?) by Can Ul. The military companies were on the move again (Many Skunks, Hanging Rabbits, Foxes, and Flags), and, again early in the *katun*, Caesar Augustus added to the confusion by seizing the priesthood at Merida and heading what sounds like a grass roots Christian revival in the name of the bishop and the Inquisition!

The curious and anachronistic sermon of the *katun* (chapter 34) brings in the shadowy figures of Antonio Martínez and Saúl (who really belong in the nineteenth century, along with their frigates and the War of Havana that are also mentioned), but its content suggests the message of Caesar Augustus: an all-out drive to Christianize the Itza. Chichen Itza and Zuyua are specifically mentioned. The pressure produced by this movement spurred a counterreaction, apparently begun at Tihosuco, which was called the Chan War and had as its objective the recapture of Valladolid, Emal, and Uaymil from the Christian party. In this it was successful, and the anti-Christians seated the following *katun* at Valladolid.

The career of Caesar Augustus marks the last gasp of the mystique of the *katun* in Merida, and 1 Ahau was the last *katun* that it claimed to seat. However, even though they were slowly being Christianized, the Itza continued the *katun* system for another two hundred years.

Yax Chuen was seated as Jaguar of 12 Ahau at Valladolid in 1658. This is the only *katun* in the history of Yucatan which is frankly admitted to be "good." The military companies were finally brought under control and disappeared from history. (The Foxes, Earth Lions, Hanging Rabbits, Flags, Lions, Weasels, and Turtles are all mentioned as being finished off, either in the Chumayel or in the Tizimin.) There is some indication that Yax Chuen achieved all this through a policy of democratization: the lords and priests made common cause with the curers and other commoners, putting an end to the class warfare that had previously precluded unity. Yax Chuen also sounded a note which will be heard increasingly in the future—to the effect that the Itza are the real Christians. Temporarily the war was over. Uuc Uitz and Chac Ek were designated as Jaguar and Spokesman of the next *katun*, but there is no evidence that they ever took office. A hurricane of 1665 is said to have killed Father Agustín Gómez. It is not clear where.

Mayan nativism, as represented by the tradition of the Itza, moved increasingly eastward, became increasingly Christian, but clung doggedly to the traditional calendar and its rites. *Katun* 10 Ahau was seated in 1677 at Chable (which I believe to have been at or near Felipe Carrillo Puerto), with Uat Hom as Jaguar, according to the Chumayel. (The other *Books* say it was Lahun Chan, presumably an heir of the Chan War of forty years earlier.) Eight years later the calendar round began, and there are suggestions that sacrifices were held, possibly of animals.

Eighteenth Century. 8 Ahau was reseated at Chable in 1697. Amayte Kauil was installed as Jaguar. A plague described as fever rash (*zan kak*) occurred in 1709. The Chumayel contains no *katun* history for this period or for the one that followed. (6 Ahau was seated by Kak Mo at Teabo in 1717, according to the Tizimin.) Sometime during 8 Ahau another summary chronicle was composed (chapter 37), apparently at Tixkokob. It is confused by an anachronistic use of the Valladolid calendar attributable to some later eighteenth-century copyist, who may also have been responsible for copying chapter 27. Indeed, chapter 37 could be regarded as simply an updating of chapter 27.

The longest *katun* in Mayan history was 4 Ahau, seated at Teabo in 1737 and not ended until 1776. The Tizimin tells us that Mac Chahom was seated as Jaguar. The *katun* was also seated at Bacalar in the south and Tan Hom in the west. A courier was sent out from Merida to order the suspension of the Itza tribute collected in the name of Chichen Itza, and things looked bleak for the Itza: it was only two *katuns* to the end of the Itza *may*.

A solution was found: change the calendar! The result was the Valladolid calendar, inaugurated in 1752, five years before 4 Ahau was due to end, but apparently decided upon at the mid-*katun* ceremonies five years before that (line 5330). The beginning of 4 Ahau coincided with the beginning of the calendar round in 1737. That was enough in itself to make this a portentous *katun*, and it is likely that heart sacrifices were made at the ceremonies inaugurating the *katun* (line 5326).

Proposed or at least backed by Pat Ay, the new calendar set up a *may* of twenty-four *katuns* of twenty-four *habs* each, thus putting a definitive end to the Long Count (*baktun*) dating system but also bringing the Mayan calendar into a much closer and equally permanent relationship to the Christian one. Henceforth the Mayan *katun* would always begin (as it did "accidentally" in 1752) on the second day of the Mayan year and (barring leap years) on the same European date. (This is also the last *katun* that gives evidence of glyphic writing.)

So it was ordained that Op Ik would be designated Jaguar at Valladolid for 2 Ahau at the mid-*katun* ceremonies of 1747 (at Teabo?) and that *katun* 4 Ahau would be reinaugurated at the three-quarter *katun* ceremonies of 1752. We know nothing of the later history of this *katun*, but the prominence of this calendar in the Chumayel implies its acceptance by the Xiu. (The noteworthy nativistic movement of Jacinto Canek at Cisteil in 1761 is not registered in any of the *Books*.)

As scheduled, 2 Ahau was seated by Op Ik at Valladolid in 1776, and Valladolid became the seat of the *may* as well as of the *katun*. To underline the importance of the occasion, the Chumayel records the highly syncretistic myth "The Sevenfold Creation" (chapter 41), which is relatively traditionalistic, but then counters this with a final attack on the sins of the Itza (chapter 42) and a completely orthodox (and probably non-Indian) sermon on the Last Judgment (chapter 43). In chapter 44 there is a note of a hurricane on August 18, 1766 (line 6152), and a plague at Chumayel on January 20, 1782 (line 6160).

Nineteenth Century.   Chapter 45 provides a *katun* history of 13 Ahau (1800–1824). It is almost entirely *pro forma*, seating the *katun* at Coba under Kin Chil, just as in the preceding 13 Ahau, and referring to Yax Chac, the Jaguar of 11 Ahau (1539), as well as to Itzam Na and Itzam Tzab. Presumably this was the occasion for the last performance of the ceremonial of the *may*, and the anachronistic references may be to that performance. There is insistent reference to a solar eclipse—in 1834, according to the Tizimin, and indeed a partial eclipse would perhaps have been visible in Yucatan on November 30 of that year (see Oppolzer 1887:

292–293). The word of the *katun* is a fifty-year famine, which would have covered the first half of the nineteenth century. Perhaps it did.

The sketchy ritual references of chapter 45 do not match the fuller ones of chapter 46, which reports the seating of Onetzihuitl as Jaguar, ostensibly at Tizimin. Possibly two different performances of the ceremonial of the *may* come into play. Eight of the thirteen acts are described, and act 17 gives the historical and commemorative drama of Antonio Martínez in some detail, including dialogue. Unlike the other historical dramas in the Chumayel, this one cannot be pinned down in time—Antonio Martínez remains unidentified. Many of the details, in fact, appear to be entirely contemporary, belonging to *katun* 11 Ahau (1824–1848) and not "historical" at all. The prophet Antonio Martínez identifies himself as Jesus Christ and offers to lead a fleet of frigates against the French and the king of Havana in order to guarantee the Christianization of the Itza and the acceptance of the "six-part bull," suspending tribute in accordance with the treaty of 1543 (in the previous 11 Ahau, three hundred years earlier). His arrival is predicted for 1838 and the suspension of tribute for 1843, which can hardly be accidental.

The chronology of the passage is further confused by the retroactive insertion of Antonio Martínez, Saúl, their frigates, and the War of Havana into the *katun* history for 1 Ahau (1638), exactly two hundred years earlier. The tale of Antonio Martínez must belong to the earlier part of 11 Ahau, since Pío Pérez transcribed it from the Mani in 1837. The bull suspending tribute may be anything from the Cortes of Cadiz in 1806 to the Revolution for Independence, which ended the *may* as 11 Ahau began in 1824.

The last *katun* mentioned in the Chumayel is 9 Ahau, which began in 1848. Again, it can hardly be coincidence that this marks the outbreak of the Caste War at Tihosuco, Ichmul, Valladolid, and Tizimin—all late Itza centers (Reed 1964). The word *katun* not only meant 'two dozen years,' it also meant 'war'. And there are Maya who are still aware that 1980 was the twelfth year of 12 Ahau. At Xcacal the *Books of Chilam Balam* are still read publicly each year (Burns 1980: 6). It is ominous that both the year 2000 and the next *baktun* and calendar round endings fall in the coming *katun* 8 Ahau.

HEAVEN BORN MERIDA AND ITS DESTINY

Q.: What is a man on a road?
A.: Time.
                    —Mayan riddle

6 Ahau

1. The First Chronicle

(74) 9: U kahlay*	The account
U xocan katunob uchc i	Of the counted *katuns*
U chictahal u chi ch'een ytza	Of the appearance of the Chichen Itza
U chi lae	Says this.
Lay tz'iban	5 This has been written
Ti cab lae*	In this country—
Uchebal	What may have happened,
Y oheltabal	What may be known
T u men hij mac y olah	By anyone who may sense
Y ohelta	10 And may understand
U xocol	The counting
Katun lae.	Of the *katun*.
9.14.0.0.0 *VI.* Uac ahau uchc i*	In 6 Ahau occurred
U chictahal u chi ch'een ytza*	The appearance of the Chichen Itza.
IIII. Can ahau lae	15 4 Ahau then,
II. Cabil ahau	2 Ahau,
XIII. Oxlahun ahau tzolc i	And 13 Ahau was the ordering
Pop	Of the mat.

1. For a list of the numerous published translations of this chapter, see the concordance in appendix A. The text is punctuated occasionally, as in this line, by a kind of rubric or paragraph mark resembling nine colon (9:).

6. Roys 1967: 135 has 'for the town', apparently reading *cah* for *cab*.

13. The Mayan text gives the coefficients of the *katuns* in roman numerals. Note the archaic listing of IIII for IV in line 15.

14. Roys 1967: 135 translates *chictahal* as 'discovery'. The form is causative from the root *chic* 'appear', hence the sense is 'the causing to appear'.

The chronology of this chapter has been subject to various interpretations, thus displacing the sketchily related events over many centuries of European time. Because the Maya believed that each *katun* cycle predicted all the others, they often repeated the same cycle with slightly varying details. The present chronicle contains one such repetition (see note 103). Taking this into account, the first date mentioned would be *katun* 6 Ahau ending on 9.14.0.0.0 (711). Even so, I doubt that any of the events chronicled can be accepted as actually historical before the tenth-century *katun* 8 Ahau ending on 10.6.0.0.0 (948). The present passage remains important as a mythological status claim that the Itza seated the cycle at Chichen Itza in the seventh century. For a description of the ruins of Chichen Itza, see Tozzer 1941: 173ff.

	XI. Buluc ahau	11 Ahau,
	IX. Bolon ahau	20 9 Ahau,
	VII. Uuc ahau	7 Ahau,
	V. Hoo ahau	5 Ahau,
	III. Ox ahau	3 Ahau,
	I. Hun ahau	1 Ahau,
	XII. Lahca ahau	25 12 Ahau,
	X. Lahun ahau	10 Ahau.
10.6.0.0.0	Uaxac ahau paxc i	8 Ahau it was destroyed,
	U chi ch'een ytza uch i*	The Itza's Chichen: so it was.
	Oxlahun uutz' katun ca cah i	Thirteen folds of *katuns* they resided
	Chakan putun*	30 At Champoton,
	Ti y otoch ob	Which was their home
	U katunil	In this *katun* cycle.

10.7.0.0.0	*VI.* Uac ahau	6 Ahau.
	IIII. Can ahau chucc i	4 Ahau and it was conquered,
	U lumil	35 The land,
	T u men ob chakan putun*	By those of Champoton.
	II. Cabil ahau	2 Ahau,
	XIII. Oxlahun ahau	13 Ahau,
	XI. Buluc ahau	11 Ahau,
	(75) *IX.* Bolon ahau	40 9 Ahau,
	VII. Uuc ahau	7 Ahau,
	V. Hoo ahau	5 Ahau,
	III. Ox ahau	3 Ahau,
	I. Hun ahau	1 Ahau,
	XII. Lahca ahau	45 12 Ahau,
	X. Lahun ahau	10 Ahau.
10.19.0.0.0	*VIII.* Uaxac ahau paxc i*	8 Ahau were destroyed
	Chakan putunob	Those of Champoton
	T u men ob ah ytza uinicob	By the men of the Itza,
	Ca tali ob	50 Who came away
	U tzacl e u y otochob*	And cursed their homes
	T u ca ten	Again.
	Oxlahun uutz'	Thirteen folds
	U katunil	Of the *katun* cycle

28. Roys 1967: 136 omits *u*: the text clearly specifies the well mouth (*chi ch'een*) of the Itza. The "destruction" of the cycle seat at the end of the cycle may have been largely ritual.

30. *Chakan putun* 'plain of the Chontal' or 'of the *putun* chiles' is probably the modern Champoton, a likely route of migration for the Itza from the Chontal territories farther west in Tabasco and Chiapas.

36. That is, by the Itza of Champoton.

47. I do not know why Roys 1967: 136 and elsewhere consistently translates *pax* as 'abandon'. The usual meaning is 'break, destroy'. This date brings us to *katun* 8 Ahau on 10.19.0.0.0 (1204).

51. Roys 1967: 136 translates *tzac* as 'seek'. I don't know why.

Cahan ob chakan putunob
  Ti y otoch ob
Lay li u katunil
  Binci ob ah ytzaob
Y alan che
  Y alan haban
Y alan ak
  Ti num ya ob lae
11.0.0.0.0 *VI*. Uac ahau
  IIII. Can ahau
II. Cabil ahau
  XIII. Oxlahun ahau
XI. Buluc ahau
  IX. Bolon ahau
VII. Uuc ahau
  V. Hoo ahau
III. Ox ahau
  I. Hun ahau
XII. Lahca ahau
  X. Lahun ahau
11.12.0.0.0 *VIII*. Uaxac ahau paxc i*
  Ah ytza uinicob
Ti y otoch ob t u ca ten
  T u men u keban than Hunac
  Ceel
T u men u uahal uahob*
  Y etel ah ytzmal
Oxlahun uutz' u katunil cahan ob
  Ca paxi ob t u men Hunnac
  Ceel
T u men u tz'abal
  U nat ob ah ytzaob lae*
11.0.0.0.0 *VI*. Uac ahau
  IIII. Can ahau chucc i
U luumil ich paa
  Mayapan
T u men ah ytza uinicob
  Likul ob ti y otoch ob

55 The Champotons lived
  In their homes.
For that was the *katun* period
  When the Itza went away
Under the trees,
60 Under the bushes,
Under the vines,
  Which was their suffering here.
6 Ahau,
  4 Ahau,
65 2 Ahau,
  13 Ahau,
11 Ahau,
  9 Ahau,
7 Ahau,
70 5 Ahau,
3 Ahau,
  1 Ahau,
12 Ahau,
  10 Ahau.
75 8 Ahau were destroyed
  The men of the Itza
In their homes again
  Because of the sinful words of
  Hunac Ceel,
Because of his making tortillas
80 With those of Izamal.
Thirteen folds of the *katun* they
stayed
  And were destroyed by Hunac Ceel
Because of his giving up
  The understanding with the Itzas.
85 6 Ahau.
  4 Ahau it was conquered,
The land inside the walls
  Of Mayapan,
Because the Itza men
90 Arose from their homes

---

75. This brings us to *katun* 8 Ahau ending on 11.12.0.0.0 (1461), the period of the fall of Mayapan.

79. Roys 1967: 136 and Barrera 1948: 63 accept Brinton's translation of *uahal uah* as 'banquet'. I believe it is an idiom for 'conspire' and is thus parallel to the 'sinful words' of the preceding line. According to the Tizimin, Hunac Ceel, who was governor of Uxmal, conspired with a usurping governor of Izamal, Can Ul, to destroy the League of Mayapan.

84. Roys 1967: 137 has 'because of the giving of the questionnaire of the Itzá'. I think the sense is that Hunac Ceel broke the Itza treaty that had been the basis of the joint Xiu-Itza government of Mayapan. The Mani specifies that the plot came to a head in 1451 (Craine and Reindorp 1979: 139).

	T u menel ah ytzmalob		Because of the Izamals—
	T u men u keban than Hunnac		Because of the sinful words of
	Ceel lae		Hunac Ceel.
	(76) *II.* Cabil ahau		2 Ahau,
	XIII. Oxlahun ahau		13 Ahau,
	XI. Buluc ahau	95	11 Ahau,
	IX. Bolon ahau		9 Ahau,
	VII. Uuc ahau		7 Ahau,
	V. Hoo ahau		5 Ahau,
	III. Ox ahau		3 Ahau,
	I. Hun ahau	100	1 Ahau,
	XII. Lahca ahau		12 Ahau,
	X. Lahun ahau		10 Ahau.
11.12.0.0.0	*VIII.* Uaxac ahau uchc i*		8 Ahau there occurred
	Puch' tun		The stoning
	Ych paa	105	Inside the fort
	Mayapan		Of Mayapan,
	T u men u pach paa		Because it was behind the ramparts,
	U paah tulum		Behind the walls,
	T u men mul tepal*		Because of crowd rule
	Ych cah *mayapan* lal lae	110	Inside the city of Mayapan there.
	VI. Uac ahau		6 Ahau.
	IIII. Can ahau uchci ma ya		4 Ahau there occurred painless
	cimlal*		death;
	Uchci oc na		There occurred the Entering of the
			House,
	Kuchil ych paa*		Appearing in the fort.
	Cabil ahau uchci kakil	115	2 Ahau there occurred the fire
	Noh kakil e*		And the great fever.
11.16.0.0.0	*XIII.* Oxlahun ahau cimci ah pul a		13 Ahau the water priest died,
	Uac p'el hab u binel		Six years before there came

103. The preceding lines (93 through 103) repeat the dates of the preceding
cycle, so we come again to 11.12.0.0.0 (1461). Hunac Ceel and seven other lords
with Nahuat names seized the walls of Mayapan and expelled the Itza, who then
counterattacked and tore down the walls.

109. Roys 1967: 137 reads *mul tepal* as 'joint government'. I would expect *et
tepal* or *et ahaulil* for that, and I think my quite literal translation makes more
sense in the context.

112. Roys 1967: 138 reads *maya cimlal* as a reference to pestilence. It could be
read as 'Maya death'. Barrera 1948: 65 reads it as 'sudden death'. I believe it to be a
reference to sacrifice and have so interpreted it throughout. I believe the reference
is to the beginning of the calendar round in 1493 in the Tikal calendar.

114. Roys 1967: 138 and Barrera 1948: 65 have 'the vultures entered the houses'
and Roys comments that Mayapan was already destroyed. The Tizimin agrees that
Mayapan fell in 8 Ahau but asserts that its destruction was not complete until
4 Ahau. Oc Na 'entering the house' was the name of the calendar round ceremony
(Tozzer 1941: 161) and *kuchil* means 'appearance' as well as 'buzzard-kind'.

116. Roys 1967: 138 interprets this as smallpox, which is possible at this date. I
think *kakil* may reasonably be read either as 'fever' or as 'conflagration'. See
Tozzer 1941: 40, note 1.

U xocol haab ti lakin c uchi e		The occurrence of the year count in the east.
Caanil Kan cumlahci pop ti lakin*	120	4 Kan was the seating of Pop in the east.
He tun te na cici pahool*		Consequently it was a very bad
Katun haab		Year of war,
Hun hix çip*		And 15 Zip
Ca tac ox p'el i		Was nearly the third.
Bolon ymix hi	125	9 Imix in fact
U kinil lay cimc i		Was the time he died,
Ah pul a lae		The water priest
Na pot xiu		Pot Xiu,
T u habil Do.		In the year period of our lord
158 años	130	Of the year 158.
XI. Buluc ahau hulci ob		11 Ahau there arrived
Kul uinicob ti lakin*		The god people from the east.
U yahtal*		Those who came
Ca hul ob		And arrived
U yax chun	135	Were the first founders
Uay tac luumil		Of these lands
C oon		Of us
Maya uinic e		Mayan people
T u habil Do.		In the year of our lord
1513 años*	140	1513.

120. This correctly identifies the date of the end of *katun* 13 Ahau in the year 11 Ix (1539), six years before the year 4 Kan (1545). The exact date of the water priest's death is given in line 125, and it is within 13 Ahau.

The manner of expressing this date merits comment. Before 1539 the Maya were using the classical Tikal calendar (Edmonson 1976). After 1539 they used the colonial Mayapan calendar, which changed the yearbearers by two days. To facilitate calculating in the latter calendar, the author advances six years to a convenient Kan year (the senior yearbearer in the new system) and calculates backward. This led him (I can't follow quite how or why) to 9 Imix 3 Ceh, February 2, 1536. Because the Mayapan calendar numbers the days of the *uinal* from 1 through 20 while the Tikal calendar numbers them from 0 through 19 (and uses different yearbearers), the same date would have been 9 Imix 4 Ceh in the Tikal system. But it is explicit that the Mayapan calendar is intended because of the use of the colonial yearbearers. The Tikal yearbearers do not appear as such in any of the *Books*.

121. Roys omits this and the following line from his translation, though he quotes Martínez: *cesó de llevarse la cuenta del katun de los años* (Roys 1967: 138, note 3). I don't see how Martínez derived this from the text, though *katun* may refer either to twenty *tuns* or to war. Barrera 1948: 65 has *he aquí que yo hago la correlación precisa de los años del katun.*

123. Why he chooses 15 Zip is not clear to me. In 1545 that would be 6 Etz'nab, which is followed by 7 Cauac, 8 Ahau, and 9 Imix. He may have had some mnemonic for going from this to the 1536 yearbearer 8 Cauac and for locating 9 Imix in that year. If so, it is not the same as mine.

132. Roys 1967: 138 has 'mighty men'.

133. Roys 1967: 49, 138, note 4 gives the text as *y ah talzah ul* and follows Brinton and Martínez in reading *yah* as 'disease'.

140. Ponce de León reached northeast Yucatan in 1513.

(77) Bolon ahau hopci *Xρnoil*
   Uchci ca put çihil e
Lay tal ychil u katunil hulci

   Obispo tora ua xan e
Hauc i
   Kuy tab e
T u habil *Do.*
   *1546 años.**
VII. Uuc ahau cimc i
   *Obispo de landa**
V. Hoo ahau
   III. Ox ahau.

9 Ahau was when Christianity began;
   There occurred being twice born.
That came in the *katun* period when there arrived
   Bishop Toral here also.
145 He ended
   The hangings
In the year of our lord
   1546.
In 7 Ahau there died
150   Bishop Landa.
5 Ahau,
   3 Ahau.

---

148. Bishop Francisco de Toral arrived in 1562, which was in 9 Ahau. I think 1546 is a transposition of 1564, which is also in 9 Ahau. The Maya had good reason to be grateful to Toral for suspending Landa's Inquisition. (See an extensive account of the Landa-Toral feud in Tozzer 1941: 80–84.) The hangings were not a form of execution but rather of torture, though some victims died of them (Tozzer 1941: 79, note 340; 81, note 344).

150. Bishop Diego de Landa died April 29, 1579, in the first year of *katun* 7 Ahau.

4 Ahau

2. The Second Chronicle

9.15.0.0.0 (77) 9: Can ahau
   U kaba katun
Uchc i
   U çihil ob pauah aen*
C u huy
   Ahauoob
9: Ox hun te
   Ti katun lic u tepal ob

Lay u kaba ob
   Ta muk u tepal ob lae

4 Ahau
   Was the name of the *katun*
155 When there occurred
   The births of the Giants
And the touring
   Of the lords.
It was the thirteenth
160   Which was the *katun* when they ruled.
That was their name
   When they ruled there.

---

156. I agree with Roys 1967: 139 and Barrera 1948: 68, note 25 that the text here is probably corrupt. Roys reads *pauah emci u yahauob.* I read *pauah tun c u huy ahauob.* Roys footnotes A. T. Willard, who apparently reconstructed *pa ua ha en cah u y ahauob* and translated as 'those who had been destroyed by water . . .'.

10.8.0.0.0	9: Can ahau	4 Ahau
	U kaba katun emci ob	Was the name of the *katun* they descended.
	Noh h emal	165 The great descent,
	Tz'e emal u kaba ob*	The birth descent was their name.
	9: Oxlahun te	The thirteenth it was,
	Ti katun	Which was the *katun*
	Lic u tepal ob	When they ruled,
	Lic u kabatic ob	170 When they were named,
	Tii ualac u cut ob	Which was to raise their seating.
	Oxlahun cuthi u cut ob lae*	Thirteen seatings had been seated.
11.1.0.0.0	9: Can ahau	4 Ahau
	U katunil	Was the *katun* period,
	Uchc i	175 And there occurred
	U caxantic ob u chi ch'een ytza e*	The overthrow of Chichen of the Itzas,
	Tij utzcinnab i	Which was achieved
	Mactzil ti ob t u men u yumoob e	By certain of them for their fathers.
	Can tzuc lukci ob	Four Parts they raised:
	Can tzucul cab u kaba ob*	180 Four-Part Country was their name.
	Likul ti likin kin colah peten	Arising in the east, Kin Colah Peten
	Bini hun tzuc i*	Became one part.
	Kul xaman na cocob hok	Arising in the north, Na Cocob appeared
	Hun tzucc i	As one part.
	He ix hoki hun tzuci e	185 And then there appeared one part
	Hol tun çuyuua	At Hol Tun Zuyua
	Ti chikin	In the west.
	Hoki hun tzucci e	There appeared one part
	Can hek uitz	At Can Hek Uitz:
	Bolon te uitz u kaba u luumil lae 190	Bolon Te Uitz was the name of that land.
11.1.0.0.0	(78) 9: Can ahau	4 Ahau
	U katunil	Was the *katun* period

---

166. Roys 1967: 139, note 3 and Barrera 1948: 68 follow Lizana in interpreting *tz'e* as 'little' (normally *tz'etz'*). I have translated it literally. Lizana relates the Great Descent to the west, as more peoples came from there.

172. Literally 'thirteen had been seated of its seats'. Roys 1967: 139 has 'settlements', which is implied but not stated.

176. Roys 1967: 139 and Barrera 1948: 69 read *cax* as 'find'; I read it as 'overthrow'. Either is possible.

180. Unlike Roys 1967: 139, note 5 I believe that dividing by fives was the Nahua aberration. The present passage appears to me to be a western Xiu (e.g., Chumayel) attempt to legitimize a Toltec notion by Mayanizing it. It didn't work. At least three other towns claimed to seat the *katun* besides the four mentioned: Atikuhe, Chichen, and Teabo.

182. What I read as 'part', Roys 1967: 139 reads as 'came forth'. I don't know why. Barrera 1948: 69 reads 'group'.

Uchc i
   U payal ob t u can tzuccilob
Can tzuc cul cab u kaba ob

   Ca emi ob
Ti yumtal ob
   Ca emi ob
T u chi ch'een ytza e
   Ah ytza tun u kaba ob
Oxlahun te
   Ti katun lic u tepal ob i

Ca oc i
   U keban thanob i
T u men Hun nac Ceel i
   Ca pax i
U cab ob
   Ca bini ob
Tan y ol che
   Tan xuluc mul u kaba*

11.14.0.0.0 Can ahau
   U katunil
Uchc i
   Y auat pixan ob i
Oxlahun te
   Ti katun
Lic u tepal ob i
   Y etel u num ya ob i
10.19.0.0.0 Uaxac ahau
   U katunil
Uchc i
   Y ulel ob
Y ala ob
   Ah ytza u kaba ob
Ca ul ob
   Tij ca ualac
U tepal ob
   Chakan putun e*
Oxlahun ahau
   U katunil*

When there occurred
   Their separating into four parts.
195 The four seats of the land was their name
   When they came down,
Who were to be made the fathers
   When they came down
To Chichen of the Itza.
200   Itza was then their name.
At the thirteenth,
   Which was the *katuns* they had ruled,
Then came
   The lies
205 By Hunac Ceel.
   Then were destroyed
Their lands.
   Then they went
To the heart of the forest,
210   Tan Xuluc Mul by name.
4 Ahau
   Was the *katun* period.
Then occurred
   The crying of their souls:
215 The thirteenth,
   Which was the *katuns*
When they had ruled
   And suffered.
8 Ahau
220   Was the *katun* period
It happened
   That they came,
The remainder
   Of the Itzas by name.
225 When they arrived,
   That was when they were to raise
The reigns
   Of Champoton.
13 Ahau
230   Was the *katun* period

---

210. The implication is that while some of the Itza continued to be associated with Chichen and the eastern part of the peninsula, another group migrated south at the time of the fall of Mayapan to become the Itza of the Peten.

228. That is, it was the intent of the Peten Itza to repeat the cycle of Champoton (ending in 1204), which they proceeded to do.

230. The founding of Mayapan in 11.3.0.0.0 (1283) is not elsewhere noted or refuted.

	U hetz'c ob	That they seated
	Cah	The city
	Mayapan	Of Mayapan.
	Maya uinic u kaba ob	They were named Mayan people.
11.12.0.0.0	Uaxac ahau paxc i	235 8 Ahau they were destroyed,
	U cab ob i	Their lands.
	Ca uecchah i	Then they became scattered
	Ti peten t u lacal	Throughout the land.
	Uac katun i	After six *katuns*
	Paxci ob*	240 They were destroyed.
	Ca hau i	They were ended,
	U maya kaba ob	The Maya by name.
11.17.0.0.0	Buluc ahau u kaba	11 Ahau was the name
	U katunil hauc i	Of the *katun* period that ended
	U maya kaba ob	245 The Maya by name,
	Maya uinic ob	The Mayan people.
	Christiano u kaba ob	They were named Christians,
	T u lacal u cuch cabal*	And all the bearing of the lands
	Tzoma *Sanc Pedro**	Was ordered by Saint Peter
	Y etel *Rey* ah tepal e.	250 And the King Emperor.

---

240. That is, from the fall of Mayapan until the founding of Spanish Merida.
248. 'Bearing the land' means owning it.
249. I read *tzolmal*.

12 Ahau

3. The Third Chronicle

	(78) U kahlay katunob u tial ah ytzaob	The count of the *katuns* for the Itzas;
	Maya katun u kaba lae.	The cycle of the *katuns* is its name.
10.17.0.0.0	Y lahca ahau*	12 Ahau,
	Y lahun ahau	10 Ahau,
	Y uaxac ahau	255 8 Ahau.
11.0.0.0.0	Y uac ahau*	6 Ahau
	Paxci ob	Were destroyed
	Ah coni(1)*	Those of Conil.
	Y can ahau	4 Ahau,
	Y cabil ahau	260 2 Ahau,
	(79) Y oxlahun ahau	13 Ahau,
	Y buluc ahau	11 Ahau,
	Y bolon ahau	9 Ahau,
	Y uuc ahau	7 Ahau.
11.7.0.0.0	Y hoo ahau paxc i	265 5 Ahau there was destroyed
	U cab y ahau ah ytzamal*	The land of the lord of the Izamal,
	Kin ich	The sun face
	Kak moo*	Kak Mo,
	Y etel pop hol chan	And Pop Hol the Younger
	T u menel hun nac ceel	270 By Hunac Ceel.
	Y ox ahau	3 Ahau.
11.9.0.0.0	Y hun ahau	1 Ahau

253. *Y* could be Spanish 'and' but is more likely *y* for Mayan *y eetel* 'and'.
256. This would be the *katun* ending 11.0.0.0.0 (1224).
258. Conil is twenty-five miles southwest of Cabo Cotoche.
266. Roys 1967: 140 reads *cah* 'town' for *cab* 'land'.
268. Kin Ich Kak Mo 'sun eye/face fire macaw' is interpreted as a god by Roys 1967, Barrera 1948, and a number of other people. The major surviving pyramid of Izamal still bears the name, which is also associated with Champoton and Coba. I believe that it was a prestige name borne by various people, in this case a lord of Izamal in 11.7.0.0.0 (1362). Hunac Ceel in the same sentence is a century too early to have been the author of the conspiracy of Mayapan, which poses a greater problem. The lineage names Kak and Mo appear elsewhere. Hunac and Ceel do not.

	Paxc i	Were destroyed
	Yala ah ytza t u chi ch'een	The remainder of the Itza at Chichen.
	T u y ox piz tun	275 On the third measured *tun*
	Ychil hun ahau*	In 1 Ahau
	Paxc i	Was the destruction
	U chi ch'een	Of those of Chichen.
	Y lahca ahau	12 Ahau,
	Y lahun ahau	280 10 Ahau.
11.12.0.0.0	Y uaxac ahau	8 Ahau
	U katunil	Was the *katun* period
	Hetz'c i	Of the seating
	Cab yala ah ytza	Of the land of the remainder of the Itzas,
	Likul y an che	285 Rising under the trees,
	Y alan haban	Under the bushes.
	Tan xuluc mul u kaba	Tan Xuluc Mul was its name,
	Ti likul ob	Which they raised
	Ca u hetz'ah ob	When they seated
	Luum çac lac tun	290 The land of the Plaza
	Mayapan u kaba	Called Cycle City,
	T u uuc piz tun	On the seventh measured *tun*
11.12.0.0.0	Uaxac ahau	Of 8 Ahau
	U katunil*	In the *katun* count.
10.19.0.0.0	La ix u katunil	295 And that was the *katun* count
	Cimc i	Of the death
	Chakan putun	Of Champoton
	T u men Kak u pacal	Because of Kak u Pacal,
	Y etel *tecuilu* e*	The sodomist.
	Y uac ahau*	300 6 Ahau,

276. The date was 1385. The "remainder" of the Itza appear to have been the Peten Itza, who were at odds with both the Itza of Chichen and the western Xiu.

294. This appears to date the founding of Tan Xuluc Mul as cycle seat of the Peten Itza in 1448, three years before the conspiracy of Mayapan came to a head. Zac Lac Tun 'white flat stone' was an honorific title of cycle seats, presumably referring to their plazas. (Compare Gaspar Antonio Chi, quoted in Tozzer 1941: 230: "Report of some of the customs . . . (of the people of the) province of Yucatan, Saclac(tun Mayapan). . . .") It is elsewhere applied to Mayapan, Valladolid, and Bacalar. Mayapan 'place of the well of the cycle' is similarly used, as are Ziyan Caan (Caan Zih) 'heaven born', Tan Cah 'front town', and Tan Tun 'front stone'. I believe the reference here is to Tan Xuluc Mul throughout, and not to the site we know as Mayapan. (See, however, Barrera 1948: 62, note 10.)

299. Kak u Pacal 'fire his glance' and Tecuilo (Nah. *tecuilonti* 'sodomist') are usually treated as two lords associated with Mayapan and said to be the conquerors of Izamal and Motul as well as Champoton (Roys 1967: 141, note 4). The Nahuat name makes it unlikely that they were Itza as the *Relaciones de Yucatán* would have it. I know of no instance of an Itza with a Nahuat name, even an insulting one. Barrera 1948: 72, note 29 relates *tecuilo* to *tecuilli* 'brazier'.

300. The *katun* count now repeats, starting over from 11.0.0.0.0.

	Y can ahau	4 Ahau,
	Y cabil ahau	2 Ahau,
	Y oxlahun ahau	13 Ahau,
	Y buluc ahau	11 Ahau,
	Y bolon ahau	305 9 Ahau,
	Y uuc ahau	7 Ahau.
11.7.0.0.0	Y hoo ahau ulc i	5 Ahau there came
	Tz'ul chibil uinic	The foreigners who ate people,
	Yx (80) ma pic tz'ul u kaba*	And Foreigners without Skirts was their name.
	Ma paxi peten	310 The country was not conquered
	T u menel ob i	By them.
	Y ox ahau	3 Ahau.
11.9.0.0.0	Y hun ahau	1 Ahau
	Paxc i	Was destroyed
	Peten tan cah *mayapan* u kaba	315 The area of the capital, called Cycle City.
	T u hun piz tun	On the first measured *tun*
	Ychil hun ahau u katunil e	In 1 Ahau of the *katun* count
	Lukc i	They removed
	Halach uinic *tutul*	The governor Tutul
	Y etel u ba tabil ob cab e	320 And his captains of the land
	Y etel can tzuc cul cab ob e*	And the four-division seats of the land.
	Lay u katunil	That was the *katun* period
	Paxc i	When they destroyed
	Uincob tan cah	The people of the capital.
	Ca uecchahi ob	325 Then they scattered
	U ba tabil ob cab e	Their captains of the land.
11.10.0.0.0	Y lahca ahau te ch'ab i	12 Ahau then got
	Otzmal u tunil e*	Otzmal its *tun* period.
	Y lahun ahau te ch'ab i	10 Ahau then got
	Çiçal u tinil e	330 Zizal its *tun* period.
	Y uaxac ahau te ch'ab i	8 Ahau then got
	Kan caba u tunil e	Kan Cab A its *tun* period.
	Y uac ahau te ch'ab i	6 Ahau then got
	Hun nac thi u tunil e	Hunac Thi its *tun* period.
	Y can ahau te ch'ab i	335 4 Ahau then got
	A ti kuh e u tuni lae	Atikuhe its *tun* period.

309. Brinton and Martínez believed these nude cannibals to have been Caribs; Roys 1967: 142, note 1 suggests Mosquito Indians. The raid would have been before 1362.

321. The year was 1382 and the account appears to refer to the destruction of the fields around Mayapan.

328. The following list of the *katun* seats from 1401 to 1559 is difficult to place geographically. Zizal, Kan Cab A, and Hunac Thi are near Valladolid. Roys 1967: 142, note 5 locates Hunac Thi near Mani and Otzmal was the seat of the Cupul near Sotuta. I am unable to locate Atikuhe, Chacal Na, Euan, or Colox Peten.

Lay u katunil uchc i

   Ma ya cimlal*
T u ho piz tun
   Ychil can ahau u katunil lae*
Y cabil ahau te ch'ab i
   Chacal na u tunil e
11.16.0.0.0 Y oxlahun ahau te ch'ab i
   Euan u tunil e
Y buluc ahau
   U yax chun kin*
Col ox peten chab i
   U tunil e
La ix u katunil
   Cimc i
Ah pul a
   Na pot xiu u kaba
T u hun pis tun
   Buluc ahau*
La ix u katunil
   Yax hulci ob *españolessob*
Uay
   Tac lumil lae
T u uuc pis tun
   Buluc ahau*
U katunil
   Ti ix hop'i *xp̄noil* lae
T u habil *quinientos dies y nuebe
años D°.*
   1519.*
Bolon ahau ma ch'ab i
   U tunil lae
Lay katun yax ulc i
   Obispo Fray Fran^co toral
Hul i
   T u uac pis tun*

That was the *katun* period when there was
   Painless death,
In the fifth measured *tun*
340   In the 4 Ahau *katun* period.
2 Ahau then got
   Chacal Na its *tun* period.
13 Ahau then got
   Euan its *tun* period.
345 11 Ahau,
   The new base year,
Col Ox Peten got
   Its *tun* period.
And that was the *katun* period
350   Of the death
Of the water priest,
   Pot Xiu by name.
On the first measured *tun*
   Of 11 Ahau.
355 That then was the *katun* period
   When the Spaniards first arrived
Here
   In these lands.
On the seventh measured *tun*
360   Of 11 Ahau
Was also the *katun* period that began
   Christianity,
In the year of our lord fifteen nineteen,

   1519 V (1546 M).
365 9 Ahau did not get
   Its *tun* period.
That was the *katun* there first arrived
   Bishop Fray Francisco Toral.
He arrived
370   On the sixth measured *tun*

---

338. See note 112.

340. 1485. The calendar round began eight years earlier.

346. Roys 1967: 142 has 'on the first day', but my translation is literal and refers to the introduction of the new calendar of Mayapan and the new *katun* cycle of 1539.

354. This would be 1539, but the correct date is 1536 and falls in *katun* 13 Ahau.

360. The first Franciscans did indeed reach Merida to stay in 1546 (Tozzer 1941: 68, note 306), though there was an earlier abortive attempt to initiate missionary work at Champoton in 1535 (Tozzer 1941: 67, note 303).

364. The date is in the Valladolid calendar. The correct Mayapan date is 1546.

370. This would be 1565. See note 148.

Ychil ah bolon ahau   In the 9 Ahau
  Katun (81) lae   *Katun.*
Y uac ahau ma ch'ab i   7 Ahau did not get
  U tunil lae   Its *tun* period.
Lae u katunil cimc i   375 That was the *katun* period of the
                                  death

  Obispo e lanoa lae*   Of Bishop de Landa
Ti ix ul i   And there came
  U hel *obispo* xan i   The new bishop also.
12.0.0.0.0 Y hoo ahau   5 Ahau,
  Y ox ahau (. . . . .)*   380   3 Ahau . . .

---

376. See note 150.

380. Throughout the Mayan text I have tried to fill gaps in the text with either dots or letters within parentheses corresponding in number to the apparent number of letters missing or illegible. If I believe the meaning to be completely rendered in the English I have not indicated breaks. If I consider the construal dubious I put in a (?). If I am unable to provide a translation I have used three dots. Five dots within parentheses indicate a missing line.

8 Ahau

4. Izamal and Champoton

Quarto

11.12.0.0.0 (98) Uaxac ahau katun*
U bolon tz'it katun
Ytzmal u hetz' katun
Kin ich kak mo
Emom *chimal*
Emom halal
(. . . . .)
T u pach y ahaulil cabob
Pakom u pol chakan putunob

U tz'ulil cab
U tz'oc çitz'il
U tz'oc u numçah ya ob
Ti bal cah
U than *Dios* citbil
Ban ban katunyah
Bin beltabac i
T u menel ah otoch
Nal ob e.

Quarto

Katun 8 Ahau
    Was the ninth part of the *katun*.
Izamal was the seat of the *katun*
    Under the glorious Kak Mo.
385 Descended will be the shield,
    Descended the arrows
    (Over Champoton)
    Because of the lordship of the lands.
Plastered were the heads of the Champoton,
390   Who were foreigners to the land.
Desire was ended;
    Endurance of sufferings was ended
In the world,
    Said God the remote.
395 Much waging of war
    Was to be produced
On the part
    Of the natives.

---

381. Throughout this series of *katun* histories, secondary marginal notes—arabic numerals, European dates, or Spanish words—suggest various orderings of the *katuns*. In this case the note *quarto* 'fourth' implies a *katun* cycle beginning with 1 Ahau. The illustration (p. 66) bears the numerals 9 and 13 in two different hands and depicts the lord of the *katun* crowned with a cross and surrounded by thirteen glyphs. Eleven of these are Ahau signs and the remaining two may be shield-arrow and flint-knife.

The Itza contention that the cycle ended at the end of *katun* 13 Ahau and the beginning of *katun* 11 Ahau is significantly related to the often quoted statement by Landa that the Mayan year began on 1 Imix, which is the day following 13 Ahau. What Landa should have said (and thereby saved us quite a lot of confusion) was that 1 Imix began the Itza cycle, not the year.

Top: *Kak Mo, lord of Champoton and Izamal (1441–1461). Bottom: Hunac Ceel, lord of Uxmal (1461–1480). From the Garrett Collection of Manuscripts in Middle American Languages, The Princeton University Library, The gift of Robert Garrett.*

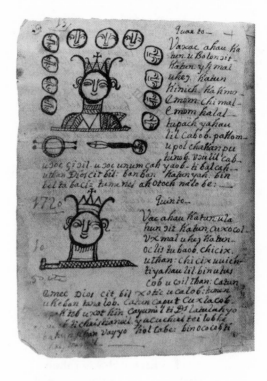

6 Ahau

5. Uxmal

Quinto

11.13.0.0.0 (98) Uac ahau katun*
　　　U lahun tz'it katun c u xocol

　　Uxmal u hetz' katun
　　　Oclis t u ba ob

　　Chic ix u than
　　　Chic ix u u ich ti y ahaulil

Quinto

Katun 6 Ahau
400　　Was the tenth part of the *katun* to be counted.
Uxmal was the seat of the *katun*.
　　They were being made to steal from themselves,
And shameful was the speech,
　　And shameful was the face in the lordship.

399. This line is preceded in the manuscript by the Spanish notation *quinto* 'fifth' in another hand, implying a *katun* cycle beginning with 1 Ahau. The accompanying illustration shows the lord of the *katun* wearing a crown bearing a cross, surmounting what may be a sword. A later annotator has added the numerals 10 and 1720.

Bin u tusc ob	405 They will tell lies
U coil than	And crazy stories.
Ca tun emec *Dios* citbil	Then God the remote will descend
Xotic u cal ob	To slit their throats
T u men u keban	Because of the sins
Tanal ob	410 Of the leaders.
Ca tun ca put cuxlac ob	Then they will be resurrected
U pakt ob u xot kin	And be made to await the judgment
Ca yumil	Of our Father
Ti *D*ˢ.	Who is God.
La t u lah y ocolob ti *christianoil*	415 That will return the thieves to
Y etel u cuchul teil ob	Christianity
He ba hun sihan uay	And the officials.
Y okol cab e	Everyone born here
Bin ococ ob	On earth
Ti *christianoil*.	Will enter into
	420 Christianity.

4 Ahau

6. Chichen Itza

(99) *Primero*	**(99) *Primero***
11.14.0.0.0 Can ahau katun*	*Katun* 4 Ahau
U buluc tz'it katun c u xocol	Was the eleventh part of the *katun* to be counted.
Chi ch'een Ytza u hetz' katun*	Chichen Itza was the seat of the *katun*;
Ulom u cahal ah ytzaob i	Come was the settlement of the Itzas.
Hulom kuk	425 Come is the quetzal;
Ulom yaxum* .	Come is the blue bird.

421. The notation above this line is the Spanish word *primero* 'first'. The accompanying illustration shows the lord of the *katun*, wearing a crown that includes both the cross and feathers and surmounting what appears to be a sword decorated with two long (quetzal?) plumes. His head is circled by four eight-pointed stars. Later notes include the numerals 11 and 1740.

423. Chichen Itza is held to have seated the *katun*, fulfilling a prophecy from the previous cycle, as Roys 1967: 161, note 6 points out.

426. "Quetzal and blue/green bird" (hummingbird) is a repeated couplet in these texts, referring to the Itza and the Xiu.

Ulom ah kan tenal*
  Ulom xe kik*
Hulom kukul can*
  T u pach ob t u ca te
U than Dˢ. lae
  Ulom ah ytza.

Come is the spirit of yellow death;
  Come is blood vomit.
Come is Kukul Can
430 Afterward for the second time.
This is the Word of God.
  Come are the Itza.

Top: *Kukul Can, lord of Chichen Itza (1480–1500)*. Bottom: *Lord of Cozumel (1500–1520) (see lines 467ff.)*. From the Garrett Collection of Manuscripts in Middle American Languages, The Princeton University Library, The gift of Robert Garrett.

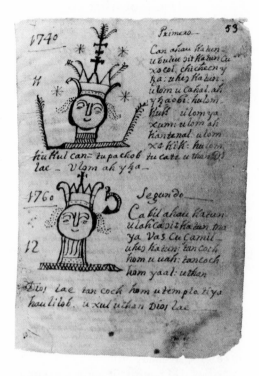

427. Roys 1967: 161 interprets Kantenal as a personal name. My translation is literal and is confirmed by the scansion. Jaundice/hepatitis is a likely possibility.

428. Roys 1967: 133, note 11 suggests that 'blood vomit' is yellow fever while acknowledging that there is some doubt that yellow fever occurred in America before the conquest.

429. Kukul Can is the Nahuatl Quetzalcoatl 'quetzal serpent'. In this case I believe it to be a personal name: both Kuk and Can are frequent lineage names. The suffixes -Vl and -il appear to me to be merely euphonic in this connection (cf. Ulil Ahau, Yaxal Chuen). Kukul Can was a prominent lord at Chichen Itza toward the end of *katun* 8 Ahau, and I believe this to be the same man, claiming the Jaguar priesthood for the second time some twenty years later. (The Tizimin makes this his fourth term, implying perhaps that he was active twice during the intervening *katun* but that Chumayel didn't know about it.)

7. The Sermon of Ahau Pech

(105) U *profeciado* Nahau Pech*
   Gran sacerdote
(*i*) T u kini
   Uil u uatal kin e
Yum e
   Ti y okçah ych ah te(*ii*)pal*

Ua lo
   T u can tz'it u katunil*

U cominal e
   U hahal (*iii*) pul t u kin ku e*
Y ok lae
   Ka u ba
Yn kuben
   Yu(*iv*)m e
Ych ex
   T u bel au ula
Ytza e
   U yum cab cah ulom
(*v*) Tal t u chi Nahau pech
   Ah kin
T u kinil ua
11.14.0.0.0   Can ahau (*vi*) katun
T u hitz'
   Bin u katunil e
Yum e
   Satom uil si(*vii*)nic uinicil*

The prophecy of Ahau Pech,
   The great priest.
435 It is time
   As the sun is rising,
My fathers,
   That the face of the ruler will be
   lifted,
Perhaps soon,
440   In the fourth part of the *katun*
   period.
This is his vessel,
   The true child of the sun god.
Believe this;
   Gather yourselves
445 That I trust in you,
   My fathers,
In you
   And in the way of your welcome.
O Itza,
450   The father of the land is coming.
Come before Ahau Pech,
   The sun priest
At this time,
   Katun 4 Ahau,
455 Which will end
   When the *katun* period comes,
My fathers.
   Destroyed is the moon of the Ant
   people.

---

433. N(a) Ahau Pech 'lord tick', a prophet of the end of the fifteenth century. The sermon is the earliest one we have, dating to the end of 4 Ahau, 11.14.0.0.0 (1500). For some reason the manuscript numbers the nine lines of text in arabic numerals (as indicated by lowercase roman numerals in the Mayan text). The line breaks do not appear to be natural or significant, sometimes falling in the middle of a word.

438. Most translators have interpreted *ok* as 'weep'; I read it as 'above, raise'. Either is possible.

440. That is, the prophet predicts correctly that Christianity will arrive in four *katuns* (or 9 Ahau, which began in 1559).

442. As a sun priest, Ahau Pech claims to be the vessel and true child of the sun god. Surprisingly, this is the only mention of such a deity in these *Books*.

458. Bricker reads *uil* as 'hunger' in this and the following lines.

Bin y anac t u pach uijl		It is to be after the moon,
T u men u bobo(*viii*)chil uijl*	460	Because of the Many Skunks' moon,
U chuyum thulil uijl		The Hanging Rabbits' moon,
Sinic		The Ants,
Tz'iu		Cowbirds,
(*ix*) Kan		Magpies,
Pich	465	Blackbirds,
X pucil.*		And Mice.

---

460. Roys 1967: 166 reads *bob* as 'a mysterious animal' and *och* as 'possum', but I believe the word is a reduplicative form of *boch* 'skunk'.

466. The Chumayel version of this prophecy is both the fullest and the most coherent we have. The Mani (Craine and Reindorp 1979: 73–74) has:

When the time is known in which the lord takes pity (has compassion), four Katuns will have passed and the bearer of the True God will arrive. Weep when you remember what I say. Oh Itzá, lords of the land, when your guests arrive receive them with pleasure. Nahau Pech, priest in the days of the Katún 4 Ahau, tells you this at the end of the Katún.

The Tizimin (Edmonson 1982: lines 401–432) has:

The prophecy
    Of Ahau Pech
On the sun
    And moon,
Of the day of remembrance
    Of the fathers
Which removes the face
    Of the returned ruler.
Four parts of the *katun* cycle
are done
    And returned.
The true cast
    On the day of the god
Is removed
    And stands up.
Let me be seated then,
    Fathers,
Whom you saw
    On the road.
Welcome Him, O Itzas,
    Fathers of the Land.
When He is come
    That will be when you give
    up your hearts
And come
    Before
Ahau Pech
    The sun priest
In the sun
    And moon
Of 4 Ahau,
    The *katun* returning.
At the end
    It will be the return of the
    katun cycle.

2 Ahau

8. Cozumel

(99) Segundo

(99) Segundo

11.15.0.0.0	Cabil ahau katun*
	U lahca tz'it katun
	Maya uas cuçamil*
	U hetz' katun
	Tan coch hom u uah*
	Tan coch hom y aal
	U than *Dios*
	Lae
	Tan coch hom u *templo**
	Ti y ahaulilob
	U xul u than *Dios*
	Lae.

Katun 2 Ahau
　　Was the twelfth part of the *katun*.
Mayauaz Cozumel
470　Was the seat of the *katun*.
Half down was its food;
　　Half down was its water.
The Word of God
　　Is this:
475 Half down is his temple
　　Who is their lordship.
The end of the Word of God
　　Is this.

467. The suffix *-il* appears to be added to numerals somewhat capriciously as a matter of euphony, especially when counting day names.

The illustration accompanying this text (see p. 68) shows the lord of the *katun* with a crown and cross over a platform (a pyramid?). It is accompanied by a glyph which might be read as a crescent moon, half black and half striped, possibly referring to the approaching end (moon) of the *katun* cycle and to the half-and-half nature of the *katun*. The glyph is surmounted by an eyelike element. Late marginal notations include the numerals 12 and 1760. *Segundo* implies a *katun* cycle beginning with 4 Ahau. This is the cycle employed by "The Second Chronicle" (chapter 2).

469. *Mayauaz* is hard to fathom and does not occur elsewhere. On the model of Mayapan one might suggest that it is composed of the Mayan root *may* 'cycle' and the Nahuatl *uatza* 'run out of/use up'. But whereas *-apan* is a properly formed Nahuatl locative suffix, *-ua(t)z(a)* is not. I believe the composer of this text was playing word games, in that the whole phrase could be translated as 'the cycle water is used up (at) the seat of expense' or 'Mayauaz Cuzamil' . . . was the seat of the *katun*. Cuzamil as a place-name is usually glossed as 'swallows'. I have opted to treat the whole thing as a place-name here, but I think it originally meant more. Running out of food and water is a frequent metaphor for approaching the end of a *katun*, why not of a cycle?

471. Roys 1967: 162 omits here and in lines 472 and 475 the fact that either *tan* or *tan coch* may mean 'half' and that *coch* and *hom* mean both 'clear' and 'deep'. The author appears to have been punning.

475. The use of the Spanish *templo* is noteworthy.

9. The Sermon of Puc Tun

(104) *La interpretaçion**	The interpretation
Historias de Yucatan	480 Of the histories of Yucatan,
(*i*) *Sacerdotesob*	Of the priests,
Profeciado Na puc tun	And the prophet Puc Tun.
(*ii*) Elom ti cab	Burned on the earth;
Petahom canal	Rounded in the sky.
U uaom kauil*	485 Raised will be the deity,
(*iii*) Uaah tan u chamal*	Raising the ash of his cigar.
Elom ti cab	Burned on the earth,
Elom tz'itz' t u ka(*iv*)tunil*	Burned the hoof of the *katun* period,
U chamal	His tobacco
Talom e	490 That is to come.
U bixan bin ylic	His spirit will be seen;
(*v*) Bin y al u than	His word will be spoken.
Bin y okte	He may cause lamentation
U num yail uchmal e.	For the sufferings that have occurred.

479. The dating of this prophecy is frankly impressionistic. Aside from the first four lines, which constitute a sort of title and are possibly a late addition, the brief text seems to me to be non-Christian and orthodoxly Mayan. It expresses forebodings but no specific anticipation of the Spanish conquest. And it may have some archaic and glyphic elements. Customary scholarly caution induces me to place it as late as is credible, and that lands me in 2 Ahau. It is more likely to be earlier than later.

485. Roys 1967: 165, note 5 comments that Kauil is a god name, a lineage name, and an obsolete word for 'food'. I believe it is an obsolete word for 'god' too, related to the development of the more current form *kuil* (cf. Quiche *qav*).

486. Roys 1967: 165 and Barrera 1948: 195 read *uchamal* 'in time to come' here and in line 489. I believe that if it were that form it would be *uchmal*, as in line 494, and even then I don't see that it expresses the future. A literal rendering of line 494 would be something like 'its pain, suffering fulfillment'. I believe the god's smoking is intended to explain why the earth is burning. It may also imply that this was nicknamed "the tobacco *katun*" (see Tizimin, note 1860).

488. The hoof may be a glyphic pun. *Tz'itz'* 'hoof' is a synonym for *may* 'hoof, cycle'.

13 Ahau

10. The Sermon of Xopan Nahuat

(105) *Profeciado de* Chilam Balam

De Zix coyom
Ca u ich en*
Many

11.16.0.0.0 Oxlahun ahau u hijtz'
    U uil katun e
Ualac uil ytza
    Ualac (106) uil (iv) tan cah e*

Yum e*
    U chicul hunab ku canal

Hulom uaom (v) che*
    Etçahan ti bal cah e
Uchebal u sas-hal y okol cab e (vi)
    Yum e
Uch tz'uni to moctan ba

    Uch tz'uni sauinal (vii)

Ca tal on
    Ti pul chicul uchmal e

Ah kin i
    Uinic e yum e (viii)
Hun auat
    Hun lub i
Uil u tal*
    Au ilic ex mut e

495 The prophecy of the Spokesman of the Jaguar
    Which was also preached
At the two-eyed well
    Of Mani.
13 Ahau was the end:
500   The moon phase of the *katun*,
To return to the moon of the Itza;
    To return to the moon of the capital,
O my fathers.
    It was a sign of the Sole God on high:
505 Come is the standing tree.
    It is manifested in the world.
It is to be his radiance over the world,
    O my fathers.
Already there has begun tangling with each other;
510   Already they have begun to be envious.
Then we came:
    He who casts the signs which will come to pass,
The sun priest—
    This man, O my fathers.
515 One shout,
    One rest
Is the moon of his coming.
    You will see the announcement,

---

497. The cenote of Mani is called Cabal Ch'en and is so listed in the Tizimin, but as Roys 1967: 166, note 4 points out, it has two openings. Tozzer 1921: 122, note 2 says there is a town named Cau Ich Ch'en near Mani.

502. That is, the end of the *katun* cycle and of the rule of the cycle seat, theoretically still Mayapan.

503. *Yum* 'father' is a courtesy title of respect, comparable to 'sir' or *señor*. Except where God is addressed directly (line 547), I believe its implication in this chapter to be plural.

505. The cross. Barrera 1948: 197, note 119 interprets this as a preconquest use of a ceremonial pole.

517. The implication is that the arrival of Christianity is imminent.

U ti (*ix*) ppil
   Y etel uaom che
Ahom cab hun xaman

   Hun chi(*x*)kin
Ahom Ytzam Na*
   Kauil
Talel u cah ca yum
   Ytza (*xi*)
Talel u cah ca çucun
   Ah tan tun e*
Kam
   Au ula ob
Ah (*xii*) mexob
   Ah likin cabob
Ah pul t u chicul ku e
   Yum e (*xiii*)
Utz ka u than ku
   C u talel c icnal e
Talel u cah u kin (*xiv*)
   Ca cuxtal e
Ma a sahtic
   Y okol cab e
Yum e
   T ech (*xv*)
Hunac Ku
   Ch'abtic on
Utz tun ba o*
   U than ku e (*xvi*)
Yum e
   Y ah canul ca pixan
He mac bin kamic (*xvii*)
   Hach ocan ti y ol e
Ti caan
   U bin t u pach
He uac (*xviii*) u chun
   Ca kin uinicil*

The demonstration,
520   And the standing tree.
Roused will be the land now in the north,
   Now in the west;
Roused will be Itzam Na,
   The deity,
525 Coming are our fathers,
   The Itza.
Coming are our older brothers,
   The people of the capital.
Accept
530   And welcome them,
The bearded people,
   The people of the eastern land,
The diviners with the sign of God,
   O my fathers.
535 Verily good is the Word of God
   That is to come to us.
Coming is the day
   Of our life.
Have no fear
540   On earth,
O my fathers.
   Thou
Who art the Sole God,
   Who had us created.
545 It is good then to follow
   The Word of God,
O Father
   And guardian of our souls,
For someone will receive it
550   Very much within his heart.
To heaven
   He will go later.
That may be the beginning
   Of the two-day people.

---

523. This identifies the Itza directly with Itzam Na.

528. The prophet, identified in the Tizimin as Xopan Nahuat, is predicting the arrival of the Spanish, the establishment of a new capital (namely Merida) as seat of the *katun* and the cycle, and the triumph of Christianity. This became the political and religious doctrine of the Xiu throughout the following century.

545. Roys 1967: 168 has 'it is sufficient then that the word of God is good', perhaps reading *ba* as *baal*. My translation is textual and literal.

554. "Two-day people" is a frequent reference to fly-by-night lords who are unable to complete their terms in office.

(i) Ca uacun to u chicul canal | 555 Then may be raised the sign of heaven;
Ca uacun to y etel uaom (ii) che | Then also may be raised the standing tree.

Numtetah u kex a | Then may it suffer division of the successor,

U hokol hel e | There appearing the changer
U hel t u (iii) pach u yax cheel cab* | To succeed behind the Ceiba Land;
Etçahan helel ti bal cah e (iv) | 560 The succession being manifested to the world.

La u chicul hunab ku canal e | That is the sign of the Sole God on high;

Lae a kult ex (v) ah ytza e | That then will you worship, O Itza.
Ca a kulte helel u chicul canal e* | Then will you worship the changing of the sign on high.

Ca a kul(vi)te to t u hahil colah | Then will you worship that in the planting of truth.

Ca kulte hahal ku hele lae* | 565 Then will you worship the True God of this change,

Yum e (vii) | The Father.
Ocezta ba u than hunab ku e | May it establish itself as the Word of the Sole God,

Yum e | The Father.
Tali ti caan | He is come from heaven,
A (viii) u ah than be | 570 Your speaker of the way,
Cuxcin ka au ol ah ytza e | To revive your hearts indeed, O Itza.
A(ix)hom uil cab | Wakened will be the moon of the earth

Ti ob | For those
Occic ob ti y ol e | Who take into their hearts
Ychil u y a(x)nal katun e* | 575 The existence of the *katun*,
Yum e | O fathers.
Y ok t u ba yn than (xi) | May my word raise itself,
C en Chilam Balam | I who am Spokesman of the Jaguar,
Ca in tzolah u than (xii) hahal ku | When I recount the Word of the True God

Tuçinil e y okol cab e | 580 And the lies of this earth.
Y ub i (xiii) | Hear then
Hunac | That it may unite
Tzuc ti cab e | The division in this land,
Yum e | O fathers,
U than *Dios* | 585 The Word of God,
U yumil (xiv) | The Father

559. Yucatan was the "Land of the (sacred) Ceiba."
563. Roys 1967: 168 reads *helel* as *behelae*.
565. Roys 1967: 168 reads *hele lae* as *behelae*.
575. The English metaphor would be: the sun is already setting upon the believers in the *katun*.

Caan
   Y etel luum
Hach utz ka u than ti caan (*xv*)

   Yum e
C okol y ahaulil
   Y okol ix ca pixan (107) hahal
   (*xvi*) ku
He uac he ob ti ules lae

   Yum e
Ox al a mukil (*xvii*)
   X cuch lum ytz'inil

Tz'aman y ol
   Cimen ix u puc (*xviii*) çikal t u
   nicteob xan
Ah uaua t u lupoob

   Ah ua(*xix*)tan çinoob
Nacxit
   Xuchit
T u nicte u lakob (*xx*)
   Ca ca kin y ahaulilob
Coylac te t u tz'amoob (*i*)

   Coylac te t u nicteob

Ca ca kin uinicil u than(*ii*)n ob
   Ca ca kin u xec ob
U luch ob
   U p'ooc ob (*iii*)
U co kinn ob
   U co akab
U maxil ob y okol (*iv*) cab
   Kuy c u cal
Mutz' c u u ich
   Putz' c u chi (*v*)
Ti y ahaulil cabob
   Yum e
He c u talel minan (*vi*) hah

   T u than ob u tz'ulilob cah

Bin y al ob (*vii*)
   Hach talanil ob

Of heaven
   And earth.
For very good indeed is the word from
heaven,
590   O fathers.
Let us glorify the lordship,
   Glorifying also our soul the True
   God.
These may be just the things which
will bring it about,
   O fathers,
595 Thrice-born is thy strength
   And the bearing of the land of the
   younger brothers.
Surrendered is their spirit,
   And dead are the hearts of the
   flowers too:
Those who constantly rise to be
baptized—
600   Those who raise quarrels—
Nacxit,
   Xuchit,
With the rest of the Flowers
   Of the two-day lordships,
605 Who will be crooked there on their
thrones,
   Who will be crooked there in their
   Flowers.
Two-by-two-day people is their word;
   Two by two days their seats,
Their gourds,
610   Their hats.
Crazy are their days;
   Crazy are the nights
Of the monkeys of the world.
   Their necks are bent,
615 Their faces wrinkled,
   Their mouths slack
In the lordship of the lands,
   O fathers.
Indeed it came about that there was no
truth
620   In the words of the foreigners to the
   place.
It will be said
   That they were very troublesome,

U mehen uuc tocoy naob (*viii*)	The engendered sons of the seven Burned Houses,
Y alob uuc tocoy naob e*	The born sons of the seven Burned Houses.
Yum e mac to ah (*ix*) bouat	625 O Father, who will be the prophet?
Mac to ah kin	Who will be the sun priest
Bin tohol cantic (*x*)	Who will correctly interpret
U than uooh lae.*	The word of these glyphs?
Finis	The End

624. Roys 1967: 169, note 10 speculates that this refers to the origins of the Itza from the ruined cities of the Peten; I think it refers to the Itza claim to come from Chichen Itza, which is explicit elsewhere. Barrera 1948: 203 translates as 'seven deserted houses'. Bricker agrees with him.
628. Roys 1967: 169 reads *huun* 'book' for *uooh* 'glyph'.

11. Coba

(100) *Terçero juiçio*

(The Third Judgment)

11.16.0.0.0 Oxlahun ahau*	13 Ahau
Katun c u xocol	630 Was the *katun* that was counted.
Kin chil coba u hetz' katun	Kin Chil of Coba seated the *katun*,
Y oxlahun tz'it katun	The thirteenth part of the *katun*.
Etlahom utz'ub*	Equalized were the folds
Y ahaulil cabob i	Of the lordship of the lands.
U yuk xot kin ca yumil	635 It was a general judgment of our Father
Ti *Dios*	Who is God.
Emom u kikel che	Descended will be the blood of sticks
Y etel tunich	And stones.
Elom caan	Burned will be heaven
Y etel luum	640 And earth.
U than *Dios* citbil	The Word of God the remote
Y etel *Dios* mehenbil	And God Made Son
Y etel D^s. *espiritu*	And God the Holy
Sancto	Ghost
Santo xot kin lae	645 Was a sacred judgment then,
Santo juiçio	A sacred sentence

629. At the head of this text is the Spanish notation *Terçero juiçio* 'third judgment/argument'. The Spanish annotator was simply wrong about the order of the *katun* cycle. The Mayan text ties in correctly with the Itza cycle.
633. Roys 1967: 162 apparently reads *es* or *ets* for *et*. Again I believe the reference is to the ending of the cycle. Roys reads *u tz'ub* but I think *uutz'ob* is more likely.

*Kin Chil, lord of Coba (1520–1539).
From the Garrett Collection of
Manuscripts in Middle American
Languages, The Princeton University
Library, The gift of Robert Garrett.*

T u menel ca yumil	By our Father
Ti D^s.	Who is God.
Bin minanac u muk caan	For there will be no strength in heaven
Y etel luum	650 Or on earth.
Bin ococ	They will enter
Ti *christianoil*	Into Christianity:
Nucuch cahob	The great towns
U cahal mac nalob	And the settlements of
	householders,
U nohochil cah	655 The great people of the towns
Max u kaba bay u cah	And the monkeys as they are called
	and their towns
T u yukul lay mehen cahob lae	And the whole of the descendant
	towns;
T u yukul lay ca petenil	The whole of this country of ours
Maya cu çamil	Has the expense of the cycle seat
Maya patan	660 And cycle tribute.
Licil ca ca kin uinicil	Since they were two-by-two-day people
Tucal coil tz'itz' i	Full of madness and lust,
Mehenil t u xul ca satmail ylil	The young in the end neglected to look
Y etel subtalil cux y ol	And shamed the living spirit
Ca mehenob	665 Of our youth
T u nicteob*	In the flowers.

---

666. I agree with Roys 1967: 162 that flowers allude to sex here, though there
are a number of alternative metaphoric meanings, including war. Barrera 1948: 141
interprets the passage as a reference to infant sacrifice.

Minan y utz kin t oon lae	There was no good time for us then.
U chun cimil t u lobil kik	They began to kill in bad blood.
Be hokol u	There appeared the moon;
T u bin u	670 The moon left.
Tulis i	It returned,
Uil u uchac	And the moon of the moon occurred.
C uchi e	There occurred
Tulis kik	The return of blood.
Bay ti utzul *planetaob* e	675 Thus in the favor of the planets
Ylabil y utzil lae	Some good was to be seen.
U xul u than *Dios*	It was the end of the Word of God.
Bin tac y oktob y alil*	They will stop sprinkling the water
Ca put sihil	Of the twice-born,
Santo pixan	680 The Holy Spirit.
U kam ob *santo olio*	They received holy oil
Ma tz'albil u pach ob i	Without pressing to return
Tal ti *Dios*	And come to God.
Hach manal bin *christiano*	Nearly all will be Christians,
Ah bal ob	685 Twisted
T u *santo* oc olall ob	In the holy faith
Ah ytzaob	(By) the Itza
Y etel Balamoob*	And the Jaguars.
Tz'ocan tun ca satic	It winds up then that we forget
Ca . . .*	690 Our . . .

678. Roys 1967: 162–163 apparently reads *octob* for *oktob* and interprets *tac* as 'so' rather than 'impede'.

688. The Itza Jaguars, priests of the *katun*, remained staunchly pagan until the end of the sixteenth century. The Xiu Jaguar (Tutul Xiu) was converted to Christianity at the time of the invasion of Campeche.

690. The text breaks off incomplete. The following page in the MS bears the notation in a modern hand: *aquí falta una hoja* 'here a page is lacking'.

11 Ahau

12. The Ceremonial of the *May*

(3) Ah itz:	The sorcerer,
Tzim thul chac:	Tzim Thul the rain priest,
U mektann ob:	Was their ruler
Ych can si hoo:	In Heaven Born Merida.

Uayom ch'ich:*	695 Uayom Ch'ich'
Chich i	The Strong
Y ah kin ob:	Was their sun priest
Ych can si hoo:	In Heaven Born Merida,
Can ul:	And Can Ul
Yx pop ti balam:	700 Was the counselor to the Jaguar.
U ca tul = ah kin chable:*	There were two sun priests: Chable
U y ahau ob:	Was their lord (in Mayapan);
Cabal xiu:	And Cabal Xiu
Y ah kin ob:	Was their sun priest;
Uxmal chac	705 Uxmal Chac
U mektan ob:	Was their ruler (in Uxmal).
Lay	This
Y ah kin cuch i:	Was the sun priest office.
Ca ulsab i: hapai can =	Then Hapay Can was brought
T u chem chan:	710 To Chem Chan.
Lay hal i:	This was the piercing;
Ca uchi kikil	Then bloodletting occurred
Pak: te	On the walls there
Uxmal e:	At Uxmal.
Tii, ca colab i.	715 And then were seized
U cangel.	The yearbearers:
Chac xib chac e:	The East priest Xib Chac
Sac xib chac: colab i u cangel:	And the North priest Xib Chac were seized as yearbearers,
U cangel ix. ek yuuan chac:*	And the yearbearer, the West necklaced rain priest,
Colab i. xan:	720 Was also seized.
Yx sac bel is:*	And the North priest Bel Iz was the name
U kaba u chich ob chac:*	Of the mother's mother of the rain priests.
Ek yuuan chac:	The West necklaced rain priest
U yum ob:	Was their father.
Hun yuuan chac:	725 A certain (other) necklaced rain priest
U thupil ob	Was their youngest brother.

695. Unlike Roys 1967: 66 I consider Uayom Ch'ich' to be a personal name. It is followed by a nickname *Chich* 'the strong', which Roys ignores. Such nicknames are not uncommon; compare (Na) Tzin Yabun Chan: Tzin Yabun the Younger.

701. The sign = is employed somewhat irregularly as an approximate equivalent to a comma.

719. *Yuuan* does not appear elsewhere as a lineage name; I believe it to be a title.

721. Roys 1976: 68, note 1 interprets *ix* as a feminine marker but I believe it is simply 'and'.

722. I think 'mother's mother of the rain priests' is a title rather than a reference to a woman; perhaps she corresponds, however, to the Ix Mol mentioned by Landa (Tozzer 1941: 159).

Uooh: puc
  U kaba =
Lay tz'ibtab i:
  Uooh t u tan u kab:
Ca tz'ibtab i
  Uooh. y alan u cal
Ca tz'ibtab i:
  T u tan y oc:
Ca tz'ibtab i:
  Ychil u p'uc u kab ti ah uooh
  pucil:
Ma ku i:
  Chaccob: =
9: Ha li li hahal ku
  Ca yumil
Ti *Dios* e:
  U kul ob
T u than
  T u y itz'atil: *mayapan:*
Ah kin coba:
  (4) Ah kin te ych: paa: e.
Tzulim chan:
  Ti chikin:
Nauat: y ah (can)il:
  U u ol pa ti nohol e:
Co Uoh: y ah canul:
  U ol pa til lakin:
Ah ek: u lak:
  He y ahauob e.
Ah tapai nok cau ich:
  U kaba u hal ach uinic ob:
Hunnac ceel:
  U pulbeen: ah mex cuc i:
Ca u katah*
  Hun tul is nicte:*
Ca u katah:
  Sac pop:
Ca u katah:
  Ca p'el u tan nok:
Ca u katah
  Yax ulum*

Uoh Puc
  Was his name.
There it was written
730 As a glyph on the palm of his hand.
Then there was written
  A glyph where his neck was.
Then one was written
  On the sole of his foot.
735 Then one was written
  On the ball of the thumb of Uoh Puc.

They were not gods:
  The rain priests were chiefs.
In truth the True God
740 Is our Father
Who is God.
  They worshiped him
In the words,
  In the wisdom of Mayapan.
745 The sun priest of Coba
  Was the priest there in the fort.
Zulim Chan
  Was in the west.
Nahuat was the guardian
750 Of the spirit of the fort to the south.
Co Uoh was the guardian
  Of the spirit of the fort to the east.
Ah Ek was the other one;
  These were their lords.
755 Cau Ich of the Embroidered Mantle
  Was the name of their governor.
Hunac Ceel
  Was the sacrificer of Mex Cuc.
Then he demanded
760 One yam blossom.
Then he demanded
  A white mat.
Then he demanded
  Two-faced mantles.
765 Then he demanded
  A green turkey.

---

759. The following lines allude to the holding of the examinations for the priests, performed during the ritual progression of the newly installed lord of the *katun* through the towns and villages (see chapters 29 and 30). The various things asked for are riddles for ceremonial foods.

760. Bricker reads *hun tulis nicte* as 'one complete blossom'.

766. Bricker reads as *yax ulum* 'a gray turkey'.

Ca u katah   Then he demanded
  Ul e   A mottled snail.
Ca u katah: Then he demanded
  Sac homa ob: 770   White drinking gourds.

Act 8   ## Act 8

Ti likulob*   They rose up;
  Ca kuch ob: p'ool e*   Then they reached P'ool (1).
Ti p'olh ob: To the P'ool people
  Y ala ah ytza i: The Itza spoke.
Ti tun u naaintah ob   775   And it was then that they established
  Yx p'ol i: P'ool.
Ca kuch ob: ake: Then they arrived at Ake (2);
  Ti sih ob: ti x ake i: There they were born at Ake.
Ake: u kaba uaye: Ake was the name then
  C u than ob: 780   That they called it.
Ca tun kuch ob: alaa: So then they reached Al A (3).
  Alaa: u kaba uaye: c u than ob   Al A was the name then that they
                                                called it.
Ca tal ob: kan hol aa.   Then they came to Kan Hol A (4);
  Ca tal ob: ti x chel:*   Then they came to Ix Ch'el (5)
Ti chelhi: u than ob i: 785   And prolonged their words
  Ti chelhi: u can ob i: And prolonged their talk.
Ca tun kuch ob: So then they reached
  Ninum: Ninum (6);
Ti numhi: u than ob i: And many were their words,
  Ti numhi: u canob i: ah ytzaob   790   And many were their talks of the
  i =*   Itzas.
Ca tun kuch ob: So then they reached
  Chikin: tz'onot: Chikin Tz'onot (7):
Ti chikin tanhi u u ich ob i:*   To the west were their faces;
  Chikin tz'onot u kaba uaye: c u   Chikin Tz'onot was the name then
  than ob: that they called it.
Ca tun kuch ob: 795   So then they reached
  Tzuc oopp: Tzuc Op (8),
Ti u tzucah u ba ob i: Where they separated themselves
  Y alan: op i: Under the annonas.

---

771. See the introduction for a discussion of this chapter as the ceremonial of
the *may*.
     772. From here to line 1080 we are supplied with 171 places listed in the order
of a double counterclockwise circuit of Yucatan. The places are listed in appendix
B and are given numbers there, in the translation, and on figure 44. This will provide approximate locations for those that have not been precisely identified. Except for the very first (P'ool), all the places listed lie in the state of Yucatan.
     784. Ix Chel is the goddess of the rainbow. The naming of the town is explained
by a pun on *chel* 'prolong'.
     790. A pun on *num* 'prickly pear' and '(too) much'.
     793. A semi-pun on *chikin* 'west'.

Tzuc op: u kaba uay e:*
    C u than ob:
Ca tun kuch ob:
    Tah cab:
Ti u huytah cab. ytza i:*
    Ca uki t u menel x koh takin:

Ca huytab i: ti cab:
    Ca y ukuh: cabil neba: u kaba:*

Ca kuch ob (5) kikil:
    Ti u canah ob: kik nak i:*
Kikil u kaba uay e:
    C u than ob:
Ca kuch ob: panab haa:
    Ti u panah ob ha i:*
Ca tal ob: cucuchil: haa:
    U cuch ob: t u tamil haa i:*
Ca kuch ob: yal sih on:
    Yal sih on u kaba uay e:
Cahlic
    Cah =
Ca kuch ob: x pitah:
    Cah xan:
Ca tun kuch ob: kan cab: tz'onot:

    Ti likul ob: ca kuch ob: tz'ul a:

Ca ix tal ob: pibhaal tz'onot:

    Ca tun kuch ob: tah: aac: u kaba:

Ca tal ob: t cooh:
    U kaba:
Ti u manah ob: than cooh i:*
    Ti u ma nah ob: can i:
Ti coh
    U kaba uay e:

Tzuc Op was the name then
    800   That they called it.
So then they reached
    Tah Cab (9),
Where the Itza stirred honey.
    Then it was also drunk by those of
    Koh Takin (10).
805 When it had been stirred for honey,
    Then it was drunk by Cabil Neba,
    as he is called.
Then they reached Kikil (11),
    Where they had bloody guts.
Kikil was the name then
    810   That they called it.
Then they reached Panab Ha (12),
    Where they dug for water.
Then they came to Cucuchil Ha (13);
    They carried them into deep water.
815 Then they reached Yal Zihon (14).
    Yal Zihon was its name then,
And they settled
    The town.
Then they reached Ix P'itah (15),
    820   Also a town.
Then they reached Kan Cab Tz'onot
(16);
    From there they reached Tz'ul A
    (17);
And then they came to Pib Haal
Tz'onot (18);
    And then they reached Tah Aac (19),
    as it is called.
825 Then they came to Cooh (20),
    As it is called,
Where they bought words dear,
    Where they bought talk.
Cooh
    830   Is its name here.

---

799. Modern Sucopo. A pun on *tzuc* 'copse' and *tzuc ba* 'separate oneself'.

803. Pun on *tah cab* 'division of land' and *huytah cab* 'stir honey'.

806. Cabil Neba could also be a place-name.

808. Kikil as a place-name could well relate to 'rubber, sap'; the pun relates it to dysentery: *kik nak* 'bloody guts'.

812. Panab Ha 'dug water' or 'plum water' or 'flag water', here played against *panah* 'dig'.

814. Roys 1967: 70, note 14 reads Cucuchil Haa as 'very full of water'; the pun is on *cuch* 'carry'.

827. Probably a pun on *coh* 'thatch' and *cooh* 'dear'.

Ca kuch ob: ti kal:	Then they reached Kal (21),
Ti u kalah: u ba ob i:*	Where they closed themselves in;
Ti kal	Kal
U kaba uay e:	Was the name of it there.
Ca tal ob: ti maax:	835 Then they came to Maax (22),
Ti u maaxtah u ba katunob i:*	Where the warriors crushed themselves.
Ca kuch ob buc tzotz:	Then they reached Buc Tzotz (23),
Ti c u bucinah ob u tzotzel u poll ob i:*	Where they clothed the hair of their heads.
Buc tzotz u kaba uay e	Buc Tzotz was the name there
C u than ob =	840 That they called it.
Ca kuch ob: tz'itz'on tun:	Then they reached Tz'itz'on Tun (24),
Ti hop' ob: chuc lum tz'itz' i:*	Where they began to finish the earth with their nails.
Tz'i hol tun	Tz'i Hol Tun
U kaba uay e:	Was its name there.
Ca kuch ob: yob ain:	845 Then they reached Yob Ain (25),
Ti u uayintah ob ayin i: t u men u mam ob i:*	Which the alligators transformed for their maternal grandfather,
Ah yamas i:	Ah Ya Maz,
9: Y ahaulil t u chi kaknab:	The lord at the seashore.
Ca kuch ob: sinan che:*	Then they reached Zinan Che (26),
Ti u uayintah ob cicin	850 Where they transformed devils.
Sinan che	Zinan Che
U kaba uay e:	Was the name of it there.
Ca kuch ob ti cah: chac:*	Then they reached the town of Chac (27);
Ca kuch ob: tz'e uc:	Then they reached Tz'e Uc (28).
Pisil ba: u cah ob u lak ob	855 Their neighbors' villages were surveyed;
Ca kuch ob u mam ob: u lak:	Their other maternal grandfathers arrived.

832. Possibly a pun on *tikal* 'dryness' and *kal* 'shut in'.

836. Pun on *maax* 'monkey' and *maaxtah* 'mash'.

838. Perhaps a pun on *buc tzotz* 'frayed clothes' and *bucinah tz'otz'el* 'dress hair'.

842. Tz'itz'on Tun could mean 'disputed stone'. The pun relates to *tz'itz'* 'hoof'. Roys 1967: 71, note 4 cites another folk etymology from the *Relaciones de Yucatán*, but it doesn't seem to relate to the name as such. He considers *chuc lum tz'itz'i* "a stock phrase" and translates line 842 as 'where a malevolent man began to seize the land'. I don't follow this. From the following line, the possibility emerges of a sexual pun on *tz'i* 'desire' and *tz'iz* 'copulate'.

846. Possibly a play on *(h)ob* 'five, fifth' and *ob* 'they, them', but it remains obscure.

849. Roys 1967: 71, note 6 identifies Zinan Che 'scorpion tree' as *Zanthoxylum*.

853. Roys 1967: 71, note 7 suggests that Telchac is intended; he may be right.

Ti mul tz'emlah y ol ob i
 Tz'e mul u kaba uay e:*
Ca kuch ob: kin i:
 Y icnal x kil: ytzam pech

X tz'e uc: u lak ob
 Ca ku(6)ch ob icnal x kil.

Ytzam pech:
 Y ah u kini ob:
Ca tun kuch ob: bac a:
 Ti bacchah i: haa ti ob i:*

Bac a: uay e:
 C u than ob:
Ca tun kuch ob: sabac nail:
 Y icnal u mam ob:

U chun u uinicil ah na e:
 Lay chel na e: u mam ob:

Ca tun kuch ob: tebe naa e:*
 Ti kah i u naa ti ob i:

Ca tal ob: yxil:
 Ca tun bin ob: chulul:
Ca kuch ob. chi chicaan:
 Ca tun bin ob hol tun chable:

Ca tal ob. ytzam na:
 Ca tal ob. chubul na:
Ca kuch ob: cau cel:*
 Ti ceelchah ob i:
Cau cel: uay e
 C u than ob:
Ca tun kuch ob: ucu:
 Ti y alah ob: ya u cu:*
Ca bin ob: hunuc ma:
 Ca kuch ob: kin chil:

They calmed their hearts together.
 Tz'e Mul was its name there.
Then they reached Kin (29),
860 The place of the Kil and Itzam Pech (30).
And Tz'e Uc was their other one.
 Then they reached the place of the Kil
And Itzam Pech,
 The lord of the Kin.
865 So then they reached Bac A (31),
 Where the spring was captured by them.
Bac A there
 They called it.
So then they reached Zabac Na (32),
870 The place of their maternal grandfather,
The head of the Na lineage,
 For Ch'el Na was their maternal grandfather.
So then they reached Tebe Na (33),
 Which recalled their mother to them.
875 Then they came to Ixil (34)
 And then they went to Chulul (35);
Then they reached Chi Chicaan (36)
 And then they went to Hol Tun Chable (37).
They came to Itzam Na (38);
880 They came to Chubul Na (39);
They reached Cau Cel (40),
 And they shook with cold.
Cau Cel there
 It was called.
885 Then they reached Ucu (41),
 Where they said, "Oh, ah!"
Then they went to Hunuc Ma (42);
 Then they reached Kin Chil (43);

---

858. Tz'e Uc, perhaps 'mourning *Bassarica*'; *tz'e mul* 'mourning mound'; *tz'em* 'to calm'.
 866. Bac A, perhaps 'bird water'; pun on *bacchah* 'to pour'.
 873. *Te be na*, perhaps 'tree road house'.
 881. Cau '?a plant', Cel 'crack (corn), vigor, cold'.
 886. Roys 1967: 71, note 12 says, "Probably an expression of sorrow or pain." I agree: *ya* is 'pain', and *ay, aya*, and *ayano* are expressions of it; *u* is simply 'uh, ooh, oof'; *uk* is 'ah!'.

Ca bin ob: kan a:	Then they went to Kan A (44);
Ca kuch ob: t ix peton cah:	890 Then they arrived at Ix Peton Cah (45);
Ca kuch ob sahab balam:	Then they arrived at Zahab Balam (46);
Ca kuch ob tah cum chakan:	Then they arrived at Tah Cum Chakan (47);
Ca kuch ob: t ix bal che:	Then they arrived at Ix Bal Che (48);
Ca kuch ob: uxmal:	Then they reached Uxmal (49);
Ti tun likul ob ca kuch ob: t ix y ub ak:	895 When they left there then they went to Ix Yubak (50);
Ca kuch ob: mun aa:*	Then they went to Muna (51),
Ti munhi: u than ob:	Where they softened their words,
Ti munhi u can ob i:	Where they softened their teachings.
Ca bin ob: ox loch hok:	Then they went to Ox Loch Hok (52);
Ca bin ob chac akal*	900 Then they went to Chac Akal (53);
Ca bin ob. xoc ne ceh:	Then they went to Xoc Ne Ceh (54);
Ceh u uay ob ca kuch ob i:	Deer was their nagual when they arrived.
Ca bin ob p'us tunich.	Then they went to P'uz Tun Ich (55);
Ca bin ob puc nal chac:	Then they went to Puc Nal Chac (56);
Ca bin ob p'en *cuyut*:	905 Then they went to P'en Cuyut (57);
Ca bin ob. pax *ueuet*:*	Then they went to Pax Ueuet (58);
Ca kuch ob ti xay a:	Then they arrived at Xay A (59);
Ca kuch ob: tistis: u kaba:	Then they arrived at Tistis (60), as it is called;
Ca kuch ob t u chican:*	Then they arrived at Chi Can (61);
Ca kuch ob t ix meuac	910 Then they arrived at Ix Meuac (62);
(7) Ca kuch ob hunac thi:	Then they arrived at Hunac Thi (63);
Ca kuch ob u tzal:	Then they arrived at Tzal (64);
Ca kuch ob: tamus bul na:	Then they arrived at Tamus Bul Na (65);
Ca kuch ob: t ix can:	Then they arrived at Ix Can (66);
Ca kuch ob: lop*	915 Then they arrived at Lop (67);
Ca kuch ob: chee miuan(h): uan	Then they arrived at Che Mi Uan (68);
Ca kuch ob: ox cah uan ka:	Then they arrived at Ox Cah Uan Ka (69);
Ca bin ob: sac bacel caan:	Then they arrived at Zac Bacel Caan (70);

---

896. Roys 1967: 72, note 1 cites the folk etymology *muan a* 'sparrowhawk well' and the pun on *mun* 'soft'. I believe he is correct.

900. Roys 1967: 72, note 2 suggests that this is the modern Yakal.

906. The juxtaposition of two Nahuatlisms is of interest: *p'en cuyut* 'lusting coyote' and *pax ueuet* 'beat (drum) the drum'. In both cases the first element is Mayan, the second Nahuatl.

909. Roys 1967: 72, note 5 suggests that this is Chichican, footnoting Stephens.

915. Modern Tiholop (Roys 1967: 72, note 8).

Ca kuch ob: cetelac:*   Then they arrived at Cetelac (71).
  U kaba cah.   920   These are the names of the towns
Macalob:*   Of the dam people
  Y etel u kaba cheenob: And the names of the wells.
Ca utzac y oheltaual t ux man ob: So that it may be known where they
                                        passed,
  T an u ximbaltic ob: y ila ob   When they explored to see
Ua utz: lay peten: 925 Whether this country was good,
  Ua u nahma cahtal ob: uay lae: Whether it was really suitable that
                                          they live here.

Tzol peten u kaba   The Ordered Country was its name,
  T u than ob   They told
Ca yumil   Our Father
  Ti *Dios*   930   Who is God.
Lay tzol peten.   It was he who ordered the country;
  Lay sihes y okol cab. t u lacal   It was he who created the whole
                                          earth around,
                                        So he ordered it too,
La yx tzol xan::   But really it was they
  He ob la e
Kabansah peten u cah ob: 935 Who named the lands of their towns,
  Kabansah ch'een u cah ob: Who named the wells of their
                                          towns,
Kabansah ca cab u cah ob   Who named the villages of their
                                          towns,
  Kabansah luum u cah ob: Who named the fields of their
                                          towns.
T u men ma mac kuchuc uay e: Because no one had come here,
  Uay: u cal peten   940   Here to the neck of the country,
Ca kuch on. uay la e:*   When we came here:
  Subin che: To Zubin Che (72),
Kau a: Kau A (73),
  Cum can ul:*   Cum Can Ul (74);
Ti em tun ti: 945 To Eb Tun (75),
  Em ob ti tun i:*   Where they descended on the
                                          stones;
Siçal: To Zizal (76),
  Sac ii: Valladolid (77);
Ti tz'ooc: To Tz'ooc (78),
  Ti tz'ooc u than katun i:*   950   Where they finished the word of the
                                          katun;

---

919. Roys 1967: 72, note 9 locates Cetelac at Yaxuna, the west end of the
causeway that leads to Coba.
   921. Roys 1967: 72 has 'whatever towns there were', which is mysterious
to me.
   941. Roys 1967: 72, note 11 infers a temporal break here. I don't think so: the
geographic order of the towns listed is smoothly continuous.
   944. Now Cuncunul.
   946. A pun on *eb* 'stairway' and *em* 'descend'.
   950. Possibly a pun on *tz'oc* 'coconut' and *tz'ooc* 'finish'.

Ti mocon popol a:	To Mozon Popol A (79),
Ti hay u pop katun i—*	Where they spread the mat of the *katun*;
Ti pixoy:	To Pixoy (80),
Ua yum haa:	Uayum Ha (81),
Sac ba	955 Zac Ba(cel) (82),
Can:*	Can (83);
Ti num	To Num (84),
Ti num chi thantab ob i*	Where many details were told them;
Ti macal popol a:	To Macal Popol A (85),
Ti u tzolah ob u pop: katun i:	960 Where they arranged the mat of the *katun*;
T ix macculum:	To Ix Mac Ulum (86),
Ti u ma cah ob than i:	Where they did not settle the word;
Tz'it haas	Dzitas (87),
Bon kauil:	Bon Kauil (88);
T ix mex:	965 To Ix Mex (89),
Kochilla:*	Kochil (90) there;
T ix xocen:	To Ix Xocen (91),
Chun pak:	Chun Pak (92),
Piba hul:	Piba Hul (93),
Tun kaas:	970 Tun Kaaz (94),
Haal tun haa:	Hal Tun Ha (95),
Kuxbil a:	And Kuxbil A (96) there,
Tz'itz'il che:	Tz'itz'il Che (97);
Ti cool:	To Cool (98),
Sitil	975 Zitil (99),
Pech:	Pech (100),
Chalam te:	Chalam Te (101),
Ti chalh i*	Which was to cleanse their hearts;
Y ol ob i:	Itzam (102),
Ytzam thulil:	980 Thulil (103);
Ti pakab:	To Pakab (104),
Ti paklah ob i:*	Which was expecting them;
(8) Ti ya . . .	To Ya (105),
An sah cab:	(C)an Zahcab (106),

---

952. Possibly a pun on *pop* 'wide' and *pop* 'mat'. See also Roys 1967: 72–73, note 13. The Mayan — is my ;.

956. Cf. Zac Bacel Caan; line 918.

958. This is a pun on *num* 'thorn' in the place-name and the verb *num-chi* 'notify, explain'.

966. Roys 1967: 73, note 1 locates Kochil just north of the Coba-Yaxuna causeway.

978. Possibly a pun on Chalam Te 'flattened tree' and *chal* 'wash'.

982. Roys 1967: 73 identifies Itzam Thulil as Izamal and Tipakab as "(?Tepakam)." In the latter case there appears to be a pun on *pak* 'plant' and *paklah* 'expect', and Roys finds 'unite' as well.

Tz'itz'om tun

    Yc tun u mam ob: ti che choc

    tz'iitz':*

Tz'itz' hol tun: popol a:

    T u nohol sinan che:*

Ca tal muc i:

    Sac nicte cheen:

Sotz'il:

    Uay

T u mul tumtah ob katun e.*

    Mul tumut u kaba: uay

Mutul e:

    Muxup'ip':

Ake:

    Hoc tun:

Ti cumlah ob

    T u chun tun i:

Xoc ch'el

    Boh e

Sah cab haa

    Tzan lah cat*

Human

    Ti humn i

Than y okolob i

    Ti human i

U pectzilob i*

    Chalam te:

Pa cax ua:*

    U kaba uay e: c u than ob:

Te kit:

    Ti kit y ala ytzaob i:*

Y okol cheen

    Ppuppul ni huh*

985 Tz'itz'om Tun (107),

    At the stone of their maternal

    grandfathers in Che Choc Tz'iitz'

    (108);

    Tz'itz' Hol Tun Popol A (109),

    To the south of Zinan Che.

    Then came Muci (110)

990   And Zac Nicte Ch'een (111)

    And Zotz'il (112).

    Here

    They commemorated that *katun*.

    Mul Tumut (113) was its name here,

995 And Motul (114),

    Muxu P'ip' (115),

    Ake (116),

    Hoc Tun (117),

    Where they settled

1000   At the base of the stone;

    Xoc Ch'el (118),

    Bohe (119),

    Zahcab Ha (120),

    Tzanlah Cat (121),

1005 Human (122),

    Which was strengthened,

    Said their belief,

    Which was strong—

    Their awareness;

1010   Chalam Te (123),

    Pacax Ua (124);

    "This is its name," they said;

    Tekit (125),

    "Which is spread out," the Itzas

    said;

1015 Y Okol Ch'een (126),

    P'up'ul Ni Huh (127);

---

986. Roys 1967: 73, note 2 suggests reading *chochoc* as 'loosely tied', which is possible but doesn't seem to go anywhere. I confess that I am stumped.

988. It is.

993. I know of no independent validation for Roys' 1967: 73 'council of war' or my own 'commemoration of the *katun*'. Take your choice.

1004. Roys 1967: 73 queries "(Sancaba?)" and identifies Tzanlah Cat as "(Sanahcat)."

1009. Roys 1967: 73 has 'where there were noisy talks and rumors about them'; *hum* means 'strong, hum', *y okol* 'around, about', and *pectzil* 'awareness, compression'.

1011. Roys 1967: 73, note 3 puts Pacax Ua on the border of the province of Mani between Chumayel and Sotuta (citing Stephens).

1014. Pun on Tekit '(?)' and *ti kit* 'which is strewn'.

1016. Roys 1967: 73 suggests that this may be Huhi.

Huh u uay ob	Iguana was their nagual.
Ca hok ob i:	Then there appeared
Tz'otz'il e:	The bat people
Ti ab:	1020 At Teabo (128)
Bitun ch'een uchc i	And Bitun Ch'een (129);
Y ocol ob ti pikal	They came from Pikal (130);
U kaba cheen: uchc i	The well had been named
U *tippilob**	By their constables.
Ca bin ob poc huh u kaba cheen:	1025 Then they went to Poc Huh (131), the name of the well,
Uchci u pocicob huh:	And they roasted iguanas.
Ca bin ob: manii:	Then they went to Mani (132)
Ti man kah i than ti ob i:*	And purchased pinole, they told them.
Ca kuch ob ti tz'aan	Then they came to Tz'am (133)
Ox kin tz'amann ob i*	1030 And soaked for three days.
Ca bin ti cul:	Then they went to Ticul (134),
Sac luum cheen:*	To Zac Luum Ch'een (135),
Ti x tohil cheen:*	And Ix Tohil Ch'een (136),
Ti tohci: y ol ob i:	Which straightened then their hearts;
Ca bin ob balam kin	1035 Then they went to Balam Kin (137),
U petennil ah kinob:	The country of the sun priests;
Ch'een ch'omac:	Ch'een Ch'omac (138),
Sac nicteel tz'onot:	Zac Nicteel Tz'onot (139),
Ti yax cab:	Yax Cab (140),
Uman:	1040 Uman (141),
Ox cum:	Ox Cum (142),
San hil:*	Zan Hil (143),
Ych caan si	And Heaven Born
Hoo:	Merida (144),
Ti noh naa	1045 Noh Na (145),
Noh pat:	Noh Pat (146),
Poy che na:	Poy Che Na (147),
Chulul:*	Chulul (148);
Ca kuch ob t u titz luum cum kal:*	Then they appeared at Titz Luum (149) and Cum Kal (150)
Ti cumlah u titz paten i:	1050 And softened the point of the country;

1024. Roys 1967: 73 omits this line.

1028. Pun on Mani, possibly 'passing sparrowhawk', and *man* 'purchase'. Roys 1967: 73 has 'where their language was forgotten by them'.

1030. Pun on *ti tz'an* 'at the gathering' and *tz'aman* 'soaked'. Roys 1967: 73 identifies the place as Tz'am.

1032. Sacalum, according to Roys 1967: 73.

1033. Xtohil, according to Roys 1967: 73.

1042. Samahil, according to Roys 1967: 73.

1048. Cholul, according to Roys 1967: 73.

1049. Titz Luum 'point of land'. Roys 1967: 73 respells Cum Kal as Conkal.

Sic pach: Zic Pach (151),

Sic pach:	Zic Pach (151),
Yax kukul:	Yax Kukul (152),
(9) Ti x kokob:	Ix Kokob (153),
Cuc a:	Cuc A (154),
Ch (. . . . .)	1055 Ch . . .
(. . . . .) xan:*	. . . also,
Ekol	Ek Ol (155):
Ekol: u kaba ch('een)	Ek Ol is the name of the well.
(. . . . .): ti x *ueue:*	(Then they reached) Ix Ueue:
Ti x *ueue* u kaba ch'een uay e: 1060	Ix Ueue (156) is the name of that well.
Uhumtal	Uhumtal (157)
Tal hun hatz i:	Came to one division;
Ti x kani macal:	To Ix Kani Macal (158),
Ti x Xaan*	To Xaan (159),
Yum xul: uchc i	1065 To Yum Xul (160),
U yumtic u haan:	For the adoption of sons-in-law;
Hol tun ake:*	Hol Tun Ake (161),
Acan queh:	Acan Ceh (162),
Ti cooh:*	Cooh (163),
Ti ch'ahil.	1070 Ch'ahil (164);
Ti chac*	To Chac (165)
Mayapan: ych paa:	And Mayapan (166) inside the walls.
Y okol haa:	Over the water
Ca bin ob:	Then they went:
Nabul a:	1075 To Na Bul A (167),
Ti x mucuy:*	Ix Mucuy (168),
Ti x kan hub e:	Kan Hub (169),
Tz'oyil a:*	Tz'oyil A (170).
Ca kuch ob	Then they appeared
Ti sip	1080 At Zip (171):
Ti sip u than ob i:	In sin they spoke;
Ti sip u can ob i:*	In sin they taught.

1056. Two lines missing. Roys 1967: 18 supplies them from Berendt:
 Ch'een Balam,
  Bolon Nic xan.
1064. Texan, according to Roys 1967: 73.
1067. Roys 1967: 73 says "(Ake?)."
1069. Tecoh, according to Roys 1967: 73.
1071. Roys 1967: 73 says "(Telchaquillo?)."
1076. Timucuy, according to Roys 1967: 73.
1078. Tz'oyola, according to Roys 1967: 73.
1082. The ceremonial circuit ends here, and an account begins of the more serious business of distributing land titles.

Act 9

Ca hop i:
  U hetz' luumob
Y ahauob i:
  Ti y anah
Y ah kin palon cab i:
  Heklay y ah kinob e

Mutecpul u kaba;*
  He ah kin palon cab e: ah may

He ah kin *mutecpul* e:
  Ah canul:
Uayyom ch'ich' ix xan
  Nunil i xan:
Y u ca tun ah chable:
  Ah ych caan si hoo:
Hol tun balam:
  U mehen:
Lay u chaah
  Yx yaxum chakan e:
Ti tun kuch i:
  U lak ahauob i:
La ob i ahau
  U nup u than ob e
Ti y ahaulilob
  Ti buluc ahau tun: u kaba c uch i:

Ca u hetz'ah cabob i:
  Ca ix ti hetz' luum nahob i

Act 10

Ca ix cahlah ob i:
  Ych caan si hoo:*
Ca em ob
  Ah hol tun ake:
Ca em ob:
  Ah sabac nailob:

Act 9

Then began
  The seating of the lands
1085 And the lords
  Who were
The sun priests of the ceded land.
  This is the account of their sun
  priest
Named Mutecpul;
1090   He was the sun priest of the ceded
  land, the cycle priest.
He was the sun priest Mutecpul
  And Can Ul,
And Uayom Ch'ich' also,
  And also Nunil,
1095 On the second *tun* of Chable
  Of Heaven Born Merida.
Hol Tun Balam
  Was his son.
This was the cession
1100   Also of the blue bird to Chakan;
It then appeared
  And the rest of the lords.
These are the lords
  Who talked back
1105 To their lordship
  For the 11 Ahau time as it was
  named.
Then they seated the lands,
  And then their lands and houses
  were seated.

Act 10

And then they settled
1110   Heaven Born Merida
And went down
  To the Hol Tun Ake people.
Then they went down,
  The Zabac Na people,

1089. Roys 1967: 73 reads this as Motul, but it clearly isn't. I read it as Nah. *motecpilli* 'your noble', here identified as Jaguar or lord of the *katun* (cycle priest), destined to rule in 11 Ahau (1539). Like the other lords mentioned, Mutecpul was a Xiu.

1110. There follows a listing of the towns in which titles to lands and houses have been settled: Merida, Ake, Zabac Na, Copo, Chac Te, and Tabi. All of these are in Xiu territory.

Ca tun kuch ob
  Y etan
Y et ahaulilob:
  He ah sabac nail e:
U chun u unicil:
  Ah na:
Ca tun u molah u ba ob
  Te ych caan si hoo e:
Ti y an yx pop:
  Ti balam.*
Ti lic y ahaulil i:
  Hol tun ba tz'am:
(10) (. . . . .)*
  (. . . . .)
(. . . . .) ti le y ahaulil

  (. . . . .) tz'oy*
Lay u chun u uinicil
  Copo e:
(. . . .) xiu*
  Ix *tloual* xan:*
Chac te ahau
  Chac te u lumil uchuc y ahaulil
ob

1115 And then they appeared
  Together
With their fellow lords.
  These were the Zabac Na,
The root of the people
1120   Of the Na lineage.
And then they gathered together
  There in Heaven Born Merida,
Which also had the mat
  For the Jaguar,
1125 Which was like the lordship,
  The Jaguar Spring throne.
(. . . . .)
  (. . . . .)
(Which was the) generation of the
lordship
1130   (Of Pochek Ix) Tz'oy.
He was the head of the people
  Of Copo
And was a Xiu
  And Spokesman as well.
1135 Chac Te was the lord;
  Chac Te's was the land where their
lordship occurred.

Act 11

Teppanquis y ah kin ob:*
  Lay ych tabi lae:*
Lay ah p'is te
  P'is u lumil ob e:
He tun lubte u lumil

  U luubob e:
Uuc lub cab:*
  Ah may he tun:

Tep'anquiz was their sun priest
  Who was in Tabi then.
He was the surveyor
1140   Who measured the lands.
He then was to be the marker of the
lands:
  He marked them
In seven steps of land.
  And it was the cycle priest

1124. There follows a listing of the lords important to the *katun* ending ceremonies: the Jaguar (Mutecpul), the Spokesman of the Jaguar (Pochek Ix Tz'oy),
Surveyor (Tep'anquiz), Sweeper, and Wakener of the Land.

1127. Two lines missing.

1130. Missing words supplied by Roys 1967: 18 from Berendt to read: *Hol tun
Balam ti t u ch'eene tili c y ahaulili Pochekix tz'oy.*

1133. Berendt says Tutul Xiu (Roys 1967: 18).

1134. I read Nah. *tlatoani* 'speaker'.

1137. Nah. *tepanquiz* 'supervisor'.

1138. Roys 1967: 74 reads 'he was looked upon as such'.

1143. Roys 1967: 74 considers a *lub* 'rest stop' as the equivalent of a league.

Accunte u xukil u luumob	1145 Who then began to scrub the land,
Ah accunte u xukil	Who began the scrubbing.
Ah mis miste u luum ob	And the sweeper was to sweep the land.
Lay mis cit ahau e:	He was the lord Sweeper and
	Remover.
He tun hetz'ci cab	He then seated the lands
Ti ob e:	1150 For them.

Act 12

Lay ho y ahel cab e:	And then the fifth priest was the
	Wakener of the Land:
He tun te y ahal cab ti ob e:	He was to mark the dawn for them
Tum te ahau:*	And as lord Renewer
Tum te y ahal cab ti ob o:	Was to renew the dawn for them.
Ca hoppi y ocol patan ti ob e:	1155 Then began the theft of tribute by
	them
T u chi ch'een:*	At Chichen,
Ti kuch uchc i.	Which had come
U kuchul u patan: can tul	To be the collector of tribute of the
uinicob e:	four men.
Buluc ahau u kaba	11 Ahau was the name
U katunil: c uch i:	1160 Of the *katun* that was occurring,
Ti baax lah i patan	Which drove down the tribute
Te. cetelac e:	There at Cetelac.
U pakte:	And they had expected
U chi y anil e:	That it would be there.
Ca tun em i	1165 So then bringing down
U patan hol tun Suhuy	The tribute of Hol Tun Zuyua,
Ua te: cetelac e:	There at Cetelac,
Ti cet-hi u thanob i	They compared their records
Ox lahun ahau	For 13 Ahau,
U katunil c uch i:	1170 The *katun* period that was
	occurring.
Ti u kamah ob patan hal ach unicob i	The governors received their tribute
	there;
Ca hop i u tepall ob i:	Then began their rule.
Ca hop' i ti (pa) y ahaulil ob i:	There began what were their lordships;
Ca hop' i u tanlabalob:	Then began their divisions.

1153. I can't trace Roys' 1967: 74 references to 'reason'.

1156. Merida had hoped to be able to collect tribute from the eastern towns for confirming their land titles too, but the Itza beat it to it, collecting tribute at Cetelac in the name of Chichen Itza and its Ba Cabs. It was a particular indignity that it collected tribute from Hol Tun Zuyua, in Xiu territory. Eventually the Itza seated *katun* 11 Ahau at Emal, a fact which the Chumayel ignores (see the Tizimin).

Act 13

Ca hop' i u kuchul u pulul te ob:

   Ca hop' i u pulic ob ych ch'een:

Ca u y abac u than ob t u menel y
ahaulil i:
   Ma hul u than ob
Lay Cau ich
   Hun hunah ceel e:
Lay cau ich u kaba u kaba u uinicil e:
   Ti cuthical
T u hol ch'een
   (11) Cheen ti nohol*

Act 14

Ca tun bin i ch'abil
   Ca tun hok i y alab u than:

Ca hop' u ch'abal u than:
   Ca tz'uni u than:
Ca hop' i y alabal ahauil:

   Ca culhij:
T u cuchil ahauuob: t u men ob.
   Ca hop'iy(.) kubal hal ach uinicil:

Ma ahau c uch ij =
   Chen u bel ah mex cuc:*
Ca ix alab i
   Ahaui(1) u pulben: ah mex
   cuc =
Coot. bin: u naa
   Ca bin cax ta ui
T u uitzil:
   Ca bin: tz'un i: u ch'abal u than
   lay ahau:
La: ci tun y alabal:
   Ca tun hop'i: u nacsabal: canal
naa:
Ti (. .) ti ahaulil.
   Ca hop'i: u pakal y ebal:

Act 13

1175 Then began the coming of their
throwing sacrifice:
   Then began their throwing people
   in the well.
Then their words were to be used up
for the lordship,
   But their words were not used:
It was "Cau Ich
1180   And a certain Hunac Ceel."
This Cau Ich was the name of the man
   Who was being seated
At the head of the well
   To the south.

Act 14

1185 So then he went to create it,
   And then he asked to speak his
   word,
And he began the creation of his word.
   Then he began to speak it.
Then began the speaking of the
lordship
1190   When he was seated
In the burden of the lords by them.
   Then began the speeches of the
   governors.
But the lord was not seated,
   Only the path of Mex Cuc.
1195 And then it was said
   That the lordship was the sacrifice
   of Mex Cuc.
Eagle will be his mother;
   Then he will be found in disguise
In the hills.
   Then this lord began to create his
1200   word.
Sweet then was the speech.
   Then began the erection of the high
   house
For the lordship.
   Then began the use of steps.

1184. Roys 1967: 75, note 3 quite rightly points out that the sacrificial platform is on the south side of the cenote at Chichen Itza.
   1194. Cau Ich was not seated; Mex Cuc was.

Ca tun culhi
  Ti canal na:
Ychil ox lahun ahau
  Uac tepal.*

1205 And then he was seated
  In the high house
  In 13 Ahau,
    The sixth rule.

Act 15

Ca tz'uni: u kuchul
  U y abil u th(an:) u kin:
U ua ah mex cuc: u kaba
  Ca u pulal
Natz'an ba
  Ca u kin ah mex cuuc*
Ci: ca yac, cuntab i:
  Ca hop'i u yum in taual i:

Ca hop'i u tzicil i:
  T u kaba ah mex cuuc:
Ca tun tzic i
  Ca tun tanlab i.
Te t u chi ch'een e:
  Chi ch'een ytzam. u kaba =*

T u men ti bin ytza
  Ca u lukah u tunil cab i:

U tunil uiil*
  Cuch itzam:
Luk ca bin ychil haa:*

Act 15

Then he began to come
1210   To speak the word of the day,
  The elevation of Mex Cuc by name,
    Then his throwing.
  And they were close together—
    The two days of Mex Cuc.
1215 Truly when he was elevated,
  Then began the father of my
    pretended return:
  Then began the homage
    To the name of Mex Cuc.
  So then they honor him
1220   And then they face toward
  The direction of the well,
    The mouth of the well of the Itza by
    name.
  Because it will be the Itza
    Who then remove the stones of the
    earth,
1225 The stones of the moon.
    The burden of the Itza
  Will be removed when he shall be in
  the water.

Act 16

Ca tun hop'i y ocol num ya.

Te chi ch'en ytza e:
  Ca tun bin i te likin e:

Act 16

So then began the entrance of
  suffering
There at the well mouth of the Itza.
1230   And then they will go there to the
  east,

1208. That is, they constructed a stepped platform and enthroned Mex Cuc on it. The sixth rule may refer to the fact that there were six claimants to the seat of the *katun* in 13 Ahau. (There were actually more, but not all of them appear in the Chumayel.)

1214. He didn't rule for long.

1222. The MS has Itzam here and in line 1226. Shades of Itzam Na! I think this is left over from some earlier version that was an Itza status claim.

1225. That is, it was time to deface the *katun* monuments, since 13 Ahau ended the Itza cycle.

1227. That is, the rule of the Itza was supposed to end.

Ca ku y icnal
   Ah kin cob(.)*
Talel u cah uaxac ahau katun
   Chi chi uaxac ahau u kaba katun:
   uchc i ta pa(.)*
Ca tun hoki u hel katun

   Ca t(un) hok i (. .) hel y ahauob i

(. . . . .)*
  (. . . . .)

The two gods together with
   The sun priest of Coba,
Coming to begin *katun* 8 Ahau.
   Tiny little 8 Ahau was the name of
   the make-believe *katun*.
1235 And then appeared the change of the
   katun:
   And then appeared the change of
   the lords.

(. . . . .)
  (. . . . .)

Act 17

(. . . . .)
  C(a tun hok i
(. . . . .)*
  (. . . . .)
(. . . . .)
  (12) Ti numn i.
Ca ahaulil i:
  C u than ob y ah kin ti ob:
Ca ti y ocsah ob kin tu(n) y abil:
  He c u talel: kin tun y abil a.

C u than ob:
  Ti el i:
Tz'itz' ti el i:
  U chi kaknab:
U kaknabil:
  Num ya la e:
Ciy y alabal canal lae:
  Cij y alabal ob:
Ca chiib i:
  U cuch kin e:
Ca oklemhij:
  U u ich kin e:
Ca tup i
  U u ich:
Ca hok i:
  Y olob canal:

Act 17

(. . . . .)
1240   And then appeared
(. . . . .)
  (. . . . .)
(. . . . .)
  Which was endured
1245 During the lordship,
  The sun priests told them
When they ended the calendar round.
  This is the coming of this calendar
  round,
They say,
1250   Which burns,
It is a cycle which burns
  The edge of the sea
And the sea itself:
  The suffering is that.
1255 Just the judgment of heaven it was,
  Just their judgment.
Then was set down
  The burden of the sun.
Then was perhaps the departure
1260   Of the face of the sun.
Then was quenched
  Its high face.
Then were strangled
  The orbs of heaven,

1232. That is, Cau Ich and Hunac Ceel join the sun priest of Coba in termi-
nating the ceremony, moving to the east to do so.

1234. This ends the drama, which is followed by the inauguration of the new
lords for 11 Ahau. Roys 1967: 19 reads *tepal(lob)*, supplying the last syllable from
Berendt. I think it is *ta pa* 'false appearance', which is what the MS says.

1237. Three lines missing.

1241. Three lines missing.

Ti el i:
  C u than y ah kin ti ob:
Ti tz'oci u than:
  Ca ahaulil i:
C u than y ah kin ti ob:

1265 Which burned,
    The sun priests told them.
"That has ended the word
    Of our lordship,"
The sun priests told them.

Act 18

  Ca hop' i
U tucul tz'ib pach kin:
  Ca y ubah
Ca ix y ilah ob:
  U:

Act 18

1270 Then they began
    Thinking of writing the past sun.
    Then they listened
And then they saw
    The moon.

Act 19

Ca tal ob y ahaulil i:
  Boob:
He ix tziu
  Nene:
Lay ti oces keban t oon:
  U munnal cab:
Ca ti tal i:
  Ca bin tz'ococ u than katun:

U tzacil katun:
  Ca ti talsab i:

Bi c a than ex
  C ex
Y ahaulil ex
  Cab ex e:
Ti oc tun u than
  U y anal katun:
U tz'oc katun
  Talsab i
Yx tziu
  Nene:

Act 19

1275 Then came the lordships,
    The stalks,
And they were Centipedes
    And Gnats.
That was what brought sin to us,
1280 The slavery of the land,
Which is what is coming
    When the word of the *katun* shall
    be accomplished,
The curse of the *katun*.
    Then that is what will be brought
    about,
1285 Just as you say:
    You,
Your lordships,
    And your lands.
So goes then the word,
1290 The nature of the *katun*.
The *katun* is finished
    And accomplished.
And the Centipedes
    And Gnats.

Act 20

  Ca ylab i
  U picul katun ti ob:
Ca hop' i
  U cimsabal ob:
Ca utzcinab i
  U y oyteel:

Act 20

1295 Then were seen:
    Thousands of soldiers of them.
Then began
    The slaughter of them.
Then was attained
1300 The weakening of them:

U sak cheil: The white stick
  U chebal u cimil   And clubbing to death.
Ca hop'i u chulul: Then began shooting
  T u menel: ox halal chan: With three-pronged arrowheads.
Ca hop'i   1305 Then began
  U payal y ahaulil i: The division of the lordships
Cab oob: And their lands.
  Ca bini   Then will be
U kikel: Bloodshed
  Ca ch'ab i.   1310 When it is seized
T u men ah cehob:*   By the deer people.
  Ca tun hak y ol ob*   So then it will strangle their will.
(. . . . .)   (. . . . .)
  (. . . .) kin   . . . sun
U tz'oc katun: 1315 The end of the war
  Ti ob: For them
(. . . . .)   (. . . . .)
  (. . . . .)   (. . . . .)
(. . . . .) tich':   . . . raise
  Na tz'an u   1320 Approaching the
(. . . . .)   (. . . . .)
  (. . . . .)   (. . . . .)
(. . . . .)   (. . . . .)
  (. . . .)al ka   . . . ness indeed
(. . . . .)   1325 (. . . . .)
  (. . . . .)   (. . . . .)

1311. Roys 1967: 77 translates *ah cehob* as 'archers'.
1312. The next fourteen lines are largely missing.

13. The Sermon of Tzin Yabun

(105) U *profeciado*   The prophecy
  Na tzin yabun chan   Of Tzin Yabun the Younger:
U chi   His mouth,
  U than (*i*)   1330 His word.
Hahal ku   Sole God
  Ti peten   In the country:
Lay a pak   This is your expectation:
  U hokol e yum e (*ii*)   The appearance of your Father.
Y ah kinob   1335 The sun priests
  Uil bin puchc ob uchmal e   May be going to return.

Tz'a		Give
C ex (*iii*)		Ye
Ka a nat t u than		Indeed help in the Word,
T u tzacil ka e	1340	And indeed direct
A pixan ex (*iv*)		Your souls,
Ca h bin hahal kamic e		And you will begin to receive the truth.
Xeth a u ol		Broken is your spirit
T a kul ah (*v*) ytza e		In your worship, O Itza.
Tubes a hauay ku	1345	Forget your finished gods;
A sat a tay ku		Destroy your ended gods.
Lo e (*vi*) t u lacal		That is all
Y anil		That exists:
Ah tepal e		The ruler
Yum e	1350	And Father,
Y ah ch'aabul caan (*vii*)		Creator of heaven
Y etel luum tuçinil		And the lying earth.
Lay ya t a u ol		This is the pain in your hearts
Yn u alic t ech o		That I speak to you then,
Maya (*viii*)	1355	O Maya
Ah ytza e*		And Itza.
Ma a kat a u uy y anil *Dios*		You did not seek to hear of the existence of God,
Haaha (*ix*) kul t a than o		The truth of your God that you speak of.
Lay u y ocol tun t a u ol		This is his entry then into your hearts.
U than (*x*) yn tzec lae.	1360	The word of my punishment is this.

1356. The implication is explicit here (but diffuse elsewhere) that the "Maya" were the Xiu or western Maya, while the "Itza" were the eastern Maya. This usage is specific to the Chumayel; the Tizimin refers directly to the "Xiu."

14. The Building of the Pyramids

(15) Ti haab		In the year
De mil quinientos quarenta y uno.		Of 1541.
181 Tz'uul		The midyear of the foreigners
A t. 5:		At Merida
Dik: 9	1365	Was the ninth of December
2n hel e*		Of the yearbearers.

(*note 1366 on following page*)

9: U kahlay t in tz'ibtah uchc i
Utzcinnabal mul t u men
heregesob
8.0.0.0.0 Ox kal katun utzcinnabc i
Ca tac holhun pis katun*

11.15.0.0.0 T u men tah ob
Nucuch uinicob
Ca ix ta bin y ala

U unicilob *Cartabona**
U kaba u lumil
Y anil ob hele lae
Ti y an ob i
Ca ul i
*Sn. Bernabe**
Ti cambesah
Ca cimsabi ob
T u men uinicob
Heregesob
U kaba u uinicilob.

156 u cuch hele e
*15 años**

The account that I have had written
Of the completion of the mounds
by the heretics.
Three score *katuns* were completed;
1370 Then it approached fifteen
measured *katuns.*
Because they did it,
The great peoples.
And then while they were going to
speak,
The peoples of Constantinople,
1375 The name of the land
Where they had moved then,
There they were
When there came
Saint Barnaby.
1380 Who had them instructed.
Then they had him killed
By the people,
The heretics,
As the people were called.

1385 In 1556 the burden changed.
It was fifteen years.

1366. Roys 1967: 79, note 10 comments, "Probably a confused imitation of the chapter-heading in some Spanish history." Actually this is something much more interesting: it is a calendrical correlation and at the same time the only example of rebus writing in the *Books of Chilam Balam* (Edmonson 1976). It works like this: 181 is a reference to the number of days from January 1 to June 30 in the Christian calendar in a non–leap year. The colonial Maya correlated their calendar to the Julian one at the convenient year 1 Ix, which began on July 16, 1555. This was convenient because all Ix years are leap years. They did not write down the leap year correlation because it could easily be computed mentally. The reference to December 9 is the date of the winter solstice. In 1541 this would have had to be corrected by adding 3 Ix (leap) year days, thus giving the correct Julian date, December 12. The whole assertion here is simply that the middle of the Christian year is analogous to the winter solstice, the middle of the Mayan one. The year 1541 is selected for comment because that was the date of the Spanish founding of Merida.

There are three rebus elements in the text: *t.* (Sp. *te*) for Mayan *ti* 'at'; 5, Mayan *ho* 'five' (hence *Ti Ho* 'Merida'); and 2, Mayan *ca* 'two', which thus initiates the expression *can hel* 'four changers', the usual expression for 'yearbearers', who here personify the Mayan year count.

1370. Three score *katuns* would be three *baktuns.* I believe the assertion here is that the Maya began building the pyramids in 8.0.0.0.0 (46) and finished seventy-five *katuns* later in 11.15.0.0.0 (1520). A more precise date is given later.

1374. *Cartabona* appears to me to be a garbled reference to Constantinople. It is certainly a foreign word (Maya has no *r*).

1379. Roys 1967: 80, note 2 says, "Possibly a reference to the battle on the day of San Bernabé at Merida." Saint Barnaby became Merida's patron saint.

1386. It is not clear what burden changed. This would be the seventeenth year

(*note continued on following page*)

9: Hel e t in tz'ibtah uchc i | In return I have had written
Y utzcin (16) nabal nucuch muullob | The completion of the great mounds
T u men ch'iballob | By the lineages,
Y etel he c en baal u mentah ahauuob | 1390 And that was something the lords had done.
He x lic u mentic ob mull e | Hence in fact they built these mounds
Ox lahun te katun | In thirteen *katuns*
11.13.6.0.0 Ca tac uac p'el haab i* | And just about six years.
Lic y utzcinnic ob cuch i | Then they finished the job.
He ix u chun mul | 1395 Thus then was the origin of the mounds

Y utzcinnah ob e | They completed.
Holhun baak u kaalal u mullil | Some six thousand pyramids were walled,

Ca tac lahu y ox kal u much' *cuentail* mul* | And nearly fifty more made the total count of the mounds.
Y utzcinnah ob | They finished them
T u yuklah | 1400 And they spread all over
Cabil | The land
Peten | And the country.
Bay ti kaknab | Thus it was from the sea
Tac t u chun cab | Nearly to the base of the land.
U patah | 1405 They labeled
Ix u kaba ob xan | And also named them,
Y etel u ch'eenil | Together with the wells.
Ca tun utzcinnab i | And then was performed
Mactzil ti ob | A miracle for them
T u men *Dios* lae | 1410 By God there.
Caa el ob | And they were burned
T u men kak | By fire
T u cahal *ysrael* | In the town of Israel,
Y etel bobil lay a | Together with the stalks there.
U kaahlay katunob | 1415 This is the count of the *katuns*
Y etel haabob | And years

(*note continued from preceding page*)
of *katun* 11 Ahau, or 1556, and the fifteenth after the Spanish reached Merida. Although early, it is a plausible date for the composition of this text. As noted above (note 1366), the preceding year was 1 Ix, initiating the second half of the calendar round.

1393. I believe this is intended as a refinement of the vague date 11.15.0.0.0 cited earlier, hence 11.13.6.0.0 (1467), or shortly after the fall of Mayapan. It is quite possible that major monumental construction was indeed suspended at about that time.

1398. I don't know of anyone who has tried to count the pyramids of Yucatan in modern times, and 6,050 seems like a lot of pyramids. Depending on the area included, it could come to something like five to six pyramids per square mile, or one pyramid for every one hundred or so people. But if small "mounds" are included, the figure might be credible, and it would be just like the Maya to have counted them.

Lukci te   They were removed there
  Viroa*   At Babylonia.
Chac u nescab   They show the relations
  U ch'ibal *Tutul* Xiuob e.   1420   And lineage of the Toltec Xiu.

1418. *Viroa* is another garbled foreign name. I reconstruct *(ba)viro(ni)a* and suppose it to be a vague reference to the Babylonian captivity of the Jews.

---

15. The Ceremonial of the *Hab*

(1) U chun u unicil   The head of the (?) family
  Ah canul e   Was Can Ul.
Yx sac (. . . .)*   And the northern (Uaxim)
  Yx culux chacah: (Had) Culux Chacah.
Y ix mehen pa(sel)(. .)*   1425   And a little (west) hut
  U pasel y(ax)um: Is the hut of the Yaxum,
U chu u uinicil   Whose head of the family
  (. . . . .)*   Was (Cau Ich),
9: Y ahau ah nohol.   And the lord of the people of the south
  U chun u unicil ah noh   1430   Is the head of the family of the
                         southerners,
Ix kan tacay u kaba   And Kan Tacay is the name
  U chun u uinicil ah puch e: Of the head of the family of the
                         Puch.
Bolon p'el y oc haa u cananma ob:*   Great valleys do they guard;
  Bolon p'el uitz u cananma ob: Great mountains do they guard.
Chac tok tun   1435   Red flint stone
  U tunil =   Is the stone;
Ah chac mucen   Red harvest
  Cab e   Is the honey;
Chac ymiix (9:) yax che.   Red alligator ceiba
  U tz'ulbal: y an ti lakin: 1440   Is the arbor to the east.
Chacal puc te:*   Red bullet trees
  U cheob: Are their trees,

1423. Roys 1967: 15 supplies *uaxim 'guaje'* from Berendt. *Zac* 'white' is the color of the north.

1425. Roys 1967: 15 supplies *ek* 'black, west' and the *ax* of *yaxum* 'blue bird' in line 1426 from Berendt, as well as the Cau Ich in line 1428.

1428. See line 1539.

1433. *Bolon* may mean either 'nine' or 'great', and the meaning of this frequent couplet is far from clear. In this context it seems to make sense that the writer intends to assert the greatness of the lords of the four directions.

1441. Identified by Roys 1967: 64, note 7 as a bullet tree (*Bucida*).

Yx chac ya	And red sapotes
Ybillo(b)*	Are their lima beans,
Yx chac*	1445 And red (?)
Akbilob:*	Are their greens.
Chac yx kan tz'ulob	And red yellowbreasts
Yulum oob:	Are their turkeys,
Yx chac op'ool*	And red annonas
Y ixim ob	1450 Are their corn.
Sac tok tun u tunil:	White flint stone is the stone
U tunil ti xaman:	That is their stone to the north.
Sac ymix yax che.	White alligator ceiba
U tz'ulbal:	Is their arbor.
Sac mucen	1455 White harvest
Cab:	Is the honey
Yx sac tan	And whitebreasts
Ý ulum ob:	Their turkeys.
Sac yb	White lima beans
Y akbil ob:	1460 Are their greens;
Sac yxim	White corn
Y ixim ob: =	Their corn.
9: Ek tok tun:	Black flint stone
U tunil. ti chikin:	Is their stone to the west.
Ek ymix yax che	1465 Black alligator ceiba
U tz'ulbal:	Is their arbor.
Yx ek hub:*	And black conch
Y ixim ob:	Is their corn,
Yx ek chuch ys:	And black stem yams
Y isil ob:	1470 Are their yams.
Yx ek ucum:	And black roadrunners
Y ulum ob:	Are their turkeys.
Ek akab	Black-as-nights
Chan u nal ob:	Are their corn ears.
Yx ek buul:	1475 And black beans
U buul ob:	Are their beans.
Ek yb:	Black lima beans
Y ibil ob:	Are their lima beans.
Kan tok tun.	Yellow flint stone
U tunil: u nohol	1480 Is the stone of the south.

1444. Roys 1967: 64 omits *ybil(l) ob* 'their lima beans'.

1445. Red what is not specified, but there is no gap in the text, as Roys 1967: 64 implies.

1446. Roys 1967: 64, note 8 sees this as *chac ak* 'red vine' and does not account for *-bil o*.

1449. Roys 1967: 64 reads *op'* as 'toast', which is quite possible. I read it as 'annona'. There is, however, no way I can accept *op'ool* as 'toasted'. The inflection is gerundive with verbs. With nouns it may be merely generalizing.

1467. Roys 1967: 64 has 'black speckled corn'. I don't know how he gets there.

Ymix yax che: — kan ymix yax
che:
   U tz'ulbal ob:
Kanal puc te
   U che ob:
Yx kan puc te
   Y isil ob:
Yx kan puc te ucum
   Y ulum ob:
Yx kan kan nal
   U nal ob
(. .) kan u uih
   U buul ob:
Cabal (. . . . .)
   (2) Cab ob =
9: Buluc ahau
   U katunil
Uc(hc i)
   T u pach cuch ob:
Ca hop' talel ah p'is (luum) lay ah
p'is te:
   Y ah p'i(s . . .) lub ob.*
Ca tun tali chac te: aban.
   Chac tetic u (. .)b ob:
Ca tali uac hab nal hoch*
   Xiu tic u lub ob =
Ta muk u talel: mis cit ahau:
   Mis tic u lub ob:

Ta muk u talel y ah p'is
   Ul u lub ob:
Heklay coch. lub
   C u p'isc i:
Ca cah i:
   U hool poop:*
Yx noh: uc:
   U hool u poop ah lakin:
Ox tocoy moo*
   U hol u poop ti lakin

Alligator ceibas—yellow alligator
ceibas
   Are their arbors.
Yellow bullet trees
   Are their trees.
1485 And yellow bullet trees
   Are their yams.
And yellow bullet tree roadrunners
   Are their turkeys.
And bright yellow corn ears
1490   Are their corn ears.
And yellowbacks
   Are their beans.
Honey water (?)
   Is their honey.
1495 11 Ahau
   Was the *katun* count
That occurred
   After they gathered.
And the Surveyors began to come there
to P'iz Te
1500   And P'iz Te is their stopping place.
And then came the Red Tree Shrubs
   And Chac Te is their stopping place.
Then came the Six-Year Corns
   And Xiu Tic is their stopping place.
1505 While there came the Sweeper lords
   And Miz Tic was their stopping
   place.
While there came the Surveyors
   And reached their stopping places.
Open there was a wide stopping place
1510   Which was measured there.
Then came
   The counselors:
And Noh Uc,
   The counselor of the east people.
1515 The third (priest) Tocoy Mo,
   The counselor of the east.

   1500. The "stopping places" are all apparently puns: *p'iz te* 'measuring stick',
chac te 'red (brazil) tree', *uac y ab nal* 'six-year corn', *xiu tic* 'spread grass', *miz tic*
'spread sweeping/cause to sweep (something)'.
   1503. Roys 1967: 65, note 4 suggests that Uuc y Ab Nal is intended: the modern town of Teabo.
   1512. Most of the counselors have lineage names documentable elsewhere. Ex-
ceptions are Tocoy, Paua, Hel, Ak, E, I, Ban, Tuc, and Uch.
   1515. *Ox* 'three' here and in line 1517 may mean 'third (priest)'.

Ox paua hel	The third (priest) Paua Hel,
U hol u pop. ti lakin.	The counselor of the east.
Ah mis:*	Ah Mis,
U hol u pop. ti lakin. — 1520	The counselor of the east.
Ba tun	Ba Tun,
U hol u pop ti xaman.	The counselor of the north.
Ah puch	Ah Puch,
U hol u pop ti xaman	The counselor of the north.
Balam na. 1525	Balam Na,
U hol u pop ti xam(an)	The counselor of the north.
Ake	Ak E,
U hol pop. ti xaman	The counselor of the north.
Y ban	I Ban,
U hol pop. ti chikin 1530	The counselor of the west.
Ah chab.	Ah Chab,
U hol pop ti chikin =	The counselor of the west.
Ah tu cuch.*	Tuc Uch,
U hol pop ti chikin.	The counselor of the west.
Ah yamas 1535	Ya Maz,
U hol pop ti nohol.	The counselor of the west.
Ah puch	Ah Puch,
U hol pop ti nohol.	The counselor of the south.
Cau ich	Cau Ich,
U hol pop. ti nohol = 1540	The counselor of the south.
Ah co uoh	Co Uoh,
U hol pop ti nohol.	The counselor of the south.
Ah puc	Ah Puc,
U hol pop ti nohol —	The counselor of the south.
Chac yx chuuah cabob* 1545	Little red honeybees
Ti lakin:	Are the bees in the east.
Chac lol	Red blossoms
U luch ob:	Are their cups.
Chachac nicte:	Bright red flowers
U nicte ob: 1550	Are their flowers.
Sac yx chuuah cabob.	And white honeybees
Ti xaman	Are in the north.
Sac ix pach tz'au*	And whiteback buds
U nicteil ob —	Are their flowering plants.

1519. *Ah* 'cane' is sometimes, as here, a lineage name; sometimes (line 1533) it is 'he (who)' and the usage seems to suggest something like 'Mr.'. The latter usage may be honorific, as it occurs rather randomly.

1533. See note 1519.

1545. The separation of this insignia section from the previous ten insignia (lines 1435 ff.) may be intended to emphasize the role of honey in the ceremony being described. See lines 1570 ff.

1553. I know of no meaning for *tz'au*. Roys 1967: 65, note 7 says, "There is little doubt that here the *pah tz'a* is meant . . ." He identifies it as either *Commelina* or *Callisia*.

Sac lol	1555	White flowers
U luch ob: —		Are their cups.
Ek yx chuuah cab		And black honeybees
U cab ob ti lakin.		Are their bees in the west.
Ek ix lau nicte*		And black laurel flowers
U nicteil ob:	1560	Are their flowering plants.
Ek lol		Black blossoms
U luch ob —		Are their cups.
Kan yx chuuah cab ob		And yellow honeybees
Ti nohol.		Are to the south.
Kan lol*	1565	Yellow blossoms
U lu(chob)(. . .)		Are their cups.
(Ka)n tzac nicte.		Bright yellowbell flowers
U nicteil ob =		Are their flowering plants.
Ca tun y anh iy		So when there is
U numte aal cab	1570	A run of suffering for honey,
Tz'(.) c u samil. u (aal)cab		They provide their honey
Y etel u luch cab:*		And their honey cup.
Kin pauah tun		The Sun Giants
Y ah kin ob: =		Are their sun priests.
Lay mektanmail: u picul katun.	1575	These are the supervisors of the *katun* cycle,
		The *katun* keepers:
Cananmail		The *katun* keepers:
Ah hul neb.*		Sire Hul Neb,
Tan tun. cusamil. =		The capital, Cusamil,
Ah yax: ac: chi nab:		The new one, Chi Nab,
Kin ich kak mo = —	1580	And the glorious Kak Mo.

1559. I know of no meaning for *ix lau*. Roys 1967: 65, note 8 says, "The *Ix-laul*, called *laurel* in Spanish, is *Stemmadenia* . . . , the flowers of which are white, not black."

1565. Identified by Roys 1967: 65, note 9 as *Tecoma*.

1572. A couplet of the text has been inadvertently omitted:

Y etel u yax cheel cab	And their green tree honey,
U chululil cab	Their dripping honey.

1577. All four are titled as well as named; hence my interpretation of *ah* (see note 1519). Most of the names are rare, and some of them are unique, *viz.*, Neb, Zamil, and Chinab.

16. Christianity Reaches Merida

11.17.0.0.0	(13) Buluc ahau	11 Ahau
	Katun	Was the *katun*
	C u maan ti pop	That came to the mat,
	C u maan ti tz'aam	That came to the throne,

Ti ualaac u than	1585	Which raised its word,
Ti ualaac y ahaulil i		Which raised the lordship.
Yax xaal chac		Yaxal Chac
U u ich ti y ahaulil i:		Was the face in the lordship.
Emom caanil ual		Descended was the high fan;
Emom caanil tz'ulub	1590	Descended were the high branch
Caanil		And the celestial
Utz'ub		Incense.
Pecnom u pax		Sounded was his drum;
Pecnom u soot ah buluc ahau		Sounded was the rattle of the lord of 11 Ahau,
Ti y octe tok y ubte	1595	Who had flint brought to be colored
Takin yax utz t u ba		And money and fresh turkey for himself.
T u kin y an sulim chan		At that time there was Zulim Chan;
T u kin y an chikin putun*		At that time there were western Chontal.
Uiilnom che		Hungering were the trees;
Uiilnom tunich	1600	Hungering were the rocks.
Ah satal uiil		The destroyer hunger
Ychil ah buluuc ahau katun		Was during the *katun* of the lord of 11 Ahau.
Buluuc ahau u hop'ol u xocol		11 Ahau was the beginning of the count
Y oklal lay katun y an ca uli		Because this was the *katun* when the foreigners arrived.
tz'ulob		
Ti u talel ob	1605	When they came,
Ti likin ca uli ob e		They arrived from the east.
✠ Ti ix hop'i *christianoil* xan i		When Christianity began also,
Ti lakin u tz'oc than		In the east was its word completed.
Ych can si hoo		Heaven Born Merida
U hetz' katun	1610	Was the seat of the *katun*.
He u kahlay uchc i		This is the account of what occurred,
Bal t u mentah ob		Of what they did.
Manlahci u thanah		The relation is not finished
Y etel u than ob		With their words.
He uac manan u nucul t u lacal	1615	It may be there is no meaning to it all:
He uac hun tatz' manci bay tz'ibannil e		It may be an error and not true as it is written.
He ca cici nucbesabac t u lacal e		If the real meaning is mastered entirely,
Ma i u il ob e		Why didn't they see it?
Ma i tun ba hun tz'ibtil ob e		How much may they not have written then?
Ma ix hach yab tz'iban	1620	Was not much more written,

1598. Roys 1967: 77 and Barrera 1948: 96 read this as Chakan Putun, which is the way it stands in the Tizimin. This is almost certainly correct; see line 1830.

T u cuch u keban than ob	Accusing them of conspiring
T u ba tan ba ob	Against each other?
Bay u cah y ahau ah ytza ob e	Thus was the way of the Itzas
Bay ix ah ytzmal	As also of the Izamal,
Ah ake	1625 The Ake,
Bay ah uxmal	As of the Uxmal,
Bay ah ych can si hoo	As of those of Heaven Born Merida,
Bay ah citab co uooh xan e	And as of those of Ci Tab and Co Uoh as well.
Hal ach yab	The chiefs were many,
Ha(14)l ach uinicob	1630 And the governors
Ma concon u keban than	Did not buy and sell their conspiracies;
U cibah ob t u ba tan ba ob e	They came to agreements with one another.
He uac ma chicaan ychil y an uay e	If this is not established in what there is here,
Ma ba hun bin tzoloc i	How much more cannot be told!
He x ohelmail talc i	1635 For in fact the knowledge comes
Ca ch'ibal c on maya uinic e	From the ancestry of us Maya.
	This stone knows its meaning,
Lay tun y ohel u nucbes	Which comes from their count that
Ca bin u xoc ob y an uay e	is here.
Ti tun y ilic	One looks at the stone
Ca tun u nucbes	1640 And divines its meaning.
Ua bic chucanil u sauin katun	Whenever the aspirations of the *katun* are found
T u men c ah kinob	By our sun priests,
Ah kin xuluc	The Xuluc sun priests,
Ma ix xuluc u kaba cuchi xan i	But Not Xuluc was also the name they had.
Chen t u men lay c u kinil	1645 Only by this was the divination,
Lay cu ah kinil	And these were the diviners.
Ca oci num ya	When misery came,
Ca oci *christianoil*	When Christianity came
T u men lay hach *christianoob*	From these many Christians
Ti ul i	1650 Who arrived
Y etel hahal ku	With the true divinity,
Hahal Dˢ.	The True God.
He uac u chun num ya	For this indeed was the beginning of misery
T oon	For us,
U chun patan	1655 The beginning of tribute,
U chun *limosna*	The beginning of tithes,
U chun hoc mucuuc tza	The beginning of strife over purse snatching,
U chun tz'on bacal tza	The beginning of strife with blowguns,

U chun cumtan tza		The beginning of strife over promotions,
U chun tocluksah	1660	The beginning of the creation of many factions,
U chun tz'al pach p'ax		The beginning of forced seizure for debts,
U chun pak pach p'ax		The beginning of forced imprisonment for debts,
U chun caca tza		The beginning of village strife,
U chun numsah ya		The beginning of misery and affliction,
U chun tocluksah	1665	The beginning of forcible separation,
U chun u meyahtabal españolesob		The beginning of forced labor for the Spaniards
Y etel ah kinob		And the sun priests,
U meyahtabal ba tabob		Forced labor for the town chiefs,
U meyahtabal camsahob		Forced labor for the teachers,
U meyahtabal fiscalob	1670	Forced labor for the public prosecutors,
T u men mehen palalob		By the boys,
U palil cahob		The youths of the towns,
Ta muk uchac numsabal ti ya		While the force of great suffering
Ah num yaob		Afflicted the suffering people.
Lay hach otzilob e	1675	These were the very poor,
Lay hach otzilob ma likul ob i		These were the very poor who did not rebel
Ti lic u mentic		At the oppression
(15) Cij u tz'aal pach		That was inflicted on them.
Lay u antachristoil		This was the Antichrist
Y okol cabob lae	1680	Here on earth,
Uh cab cohil cahob		The Earth Lions of the towns,
U chamacil cahob		The Foxes of the towns,
Uh picil cahob		The Bedbugs of the towns
Y ah tz'utz'il otzil maseualob lae		Are the bloodsuckers of the poor peasants here.
He uac bini to kuchuc	1685	For indeed the time is coming soon
T u kin u kuchul		Of the day of the coming
Y alil u u ichob		Of tears to the eyes
Y icnal ca		And the presence
Ca yumil		Of our Lord
Ti Dˢ.	1690	Who is God.
Emon u justisia ca yumil		The justice of our Lord
Ti Dˢ.		God will descend
Hun yuk		Everywhere
Ti bal cah		In the world.
Hach likul ti Dˢ.	1695	God will be very angry
Bin tal bal		And something will come

Ah kan tenal   From Yellow Death
   Yx puc y ol a   And the Destroying Spirit,
U tz'utannilob   The oppressors
   Y okol cab lae.   1700   On the face of this earth.

---

17. The Count of the *Katuns*

---

(71)MS Tzaay nitic tun   A collection of flower stones:
   Chac tun   Red stones
U uayas ba kab caan   Shaped by the juice of heaven:
   Ytz caan u uayas ba   By dew of heaven shaped,
U uays ba a ch'aabtac kin   1705   Shaped by thy creation of day:
   A ch'aabtaci ti acab   Thy creation of night,
U uayas ba ytz caan   Shaped by dew of heaven:
   Kab caan   By the hand of heaven,
Kan lol caan   Yellow blossoms of heaven
   U uayas ba ba c in   1710   Shaped by whatever I am.
In ch'aabtahci a kinil   I have been created by thy sun,
   Ch'abtabci a u il   Created by thy sight.
Ba cit   Whatsoever,
   Ba cin in ch'aabta tunil   Whatever I have had created of
     stone,
Yn ch'aab ech   1715   I have created you
   Ti cumtal   In darkness.
T a hoyobal ak   Thou hast been sprinkled with
   moisture
   Ah cunic u kinam   By the curer of wounds.
T a yam kin   Thou hast changed the sun
   Ca ti t u tuxchi*   1720   Whenever it was time.
Tab ech   Where wast thou?
   T a chacit ti mucc e   Thou hast appeared secretly.
Yn ch'ab ech   I created thee;
   Yn cumcinn ech tac helel   I have transformed thee.
Yn ch'aic   1725   I have arranged
   U uyic a kinam e   To listen to thy injuries
T u menel a yum   Because of thy father,
   A mucut   Thy secret,
Ti cit   Who is distant,
   Ti tun e   1730   Who is stone.

1720. Bricker reads *ca ti t u tuxchi* 'when he sent it'.

In colobta

   T a chi e u kan ti tun e

Lay c u bin

   U ximbal u tz'olic lae

Lay ahauob

   Tzolanob lae

Xic u bin a xoc

   Ca a nucte lae

(72) Ti likin uay e*

   Buluc ahau

Buluc ahau u hetz' katun

   Ich caan ci hoo

Yax haal hop'c i

   Christianoil lae

Bolon ahau

   Ti uuc y ab nal

U hetz' katun

   Ti bolon ahau

Uuc ahau

   Ti *mayapan*

U hetz' katun

   Ti uuc ahau

Hoo ahau

   Ti çotz'il

U hetz' katun

   Ti hoo ahau

Putzhom

   Kohom

Uil ti y ahaulil

   Ah hoo ahau katun

Ti nohol uay e

   Ox ahau

Ti *çuyua*

   U hetz' katun

Ti ox ahau

   Katun

I have been separated.

   Thou hast shown the yellow in the stone.

This is going to be

   The course of this count.

1735 These are the lords

   Who have been counted.

Go on and do thy count

   When thou canst understand this.

To the east here

1740   In 11 Ahau the

Seat of the *katun*

   Was Heaven Born Merida.

Yax Haal began it;

   It was Christianity.

1745 In 9 Ahau,

   At Teabo

Was the seat of the *katun*

   In 9 Ahau.

7 Ahau:

1750   At Mayapan

Was the seat of the *katun*

   In 7 Ahau.

In 5 Ahau:

   At Zotz'il

1755 Was the seat of the *katun*

   In 5 Ahau.

Dust

   And drought

May have been in the lordship

1760   Of *katun* 5 Ahau.

To the south here

   In 3 Ahau:

At Zuyua

   Was the seat of the *katun*

1765 In the 3 Ahau

   Katun.

1739. The *katuns* are numbered clockwise and the directions counterclockwise on this *katun* wheel. The premise seems to have been that the direction points remain fixed while the wheel is rotated counterclockwise, thus bringing each *katun* in turn to its seating in the east, beginning with 11 Ahau. Roys 1967: 132, note 1 assumes that the *katuns* are named by ending date, which was true in the Tikal calendar (before 1539). In the colonial Mayapan calendar they were named by initial date (Edmonson 1976). The list of *katun* seats that follows is a later interpolation, possibly belonging to 6 Ahau (1717). The last three seatings disagree with those on other lists. Since I cannot date the passage firmly, I have left it here.

Hay lic u keulel can	Spread like the skin of the serpent
Y etel u keulel balam	And the skin of the jaguar.
Yax coc ay mut	The center priest Coc Ay the Crier
U u ich ti y ahaulil i	1770 Was the face in the lordship
Ah ox ahau	In the 3 Ahau
Katun	*Katun.*
Hun ahau	In 1 Ahau:
Emal	Emal
U hetz' katun	1775 Was the seat of the *katun*
Ti hun ahau	In 1 Ahau.
Emom tab	Descended will be the rope,
Emom çum	Descended will be the cord
T u kin y emel ix yom	At the time of the descent also of Yom
Yx ual icay	1780 And Ual Icay.
Lahca ahau	In 12 Ahau:
Ti çac lah tun	At Valladolid
U hetz' katun	Was the seat of the *katun*
Ti lahca ahau	In 12 Ahau.
Yaxaal chuen	1785 Yax Chuen
U u ich ti y ahaulil i	Was the face in the lordship.
Ti chikin uay e	To the west here
Lahun ahau	In 10 Ahau:
Lahun chable	10 Chable
U hetz' katun	1790 Was the seat of the *katun*
Ti lahun ahau	In 10 Ahau.
Uaxac ahau	In 8 Ahau:
Ti lahun chable	At 10 Chable
U hetz' katun	Was the seat of the *katun*
Ti uaxac ahau	1795 In the 8 Ahau
Katun	*Katun.*
Uac ahau	In 6 Ahau:
Ti uuc y ab nal	At Teabo
U hetz' katun	Was the seat of the *katun*
Ti uac ahau	1800 In the 6 Ahau
Katun	*Katun.*
Ti xaman uay e	To the north here
Can ahau	4 Ahau:
Ti can ahau	In 4 Ahau
Uuc y ab nal	1805 At Teabo
U hetz' katun	Was the seat of the *katun*
T u chi ch'een ytza	At Chichen Itza.
Cabil ahau	2 Ahau:
Ti cabil ahau	In 2 Ahau
Maya cuçamil	1810 Maya Cusamil
Mayapan	Mayapan.
Oxlahun ahau	13 Ahau:
Oxlahun ahau	In the 13 Ahau
Katun	*Katun*

Kin colah peten
  U hetz' katun
Oxlahun ahau
  Katun.

1815 Kin Colah Peten
    Was the seat of the *katun*
  In the 13 Ahau
    Katun.

18. Merida Seats the Cycle

Katun *wheel (1539). From the Garrett Collection of Manuscripts in Middle American Languages, The Princeton University Library, The gift of Robert Garrett.*

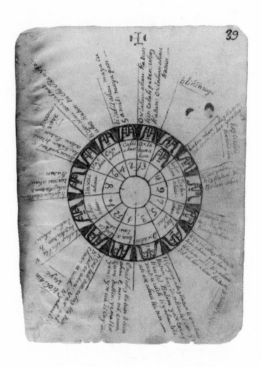

11.17.0.0.0 (73) Buluc ahau
  U hetz' katun
Ych caan çi hoo
  Yaaxhaal u u ich*
Emom canal u al

Emom canal utz'ub

Pecnom u pax
  Pecnom u çoot

11 Ahau
1820   Seated the *katun*
  At Heaven Born Merida.
    Yax Haal was lord.
Descended from heaven will be its juice;
    Descended from heaven will be its perfume.
1825 Sounded will be its drum;
    Sounded will be its rattle,

1822. Yax(al) Chac was the lord of this *katun*. See line 1587.

Ah bolon y oc te*	That the great one might be installed.
T u kin y an yax cutz*	At the time there was Yax Cutz,
T u kin y an çulun chan*	At the time there was Zulun Chan,
T u kin chakan putun 1830	At the time of Champoton.
Uilnoh che	And the famine of sticks,
Uilnom tunich	And the famine of stones;
Ah çal i	The spirit of drought
Uiil	And famine
Ychil ah buluc ahau 1835	In 11 Ahau
Katun lae.	*Katun.*

1827. *Bolon y octe* is obscure. *Bolon* is 'nine, great'; *oc* is 'foot, enter'; *te* is 'tree' or a verbal suffix. Possible readings are 'nine-foot rounds', 'the nine priest Oc Te', 'tree of nine-foot (roots)' or 'the great one might be installed'.

1828. Yax Cutz may have been a pretender to the lordship.

1829. Zulim Chan is named by the Tizimin as lord of the *katun* at Emal. Here he seems to be awarded the same office at Champoton, but the text is inexplicit.

19. The New Cycle of Merida

(87) *Capitulo del Año*	Chapter of the year:
Katun	The *katun*
11.17.0.0.0 *Primero* Buluc Ahau	Of the first 11 Ahau,
U yax hetz' luum tz'ulob lae 1840	The first seat of the land of the foreigners here.

Primero Buluc Ahau	11 Ahau
Katun	Was the *katun*,
U yax chun u xocol katun	The first base of the count of *katuns*,
U hun tz'it katun*	The first part of the *katun*.
Ych caan çi hoo 1845	Heaven Born Merida
U hetz' katun	Was the seat of the *katun*
Ulc i	At the arrival
Tz'ullob:	Of the foreigners.
Chac u mex u mehen kin	Red were the beards of the sons of the sun,
Ah mexob ti lakin u tali ob 1850	The bearded ones who came from the east,
Ca uli ob uay tac luumil e	When they arrived here near this land
U tz'ulilob cab	As foreigners to the land:

1844. 11 Ahau was the base of the count in a triple sense: it initiated the Itza *katun* cycle, the colonial era, and also the colonial Mayapan calendar. The lords of this and the three following *katuns* are depicted with ropes around their necks.

Yax Chac, lord of Merida
(1539–1559). From the Garrett Col-
lection of Manuscripts in Middle
American Languages, The Princeton
University Library, The gift of
Robert Garrett.

Çac uinicob	White people
Chac uinicob	And red people,
U mehen cab	1855 The sons of the land,
U chun nicte*	The trunk of the flower
Ti petenob	In the lands
(. . . . .)ca ob*	They . . .
Nicte u ua ti ob	The flower raised by them
(. . . . . .) ba ob*	1860 They . . . themselves.
Bee ah ytza e	Thus were the Itza
Cah ch'aab	At the start of that creation,
Talel u cah çac o ych caan	Coming to begin the white birds in heaven,
Çac tun lah pal tal ti caan	The white stone of all the children come from heaven.
Çac uaom che bin emebal	1865 The white standing tree will be lowered
Tal ti caan	Coming from heaven.
Hun auat	One shout,
Hun lub u talel	One rest and it will come.

1856. Roys 1967: 148, note 2 routinely identifies *nicte* as the *Plumeria* flower, but it means 'flower' in general. It has a number of metaphorical meanings, including sex, war, Xiu, and Spanish. It is also the nickname for *katun* 11 Ahau.

1858. Word missing in MS.

1860. Word missing in MS.

A u ilic ex y ahal cab   You will see the dawn;
    A u ilic ex mut.   1870   You will see the news.
Bee oktabac oon ti tali ob   Thus we were made to weep for their coming,
    Ulic ob   Their arrival,
Hunac ah mol tunichob   Uniting the collectors of stones,
    Hunac ah mol cheob   Uniting the collectors of sticks.
U çac yb te el ob cab   1875   And the white lima bean trees will burn the land
    Hopom kak t u ni u kab ob   With fire beginning at the tips of their branches,
Y et mac u çaban ob   And your fellow men will be poisoned
    Y etel u taab ob   And tied up,
Uchebal   And they will be beaten
    U hich' cal u yum ob   1880   And the fathers hanged by the neck.
Bee ah ytza e   Thus were the Itza,
    He ix a kul e   And that will be your fate:
Ma bal   Poverty
    U uilal   And need.
Lay te hahal ku   1885   That will be the True God
    Ti emi lae   Who descends here.
Hun çipi u than   One blame his word:
    Hun çipi u can   One blame his teaching.
Coc ix bin u katunil   And deaf will be the *katun* period,
    Coc ix bin u chacilob   1890   And deaf will be the rain gods.
Mac to uil ah kin   Who then may be sun priest,
    Mac to uil ah bouat bin natic   Who then may be the prophet who will understand?
Ualac   He should arise,
    U talel   And come
Tan cah maya patan   1895   To the capital city of Mayan tribute,
    T u chi ch'een ytza e   To Chichen Itza.
Bee alan ytz'inil*   Thus was the burden of the younger brothers:
    Ti tali   To come in
Ychil uuc ahau   In the 7 Ahau
    Katun   1900   *Katun*,
T u cal ya   Bringing back pain,
    T u cal num ya   Bringing back suffering,

1897. "Younger brothers" is a metaphor for Maya as opposed to Spaniards, but also for peasants as opposed to nobles. The decision of the Itza to declare Chichen Itza a capital (*tan cah*) and collect tribute in its name produced immediate resistance from the Spanish and the Mayan nobles of the west and the peasantry everywhere. It does not appear that this move was justified calendrically or mythologically, nor is it clear how the accommodation between the Spanish and the Xiu nobility worked. "Chichen Itza" continued to collect tribute (or tried to) until late in the eighteenth century.

T u patan tac yax cul | Paying tribute as you are first seated,
  He x tac pul ex y alan patan | As you bear the burden of tribute.
Çamal cabehe | 1905 Day after tomorrow
  Ti tali | It will come.
Mehen ex e | You will engender
  Ch'a a ba ex | And create
A manç ex u cuch num ya | And will pay the burden of suffering
  Lic u talel yam a cahal ex e | 1910   As the time has come for you to
    settle.

He ix katun | And this is the *katun*
  Ti culhi lae | Which is seated then:
U (. . .) (88) katun | The . . . *katun*,
  U katunil num ya | The *katun* period of suffering,
U katunil | 1915 The *katun* period
  U tza ciçin | Of the devil's due,
Ti culhi ychil buluc ahau | Which was seated in 11 Ahau
  Katun | *Katun.*
Kam ex | Receive them;
  Kam ex a u u la ex ob* | 1920   Receive and welcome them:
Ah mexob | The bearded people,
  Ah pulob | The guayaba people,
T u chicul ku | In the sign of God.
  Talel tun u cah ob | Coming then is the settlement
A çucun ex ob | 1925 Of your older brothers,
  Ah tan tun ob* | The people of the capital.
Lay to bin katic | That then will be the desire
  U çian ku | Of the born God
T ex | For you
  Y etell ob e | 1930   And them.
He ix u kaba | And these are the names
  Y ah kin ob e | Of their sun priests:
Ah mis | Ah Mis,
  Ni lac | Ni Lac,
Pe coh | 1935 Pe Coh,
  Antachristo u u ichob | And Antichrist are their faces
T u kinil te u talel | At the time when they come,
  U kinil t atan ex e | The time that you are paid.
Bee t u yabal num ya mehen ex e | Thus will be endured suffering, O sons,
  Lay u than ca yum | 1940 This is the word of our Father.
Elom ti cab | Burnt will be the land—
  Çac petahom caanal | And a white circle will be in the
    sky

1920. This is the Xiu counterattack against the Itza: convert to Christianity
and accept Spanish rule, a proposal which must therefore have been reasonably advantageous from the Xiu point of view.

1926. Here the older brothers are the Spanish, but the reference to the capital is
a scarcely veiled attempt to make the Xiu nobility senior to the Itza.

T u katunil uchmal e	In the *katun* period that occurred,
Tali t u chi *Dios* citbil	Coming before the face of God the remote
Ma tusbil thann i	1945 With no lying words.
Bee hach al	Thus very heavy
U cuch katun	Is the burden of the *katun*
Ti culhi ychil *christianoil*	That was seated in Christianity.
He ualac	That will arise
C u talel e	1950 And come:
P'entacil than	The lusting of words,
P'entac (can	Lustful (teaching,
P'entac) tun ich	Lustful) faces,
P'entac uinic	Lustful people
Ti talij	1955 Who come
Bin ku (. .)	And will arrive
(. . . . .) in a u ilic ex	And then you will see them.
Talel u cah	They are coming,
He ix hal ach (uinic)	And they will be the governors
(C uchi e)	1960 Who occur:
Ah ca kin tz'amoob	Those of the two-day thrones,
Ah ca kin popoob	Those of the two-day mats,
Ychil uay yab haab	In these painful years,
Ti u coy kinilob i	In the crooked times.
Ha li li	1965 In truth
U xul u than *Dios*	It is the end of the Word of God.
Buluc pis u luch*	The eleventh bundle is his gourd.
Mol yam u mut	The pile of change is the news
U u ich	Of the face
Ti y ahaulil i	1970 In the lordship.
Mol tun u can*	Piled stone is his teaching;
Mol tun u than	Piled stone is his word.
Bin ex cimic	You will die
Bin ex cuxlac	But you are to live.
Me x ca a naat ex	1975 And then you will more or less understand
U than cuxul uooh lae	The word of this living glyph.
Ah *maypan* e	The man of the cycle city,
U mehen u ba t u hunal	Engendering himself all alone,
U *justisiail*	Is tried
Lay ti tz'aic ti mas cab	1980 And put in irons.
Lay ti hoksic	He is tied up.
Ca u kax	When he is tied

1967. Compare references to the ninth and thirteenth "burdens."

1971. Here to the end of the chapter (line 1990) is a Xiu reading of Christian doctrine in the first generation of the conquest: you will die but you will live when you understand the Word. The Lord is self-born, is tried, imprisoned, tied up, and beaten. Then he is seated (as God) with a crown and insignia of majesty. It is apparent that the Franciscans communicated something.

Ca u hatz'ab*	Then he is beaten.
Ca tun tac ti cutal	Then next he is seated.
Ca y al	1985 Then he speaks
U xicin u mehen	To the ear of his son.
Ti y an u p'oc t u hol e	He has his hat on his head
Y etel u xanab ti y oc e	And his sandals on his feet.
Ti kaxan u taab t u nak e	He has his sash tied around his waist,
He ualac u talel e.	1990 And thus perhaps is his coming.

1983. Bricker has strenuous objections to my translating this as present passive. She sees some -ab constructions as simple future: see also 2007–2008.

9 Ahau

20. The Birth of the *Uinal*

(60) Bay tzolci yax ah miatz	Thus it was read by the first sage,
Merchise	Melchisedek,
Yax ah bouat	And the first prophet,
Na Puc Tun*	Puc Tun,
Sacerdote*	1995 The priest,
Yax ah kin	And the first sun priest.
Lay kay uchci*	This is the sermon of the occurrence
U çihil uinal*	Of the birth of the *uinal*,
Ti ma to ahac cab cuchi e	Which was before the awakening of the world occurred,
Ca hop'i u ximbal	2000 And it began to run
T u ba	By itself,
T u hunal	Alone.
Ca y alah u chich*	Then said his mother's mother,
Ca y alah u tz'e naa	Then said his mother's sister,

1994. A prophet of the early sixteenth century. See chapter 9.

1995. Melchisedek is identified as a Christian priest and Puc Tun as a Mayan one, the implication being that what follows is universally accepted truth.

1997. *Kay* is 'song'; *kaay* is 'sermon'.

1998. The *uinal* is the sacred cycle of twenty named days that form the base of all the larger cycles of the Mayan calendar. Its birth is the birth of time itself.

2003. Personification and deification of the world, *mundo* in Spanish, is a widespread conception among the colonial Maya. It is not clear why these particular relatives are singled out. They are all women, of course, searching for a male god.

Ca y alah u mim
   Ca y alah u muu*
Bal bin c alab
   Ca bin c ilab uinic ti be*
C u than ob
   Ta muk u ximbal ob cuchi e
Minan uinic cuch i
   Ca tun kuchi ob
Te
   Ti likin e*
Ca hop'i y alic ob
   Mac ti mani
Uay
   Lae
He y ocob
   Lae
P'iz t a u oc i*
   Ci bin u than u colel cab*

Ca bin u p'izah y oc ca yumil

   Ti D⁵. citbil*
Lay u chun y alci
   Xoc lah cab oc*
Lae
   Lah ca oc
Lay tzolan çihci
   T u men oxlahun oc uchci*

2005 Then said his father's mother,
   Then said his sister-in-law,
   "What is to be said
   When a man is seen on the road?"
So they said
2010 Whilst they were going along,
But no man occurred.
   And then they arrived
There
   At the east.
2015 And they began to say,
   "Who is it that passed
By here,
   Now?
Here are his tracks,
2020 Right here.
Measure them with your foot
   According to the word of the planter
   of the world."
Then they were to measure the
footprint of our Father
   Who is the holy God.
2025 This was the beginning of saying
   The count of the world by footsteps.
This was
   12 Oc.
This is the account of his birth.
2030 For 13 Oc occurred,

2006. *Mu* is 'sibling's spouse' but here it would appear to refer specifically to '(?older) brother's wife', possibly reflecting the levirate. The term may also have applied to father's sister, as the scansion suggests.

2008. The answer to all questions is the riddle of the Word, in this instance the word 'man' (*uinic*), which also means 'twenty' and shares its root with *uinal*. The root *uin* by itself means 'model, being'. The road is important too, as the Maya conceived time as a road on which the gods traveled endlessly, carrying by turns the burden of 'fate, time, and the sun'—all of which are meanings of the word *kin*.

2014. All things begin in the east with the rising sun and proceed counterclockwise.

2021. The day name 'foot' (Oc) provides a punning rationale for the 'measurement' (elsewhere 'pacing') of time. It may also have been selected because it is a member of a set of potential yearbearers (Chicchan, Oc, Men, Ahau) who are the focus of the still extant cult of the Burners. See lines 2161 ff. Perhaps they were the yearbearers in some ancient version of the Mayan calendar.

2022. Roys has 'the mistress of the world'. *Col* is both 'wife' and 'plant'.

2024. This is the Christian god, Sp. *Dios*.

2026. Another pun: *xoc lahcab oc* is 'count 12 Oc'; *xoc lah cab oc* is 'count the whole world (by) paces', as Roys 1967: 116, note 11 points out.

2030. The days 12 Oc and 13 Oc are 40 days apart in the *tzol kin*, or 40 years apart in the calendar round. They would be 120 *tuns* apart in a hypothetical *katun* cycle based on Oc, but there is no evidence that such a cycle ever existed.

U nup tan ba y oc   And they matched each other's paces
  Likci ob   And arrived
Te   There
  Ti likin e   At the east.
Ca y alah u kaba   2035 They said his name,
  Ti minan u kaba kin cuchi e   Since the days had no name then,
Ximbalnahci y etel u chich   And he traveled on with his mother's
                                     mother,
  Y etel u tz'e naa   And his mother's sister,
Y etel u mim   And his father's mother,
  Y etel u muu   2040 And his sister-in-law.
Çi uinal   The month was born
  Çihci kin u kaba   And the day name was born,
Çihci caan   And the sky was born
  Y etel luum   And the earth,
Eb haa   2045 The pyramid of water
  Luum*   And land,
Tunich   Stone
  Y etel che   And tree.
Cihci u bal kaknab   There were born the things of sea
  Y etel luum   2050 And land.
Hun Chuen u hokçici u ba*   On 1 Monkey (Chuen) he manifested
                                       himself
  T u kuil   In his divinity
U mentci caan   And created heaven
  Y etel luum   And earth.
Ca Eb*   2055 On 2 Peak (Eb)
  U mentci yax eb   He made the first pyramid.
Emci   He descended,
  Likul   Coming from
Tan y ol caan   There in the heart of heaven,
  Tan y ol haa   2060 There in the heart of the water.
Minaan   For there was nothing
  Luum   Of earth,
Y etel tunich   Or stone,
  Y etel che   Or tree.
Ox Men*   2065 On 3 Ben
  U mentci t u lacal bal   He made all things,
Hi ba hun bal   Each and every thing,
  U bal caanob   The things of the heavens
Y etel u bal kaknab   And the things of the sea
  Y etel u bal luum   2070 And the things of the land.

2046. The Maya conceived the cosmos as a pyramid of thirteen levels in the upper world and an inverted pyramid of nine levels in the lower.
    2051. Possible pun on *chuen* 'monkey' and *ah chuen* 'artisan', hence creator.
    2055. Pun on *eb* 'stairway, pyramid' and *em* 'descend'.
    2065. Pun on *ben* '(?corn)' and *men* 'make'.

(61) Can Ix uchci*
  U nixpahal
Caan
  Y etel luum
Ho Men uchci*
  U meyah t u lacal
Uac Cib uchci*
  U mentci yax cib

Uchci u çasilhal
  Ti minan kin y etel u
Uac Caban*
  Yax çihci
Cab
  Ti minan t oon c uchi
Uaxac Etz'nab*
  Etz'lahci
U kab
  Y etel y oc
Ca u ch'ich'aah
  Y okol luum
Bolon Cauac*
  Yax tumtabci *metnal*
Lahun Ahau*
  Uchci u bin ob
U lobil unicob
  Ti *metnal*
T u men D⁵. citbil
  Ma chicanac c uchi e
Bulu Yx*
  Uchci u patic
Tunich
  Y etel che
Lay u mentah
  Ichil kin
Lahcabil Yk*
  Uchci u çihcic Yk
Lay u chun u kabatic Yk

  T u men minan cimil ichil lae

On 4 Ix
  There occurred the separation
Of heaven
  And earth.
2075 On 5 Men
  Occurred the working of everything.
On 6 Cib
  Occurred the making of the first
  candle:
There occurred the illumination,
2080 For there was no sun or moon.
On 7 Caban
  There was first born
The earth,
  Which we didn't have before.
2085 On 8 Etz'nab
  He planted
His hands
  And feet
And made birds
2090 Upon the earth.
On 9 Cauac
  Hell was first tasted.
On 10 Ahau
  Occurred the going
2095 Of evil men
  To hell,
Because the holy God
  Had not yet appeared.
On 11 Imix
2100 Occurred the shaping
Of stones
  And trees.
This was what was done
  On this day.
2105 On 12 Wind (Ik)
  Occurred the birth of breath.
This was the beginning of what is
called breath,
  Because there is no death on it.

2071. Pun on *ix* 'jaguar' and *nix* 'separate'.
2075. Pun on *men* 'make' and *mey* 'work'.
2077. Pun on *cib* 'wax, candle'.
2081. Pun on *caban* '(?earth)' and *cab* 'earth, honey'.
2085. Pun on *etz'nab* 'flint' and *etz'lah* 'plant'.
2091. There may be a pun on *cauac* but I don't see it.
2093. *Ahau* 'lord' is associated with God and with the Lords of Hell.
2099. No pun on *imix*.
2105. Pun on *ik* 'wind, breath'.

Oxlahun Akal uchci u ch'aic haa*		On 13 Akbal occurred the taking of water.
Ca y akzah luum	2110	Then he moistened earth
Ca u patah		And shaped it
Ca uinic-hi		And made man.
Hunnil Kan*		On 1 Kan
U yax mentci		He was first
U lep'el y ol	2115	Disturbed at heart
T u menel u lobil u çihçah		By the evil that had been created.
Ca Chicchan*		On 2 Chicchan
Uchci u chictahal u lobil hi bal		Occurred the appearance of everything evil,
Y ilah		And he saw it
Ychil u u ich cah e	2120	Even within the towns.
Ox Cimil*		On 3 Death (Cimi)
U tusci cimil		He invented death.
Uchci u tusci		It happened that then was invented
Yax cimil		The first death
Ca yumil	2125	By our Father
Ti Dˢ.		Who is God.
(Can Manik)		(On 4 Manik)
(. . . .)*		(. . . .)
Ho Lamat lay u tusci*		On 5 Lamat there was the invention
Uuc lam chac	2130	Of the seven floods of rain,
Haal		Water,
Kaknab		And sea.
Uac Muluc*		On 6 Muluc
Uchci u mucchahal		Occurred the burial
Kopob t u lacal	2135	Of all caves
Ti ma to ahac cab e		And this was before the awakening of the world.
Lay uchci		This occurred
Y ocol u tus thanil		By the commandment
Ca yumil		Of our Father
Ti Dˢ.	2140	Who is God.
T u lacal ti minan		Everything that there was not
Tun than ti caan		Was then spoken in heaven,
Ti minan tunich		For there had been no stones
Y etel che c uchi		And trees.

2109. Pun on *akbal* 'night' and *aksah* 'moisten'.
2113. No obvious pun on *kan*.
2117. Pun on *chicchan* 'snake' and *chictahal* 'appearance'.
2121. Play on *cimi* 'death'.
2128. The day 4 Manik has been omitted.
2129. Pun on *lamat* '(?)' and *lam* 'flood'.
2133. Pun on *muluc* '?rain' and *muc* 'burial'.

Ca tun bin ob u tum t u ba ob	2145 And then they went and tested each other,
Ca y alah tun bay la	Then he spoke as follows.
(62) Oxlahun tuc	"Thirteen heaps
Uuc tuc hun*	And seven heaps make one."
Lay y alah ca hok u than	He said for speech to emerge,
Ti minan than ti	2150 For they had no speech.
Ca katab u chun	Its origin was requested
T u men yax Ahau kin	By the first lord day,
Ma ix hepahac u nucul than ti ob	For their organs of speech were not yet opened
Uchebal u thanic u ba ob e	So that they could speak to each other.
Ca bin ob t an y ol caan	2155 They went there to the heart of the sky
Ca u machaah u kab t u ba tan ba ob e	And took each other by the hand.
Ca tun ualah	And then they stood there
Tan chumuc peten	In the middle of the country
Heklay ob lae	And divided it up,
Hekla ob i	2160 And they divided
Ah Toocob*	The Burners,
Can tul ob lae	The four of them.
Can Chicchan Ah Toc	4 Chicchan the Burner,
Canil Oc Ah Toc	4 Oc the Burner,
Ca Men Ah Toc	2165 4 Men the Burner,
Can Ahau Ah Toc	And 4 Ahau the Burner.
Lay Ahauob	These are the lords:
Can tul ob lae	The four of them.

Uaxac Muluc*	8 Muluc
Bolon Oc	2170 9 Oc
Lahun Chuen	10 Chuen
Buluc Eb	11 Eb
Lahca Men	12 Ben
Oxlahun Yx	13 Ix
Hun Men	2175 1 Men
Ca Cib	2 Cib
Ox Caban	3 Caban
Can Etz'nab	4 Etz'nab

2148. This mystical statement justifies the unity of the *uinal* by adding 13 and 7 to produce 20 (*uinic*). This also produces man (*uinic*) and the cycle itself (*uinal*).

2161. The Burners (Ah Toc) were the focus of the fire cult, which divided the *tzol kin* into sixty-five-day quarters, each governed by a Burner. Each cycle was initiated on a day 3, and special ceremonies were held on the following occurrence of the same day with the coefficients 10, 4, and 11, for a total of sixty days. Then there was a five-day break and a new Burner cycle began.

2169. Roys 1967: 118, note 5 observes that this could be the first *uinal* in a year 8 Muluc. I believe he's right and that this dates the text to 1562.

Hoil Cauac	5 Cauac
Uac Ahau	2180 6 Ahau
Uay Imix	7 Imix
Uaxacil Yk	8 Ik
Bolon Akabal	9 Akbal
Lahun Kan	10 Kan
Buluc Chicchan	2185 11 Chicchan
Lahca Cimiy	12 Cimi
Oxlahun Manik	13 Manik
Hun Lamat	1 Lamat

Lay çihci uinal — This was the birth of the *uinal*
  Y etel uchci y ahal cab — 2190 And the occurrence of the
    awakening of the world.

Tzolci caan — There was finished heaven
  Y etel luum — And earth
Y etel cheob — And trees
  Y etel tunich — And stones.
Çihci t u lacal — 2195 Everything was born
  T u men ca yumil — Through our Father
Ti *Dˢ*. lae — Who is God, then;
  Lay citbil — Who is holy.
(63) Ti minaan caan — For there was no heaven
  Y etel luum — 2200 Or earth,
Ti bay y anil t u *Diosil* — So there he was in his divinity,
  T u muyalil — In his nebulousness,
T u ba — By himself,
  T u hunal — Alone.
Ca u çihcah — 2205 And he caused to be born
  Bal cah tuçinil — Everything that was invented.
Ca pecnahi t u caanil — And he moved to heaven
  T u kuil — In his divinity,
Ti bay noh uchucil — Which was thus a great event,
  Y anil ah tepal e — 2210 And he was the ruler.
U tzolan kin çançamal — The account of all the days
  Licil u xocol u chun — Through which the beginning is
    counted

Ti likin e — Was in the east,
  He bix tzolanil e. — As has been told.

21. The Sermon of Kauil Ch'el

(104) U *profeciado*
    Ah Kuil Chel *sacerdote*
(*i*) C u hitz'ibte katun e*
    Yum e
Mex ca *anate**
    Ualac (*ii*) u talel
Mac bin ca tz'ab*
    T u cotz' pop katun e*
Yum e (*iii*)
    Bin uluc
Holom uil
    T u cal ya
Tali ti xaman (*iv*)
    Tali ti chikin e
T u kin ob
    Uil y an e yum e*
Mac (*v*) to ah kin
    Mac to ah bouat
Bin toh alic u than (*vi*) uooh e yum e

11.18.0.0.0   Ychil Balam ahau
Mex ca a(*vii*)naate
    Hunac tzuc ti cab
Hun tz'al pixan
    (T u me)(*viii*)nel tzutzuc chac

Be ci oltzil i
    Uil tan tun (105)(*ix*) tepal c
    uchi e
Cij uil y okol y ahaulil cabob e (*x*)
    Kahcun a u ol ah ytza e.

2215 The prophecy
    Of Kauil Ch'el the priest:
The *katun* may be ended,
    O father.
Poor are our books
2220   To make it come back.
To whom will it be given
    To roll the mat of the *katun*,
O father?
    It will return
2225 Spreading want
    And the suffering of pain,
Coming to the north,
    Coming to the west.
In their sun
2230   Will be the moon, father.
Who will be the sun priest:
    Who will be the prophet
Who will correctly speak the word of
the glyph, father,
    In 9 Ahau?
2235 Poor are our books
    To unite the parts in the land.
There is much groaning of the soul
    Because of the factionalism of the
    rain priests.
Thus delighted
2240   May be the ruling capital,
Really perhaps over the lordship of the
lands:
    Remind your hearts, O Itza.

2217. The lines are numbered in the MS as indicated by italicized roman numerals in the text.

2219. Bricker reads this as *me(hen e)x ca a nate* 'you sons, you might know', which is possible in context.

2221. Roys 1967: 165 gets 'believe' out of this line. I don't know whence.

2222. To roll the mat of the *katun* is to end it.

2230. The implication is that when 9 Ahau has moved to the north and to the west the *katun* system will come to an end, i.e., in 5 Ahau. Being a Xiu, Kauil Ch'el blames this impending catastrophe on Itza factionalism. The Xiu seating of the *katun* did end one *katun* later than that according to the Chumayel, two *katuns* later according to the Tizimin. The moon is a metaphor for 'end'.

22. The Cathedral of Merida

Top: *Ul Uac, lord of Merida (1559–1579)*. Bottom: *The heavenly bodies (1559)*. From the Garrett Collection of Manuscripts in Middle American Languages, The Princeton University Library, The gift of Robert Garrett.

(89) *Segundo*

11.18.0.0.0 Bolon ahau katun*
    U ca tz'it katun c u xocol

    Ych caan çi hoo
      U hetz' katun
    Ti jx t u kamah u patan ob i
      U tz'ullilob cab i
    Ti jx uli ob u yumil ca pixann i
      Ti jx hun molhi cah i
    Ti tzucen tzucil
      T u hol u poopob i
    Ti yx ti hop'i u canal *santo* ok olal i

    Ti x hop'i y ocol haa tac polob

    Ti jx etz'lahi
      U chun

(89) *Segundo*

Katun 9 Ahau
    Was the second part of the *katun* to
    be counted.
2245 Heaven Born Merida
    Was the seat of the *katun.*
And it received their tribute
    For the foreigners to the land.
And the fathers of our souls came,
2250   And brought together the towns,
Which were divided into factions
    Over the headship of the mats.
And it was it that began the elevation
of the holy faith.
    And it began to bring water to their
    heads.
2255 And it established
    The foundations

2243. The word *segundo* at the head of this text is a late interpolation.

Santa yglesia mayor i		Of the holy primate church,
U kakal na *Dios* i		The fiery house of God,
U xiuil		Erecting
Xitel na *Dios* citbil	2260	And decorating the house of God the remote.
Ti x etz'lahi		And it established
U chun		The foundations
Uuc p'el *sacramento*		Of the seven sacraments
Y çatebal kebanoob		And the forgiveness (of sins?).
Ti x hop'i ban meyah chumuc cah	2265	And it began piles of work in the middle of town,
U (. . . . .) num ya bal cah i		The . . . of the suffering world.
Ti x u uatal ca ui (. . . . .)		And it erected our . . .
Lic u than ku i		According to the Word of God,
Xanomistali		Which has sent for them to come
T u chi *Dios* citbil	2270	Before the face of God the remote.
Ti y ulel çac tunlah pal		That will be the arrival of the white stone child
Tal ti caan		Come from heaven
Çuhuy ch'uplal u kaba		To the Virgin Lady, as she is called,
U na uuc p'el chachac ek*		The mother of the seven great stars.
Uchucma t u bolon pis y abil	2275	This came about on the ninth measure of the years
Ah bolon ahau		In 9 Ahau,
T u taninah		The confrontation
Christianoil		Of Christianity.
Bay tz'ibanil		Thus it has been written
T u men *propheta* Chilam Balam	2280	By the prophet and Spokesman of the Jaguar
T u bolon tz'al ab tun		On the ninth giving of the date stone
Te caanal e		There in heaven.
Oxlahun etz'nab u ki*		13 Etz'nab was the day,
Kinil te ti caan e		The time there in heaven.
Bay x uay	2285	And as it is here
Ti luum e		On earth,
Ti caanil xol		In heaven there is grain;
Ti caanil u al*		In heaven there is water.
Emtab u than *Dios**		The Word of God is brought down,
Tal ti canal*	2290	Coming from heaven.

2274. This line is followed in the MS by seven eight-pointed stars.

2283. July 11, 1568.

2288. Roys 1967: 150 has 'the heavenly staff, the heavenly fan', which is also possible.

2289. Roys 1967: 150 reads *em tab* as 'the cord descended'.

2290. A couplet of the text has been inadvertently omitted:

Hun y uk	A drink
Ti bal cah tuxinil	For the lying world.

Bolon pis u lac | The ninth measure is his bowl;
Bolon pis u luch | The ninth measure is his gourd.
Bee ch'aaba ah ytza e | Thus were the Itza seized:
Ma tub a tz'aic a u ula ex | Nowhere did you surrender and accept it.

Bi a hant ex ob | 2295 You will feed them,
Bin ix u hant ex ob xan* | And they will feed you too,
Ti tali | When they come
Lae. | Here.

2296. The order of the pronouns appears to be confused here. I read it as *u hant ob ex*, as Roys 1967: 151 does.

---

23. The Shield of Yucatan

Coat of arms of Yucatan (1559). From the Garrett Collection of Manuscripts in Middle American Languages, The Princeton University Library, The gift of Robert Garrett.

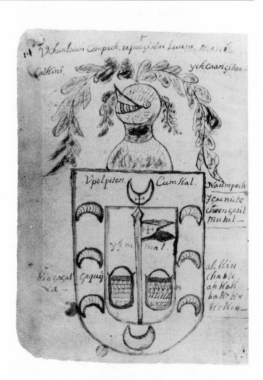

(25) U chun luum Campech* | The base of the land is Campeche;
U pucçikal luum Mani | 2300 The heart of the land is at Mani,
Calkini | Calkini,
Ych can çi hoo | And Heaven Born Merida.

2299. It is of interest that thirteen towns are named.

U pol peten Cumkal	The head of the land is Cum Kal;
Ytzmmal	Izamal,
Kin çaçal Xa*	2305 Kin Zazal Xa,
Çaquij	Valladolid,
Naum pech y etel cac nicte ch'een*	Um Pech at Zac Nicte Ch'een,
Çotz'il	Zotz'il,
Mutul	Motul,
Ah kin Chable	2310 The sun priest of Chable,
Ah Kok bak	Cooker of the meat
T ix kokob.	At Tixkokob.

2305. I am unable to locate Kin Zazal Xa.

2307. Roys 1967: 86, note 2 identifies Um Pech as governor of Motul. Zac Nicte Ch'een is five or ten miles from Motul (see line 990).

24. The Inquisition in the East

The thirteen katuns (1579). From the Garrett Collection of Manuscripts in Middle American Languages, The Princeton University Library, The gift of Robert Garrett.

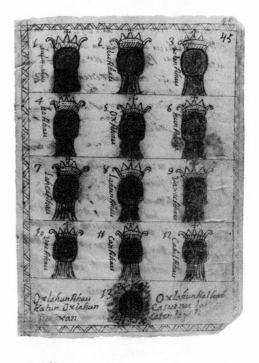

(85) Oxlahun ahau	13 Ahau
Katun	Was the *katun*
Yax hok i	2315 There first appeared
U cheem tz'ullob Campech	The ships of the foreigners at Campeche.

Mil i quinientos y quarenta y uno | A.D. 1541
U kaba hab c uch i | Was the name of the year it happened

Ca y ulçah ob | That they brought it—
U kin y ocol ob   2320 | The time of entering
Ti *christianoil* | Into Christianity
Maya uinicob | Of the Mayan people.
Hetz'ci cab | Seated was the land
Tan tun cuçamil | At the capital of Cozumel.
Tan coch hab y an ob i   2325 | Halfway through the year they were there

Ca bini ob | When they came
T u hol haa | To the port
Ti chikin e | To the west.
Ti yx oc u patan | And that was the coming of tribute
Ah chikin cheellob i*   2330 | Of the western Cheel.
Lay hab y an c uch i | This was the year it was:
D°. 1542 | A.D. 1542.
Hetz'ci u petenil ti hoo | Seated was the country at Merida,
Ych can çi ho | Heaven Born Merida.
Buluc ahau   2335 | 11 Ahau
Katun lae | Was the *katun* then,
He ix yax hal ach uinic e | And this was the first governor:
*Dn. Fran*co*. Montojo, Adelantado* | Don Francisco de Montejo, *adelantado.*

Lay tz'a e | He it was who gave
U *chinam*   2340 | Their town
Tz'ulob | To the foreigners,
Kul uinicob | The people of God.
Ychil y abil | In the year
D°. 1542 | A.D. 1542
Oc i   2345 | Was the coming
Patan | Of tribute.
D°. 1549 | A.D. 1549
Hab | Was the year
Y an c uchi | Of the settlement
Ca hul i   2350 | And arrival
Padreob | Of the fathers.
Can p'el hab huluc tz'ulob c uch i | Four years after the arrival of the foreigners,

Ti jx hop'i | Then they sailed
Y ocol haa | Over the water
T u pol uinicob i   2355 | To the P'ool people.
Ti cahal cah t u men *padreob* | That was the settlement of the city by the fathers.

2330. The "port" may have been Emal, capital of the province of Chikin Chel.

Yax ul ob e First they arrived there,
  Thoxci cah ti ob   And then the city was sprinkled by
    them.

Mil i quinientos quarenta y quatro a⁵. A.D. 1544
  Haab e 2360   Was the year,
Lahu ca bak haab 410 years
  Ca tac holhu can kal haab   And then 75 years (after)
Paxci cah They destroyed the town
  T u chi ch'een ytza*   At Chichen Itza.
Paxci 2365 They destroyed it
  U cahal ob lae   And its inhabitants;
Ca bak haab And it was 800 years
  Ca tac lahu can kal haab   And 70 years (after)
Paxci They destroyed
  Cah uxmal lae 2370   The town of Uxmal,
Paxci And destroyed
  U cab ob lae   Their lands.
Mil i quinientos y treinta y siete a⁵. In 1537
  Ti bolon cauac*   On 9 Cauac,
U kaba kin 2375 The name of the day then,
  Uchci u mol tan ba ob   They assembled together
Al The born
  Mehenob   And engendered
Ti canancil ob Who were the responsible authorities
  Ti cah mani 2380   In the town of Mani.
Uchebal u binel ob And when they had gone,
  Ti ch'a tz'ul t u cahal   They seized the foreigners in the
    town

Y oklal cimçabci hal ach uinic e Because of the governor's being killed.
  Lay u kaba ob lae   These are their names as follows:
Ah moo 2385 Ah Mo,
  Chan xiu   Chan Xiu,
Na hau es Ahau Ez
  Ah tz'un   Ah Tz'un
Chi nab Of Chi Nab,
  Na poot cupul 2390   Poot Cupul,
Na pot che Pot Che,
  Na batun ytza   Batun Itza,
Ah kin euan The sun priest E Uan
  Tal cocel   From Cocel,
Na chan uc 2395 Chan Uc
  Tal ti tz'ibil kak   Coming from Tz'ibil Kak,
Ah kin ucan The sun priest U Can
  Tal ti ekob   Coming from Ekob,

2364. This would date the destruction of Chichen Itza to 1059 and that of
Uxmal to 674.

2374. August 27, 1537: eight months after the murder of Pot Xiu, governor of
Mani, at Otzmal.

Na chi uc
   Ah kul koh
Na chan motul
   Na hau coyi
La ob i
   U nucil uincob ti thani ob
Ca bin ch'abil tz'ul
   T u cahal lae
Y oklal u cimçabci
   U hal ach uinicil cah
Ah (tz) xiu*
   (86) Otzolmal
Lahun Kan
   Ah cuch haab ca man i
Ah caxan cah
   Heklay *montejo* u kaba

Ah tz'ib cah
   Lay ix hab y an ca man i

Ah luum tz'ul
   Ah mak op tz'ul
He lay yax thox cah

   He x ca ul i
Tz'ul t u ch'a ob e
   Y ah ch'a ul e
Ti ban ob campech e
   Ti hoki u chem ob i
Ca ix bini ob al
   Mehenob u tz'aab u cijl ob i

Oxlahun tul y ah ch'a ul tz'ulob lae
   Ca ix tal ob ych caan çi hoo
Bolon ahau
   U katunil c uchi lae
U kaylay u tzolan
   U miatzil u y *anahteil*
U tzolan u ximbal katun

   Uay c u hokçabal t u lumil

Ni tun tz'ala
   Chactemal
Tah
   Uaymil

Chi Uc,
2400   Kul Koh,
Chan Motul,
   Ahau Coy.
And these
   Were the important people who said
2405 They were going to seize the foreigners
   In that town
Because of the killing
   Of the governor of the town
And the head of the Xiu
2410 At Otzmal.
10 Kan
   Was the yearbearer that passed,
And the seer of the town
   Related it to Montejo, as he was called,
2415 And the town scribe.
   And that was the year that there passed
The foreigners to the land,
   The foreign slurpers of annona.
And that was the first division of the town.
2420   And that was the arrival
Of the foreigners to seize them.
   And the seizers arrived
And grabbed Campeche.
   Thus their ships appeared,
2425 And then came the born
   And engendered to surrender their birth.
Thirteen of the foreign seizers arrived
   And came to Heaven Born Merida.
9 Ahau
2430 Was the *katun*.
This is the relation of the count,
   Of the wisdom of the books,
The count of the progression of the *katuns*.
   This was their appearance in the lands
2435 Of Ni Tun Tz'ala,
   Chetumal,
Division of
   Uaymil,

2409. I read Ah Pot Xiu.

Hol tun ytza
   Chichinila*

Ca utzac y oheltabal
   U cuch

U ximbal katun
   Hun hun tz'it katun e

Ua utz
   Ua lob y an i

Bay tz'ibanil
   T u men ah kulen tz'ib

Euangelista
   U than u yumil

Caan
   Y etel luum

(. . . .)op ich kin
   Tal canal

Lay tz'abi ti ob
   (. . . .)n ob

T u chun luum
   T u chun ca uinicil e

(. . . .)h tohil than
   T u kulem tz'ibil

T u y unil
   Repuldoryo

Minan çipan i
   Ti cici ylabil

T u tz'alal ti y unil*
   Heklay t u menel ob

Can tul ch'ibalob
   Tal ob ti caan

Ah kab caan
   Ytz caanob

U hal ach uinicob
   Y ahaulilob cab

Çacaal puc
   Hool tun balam

Hoch' tun poot
   Ah mex cuc chan

Che ychil
   He ychil

The gateway of the Itza,
2440   And Chi Chimila.
Then one will be able to understand
   The burden
Of the progression of the *katuns*,
   Each and every part of the *katun*
   period,
2445 Whether it is good
   Or bad.
Thus it is being written
   By the sacred scribe,
By the Evangelist
2450   Of the word of the Father
Of heaven
   And earth.
. . . the face of the sun
   Come from on high
2455 This was given to them
   (?) to them
At the founding of the land,
   At the founding of our people.
(This is the) right word
2460   In holy writ
In the books
   Of the *reportorio*.
There are no errors.
   It can be clearly seen
2465 In what is being given in the books,
   The account
By the four ancestors
   Come from heaven,
The juice of heaven,
2470   Dew of heaven,
The governors
   And lords of the land:
Zacaal Puc,
   Hool Tun Balam,
2475 Hoch' Tun Poot
   And Mex Cuc the Younger.
The tree is in it:
   That is in it:

2440. Roys 1967: 146, note 8 locates Chi Chimila a few miles south of Valladolid. The other places named are near Chetumal, which was, as Roys notes, a major trade gateway to Honduras.

2465. Roys 1967: 147 has 'the seal on the book' from *tz'al* 'press'. I think my translation fits the context better even though the inflection of *tz'a* 'give' seems odd.

	Uuc kal hab	The 140 years
	Ococ *christianoil* e	2480 Of the coming of Christianity
	Ti u hu mul hun ahauob i	To the 21 lords
	U chuclum tz'itz' katun i*	In the Chuclum Tz'iitz' *katun*.
	Ti jx u chacanpahal ah miatz i	And the sages will be summoned
	Ti yx u kat naat katun i	Along with those who wish to take the *katun* examination.
	Otzilhom u u ich chac	2485 Humbled will be the face of the rain priest
	Chuen coy i	Chuen Coy.
	Ca bin uluc u yumil kul na	There will arrive the fathers of the god house
	Y an chumuc cah ti hoo e	That is in the center of the town of Merida,
	Ulom tal ti lakin	Arriving coming from the east,
	Tal ti xaman	2490 Coming from the north,
	Tal ti chikin	Coming from the west,
	Tal ti nohol	Coming from the south;
	U y ub u thanil	(And bringing) the words
	U *christianoil*	Of Christianity
11.17.0.0.0	T u uuc lahun	2495 In the seventeenth
	Katun e*	*Katun,*
	Uchebal u naat	Bringing about the knowledge
	Christianoil	Of Christianity.
	(87) Ulom u *padreil*	Coming are the fatherhoods;
	Ulom u *obispoil*	2500 Coming are the bishoprics
	Sancto ynquiçicion	And the Holy Inquisition.
	U than *Dios* bin beltabac i	The Word of God will be established,
	Ma mac bin hauçic lae*	And no one will be sacrificed.
	Amen.	Amen.

2482. Chuclum Tz'itz' is the fifth of the 13 Gods (Tizimin, line 585), perhaps lending his name to the *katun* in honor of Merida's seating it (Ti Ho 'at five'). Roys 1967: 147 construes this whole passage quite differently. Beginning with line 2477, he omits *che ychil*, apparently considering it a copyist's error, then reads: 'Behold, within seven score years Christianity will be introduced amid the clamor of the rulers, those who violently seize land (during) the katun. Then suddenly appears the wise man; then there is the examination of the katun'. The passage is a difficult one, but Roys and I agree that what is involved is the confrontation of the Mayan test of orthodoxy—the examination system—and the Holy Inquisition. Chuen Coy apparently flunked the Mayan exam. I have no idea who the 21 lords were, but I don't think Roys is justified in converting them into a verb.

2496. I believe this to be a direct reference to the Long Count date 11.17.0.0.0   11 Ahau. It is of substantial interest because it indicates that Long Count dates were still being counted terminally even though *katuns* were being counted initially.

2503. I read *hau* as 'slice'; Roys 1967: 147 reads it as 'end'. Either is possible.

7 Ahau

25. The Civil War

Yax Chac, lord of Merida
(1579–1599). From the Garrett Col-
lection of Manuscripts in Middle
American Languages, The Princeton
University Library, The gift of
Robert Garrett.

(90) *Tercero*

11.19.0.0.0 Uuc ahau katun*
    Y ox tz'it katun
Yaxal chac ych caan çi hoo
    U hetz' katun
Yaxal chac u u ich ti y ahaulil

    Ti y ah miatzil
U tan pax cabal
    U tan xot cabal
Nicte uah
    Nicte haa y aal

(90) *Tercero*

2505 *Katun* 7 Ahau
    Was the third part of the *katun*.
Yaxal Chac of Heaven Born Merida
    Seated the *katun*.
Yaxal Chac was the face in the
lordship
2510   In the position of the sage.
Half destroyed was the earth;
    Half cut up was the earth.
Flower food
    And flower water was the juice of
the *katun*.

2505. The notation *tercero* 'third' is a late addition to the MS at the head of
this text.

Ti u hop'ol u tzuc a chil	2515 It was the beginning of the division
Ah miatzob i	Of the sages,
U be bech kab nicte i	The road of the Bech' Kab flower,
U be bech kab katun i*	The road of the Bech' Kab war.
Ti u hop'ol	It was the beginning
U tzintzin loc katun	2520 Of the asshole boils war
Lay bin hun yuk	That is going to spread
Katic bal cah	All over the world.
(. . . .) nicte u buc	. . . flowers are its clothes,
Nicte u u ich	Flowers its face,
Nicte u (. . . . .)*	2525 Flowers its (hat),
Nicte u xanab	Flowers its sandals,
Nicte u pol	Flowers its head,
Nicte u ximbal	Flowers its gait.
Kuy c u cal	Bent is its neck,
Kuy c u chi	2530 Bent is its mouth.
Mutz' c u u ich	Wrinkled is its face,
Putz' c u tub	Dribbling is its spittle:
T u xiblalil	For the men,
T u ch'uplalil	For the women,
T u ba tabil	2535 For the chiefs,
T u justiçiail	For the justices,
T u chun thanil	For the law givers,
T u scriuanoil	For the scribes,
T u h camçahil	For the teachers,
(. . . .)*	2540 (. . . . .)
T u nohochil	For the great,
T u chanchanil	For the very small.
Minan to nohoch can	There may be no great teacher
Ti u hach çatal	Who can really forgive
Caan	2545 Heaven
Y etel luum ti ob i	And earth for them,
Ti u hach satal subtall i	Who can really forgive their shame.
Ti u hich'il u cal	That is the knotting of the necks
U hal ach uinicil cah i	Of the governors of the towns,
Y ahaulil cab i	2550 The lords of the land,
U bouatil cahh i	The prophets of the towns,
Y ah kin maya uinicob i	The sun priests of the Mayan people,
Satal tun naat	Destroying knowledge then,
Satal tun miatz	Destroying understanding then.

2518. The name Bech Kab is associated with Coba. I assume there was a rather bloody rebellion in the east at this time. It was apparently a pain in the neck from the standpoint of the author. As often elsewhere, flowers symbolize war.

2525. Word missing from MS; supplied from the Tizimin.

2540. Line missing.

Ch'aaba | 2555 Accept it,
Ah ytza e | O Itza.
A mehen ex ob | It will be your sons
To bin ylic | Who will see
U hitz'ibte katun | The termination of the *katun*,
U baxal katun* | 2560 The smashing of the *katun*.
Coo u than | Crazy is the word;
Coo u u ich | Crazy is the face
Ti y ahaulil | In the lordship,
T u hal ach uinicil | In the governorship
Chac uen co . . . | 2565 Of the great nightmare . . .
(. . . . .)* | (. . . . .)
Uuc p'el u lac | Sevenfold is the plate;
Uuc p'el u luch u than *Dios** | Sevenfold is the gourd of the Word of God.
Ban ban hich' cal | Many many hangings
U cuch katun lae. | 2570 Is the burden of this *katun*.

2560. This repeats the prophecy of the ending of the *katun* system in 5 Ahau or a little later. See note 2230. Roys 1967: 151 translates as 'your sons will see the mirth of the katun, the jesting of the katun'.

2566. Line missing.

2568. That is, the passing of the plate and gourd, ending the *katun*, is on 7 Ahau.

5 Ahau

26. The Military Orders

Amayte Kauil, lord of Merida (1599–1618). From the Garrett Collection of Manuscripts in Middle American Languages, The Princeton University Library, The gift of Robert Garrett.

(91) *Quarto*

12.0.0.0.0 Ho ahau katun*
    U can tz'it katun
Ych caan çi hoo
    U hetz' katun
Chich u u ich
    Chich u mut ti y ahaulil
Chibil al
    Chibil mehen ti talij

(91) *Quarto*

Katun 5 Ahau
    Was the fourth part of the *katun.*
Heaven Born Merida
    Was the seat of the *katun.*
2575 Strong was the face,
    Strong was the news in the lordship.
It was the lineage born
    And lineage engendered who came.

2571. The word *quarto* at the head of this text is a late addition to the MS.

Ti u hop'ol	It was the beginning
U tza ciçin ti bal cah i	2580 Of the removal of the devil from the world.
Ti jx u binel	And it was the coming
U u ich kauil	Of the face of the deity
Can chebil caan	In the four changes of heaven,
T u can hebil hele be	In the four changes of the road.
Tij u y uchul chuy	2585 That was the occurring of hanging
Tab ti bal cah i	And the rope in the world.
Ti ix u likil u cal	And that was the raising of the neck
Cha (. . . . . .)an ti chibal i	Of the (East priest Ahau Can) by descent;
Ti jx u likil u cal	And it was the raising of the neck
Holil (. . . .) ti chibal i*	2590 Of Holil (Och) by descent.
Con con mehen	It was very few engendered sons,
Con con aal	Very few born children
Ti talij	Who came
Ti jx (. . . . .) u hool chamal*	And who (avoided) the tip of the cigar
Ch'abci u yum bal cah	2595 Created by the father of the world.
T u ta (. . . .)	He has (approached then)
Y an bin y ubah	And will have heard
Okot bot bat	The dance of payment of death:
Ox chac	The three rain priests,
Ni cen	2600 Ni Cen,
Chac	The rain priest
Xul ab	Xul Ab,
Chac	And the rain priest
Uayah cab	Uayah Cab,
U bal	2605 Twisting
U çoot	And shaking
Y ah tz'a	As givers
Ul	And receivers
Ca pucçikal	Of our hearts
Ychil patan	2610 In tribute.
T u cal ya	One suffered the pain;
T u cal tza	One suffered the removal
Ba tab och*	Of Chief Possum,
Ba tab ch'amac	Chief Fox,

2590. Ahau Can (line 2588) could be either a personal name or the title of the Jaguar priest of the *katun*. The identification of him as east priest confirms the latter interpretation. Holil Och was presumably his Spokesman, and they were both seemingly hanged for idolatry. Both names are garbled or missing in the Chumayel text and are supplied from the Tizimin.

2594. Word missing, and 'avoided' is just a guess, as is 'approached then' in line 2596.

2613. Here again are the military companies of the countryside harassing the towns.

Ba tab ah pic
    Ah tz'uutz'
U tz'utanil
    Cahob
Cum u tal
    Xin
Ca yn lahab
    X a pax
C ech u itz'in
    Çucun
Ah xac lam pat
    T ech
U u ichil e
    Ex
Tolil och
    U katunil
Nicte u kan che
    Culic t u tz'am
Ti chaan tan kiuic
    Tan pop
Ah ca kin tz'am
    Ah ca kin pop
T u tab cah
    Cahaan uchi
U balamil cab
    T u ca tulil
Ba tab och
    Y etel ah xac lam pat
Ma ya cimlal
    Bin tz'aic ob
U chun (. .)x ob e*
    Tz'etz'ecil c uchi e
T a kabatah tun hele lae
    Ah ytza
T u chicchic çoot katun
    T u keban than katun
Tan cah maya *patan*
    Chac *Xuyua patan*
T u lachlam pach balam
    Ah cab cob
T u chibal katun
    T u chibal haab
Çitz'ob
    Ti y ahaulil
Ban ban hich' cal
    U cuch katun

2615 Chief of the Bedbugs,
    Chief of the Suckers,
The hagglers
    Of the towns.
Darkness comes
2620   And goes,
And then it is finished,
    And you are beaten,
O younger
    And older brothers.
2625 Xaclam Pat
    Art thou
In thy person,
    And thine
Is the end of the count
2630   Of the *katun* period.
Flower is his bench
    Seated on his throne,
Which is seen before the Plaza,
    Before the mat
2635 Of the two-day throne people,
    The two-day mat people.
He tied the town
    And settled
The Jaguars of the land
2640   By twos:
Chief Possum
    And Xaclam Pat.
Painless death
    Will they give
2645 The beginning of their (beating)
    And they will be crushed.
And you will name them then anew,
    The Itza.
In the full swollen *katun*,
2650   In the sinful words *katun*
Of the primate city of Mayan tribute,
    The East priest of the Zuyua tribute
Outlasted the Jaguar
    And the Earth Lions
2655 To the completion of the *katun*,
    To the completion of the year.
They lusted
    After the lordship.
Many many hangings
2660   Were the burden of the *katun*.

2645. Word missing. My 'beating' is a guess.

Ua c u hich'il u cal u ba tabil cah
te lae
    U xul u num ya maya uinicob

(92) Ti u çebtal u talel ah uaymillob

Ch'aic u toh ti bal cah i.

If they hanged the town chiefs there
then,
    It would end the suffering of the
    Mayan people.
That was the rapid arrival of the
people of Uaymil
    To take the authority in the world.

---

27. The War Indemnity

---

(16) U kahlay katunob
    Y etel haabboob
Yax
    Ch ucci
U petenil
    Yucatan
T u menel tz'ulob
    Sac uinicob
Ychil bin buluc ahau

    Katun uchci*
U chucic ob u hol haa
    Ecab
Ti lakin u talel ob
    Caa ul ob
Op
    Bin u yax kam chitah ob

Lay u chun
    U kabatic ob
Ah mak op tz'ulilob
    Ah tz'uutz' op tz'ul u kaba ob

He ix bin u kaba ah otochnalob

    U chu cah ob i e Ecab e
Nacom
    Balam u kaba
He yx yax chucite
    Ecab e

2665 The count of the *katuns*
    And years
Recently
    Completed
In the country
2670   Of Yucatan
By the aliens,
    The white men.
Within the coming of 11 Ahau V (13
Ahau M)
    Was the *katun* that occurred
2675 Their reaching the port
    Of Ecab.
From the east they came
    When they arrived.
Custard apple
2680   Was to be the first thing they put in
    their mouths.
That was the origin
    Of their name:
Foreign custard apple slurpers,
    Foreign custard apple suckers is
    their name.
2685 That was also the name of the
inhabitants
    Of the little houses of Ecab.
The captain
    Was named Jaguar.
So thus was the first arrival there
2690   At Ecab

2674. See the introduction for a discussion of the aberrant dating in this chapter.

T u men yax *capitan* e	By the first captain,
Dn. Juan	Don Juan
(17) *De Montejo*	De Montejo,
Yax *concixtador*	The first conqueror.
Uay t u petenil	2695 This was in the country
Yucatan lae	Of Yucatan here.
Lay li	It was then
U katunil uchci	The time of the occurrence
U kuchul ych caan si hoo	Of the arrival at Heaven Born Merida
Lae	2700 Here.
T u y aabil	In the year
1513 años	1513 V (1540 M)
Oxlahun ahau	13 Ahau V (11 Ahau M)
Katun	*Katun,*
Uchci u chucic ob Campech	2705 Occurred their reaching Campeche.
Hun tz'it katun y an ob i	They had one *katun* (left).
Ah kin	The sun priest
Camal likul Campech	Cam Al arose in Campeche
Oces tz'ulob uay	And received the aliens here
Ti peten lae	2710 In this country.
Helel	On the other hand
En 20 de agosto	On the 20th of August
Ti y aabil	In the year
De mil quinientos quarenta y uno	1541 V (1564 M),
T in chicbesah	2715 I have made a demonstration
U kaba haabob	Of the names of the years,
Hop'ic	And there began
Christianoil lae	Christianity here,
Mil quinientos dies y nuebe años	In 1519 V (1546 M),
Kuchic uac kal hab	2720 It came to the sixth roll of years
Ca tac	And approached
Buluc pis hab i	The eleven count of years.
Uchci *consierto* y etel tz'ulob	There was an agreement with the aliens.
Bay lic ca botic u liksah katun tz'ulob	This was so as to pay for the waging of the war of the aliens
Y etel u y anal uinicob lae	2725 And for the residence of people
Uay ti cahob	Here in the villages.
Lay u *capitanil* cahob uchi e	Thus the captaincy of the villages occurred then:
Lay tun ca botic hele lae	It was so as to pay this back.
Helel	Again
Tz'ibnah en	2730 As I have written
Ti y aabil	In the year
Mil quinientos quarenta y uno años	1541 V (1513 M)
Yax ulci tz'ulob ti lakin	There first arrived the aliens in the east
Ecab u kaba	At Ecab by name.

T u y abil	2735	In that year
Uchci u kuchul ob		Occurred their arrival
T u hol haa		At the port
Ecab		Of Ecab,
T u cahal Nacom		The town of the captain
Balam	2740	Jaguar.
T u yax chun		At the first beginning
U kinil		Of the time
U habil		Of the years
(18) U katunil		Of the *katun* period
Buluc ahau	2745	Of *katun*
Katun		11 Ahau V (13 Ahau M).
Ca pax ob ah ytzaob		When they destroyed the Itzas,
Hoolhun kal haab		It was three hundred years before
U talel		The coming
Y ulel tz'ulob	2750	And arrival of the aliens.
Ca paxi cah sac lah tun*		Destroyed was the town of the Plaza;
Ca paxi cah kin chil coba*		Destroyed was the town of Kin Chil, Coba;
Ca paxi cah t u chi ch'en ytzam		Destroyed was the town at Chichen Itza;
Ca paxi cah t u xax uxmal		Destroyed was the town at outer Uxmal,
T u nohol cah uxmal*	2755	And to the south the towns of Uxmal:
Cib u kaba y etel Kabah		Cib, as they were called, and Kabah.
Pax cah Seye		Destroyed was the town of Zayi,
Y etel Pakam*		And Pakam,
Y etel hom tun		And Hom Tun,
Ti cah t ix calom kin	2760	Which is a town of Tixcalomkin,
Y etel ake		And Ake
Hol tun ake		And Ake Gate.
Paxi cah emal chac		Destroyed was the town of Emal the Great,
Etzemal		And Izamal,
Ti em i	2765	Where there descended
Y ix mehen		The daughter
Hahal ku i		Of the True God,
U yumil caan		The Father of heaven:
Yx ahau		The Queen,
Yx suhun*	2770	The Virgin,

2751. Roys 1967: 81 suggests *zacal actun* 'white cave/white building'; I think it is *zac lac tun* 'white flat stone' and believe it refers to the Plaza of the cycle seat, in this case probably Mayapan. Elsewhere it is associated with Merida and Valladolid.

2752. Unlike Roys 1967: 81, note 9, I believe Kin Chil 'sun face' is a personal name of a ruler of Coba who was Jaguar in 2 Ahau.

2755. Cib, Kabah, Zayi, and Xcalumkin are all south of Uxmal.

2758. Roys 1967: 82, note 4 identifies this with Tepakam, northwest of Izamal.

2770. The Virgin of Izamal is the patron saint of Yucatan.

Yx mactzil	The Holy Person.
Ca y alah ahau	Then the lord said,
Emom	"Descended
Chim	Is the anger
Kin ich	2775 Of the glorious
Kak mo*	Kak Mo.
Ma paat ti ahaulil uay e	Do not expect the lordship here.
Uay ti pat i	Here you may expect
Yx mactzil	The Holy Person,
Yx tz'a yatzil	2780 The Giver of Love.
Emom sum	Descended is the rope,
Emom tab tal ti caan	Descended is the cord come from heaven,
Emom u than tal ti caan	Descended is the Word come from heaven."
Lay cicuntabi y ahaulil	Thus the lordship was announced
T u men u chucan cah ob	2785 For all of the towns,
Ca y alah ob	Which were told
Ma pat i y ahaulil ob	Not to expect the lordship
Emmal*	Of Emal.
Ca tun bin noh	Then came the great ones,
Ah ytzaob lae	2790 The Itzas here.
Oxlahun bak	5,200
U bakal u piccill ob	Was the number of their thousands,
Ca tac holhun bak	And nearly 6,000
U bakal u ho kallil i*	The number of their hundreds,
U nucteellob heregesob	2795 The great actors and heretics,
Ah ytzaob	The Itzas.
He tun bini y ah tzenulte ob	So thus sickness was to come to their breasts,
Xan numbilob	And likewise suffering came
Bin t u pach ob	To their backs
Tzentic ob lae	2800 And breasts then.
Ox hun p'is bin y iximal u pol	Thirteen measures of corn per head
U cuentail ob	Was their bill,
Ca tac bolon pis almut	And then nine almuds,
Ca tac ox oc y iximal ob	And then three feet of their corn.
Yab ix mehen cahob	2805 Many village girls
Bin uh uay	Became prostitutes

2776. Kak Mo was an 8 Ahau lord associated with Izamal, Uxmal, and Champoton.

2788. The previous passage syncretizes several time periods: a legendary destruction of cities in 4 Ahau, the appearance of the Virgin of Izamal and the teaching of Christianity in 9 Ahau, and the prestige figure of Kak Mo from 8 Ahau, all in order to magnify the opposition to the Itza seating of Emal, which took place in 5 Ahau (1599). The reference to Emal is a further confirmation of the date of composition of this text.

2794. 11,200 Itza is a lot of Itza, but then they constituted the aristocracy of thirteen out of the eighteen Mayan provinces.

Tanill ob
   T u pach ob xan
(19) Ma t y oheltah ob
   U pakt ob tz'ulob
Ma u *cristianoil* ob
   Ma y oltah ob u bot patan

Ah uayom ch'ich'ob
   Ah uayom tunob
Ah uayom sinil tunob
   Ah uayom balamob
Ox uayahob*
   Can bak hab
U xul u cuxtal ob
   Ca tac holhun kal hab
Y an ca tac i*
   Ta xul u cuxtal ob
T u men y ohel ob
   U p'is kinob t u ba ob
Tulis u
   Tulis hab
Tulis kin
   Tulis akab
Tulis yk
   C u ximbal xan
Tulis kik xan
   T u kuchul t u uay ob
T u poop oob
   T u tz'am ob
P'is u caxantic ob y utzil *oraob*

   P'is u caxantic ob y utzil kin

La t u p'is y ilic ob
   Y ocol ob u tzul ekob t u y
   ahaulil
T an u p'ix ychtic ob
   Y ocol ob y ahaulil u tzul ekob

Utz tun t u lacal
   Ca tun u takbes y al ob
T u cux olal ob
   Y an manan tun keban

Before them
   And behind them too.
They did not understand
2810   The expectations of the aliens:
Neither their Christianity,
   Nor did they understand the
   payment of tribute.
The diviners of birds,
   The diviners of stones,
2815 The diviners of flat stones,
   The diviners of jaguars
Are weak spirits.
   Sixteen hundred years
Is the end of their lives,
2820   And three hundred years
Follow.
   And so their lives have ended,
Because they know
   The count of days among them.
2825 Returned is the month;
   Returned is the year;
Returned is the day;
   Returned is the night;
Returned is the wind
2830   And gone again.
Blood is returned also.
   It has arrived and divined
On the mats,
   On the thrones.
2835 They have measured to learn the best
hours;
   They have measured to find the
   best day.
There they have measured to see
   The arrival of the best stars in
   ascendancy.
They have measured to observe
2840   The arrival in ascendancy of the
   best stars,
The best *tun* altogether.
   And so they form their opinions
In the direction of encouragement.
   There is then no sin

2817. I believe the implication is that these are inferior diviners in comparison
with calendrical diviners.

2821. Though this is stated in years, I agree with Roys 1967: 83, note 3 that it
is a Long Count date, 11.15.0.0.0. Compare line 1370, which counts from
8.0.0.0.0, while this text appears to be counting from 7.0.0.0.0 (334).

T u *santo* ok olal ob	2845 In their holy belief.
Y an u cuxtal ob	These are their lives.
Manan tun ch'apahal	There is then no seizure;
Manan tun chibil bac ti ob	There is then no rending of flesh for them.
Manan tun tz'am chacuil ti ob	There is then no groaning fever for them.
Minan tun x pom kakil ti ob	2850 There is then no excess burning for them.
Minan tun elel tzemel ti ob	There is then no burning chest for them.
Minan tun yanakil ti ob	There are then no stomach pains for them.
Minan tun tzentzem cimil ti ob	There is then no fatal chest weakness for them.
Minan tun ch'ibil pol ti ob	There are then no torn heads for them.
Tzolombil tun	2855 In sound health then
U bin u uinicilob	Will people be.
Ma bay tun u mentah tz'ulob	But not so are the actions of the aliens
Ti uli ob lae	Who have come here.
Sabtzolil ta (20) sah ob	They brought shame
Ca tal ob	2860 When they came.
Ca cuxhi y ol nicte	For spoiled is the heart of the flower;
Cuxhi tun y ol t u nicteob	Spoiled then is the heart in the flowers:
Nacxit	Four Leg Nacxit,
Xuchit	Flower Xuchit,
T u nicte	2865 In the flowers,
U lak ob	All of them.
Minan tun y utz kinn ob	There are then no good days
Y et sah ob t oon	That they have showed us.
Lay u chun ca kin xec	This is the beginning of two-day seats,
Ca kin ahaulil	2870 Two-day lordships.
Lay ix u chun cimil	And this was the beginning of death
T oon xan	For us too.
Manan y utz kin t on xan	There are no good days for us either:
Minan cux olal t oon	There is no life for our spirits.
T u xul ca satmail ylil	2875 The forgiveness of evil is over,
Y etel subtalil etlahom t u lacal	And shame will flatten us all.
Minan nohoch can	There is no great teacher;
Minan y ahau than	There is no lord speaker;
Minan ahau can	There is no learned lord
Ti lay	2880 To be the one who
U hel ahauuoob	Changes the lords
Ti uli ob lae	Who have arrived here.
Tzuc	Lust
Cep	And Sex

Ah kinil	2885	Are the sun priests
C u talel		That are coming
U mentabal ti te lae		To administer things here
T u men tz'ulob		Because of the aliens.
Ca tun		Two years
T u p'atah ob	2890	They have abandoned
Y al		The born children
U mehenob		And engendered children
Uay		Here
Tan cah lae		At the capital.
Lay tun kamic ob	2895	This year they have caught
U num yail ob		The plague.
Uchci u chibil		Its bite has come here
Lay tz'ulob lae		From these aliens.
He bin ah ytzaob e		Indeed the Itzas could come here
Ox ten hij bin uchic ob	2900	Three times over for one occurrence
tz'ulob		of aliens.
Lay tun		This year,
T u men ox kal haab*		Because it is the sixtieth,
Y an t oon		We must
T u luksic ob ca patan*		Have them remove our tribute
T u men uchci u chibil ob t u men	2905	Because of the occurrence of the
lay uincob		assault of these men,
(21) Ah ytzaob lae		These Itza.
Ma t oon t mente i		It wasn't we who did it,
T oon botic hele lae		But we are paying for it.
He uac *consierto* y anil		Whenever an agreement exists,
Y an u xul	2910	It has an end:
Ca y anac hun oolal t on		Then there would be accord between us
Y etel tz'ulob		And the aliens,
Ua ma e		But if that is not so
Bi y anac t oon noh katun.		There will be for us a great war.

2902. That is, 1603, sixty years after the *concierto* of 1543. Roys 1967: 84 has 'we were relieved from paying tribute at the age of sixty'.

2904. That is, it was the Itza who made war but it's the Xiu who are paying the tribute. There was probably some truth to this, at least in 5 Ahau.

3 Ahau

28. Caesar Augustus

*Coc Ay, lord of Merida (1618–1638).
From the Garrett Collection of
Manuscripts in Middle American
Languages, The Princeton University
Library, The gift of Robert Garrett.*

(92) *Quinto 1620*

Ox ahau katun*
  U ho tz'it katun
Ych can çi hoo
  U hetz' katun
Ek coc oh mut*
  U u ich ti y ahaulil
Ti y ah miatzil *Antachristo**
  U u ich ti y ahaulil

Fifth: 1620

2915 *Katun* 3 Ahau
    Was the fifth part of the *katun.*
  Heaven Born Merida
    Was the seat of the *katun.*
  The West priest Coc Oh the Crier
2920   Was the face in the lordship.
  In the office of sage, Antichrist
    Was the face in the lordship.

2915. The notation *quinto 1620* at the head of this text is a late addition to the MS.

2919. Elsewhere Coc Ay (line 1769). Roys 1967: 153, note 5 reads Coc Ah and relates it to an idol at Tayasal.

2921. The implication is that either Coc Ay or his Spokesman was pagan. Probably they both were.

Hopom   There will be ignited
   Kak   A fire
T u xulub yuc*   2925   At the goat horns
   Ych caan çi hoo   In Heaven Born Merida.
Haulahom u keulel   Sliced up was the robe
   Chac bol ay   Of the East priest Bol Ay
Tan kiuic   Before the Plaza.
   Pek u mut   2930   Dog was its news.
Çac pat ay chacil   The North priest Pat Ay was a rain
                                 priest;

   Thul Caan chacil   Thul Caan was a rain priest;
Bohol Caan chacil   Bohol Caan was a rain priest;
   Ch'uhum caan chacil   Ch'uhum Caan was a rain priest;
Caan il chacil   2935   Caan Il was a rain priest;
   Kuch caan chacil   Kuch Caan was a rain priest;
Thel en chacil   Thel En was a rain priest;
   Ceh il chacil   Ceh Il was a rain priest;
Ti jx y emel ox ualah   And they brought down three figures
   U leçil il   2940   Who were condemned.
Çinic balamil   Ants and Jaguars
   Çakil habil   And Locust years.
Ox ch'uytah u xuthen   Three were sentenced to hang;
   Ox cuchlahom y al max   Three bore the burden of the
                                   monkey children.

Okom bul cum   2945   Lamented is the bean bowl
   T u can xay be o   At the four divisions of the road.
La u tah hob katun   These are the sections of the *katun*.
   Auatnom u pixan   Mourning their spirits
T u holobal cah   At the gates of the city,
   Numal ytza et(. . .)talij   2950   The base of the Itza who
                                   accompanied them.

He t en   Here I am,
   C en ox ahau katun e   I, *katun* 3 Ahau,
Cumtal yn cah   Who have seated my city,
   Ych can çi hoo   Heaven Born Merida!
He t en   2955   Here I am,
   C en   I,
Ceçar Agusto e*   Caesar Augustus,
   Cah yn kam yn matan   To begin to collect my request
Tan y ol che   Among the trees—
   Tan (y ol haa) . . .*   2960   Among (the wells) . . .

2925. I persist in thinking (Tizimin) that there was a fire at a bar known as *Los Cabrones*. From the present passage I suspect a plot against the reigning Jaguar ('East priest') Bol Ay by his cousin (?) Coc Ay and the committee of eight rain priests who are then named, apparently headed by another cousin (?), Pat Ay. Coc Ay was therefore a usurper. Three of the conspirators were hanged.

2957. And "Caesar Augustus" claimed the lordship of the following *katun*.

2960. The text breaks off incomplete.

29. The Ceremonial of the *Baktun*

(42) Ti hach kabet – u bel*
   Y ocsabal ti: ol:*

Lay u tunil
   T u patah
Ca yum
   Citbil =

It is very necessary, the path
   That is the introduction to the
   heart.
This is the *tun* period
   When it was shaped
2965 By our Father
   The remote.

Act I

Lay u kam chi
   Lay baal che:
Licil ca tzicic:
   Uay
C on
   Ah tepall i*
Tic ob =
   Hach pay bentzil
U kultabal ob =
   Hahil ob
Kuob =
   La ob i =
Tunob:
   Cumlahic
Hahal ku =
   Ca yumil
Ti *Dios* =
   U yumil
Caan
   Y etel luum:
Hahal ku:
   Ba ca cix =
Yax kuob e =
   Hauay kuob =
Tz'oc:
   U than u kultabal ob=
Kaz pahi ob
   T u men u *bendision*:

Act 1

This is the taking of the occasion.
   This is the balche ceremony
As we honor him
2970   Here.
We
   The rulers
Spread
   In many separate parts,
2975 Worship them,
   The true
Gods.
   There they are
As stones,
2980   The established representation
Of the True God,
   Our Father,
Who is God,
   The Father
2985 Of heaven
   And earth,
The True God.
   However,
The first gods
2990   Were leprous gods,
Finished
   Is the word of their worship.
They have been done in
   By the benediction

2961. See the introduction for an analysis of this chapter.
2962. I agree with Roys 1967: 98 that this refers to faith, but I have translated it
literally anyway.
2972. Bricker reads this as *ah tepal incob*, presumably 'the rulers of men'.

U yumil caan =
  Ca tz'oc i:*
U lohol bal cah ca tz'oc i.
  U ca put cuxtal
Hahal ku
  Hahal D^s.
Ca u cici
  Thantah
Caan
  Y etel luum =
Ti kaspah i a kul
  Maya uinic ex e:
Xeth a u ol
  T a kul ex lae:
U kahlay cab
  T u kinil =
Lay t u men tz'iban lae =
  T u men ma kuchuc
T u kin u meyah
  Lae hun ob
Lay picilthan ob lae:*
  U ti al katabal u chi
Maya uinicob i
  Uay y ohel ob
Bix sihanil ob
  Etz'lic cab
Uay
  Ti peten lae.

2995 Of the Father of heaven.
  Then it ends.
The redemption of the world is over,
  The twice-born life
Of the True God,
3000   The True *Dios.*
When they sweetly
  Prayed
To heaven
  And earth,
3005 That put an end
  To the gods of you Mayan people.
Shattered is the belief
  In your gods then,
This is the account of the land
3010   At that time.
That is because it was written there,
  Because it wouldn't have happened
At the time of the making
  Of these books.
3015 These are millennial words here
  For the examination
Of the Mayan people here
  Who may know
How they were born
3020   And settled the land
Here
  In this country.

Act 2

Ychil buluc, ahau,
  Tij ca hok i
Ah mucen cab;
  Kaxic u u ichob,
Oxlahun ti ku;
  Ma yx y oheltah ob i:
U kaba halil i:
  U cic:
Y etel u mehenob e:
  Y alah ob;

Act 2

In 11 Ahau
  That was when there began
3025 The Muzen Cabs
  To tie the faces
Of the 13 Gods,
  And they did not know
Their true names.
3030   For their older sisters
And their engendered sons,
  Their offspring

2996. Bricker prefers this scansion for lines 2996 through 2998:
  Ca tz'oci u lohol bal cah   Ended is the redemption of the world,
    Ca tz'oci u ca put cuxtal   Ended is the twice-born life.
3015. Gates 1932: 79 has 'these many-leaved volumes'.

Coc Ay, lord of Merida (1618–1638).
From the Garrett Collection of
Manuscripts in Middle American
Languages, The Princeton University
Library, The gift of Robert Garrett.

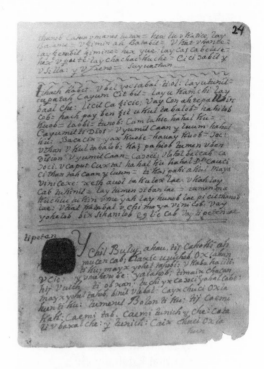

Ti ma ix chacan
  Hij u u ich ti ob xan;
T u chi yx ca tz'oc i*

And those who are not grown—
  Perhaps even their faces
3035 And their voices are gone.

Act 3

U y ahal cab e:
Ma yx y oheltah ob.
  Binil
Ulebal:
  Ca yx chuc i*
Oxlahun ti ku:
  T u menel bolon ti ku;*
Tij ca emi kak:
  Ca emi tab.
Ca emi tunich
  Y etel che:
Ca tali u baxal che:
  Y etel tunich:

Act 3

The dawning of the land
They didn't know about either,
  The going
And coming,
3040   And then there were finished
The 13 who are Gods
  By the 9 who are Gods.
They then brought down fire;
  Then they brought down the rope;
3045 Then they brought down stones
  And sticks.
Then came beating with sticks
  And stones.

3035. The old gods are being forgotten by women and children.

3040. Bricker reads *chuc* as 'capture'.

3042. The 9 Gods presided over the nine levels of the underworld. They are presumably also masked and they reenact the destruction of the 13 Gods as the *katun* cycle ends. This also symbolizes the traditional calendrical disagreement of the Xiu and the Itza, since the ninth *katun* of the Itza cycle is the thirteenth of the Xiu cycle. Thus, this is a symbolic way of finishing off the Itza and relegating them to the underworld.

Ca ix chuc i   And then were finished
  (43) Oxlahun ti ku: 3050   The 13 who are Gods.
Y etel ca ix paxi u pol: And so then their heads were beaten,
  Ca ix lahi u u ich: And then their faces were flattened,
Ca ix tubab i: And then they were forgotten,
  Ca ix cuch pach hi xan: And then they were also carted
                                                 away.

Act 4   ## Act 4

Ca ix colabi u cangel: 3055 And then were planted the four
                                           changers
  Y etel u hol sabac: Together with the Soot Heads.

Act 5   ## Act 5

Ca ch'abi yx kukil: Then was created also the quetzal
  Yx yaxun: And the blue bird.

Act 6   ## Act 6

Y etel ca ch'ab i ybnel puyem uiil: And then was created the placenta of
                                           breast plants,
  Y etel puccikal puyem çicil: 3060   And the heart of breast squash,
Y etel puyem topp   And breast pumpkin
  Y etel puyem buul: And breast beans,
U tep'ah ynah: The wrapping of the seed
  Yax bolon tz'acab:*   Of the first nine steps.
Ca bin i   3065 Then they went
  T u y oxlahun tas caan: To the thirteenth level of heaven,
Ca yx tun culhij: And so then were established
  U matz'il: His membranes,
Y etel u ni   And his nose,
  U baclil i: 3070   His skeleton
Uay   Here
  Y okol cab e: In the world.
Ca tun bin u pucçikal   So then went his heart
  T u menel oxlahun ti ku: Because of the 13 who are Gods.
Ma ix y oltah ob   3075 But they didn't know
  Bin ci u pucçikal uiil lae:*   His heart was to be a plant.

3064. The various plants in the preceding lines suggest the riddles of Zuyua
and probably refer to a ritual meal and/or procession relating to the Lords of Hell.
I do not accept the misconception, originating with Landa, that Bolon Tz'acab was
a single deity. Landa's Maya left much to be desired. (Cf. Roys 1967: 99, note 10.)

3076. Then there is another procession in honor of the thirteen heavens, accompanied by bloodletting and ending with a heart sacrifice, except that here a
plant (presumably rubber) is substituted for a real heart. Maya *kik* is 'rubber, sap,
and blood'.

Act 7

Ca ix hul lahi
  Yx ma yumob
Y etel ah num yaob:
  Yx ma ychamob:
Cuxanob
  Ix ti minan u pucçikalob:
Ca yx mucchahij:
  T u men:
U yam çuc
  T u yam kaknab:
Hun uatz' hail:
  Hulom haail:
Tij: ca uchic ol*
  Cangelil i:
Ti homocnac canal:
  Homocnac ix ti cab:
U alic can tul ti ku:
  Can tul ti ba cab:
Lay ha y eçob:
  T u chij:
Tun ca tz'oc i
  Hay cabil =
Lay cahcunah =
  U chebal ca tzolic*

Act 7

And then they all arrived,
  Even the fatherless
And the suffering poor,
3080 And the widows,
The living,
  And those without hearts.
And they began to wait
  For it:
3085 The direction of thatch grass,
  The direction of the sea.
A deluge of water,
  A storm of water
Then reached the hearts
3090 Of the four changers,
Who radiated in heaven
  And radiated also on the land.
Said the 4 who are Gods,
  The 4 who are Fathers of the Land,
3095 "This water shows them
  To their faces.
Then let us finish
  The flattening of the lands.
This is the initiation
3100 Of the future of our count."

Act 8

Kan xib yui:*
  Ca u alhi
Çac ymix che:
  Ti xaman:
Ca yx u alhi
  Y oc mal caan:

Act 8

The South priest Xib Yuy
  Then bore
The north alligator tree
  In the north.
3105 And then he bore
  The entrance to heaven,

3089. Bricker reads *ca uchi col* 'then occurred the theft'.

3100. The whole ceremony up to here has been oriented to the east, always the Mayan starting point. It now shifts to the north (always counterclockwise). You can get to the sea from Merida in any of three cardinal directions, but north is the closest. The general public—orphans, the poor, widows, even witches—is summoned and a deluge of water is released. This symbolizes both the power of the rain gods, who are equated with the yearbearers, and the power of baptism. The yearbearers announce that baptism will subjugate Yucatan and justify the calendrical mystique.

3101. It is time for another procession. It begins in the north, confirming the implication in the preceding note, and moves to the west and south and back to the center. The South priest Xib Yuy (personal name) carries the sacred tree to the north, west, and south. The latter two are symbolized by appropriately colored birds. Another South priest, Oyal Mut, then carries the "alligator tree" to the center of the Plaza. I'd bet it was a blue-green cross!

U chicul hay cabal:
  Lay çac ymix che:
U alic cuchic:
  Ca yx u alhij
Ek ymix che:
  Cu ektan pitz'oy =

Ca yx u alhi
  Kan ymix che:
U chicul hay cabal:
  Culic kan tan pitz'oy:

Cumlic ix kan xib yui:

  Yx kan oyal mut:
Ca ix u alhij
  Yax ymix che: t u chumuc

U kahlay hay cabil =
  Culic:

The sign of the flattening of the lands.
  That is the north alligator tree,
Said to be carried.
3110 And then he bore
The west alligator tree
  To seat the black-breasted weaver
  bird.
And then he bore
  The south alligator tree,
3115 The sign of the flattening of the lands
  To seat the yellow-breasted weaver
  bird,
And was seated the South priest Xib
Yuy,
  And the South priest Oyal Mut.
And then he bore
3120 The center alligator tree to the
  middle,
Signifying the flattening of the land.
  It is seated.

Act 9

U atal:
  Cumtal u cah:
U: lac:
  Canah ual katun:*

Act 9

Its being raised
  Establishes the town;
3125 And the same
  When the return of the *katun* is
  fulfilled.

Act 10

Ah pay kab*
  Ah pai oc: t u yum:

Cumtal u cah
  Chac *piltec* = t u lakin cab:

Ah pay oc
  T u yum:
Cumtal u cah:
  Çac *pilte* t u xaman cab:

Act 10

The leaders of the hand
  (And) the leaders of the foot as its
  fathers:
Establishing the town
3130 Of the red noble in the eastern
  lands,
The leader of the foot
  As its father;
Establishing the town
  Of the white noble in the northern
  lands,

3126. At this point the symbolic seating of *katun* 11 Ahau is accomplished.

3127. I believe these are the yearbearers again. As the text explains, there were two leaders of the foot (east and north) and two of the hand (west and south). They are honorifically named in this couplet in reverse order because the south is "the heart of the lands" in this ceremony. That may explain the two South priests mentioned in note 3101. However, it was the West priest (Coc Ay) who was seated at the beginning of 3 Ahau (line 2919).

(44) Ah pay oc
   T u yum =
Cumtal u cah
   Lahun chan:*
Ah pay kab.
   T u yum:
Cumtal u cah
   Kan *piltec*:
Ah pay kab
   T u yum:
He x u u ol cab
   U alic*

3135 The leader of the foot
     As its father;
     Establishing the town
       Of Lahun Chan,
     The leader of the hand
3140   As its father;
     Establishing the town
       Of the yellow noble,
     The leader of the hand
     As its father.
3145 And that is the heart of the lands
     It is said.

Act II

Ah uuc cheknal e: tal i
   T u uuc tas cab:
Ca emi u chekeb te:
   U pach: ytzam kab ain =
Tij ca emi
   T u muk u xuk
Luum:
   Caan:
Ximbal
   U cah ob.
T u can cib:
   T u can tatz:
Ti ek:
   Ma sasil cab:

Act 11

The 7 Pacers have come
     To the seven levels of the land.
     Then comes down the pacing pole
3150   On the back of Itzam Cab Ain.
     He then descended
       With the strength to bury
     Earth
       And heaven,
3155 Walking
     Through the villages
     To light candles,
     To light lamps
     In the dark,
3160   Obscure lands.

Act 12

Ti hun minan kin:
   Ti hun minan akab:
Ti hun minan: u:
   Ah ubah ob
Ti yx tan u y ahal cab =
   Ca tun ah icab:
Ua la ci to:
   Y ahal cab:

Act 12

To one who has no day,
     To one who has no night,
     To one who has no moon,
     He is their painter;
3165 And he has the dawn;
     So then it dawned,
     If that is indeed he,
     The dawn.

3138. Lahun Chan was lord of Emal in 11 Ahau (Tizimin). The expectable reference to the west is missing. Roys 1967: 101, note 2 identifies Lahun Chan as a god.

3146. Neither of these ceremonial circuits is explicit and complete. It appears that the Xiu operated on a five-point directional circuit (east, north, west, south, center) as did the Nahua. The "heart of the land" suggests the missing Center priest.

Oxlahun pic tz'ac | Thirteen thousand steps
  T u uuc | 3170 And seven
U xocan | Is the count
  Y ahal cab:* | Of the dawn.
Ca tun ah cab. ti ob: | So then the landowners among them
  Ci u ba: | Say to themselves,
Ca kin tz'am: | 3175 "Two-day thrones;
  Ox kin tz'am: | Three-day thrones."
Ca yx hop' i* | And then they begin to be
  Y okol ox lahun ti ku: | Over the 13 who are Gods,
Okol u cahob | Over the towns
  Ti y ahaulil: | 3180 In the lordship,
Chacab tun tepal: | Reddening the stone of rule,
  Chac h ix pop: | And reddening the mat,
Chac acan | Reddening the lamentation
  U yax chel cab: | Of the Ceiba Land.
Chacan u numteil cab | 3185 Reddened is the oppressed land
  T u menel ob: | Because of them.
Uuc y ol çip: | The seven priest Ol Zip (appeared),
  Ma ix t u kin u tepal: | But it was not time for his rule—
Lay lic y oktic ob: | That is when they raised up
  Bolon ti ku lae:* | 3190 The 9 who are Gods there.
Tij ca tal i | What then came
  U tzolol pop: | Was the counting of mats,
Chacc ix pop. | And it reddened the mats
  Culic bolon ti ku: | To seat the 9 who are Gods.
Tz'ut polbil ix y it. | 3195 And haggling and trading was the ass
  Ti culic tu pop: | That sat upon the mat
T u ca emi çitz' | That then brought down envy,
  Tali tan y ol caan = | Coming from the center of heaven,
Lay u çitz'il tepal | That was the envy of the ruler,
  U çitz'il ahaulil = | 3200 The envy of the lordship.

3172. Martínez 1912: 15, note 1 speculates brilliantly that *ox lahun pic tz'ac* refers to 13 *baktuns*: 13.0.0.0.0 4 Ahau 8 Cumku. I agree, but note that when you add the other seven you reach the mythological date of 20.0.0.0.0. Martínez' date lands us in 2214, mine in 4954.

3177. Bricker suggests this scansion for lines 3177 through 3180:
And then they began to cry,
  The 13 who are Gods;
They began to cry
  In their lordship . . .

3190. The 7 Pacers triumph over the 13 Gods and sacrifice them. They are apparently headed by Ol Zip, an Itza lord of Emal who became Jaguar in 1 Ahau. But since it is not yet 1 Ahau, the 7 Pacers are in turn displaced (and sacrificed?) by the 9 Gods, who are rather nasty characters.

Act 13

Ca ix cumlahij chac etz':*

   Ca cumlahi çac y etz'ebil ahaulil:

Etz': ca cumlahij: ek:
   Etz'. ca cumlahij: kan.

Etz' ca cumlahij.
   Chac tenel ahau:
Ah ten pop:
   Ah ten tz'am.*
Ca cumlahij:
   Ek tenel ahau:
Ah ten pop.
   Ah ten tz'am:
Ca cumlahij
   Kan tenel ahau.
Ah ten pop
   Ah ten tz'am:
Ti ku ix t u than:
   Ti ua ix: ma ix ku i =

Act 14

Ti minan ix u uah.*
   Ti minan ix y aal:

Act 13

And then were established the red-placed—
   Then were established the white-placed lords;
The place then established was black;
   The place then established was yellow.
3205 The place then established
   Was the Red Death Lord
As lord of the death mat,
   Lord of the death throne.
Then was established
3210   The Black Death Lord
As lord of the death mat,
   Lord of the death throne.
Then was established
   The Yellow Death Lord
3215 As lord of the death mat,
   Lord of the death throne.
And he was a god, he said,
   And it may be too he was not a god.

Act 14

And he had no food,
3220   And he had no water.

3201. Another ceremonial circuit follows, seating the Ba Cabs as Death Lords, and again it is incomplete. This time it is the Death Lord of the north who is omitted (around line 3208). Bricker scans lines 3201 through 3206 differently:

Ca ix cumlahij chac etz':	And then were established the red placed;
Ca cumlahi çac y etz'ebil	Then were established the white placed,
Ahaulil etz'	The lordly placed;
Ca cumlahij: ek etz'	Then were established the black placed;
Ca cumlahij: kan etz'	Then were established the yellow placed;
Ca cumlahij chac tenel ahau:	Then was established the Red Death Lord . . .

3208. Two couplets have been inadvertently omitted from the text:

Ca culhi	Then was seated
Sac temal	The White Death Lord
Ah ten pop	As lord of the death mat,
Ah ten tz'am	The lord of the death throne.

Correct calendrical order would have required these lines after line 3212, but the order already given (lines 3201 ff.) is the same. Perhaps the death gods were expected to be aberrant.

3219. A ritual banquet ensues that symbolizes the food and drink (i.e., the fate) of *katun* 3 Ahau and commemorates (line 3284) the inauguration of 11 Ahau. It also involves (line 3244) the ritual riddles legitimizing the lords.

Hun xel i:
　(45) Lic u alic u mul u i t ic.

Ma ix tab u tal u y abal:
　Lic u yancuntic:
Caal:
　U mut ti culic:
Cal kin
　Caal num ya
Ti tal i:
　Ta muk y ahaulil;
Ca kuch i:
　Ti culic t u pop:
(7) Top canal:
　Hopan u kak:
Colop u u ich:
　Kin:
Tocan ti cab =
　Lay u buuc: ti y ahaulil =

Lay u chun
　Licil y oktic u tepal:
T u kin = numen: chuc:
　Numen celem:
T u kin = u natal naat:
　Ahauob =
Can u alic: u ch'ic che:
　Mol t u kin:
Çatay
　Babalil i:
Can u alic: u che:
　Ah muuc =
T u ho can be:
　T u ho can heleb:
Okom bul
　Cum t u kinil:
Momolij =
　Pepen =
Ti tal i
　Chac mitan nun ya =
Lic u talel ox uin keech
　U kin
Ox ahau katun
　Ox tuc ti hab:
Lay bin nup'uc:
　Ychil ah ox ahau katun:

One fragment,
　When he ordered a pile of shoots
　　spread out;
There was nowhere to get his fruit
　As he liked it.
3225　Harsh
　Was the news that was seated.
Harsh times,
　Harsh suffering
Were what came
3230　During the lordship
When he arrived
　To sit upon the mat:
Fornication on high,
　Fires being set,
3235　Snatched away was the face
　Of the sun;
Burned on the land,
　That was the judgment on the
　　lordship.
That was its foundation
3240　As his rule became known.
It was a time to suffer fists,
　To suffer shoulders.
It was a time for the riddles
　Of the lords,
3245　Teaching him to say wooden lance
　(For) the track to the sun:
He is forgetting
　Everything.
Teaching him to say the tree
3250　For the crier
At the four crossroads,
　For the four changers.
Come is the bowl—
　Seated in the time
3255　Of the swarming
　Of butterflies.
What is coming
　Is a great plague of suffering,
Since there came three kinds of folds
3260　In the time
Of *katun* 3 Ahau,
　Threefold in a year.
That will be the closing up
　Of *katun* 3 Ahau.

Act 15

Ca bin cumlac
  U y anal katun
Ox u uah
  Ox y aal
Cup: u uah:
  Cup: y aal:
La c u hantic:
  La c u y ukic =
X ba tun =
  Ch'ich'im chay: c u hantic =
Lay culhi: uay
  T u cahal num ya e yum e:

Ychil u bolon tun =*
  T u kin y an: tz'util i =
Katal u cah
  U cuch katun:
T u lah y abil =
  Ah ox lahun ahau =
Tij ca ca u hekah y oc =
  Ah buluc ahau =
Tij ca emi u than bolon tz'acab:

  U ni y ak = ca emi:

Katal: u cah
  U cuch katun:
Katun
  Bolon te u cuch:*

Act 16

Ca emi:*
  Ti caanil =
Kan ix u kinil:
  Kaxc i = u cuch:
Tij ca emi haa:
  Tali tan y ol caan =
U chebal
  U ca put çihil:

Act 15

3265 Then will be established
  The nature of the *katun*.
Gourdroot is its food,
  Gourdroot is its water.
Breadnut is its food,
3270   Breadnut is its water.
That he will eat;
  That he will drink.
And what then?
  Scrounged cabbage for him to eat,
3275 Who is seated here
  In the city that was to suffer the
  fathers.
In the ninth *tun*,
  At that time there was haggling
Over wanting to settle
3280   The burden of the *katun*
For the whole period
  Of 13 Ahau.
Which (two by two) broke up the entry
  Of 11 Ahau.
3285 That then brought down the word of
  the nine steps.
  The tip of his tongue then came
  down,
Wanting to settle
  The burden of the *katun*,
A *katun*
3290   Which was his ninth burden.

Act 16

Then he came down
  From heaven,
And Kan was the day
  He tied his burden,
3295 Which then brought water
  Coming from the heart of heaven,
Ordaining
  Second birth,

3277. Probably a retrospective reference to the middle of 13 Ahau.
3290. The 9 Gods declare the fate of the *katun*. The symbolism of 9 reiterates the Xiu-Itza calendrical standoff.
3291. The four Ba Cabs appear, headed by the senior day, Kan (the year 1618 was 11 Kan) and symbolizing rain and baptism. Sacrifice is implied, possibly bloodletting.

Bolon haaban: | The nine bowers
Y otoch: | 3300 And homes,
Y et emcij: bolon mayal | And bringing down the nine cycle
Ch'ahuc: u chi = | Dripping at the mouth.
U ni y ak = ch'ahuc: | The tip of his tongue dripping,
Hi u tz'omel: | Perhaps his brains.
Ti ca emi: can tul: chaac = | 3305 Then there descended the four rain
Uaya: | gods,
| The *naguals*.

Act 17

Caat lae: | It was clear
Lay u cabil ob nicte:* | Those were the lands of Flowers.
(46) Lae tij ca hok ij: yx chac hoch kom: | He who then appeared also was Red Hoch Kom,
Ti: y etel yx çac hoch kom: | 3310 Who was also with White Hoch Kom,
Ti: y etel yx ek hoch kom: | Who was also with Black Hoch Kom,
Y etel yx kan hoch kom: | And with Yellow Hoch Kom,
Y etel yx haunal: | And with Hau Nal,
Y etel yx huk nab = | And with Huk Nab.
Y et hokci tun: | 3315 There also appeared Ci Tun,
Yx hoyal nicte: | And Oyal Nicte,
Y etel yx ho nixte: | And with Ho Nicte,
Y etel yx nin ich': cacau: | And with Ninich' Cacau,
Y etel yx chacuil tok: | And with Chac Uil Tok,
Y etel yx bac nicte: | 3320 And with Bac Nicte,
Y etel yx *macuil xuchit* e =* | And with Macuilxuchit,
Yx hobon y ol nicte = | And Hobon y Ol Nicte,
Y etel yx laul nicte: | And with Laul Nicte,
Y etel kouol y octah nicte: | And Kou Ol Nicte and Octah Nicte.
Lay hokob nicte: | 3325 These are the appearances of the Flowers,
La o b ix ah co mayelob: | And they are the madmen of the cycles.
Lay u naa: nicte: | This is their mother: Nicte,
Ca hoki ob: | When they appeared.
Y utz'ub ah kin: | The scent of the sun priest,
Y utz'ub ahau: | 3330 The scent of the lord,

3308. They are followed by the Flower Lords, who are named. There are eighteen of them, led by their mother, Flower (Nicte, Xochit), and they reenact the Xiu origin myth. Apparently they symbolize the *tun* (each being one *uinal*) and hence stand outside the conflict between 13 and 9, heaven and hell (line 3346). They perform flower sacrifices.

3321. Nah. *macuilxochitl* 'Five Flower' is the same as Maya Ho Nicte 'Five Flower' in line 3317.

Y utz'ub hol can:
  Lay u cuch nicte ahau =

Ca emi:
  Minan ix u y anal:
Lay uil e:
  C u than =
Ma ix uah u cuchma =
  Tij tun ca hoki
Yx haulah nicte:
  Occic u keban: bolon ti ku:

Ox te ix ti hab:
  U kin ca y alah: cuchij:

Ma ix kuchi
  Ch'ab: naci:
Ku:
  Mitnal i =
Bolon tz'acab ca emi

  T u chun nicte:
P'islim te.
  Yax bac:
Tz'unun ix
  U uayinah ca emi =

Ca u tz'utz'ah u cabil =
  Bolon y al nicte:
Lic ychil bix ca ch'a ycham nij
  Yx hoyal nicte:*
Ca tun hoki u puccikal nicte:

  U ximbante u ba:
Can hek ix
  Lae nicte: lae =

The scent of the commander,
  That is the burden of the Flower
  lords.
When they came down
  And had no existence,
3335 This was the end
  They said.
But they bore no food then
  When they appeared,
And they sacrificed flowers,
3340   Entering into the sin of the 9 who
  are Gods,
And three times in a year
  Was the day when they bore the
  burden.
But they did not come
  To create the rise
3345 Of God
  Or hell.
There were nine steps when they
descended
  To the founding of the Flowers.
P'izlim Te,
3350   The Green Bird,
Hummingbird
  Were the spirit seeds that
  descended.
Then they sucked the nectar
  Of the nine children of Flowers,
3355 And in just that way they got mates
  And little Flowers.
So then appeared the heart of the
Flower
  Moving itself along,
And with four branches.
3360   That was the Flower then.

Act 18

Ti yx culan ah kin:
  Xocbil tun chumuc:*

Act 18

And she was seated as sun priest,
  Counting the *tuns* in the middle,

3356. The Flower lineages were the Xiu. Their origin myth made them descendants of Hummingbird (elsewhere blue/green bird), who came down to suck the nectar of nine flowers and thus begot the Xiu.

3362. Roys 1967: 105, note 4 identifies Xocbiltun as a god and as another name for Pizlimtec, citing López de Cogolludo.

Tij ca uchi u huhu y ol

Oxlahun ti ku:*
Ma yx y oheltah y emel u keban
u pop:
　Ti ku ix t a than c uchi e
Nicte yx u pop:
　Nicte yx u kan che:
Nicte y em a:

Which she did for each of the middle
ones
　Of the 13 who are Gods.
3365 But she didn't know the origin of the
sin of the mat,
　And she is the god you have spoken
of.
And Flower is her mat,
　And Flower is her bench,
Flower her descent.

Act 19

　Çauin culic.*
Çauin u ximbal
　Çauin u lac
Çauin u luch
　Çauin u puccikal.
Çauin u nat.
　Çauin u tucul
Çauin u chi.
　Cool u than ti y ahaulil i.
T u kin uat uil =
　T u kin uaat. ukul.
T u xay uch i
　Lic u hanal
T u pach u xau
　Lic u uil uchijc
Ma che e =
　Et ma tunich.
Chac
　U cool
Y an ti lahun chan u u ich
　Ti culic çip u u ich
Çip u than
　Çip u can
Çip u naat
　Çip u ximbal
Kaxan u u ich ti culic
　(47) Chac cah u pop culic ta
　muk y ahaulil

Act 19

3370　Envy was seated:
Envy his walk,
　Envy his bowl,
Envy his gourd,
　Envy his heart,
3375　Envy his mind,
　Envy his thought,
Envy his mouth;
　Crazy was his word in the lordship.
In his time was the voice of hunger,
3380　In his time was the voice of thirst.
It was divided,
　Like his eating
After he got dizzy,
　As the need occurred.
3385 No sticks
　And no stones.
The rain priest
　Was his wife
In the person of Lahun Chan,
3390　Who seated the person of Spite.
Spite was his word,
　Spite was his teaching,
Spite was his knowledge,
　Spite was his gait.
3395 Tied was the face which was seated;
　A big city was the mat to be seated
　during the lordship.

3364. I get out of this that the head (mother) of the Flowers was seated and
counted off the calendrical implications of the 18 *uinals* and the 13 Gods as they
stood in the middle of the Plaza.

3370. What follows seems to be a kind of Mayan morality play in which Envy
and Spite are personified. Lahun Chan plays the part of the wife of Envy (line
3389), and the whole episode is one of comic relief. They act crazy (line 3378),
dizzy (line 3383), furtive (line 3408), bad (line 3412), and ignorant (line 3416).

T u ban u yum
   T u ban u naa =
Ma ix y ohelma u naa:
   Alintee
Thaban u pucçikal
   T u hunal.
Ychil yx ma yumil
   Ah poch' yum:
Ychil yx ma nail
   Bin ximbalnac
Calan u mut.
   Çatal u naat
Y icnal u yum
   Y icnal u naa:
Minan tibil ti.
   Minan utz t u pucçikal.
Halili y an t u ni
   Y ak tz'etz'ec lo e
Ma y ohel bix bin tz'oc cebal

   Ma yx y ohel bal y an
T u tz'oc y ahaulil i
   Lay ca bin tz'ocnac
U kinil
   U tepal e = ————*
He bolon ti ku
   Lae bolon chan u ich
Ahauuil
   Uinicob
Ah ca kin pop
   Ah ca kin tz'am:
Lay tal i
   Ychil ox ahau katun
Ti yx bin y anac
   U y anal u yumil peten

Y ah culcinnah ul u than
   U y anal katun

His father was dropped,
   His mother was dropped,
And his mother didn't know
3400   What she was to have borne,
Her heart burning
   By itself.
And in being fatherless
   The Death Lord was his father;
3405 And in being motherless
   He will be a vagabond.
Hardened was his message,
   Furtive was his mind
Through his father,
3410   Through his mother.
He had no fear;
   There was no good in his heart.
Truly it is stone,
   And his tongue is plaster.
3415 He doesn't know whatever will end his sins,
   And he doesn't know he has them.
The lordship is over,
   That is what will terminate
His time
3420   And his rule.
These are the 9 who are Gods;
   These are the nine little faces
Of the lordship:
   Commoners,
3425 Those of the two-day mat,
   Those of the two-day throne.
This comes
   In *katun* 3 Ahau.
And it will be his nature,
3430   The nature of the fatherhood of the country,
The incumbent receiver of the word,
   The nature of the *katun*.

Act 20

Ca bin tz'ococ u than
   Ah ox ahau katun
T u kinil u con con mehen
   Lay bin y anac y okol u nunil ah ytza.

Act 20

Then will be finished the word
   Of *katun* 3 Ahau.
3435 At a time of very few sons,
   This will be the lamentation of the stupid Itza.

3420. The lordship has been passed and what follows is a sermon, presumably by the Spokesman of the Jaguar, prophecying the fate of 3 Ahau.

Hun ua chuen
   Hun ua celem
Hun tz'it tunil
   U kex u keban
U nunil ah ytza.
   Lay bolon ti ku:
Lay bin tz'ocebal u than
   Ah ox ahau katun
Ti yx u natal nat
   Y ahaulil cabob i:
Tz'ocebal u than katun

   Ti x u chucanhal
U ch'ibal al
   Mehenob
Ba tabob
   Y etel u y anal ah cux olalob
Y etel u ch'ibal ba tabob
   Lay muc chektabi luum

T u u ichob e.
   Ca ma balhi ob
T u men u co kin
   U co katun
U mehen kas
   Y al x buyuk.
Lay çihob ca ah icab*

   Ychil ah ox ahau katun
Bay bin tz'ocebal u tepalob

   Ah ca p'el ychob
Ti ca yumil
   Ti *Dios*
He x ca bin tz'ocnac
   U than katun lae
Ca tun u tz'ab D͛.
   Y uchul hun y eciil t u ca ten

Lay hay cabil e:
   Lay tun c u tz'ocol e
Ca tun emec ca yumil
   Ti *jesuchristo*
Y okol (u) komil*
   Josapat.

If one is clever,
   If one is strong,
One part of a *tun*
3440   Will change the sin,
The stupidity of the Itza;
   That is, the 9 who are Gods.
That will be the ending of the word
   Of *katun* 3 Ahau.
3445 And that is the riddle
   Of the lordship of the lands,
The termination of the word of the
katun;
   And that is the manifestation
Of the descent of born
3450   And engendered children
And chiefs,
   And the existence of living souls,
And the lineage of the chiefs.
   That is the secret pacing of the
lands
3455 In the sight
   Of our poor,
Because of the madness of the time,
   The madness of the *katun*.
The wicked son,
3460   The stupid child.
That is their birth when they are
awakened
   In *katun* 3 Ahau.
Thus will be the termination of the
rulers,
   The two-faced people
3465 By our Father
   Who is God.
And he then will bring about the end
   Of the word of this *katun*.
So then God will be given
3470   The achievement of a flood for the
second time.
That will flood the lands;
   That then will finish it.
So then will descend Our Father
   Who is Jesus Christ
3475 Over the pit
   Of Jehoshaphat

3461. I read *ahzab* 'be awakened'.
3475. Gates 1932: 92 reads 'over the valley'.

T u xax cah	Beside the city
(48) *Jerusalen*	Of Jerusalem,
U chic u lohic oon	Succeeding in redeeming us
T u cilich kikel.	3480 With his holy blood.
La ix bin emec	And that will be the descent
Ti noh muyal	In a great storm,
U tz'ab u tohol	Being given the right
Canil hah	To heavenly truth.
U mançah ti çinan	3485 He will be made to pass in subjection
Ti *crus* che: c uchi e.	To the wooden cross he bore,
Tij tun y emel ti noh u chucil	Which then is the descent to the great event,
Ti noh ix u tepal xan	And to the great rule also
Hahal *Dios*	Of the True *Dios*,
Lay hahal ku.	3490 That is, the True God.
Lay çihes caan	That will bring to birth heaven
Y etel luum	And earth
Y etel y okol cab	And the world
T u lacal.	Entire.
La yx bin emec taxcuntic	3495 And that will be the descent that flattens
Y okol cab xan	The surface of the earth too,
T u y utzil	For good
Y etel lob	Or evil,
Ta cil y ah tz'oy sahul ob	Sheltering the weak and frightened
Ah nunob = ———————	3500 And the stupid.

30. The Language of Zuyua

(28) *Suyuaa* than*	Zuyua language
Y etel naat	And explanation
U ti al ca yum	For our father
Sr. Gov^{or}. Mariscal *	Sr. Governor Marshall,

3501. Zuyua (Nah. 'bloody water') is another name for Tula. It is used here to draw the mantle of the Toltecs over the ritual language of the Mayan examination system. Perhaps a better analogy than examination would be the secret ritual of the Masonic order and other kindred groups. A Mayan priest aspiring to high office was supposed to be noble on both sides of his family and also well educated, particularly in genealogy and religion. The riddles of Zuyua were a ritual test of this. Presumably they were not taught to the plebs, or "younger brothers," as the Maya would put it. They were a standard part of the ceremonies inaugurating a *katun*. The riddles of this and the following chapter have been numbered in the translation for easy reference. There are 77. (See "riddle" in the index.)

3504. Our Father the Lord Governor Marshall is not identified. Roys 1967: 88,

Lay uchic u cahtal tzuc uaxim lae 3505 Who has settled here at Tzuc Uaxim
   T u lakin ych caan çi hoo   To the east of Heaven Born Merida,
Ti y an luum uchic Where he has land
   U y antal u pakal i   And has located his orchard
Y etel u *solar* And garden
   Uchic u cahtal lae 3510   And settled here.
Bin ix kuchuc t u kin For when there arrives the time
   U holol u bel   Of the beginning of his road
Xan talel u than u hal ach uiniccil There also comes the word of the
   Mayan governor.

   Chac u than ca bin uluc   Strong is his word when it arrives,
Chac c ix u buc xan* 3515 And rather strong is his judgment too.
   He le ac t u *suyua* than   Indeed this is in Zuyua language!
Lay bin u than This will be the language,
   Lay bin u kat   These will be the questions
U hal ach uinicil Of the governing people
   Cah lae 3520   Of this town

Top: *Yax Chac, lord of Merida (1539–
1559).* Middle: *Ul Uac, lord of Merida (1559–1579).* Bottom: *Yax Chac,
lord of Merida (1579–1599). From
the Garrett Collection of Manuscripts in Middle American Languages, The Princeton University
Library, The gift of Robert Garrett.*

(note continued from preceding page)

note 2 opts for Don Carlos de Luna y Arellano, but admits that his incumbency as
governor of Yucatan (1604–1612) is a *katun* too early. The subsequent lines, however, do suggest that he had retired to his hacienda east of Merida. I cannot locate
Tzuc Uaxim. The hypothetical tone of the text (line 3546) suggests that it was a
text composed in the first half of 3 Ahau (*ante* 1628) and after the governor's re-
tirement (*post* 1612). I would bet it was before 1618.

   3515. I read *chac c(i) ix.*

Ca bin kuchuc t u kin
  U tz'ocol u than
Ah ox ahau
  Katun
Ca bin culac
  U y anal katun
Ah hun ahau
  Katun
Bay alanil lae
  He x katun hele lae
Ox ahau
  Katun
Tz'oc ix u kuchul
  T u kinil
U tz'ocol y ahaulil
  Y etel u tepal
Ha li li be
  Mahan ix u y anal
He x hun ahau
  Katun culan
Ychil y otoch ah ox ahau
  Katun lae
Y ula te
  T an u tz'abal u chaan
T u menel ah ox ahau
  Katun lae
Subtzil bin
  Bin balob t u cahal ob

(29) Kat
  Naat
C u talel ychil u katunil
  Licil u tz'ocol hele lae
Ti kuchi t u kinil u katabal
  U naat ob u ba tabil cahob
U y ohel ob uchic
  U talel ob
U uinicil ob
  Y ahaulil ob
Ua tzolan u talel u ba tabil ob

  U hal ach uinicil ob
Ua u ch'ibal ob ahauuob
  Ua ba tab u ch'ibal ob
Ti u hahcuntic ob*
  He ix u yax chun than*

When the time comes
  To finish the speech
Of 3 Ahau
  Katun
3525 And we arrive
  At the *katun* period
Of the 1 Ahau
  Katun.
Thus is the saying then,
3530   For indeed the *katun* changes then,
The 3 Ahau
  Katun.
For it is come
  To the time
3535 Of the end of its lordship
  And glory,
And therefore
  Its period ceases.
For indeed 1 Ahau
3540   *Katun* is seated
In the house of 3 Ahau
  Katun then.
He arrives there
  And is given leave
3545 By 3 Ahau
  Katun then.
He will be shamed,
  And his things will go to the villagers.
The questions
3550   And answers
Come into the *katun,*
  As it has changed then.
This comes at the time of questions
  And answers of the village officials:
3555 Whether they know
  How they came,
The people
  And the lords;
Whether they recount the coming of the officials
3560   And the governors;
Whether the lineages of the lords
  Or the officials of the lineages
Are cited correctly.
  (1.) So this is the first basic phrase

(notes 3563 and 3564 on following page)

Top: *Amayte Kauil, lord of Merida (1599–1618).* Middle: *Coc Ay, lord of Merida (1618–1638).* Bottom: *Amayte Kauil, lord of Merida (1638–1658).* From the Garrett Collection of Manuscripts in Middle American Languages, The Princeton University Library, The gift of Robert Garrett.

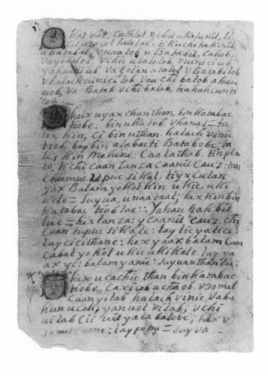

Bin katabac ti ob e
  Bin u kat ob u hanal
Taleç kin
  (. . . . .)*
Ci bin u than hal ach uinic ti ob*

  Bay bin alabac ti ba tabob e

Tal ex kin
  Mehen e
Ca a lathab
  T in *plato*
Ti ch'icaan *lanza*
  Caanil *cruz*
T an chumuc
  U pucsikal

3565 That is to be asked of them then:
  They will ask them for food.
"Bring the sun,"
  (. . . . .)
So goes the word of the governor to them;
3570 Thus should it be spoken by the officials then.
"Bring the sun,
  My son, then,
And stack it
  On my plate,
3575 Which is pierced by the lance
  Of the high cross
That is in the middle
  Of its heart,

3563. Genealogy is nowhere emphasized in the *Books*, but it must have been an effective control on upward mobility for the Maya as in other hierarchical cultures.

3564. Riddle. Sun? Egg. Cross? Benediction. Green jaguar? Green chile. Jaguar blood? Red chile.

3568. Line missing.

3569. Apparently the examinations were conducted by the local governors, but they were under the supervision of the Spokesman of the Jaguar (Chilam Balam).

Ti yx culan yax balam y okol kin

  Ukic u kikel e

Suyua

  U naataal

He x kin bin katabac ti ob lae

  Y ahau tzahbilhee

He x *lanza* y etel caanil *cruz*

  Ch'icaan t u pucsikal e

Lay lic y alic e

  Lay cici than e

He x yaax balam cumcabal y okol

  Ukic u kikel e

Lay yaax yc

  Balam y an i e

Suyua

  U than lae

He x u ca ch'ic than*

  Bin katabac ti ob e

Ca xic ob u ch'a ob u tz'omel caan

  Y ilab hal ach uinic ua ba hun u
cah

Y an u ol u ilab

  Uchi u ilab

Cii uil

  Y alabal ob e

He x u tz'omel caan e

  Lay pom e *Suyua*

(30) He x u y ox ch'ic than*

  Ben katabac ti ob e

Ca u kax ob

  Nohoch na lae

Uac thil u uaan

  Hun tz'it ti li y ocmal

He ix nohoch na

  Lay y ahau p'oc tz'oç lae

Bin alabac ti ca nacac

  Y okol y ahau sasac tzimin

Sasac u nok

  Y etel suyem

Y etel sasac çoot u machma t u kab

  Ta muk u soottic u tzimin

And with a green jaguar seated over
the sun

3580 Drinking its blood there."

Zuyua

  Is the meaning.

And so the sun they will be asked for

  Is the lord's fried egg.

3585 And so the lance with the high cross

  Piercing its heart,

That is just like saying

  These are the holy words.

And so the green jaguar piled over it

3590 Drinking its blood then,

That is green chile,

  The jaguar that is there.

Zuyua

  Is this language.

3595 (2.) And so the second secret word

  That is to be asked of them

Is that they go get the brains of heaven

  To be seen by the headman

  wherever he lives.

"I wish it to be seen;

3600 Let it be seen,"

Thus perhaps

  They will be told then.

For these brains of heaven,

  That is incense (in) Zuyua.

3605 (3.) And so the third secret word

  That is to be asked of them

Is that they tie together

  A great house

Six rows high

3610 And one jump wide.

For the great house is this:

  It is the lord's hat and hair then.

He should be told to mount

  On the lord's all-white horse.

3615 All white are his clothes

  And appearance,

And all white is the rope held in his
hand

  While he is roping the horse,

3595. Riddle. Brains of heaven? Incense.

  3605. Riddle. House six rows high and one jump wide? Hat and hair. White
horse? Sandal sole. White rope? Flowering branch. Ball of rubber? Money.

Top: *Yax Chuen, lord of Valladolid (1658–1677).* Bottom: *Lahun Chan, lord of Chable (1677–1697).* From the Garrett Collection of Manuscripts in Middle American Languages, The Princeton University Library, The gift of Robert Garrett.

Ti y an olom kik
    T u lol u soot
Ti uil
    U lukul e
He yx saçac tzimin lae
    Lay y ocbil xanab soscil kaan e

He ix sasac çoot lic y alabal e

    Lay sasac suyem e
Lay nicte e sasac tz'ulub e

    He ix olom kik
U lol soot e lic u katabal ti e

    Lay takin e y an tan chumuc e

Y oklal kikil likul
    T u kikel
Yx ma naa
    Yx ma yum u talel lae
He ix u can ch'ic than*
    Bin katabac ti ob e

Which has a ball of rubber
3620   On the blossom of the rope
Which bounces
    When it is moved.
And so the white horse is this:
    It is the sole of a maguey fiber sandal.
3625 And so the all-white rope as it is said then,
    That is its all-white appearance,
That is the flower of the white branch then.
    And so the ball of rubber
On the blossom of the rope that he is asked for then,
3630   That is money that is in the middle there,
Because of pain arising
    From the blood,
And the motherless
    And fatherless who come there.
3635 (4.) And so the fourth secret word
    Is to be asked of them:

3635. Riddle. Noon double? Invisible shadow. Puppy? Wife. Commandment of our blessed lady? Wax candles.

Ca xic ob ti y otoch

 Ca tun alabac ti ob

He ix ca bin talac ex

 A u ilben ex e

T u kak

 Chumuc kin ual e

Ca put pal ex

 Huk a cah ex

Ca bin uluc ex

 Ti y an a u al pek t a pach ex e

He yx a u al pek ex lo e

 U nachma u pixan ca cilich colel

Ca bin uluc ech y etel

 He ix ca put palil lic y alabal ti e

Kak chumuc kin ca bin xic u cumtan

 Ma u booy

Lay licil y alabal huki u binel

 Ca bin kuchuc y icnal hal ach uinic e

He ix y al pek lic u katabal ti e

 Lay u ch'uplil e

He ix u pixan ca cilich colebil e

 Y ahau *candelas hacha* cib e

Suyua

 Than lae

(31) He ix u ho ch'ic than*

 Bin katabac ti ob e

Bin alabac e ti ob

 Ca xic ob u ch'a ob u picsikal

Ku citbil

 Ti caan

He ix ca bin a tales t en e

 Oxlahun yal u tas

Tij tep'an a pach i

 Y etel çac potz

He ix lay u pucsikal ku citbil lic y alabal ti ob lae

 Lay kan e

He ix u tas lay oxlahun y al lic y alabal e

 Lay y ahau uah e

They go to the house,

 And then they are to be told,

"When you have come

 You should be seen (3640)

In the fire

 Of high noon then.

Appear double,

 Proceeding jointly,

And when you arrive (3645)

 Have your puppy behind you.

And so your puppy may then

 Be burning the commandment of our blessed lady

 Which he shall bring with him."

And the double appearance that is mentioned to him (3650)

Is that exactly at noon he will clear his darkness:

 He will have no shadow,

Which is like saying going jointly.

 Then he arrives at the governor.

And so the puppy that he is asked for, (3655)

 That is his wife,

And the commandment of our blessed lady

 Is the lord's candles of sweet wax then.

Zuyua

 Is this language. (3660)

(5.) And so the fifth secret word

 Is to be asked of them.

They are to be told

 To go get the heart

Of the blessed God (3665)

 In heaven.

"Go then and bring me here

 Thirteen folds covered

Which are wrapped behind you

 With white cord." (3670)

And so this is the heart of God the blessed, as they are told then:

 It is cordage.

And so the cover and the thirteen folds as they are told then,

 They are the lord's tortillas there,

3661. Riddle. God's heart? Cordage. Thirteen folds? Tortillas and beans. White cord? Tortilla cloth.

Top: *Amayte Kauil, lord of Chable (1697–1717).* Middle: *Kak Mo, lord of Teabo (1717–1737).* Bottom: *Mac Chahom, lord of Teabo (1737–1776). From the Garrett Collection of Manuscripts in Middle American Languages, The Princeton University Library, The gift of Robert Garrett.*

Oxlahun y al
    Buul y an ychil e
He ix sasac potz e
    Lay sasac nok e
Lay bin katabac ti ob
    U naatul *suyua*
He ix u uac ch'ic than*
    Bin katabac ti ob e
U binel u ch'a ob u kab choo
    Y etel ox bal hax
Y etel cuxul ak
    Lay bin u ciilte
Yn hanal samal
    Y an u ol yn hantante
Ma y uill ob
    U kuxul u chun cho e cij y
    alabal ob
He ix u chun cho e
    Lay chop e
He ix oxbal hax e
    Lay u ne huh e

3675 With thirteen "folds"
    Of beans in it.
And the all-white cord
    That is an all-white cloth then.
This is what is to be asked them
3680   And the answer, in Zuyua.
(6.) And so the sixth secret word
    Is to be asked of them then:
To go get the ceiba branch,
    And twisted bamboo
3685 And living vine.
    This will be said:
"I eat tomorrow;
    I wish to be fed then.
It is not necessary
3690   That this ceiba root be chewed," so
    they are told.
And so the ceiba branch—
    That is a chuckawalla.
And so the twisted bamboo—
    That is iguana tail then.

3681. Riddle. Ceiba branch? Chuckawalla. Twisted bamboo? Iguana tail. Living vine? Pig intestines. Ceiba root? Chuckawalla tail.

He ix cuxul ak e | 3695 | And the living vine there—
Lay u chochel keken e | | That is a pig's intestines.
He ix u chun cho e | | And so the ceiba root—
U chun u ne chop | | That is the root of a chuckawalla tail:

Suyua | | Zuyua
Than | 3700 | Language.
He ix u uuc ch'ic than* | | (7.) And so the seventh secret word
Bin katabac ti ob e | | Is to be asked of them then:
Bin alabac ti ob | | They are to be told,
Xen mol t en u mac y it tz'onot | | "Go gather me the man of the well bottom,

Ca p'el sasac i | 3705 | Two bright white
Ca p'el kankan i | | And two bright yellow.
Y an u ol yn hante | | I want to eat then."
He ix u mac y it tz'onot lic u katabal ti ob e | | And so the man of the well bottom that is asked of them,
Lay sasac *chicam* e | | That is bright white gourdroot
Ca p'el kankan i | 3710 | And two bright yellow ones.
U natul u chuc | | The explanation is completed:
U chucul u ba tabil cah | | The village official completes the explanation,

Ca pul t u tan ahau | | Then throws it before the lord,
Yax hal ach uinic lae | | The new governor there.
(32) He than ob lae | 3715 | These are the words then.
Ua ma t an u natabal t u men u ba tabil cahob e | | If they have not been understood by the officials of the village then
Okom moltzil ek | | Gone are the myriad stars
Taplay hom akab* | | Adorning the abyss of night,
Ch'a kax | | Seizing the forest
Thantzil y otoch | 3720 | And the sanctity of home.
Okom moltzil hom | | Gone are the myriads of the deep,
Okom bul cum* | | Gone the dark whales
T an chumuc tan cab | | Which are in the middle of the half earth

Y icnal ah al mehenilob | | Among the nobles.
Ah cimil ma u naatic ob | 3725 | The dead do not understand;
Ah cuxtal bin u naatab | | The living will.
Lay bin y anac y okol u ba tabil cahob | | This is to be placed above the officials of the villages.
Lay y et p'isan u hochbilan | | This examination will be concerted
Oheltabal yail | | And precise knowledge
Bin tz'occebal ahaulil lae | 3730 | Will finally unite the lordship here.

3701. Riddle. Man of the well bottom? Gourdroot.
3718. Metaphor. Stars go out: the end.
3722. Pun? *Bul cum* 'black beans' or 'dark whales'.

Lay kaxan u kab t u tan y etel
yuma che
    Ch'a payan u sumil*
Binsabal u cah y icnal ahau

    Yax hal ach uinic
Lay u tz'oc ba tabil

    Lay bin y anac
Y okol u co kin
    U co katun
Bin y ub ob ya
    Ca bin tz'ococ
U ball ob
    U ba tabil cahob
Lay bin y anac t u kin lae
    Hijtz'ebal u than katun

Ca bin tz'ococ
    Ah ox ahau katun*
Chucom u ba tabil cahob
    T u men minanil u naat ob lae

(33) Bay bin uch
    C u chucul u ba tabil cah lae
Kahlay
    Uchebal
U tz'aic ob u hanal yax hal ach
uinicob
    Ca bin u kat ob u hanal ob
Hich'om u cal ob
    Xotom u ni y ak ob
Colom u u ich ob*
    T u kinil lay bin tz'ocebal lae
He x ch'ibal e
    Ti ix u hoksic u ba
T u tan u yum
    Ti caclam pix*
Uchebal y oheltabal
    Y anil u cux olal ob
Ti yx u kubul u poop
    Y etel u tz'am ti ob xan i

Then, tying their hands before them
with a swaying log
    And taking the rope separately,
They will be brought to the village
before the lord,
    The new governor.
3735 This was the end of the village
chieftainship.
    It is to be done
On the mad day,
    The mad *katun*.
They will come to hear exactly
3740   When it will be the end
Of the property,
    Of the officials of the villages.
This is to be done on that day,
    The ending of the word of the
    katun.
3745 Then it will be over,
    The 3 Ahau *katun*,
Ending the office of the villages
    Because of their lack of
    understanding.
Thus will occur
3750   The completion of the village
offices.
This is the record
    Of what occurs.
They give food to the new governor;
    Then they will ask for their dinners.
3755 Knotting their necks,
    Cutting off the tips of their tongues,
Ripping out their eyes,
    That very day will be the end then.
And so the lineages there
3760   Which just present themselves
Before the father
    And kneel
Will achieve knowledge
    And be encouraged
3765 While he is seated on his mat
    And throne by them also.

3732. A graphic enough portrayal of how prisoners were transported.
3746. This dates the passage to 3 Ahau (1618).
3757. Bloodletting was part of the ritual.
3762. Kneeling was an act of submission for the Maya as elsewhere. It is attested in Classic Mayan art.

Seizure of the chiefs, possibly Pat Ay and Op Ik of Valladolid (1776–1800). From the Garrett Collection of Manuscripts in Middle American Languages, The Princeton University Library, The gift of Robert Garrett.

Lay y et p'isan y ilabal	This is the convocation and review,
U hochbilan ci otzil y ilabal	The examination and correct review
U ch'ibal	Of the lineages
Hal ach uinic	3770 Of the governors
Ti luum	In the land
Uay e	Here.
Lay bin cuxlac t u kinil	This is to be the experience of the time.
Lay ix bin kamic yax *Bara* xan*	This also then is to be the taking of new staffs.
Bay tun bin hetz' luum	3775 Thus then will be the seating of lands
Nahbal	And houses
U ch'ibal	Of the lineages
Maya uinicob	Of the Mayan people
Uay	Here
T u cahal *yucatan*	3780 In the region of Yucatan.
T u ca sut lae	And so again here
Dios pay be tz'ocebal	God divides and ends
Uay	This
Y okol cab lae	Our world.
Lay u hahil ahau	3785 He is the true lord
Bin tac u kat t oon	Who is to receive what he wants of us.

3774. Ceremonial staffs are a frequent iconographic emblem of rule in Classic Mayan art.

Coc Ay, lord of Merida, or Kin Chil, lord of Coba (1800–1824). From the Garrett Collection of Manuscripts in Middle American Languages, The Princeton University Library, The gift of Robert Garrett.

Lay ca tepalilob
  Lay ca kulob lae
Tun ob
  Kan ob
Y etel bin katic pakal cij
  Bal che
He mac minan ti e
  Cimsabil
He max bin tzicic e
  Diosil u cah t u than a
Mai uil y oltic D^s.
  Y uchul t u lacal bal tz'iban
  ob lae
(34) Bay xan he ix al mehenob
  U ch'ibal ba tabob
Y ohelma bix talic ob
  U uinicilob
Y etel y ahaulilob
  U tepalob
Ci otzil y ilabal
  U cux olalob
U mek tanma
  U tzicilteil ob

These are our lords.
  These are our gods then,
Their stones
3790 And their harvest.
And he asks for the expected wine
  And mead.
For no one of them
  Is to be killed.
3795 Who would then honor
  God in heaven in prayer?
Is it not the will of God
  That causes everything to be
  written then?
So likewise it is with the nobles,
3800 The lineages of the officials
Who know what will come
  To mankind
And to the lordships
  And the rulers.
3805 Joyful is the sight
  And encouragement
Of the government
  And the rites.

Bin ix cici	So it will be correct
Kubuc	3810 To entrust
U pop ti ob	Their mats to them
Y etel u tz'am ti ob	And their thrones to them
T u menel ca yum	Through our father
Yax hal ach uinic	The new governor.
Lay u pop	3815 That is his mat
Y etel u tz'am	And his throne.
Bax tabi u u ich popok*	Mocked then is the face of the bush;
Chektabi t u u ich luum	Paced off is the face of the land.
Bibil y ab i	Twisted is the year,
T u chocho pay	3820 And dragged apart
U co kin	Is the mad time,
U co katun	The mad *katun,*
Y al x buyuk	The child of the stupid woman,
Y al co	The child of the mad woman,
U mehen kas	3825 The son of the evil man,
(. . . .)*	(. . . .)
Ah ca kin pop	He of the two-day mat,
Ah ca kin tz'am	He of the two-day throne,
U maxil ahaulil	The monkey lordship,
U maax katun	3830 The monkey *katun.*
Lay ximbal	This was their approach
Nah,ob	And settlement
Ychil ah ox ahau	On the 3 Ahau
Katun	*Katun.*
He than bolon buth	3835 These words were rolled and stuffed
Ychil u pucçikal	Into the hearts
U ch'ibal al mehenob	Of the nobles' lineages,
Ahaulil uinicob	The ruling people.
Lic i tac y alabal ti	And they were told
U binel u ch'ab u ba tabil cahob e 3840	To go get the officials of the villages then,
Ca xic	So they went
U ch'ab	And got them.
Mehen e xen ch'a*	(8.) "Son, go get
U lol akab t en uay e	The flower of night for me here,"
Cij uil y alabal	3845 Might just be said.
Ca tun xic ti caclam pix	So then he went and knelt

3817. Three lines were omitted, suggesting a different scansion and a different translation:

Baxtabi	Mocked
Mucluum tabi	And canceled are the lands
U u ich popok	Of the wetfaces (?Christians) . . .

3826. Line missing.

3843. Riddle. Night flower? Star. Evil of night? Moon. Tender wasting vine? (Unclear.) Fig branch? (Unclear.) Big man with nine sons? Big toe. Fat woman with nine children? Thumb. Stones of clearings? Quail.

T u tan hal ach uinic
  Katic ti e
Yum e he yx u lol akab

  Lic a katic t en e
U et talic y etel u kaz akab e

  Tij y an u icnal e
Cij u than
  Ba la mehen e
Ua ti y an a u (35) icnal e
  Ti ua y an
Yax ix tz'oy t a pach e

  Y etel noh copo e
Yum e ti y an u icnal e
  U et ulic
Ba la mehen e ua a u et ulic e

  Xen payal a kob t en

Lay hun tul noh xib e
  Bolon tul u mehen e
Y etel hun tul yx nuc
  Bolon tul y al e
Yum e cij u than
  Ca bin u nucub
U et ulic
  Ua y an t in pach e
Payan be u tal ob t en
  Ca t ul en yn u il ech
Ba la mehen e
  Ua y an t a pach e
Xen molob t en u tunichil chakan

  Y etel ob ca tac ech
U lotma ob t u tzem
  C u talel
Ua hal ach uinic c ech ib e
  Ua t ech u ch'ibal ahau
Uay
  Ti luum be
Suyua
  Than
He yx u lol akab
  Lic u katabal ti e
Ek
  Ti caan

Before the governor
  Who asked him.
"Father, here then is the flower of
night

3850 As you have asked of me.
It comes together with the evil of
night here
  Which is with it."
He just says,
  "What's that, son!
3855 If you have it with you,
  If you do have it,
It is the tender wasting vine on your
back
  And a large fig branch, then."
"Father, they are with me;
3860 They came together."
"What's that, son! If you came together
then,
  Go separate your companions for
me.
There is one big man there
  With nine sons there,
3865 And one fat woman
  With nine children there."
"Father," he just says,
  "Then it will mean
It just came together.
3870 It should be on my back then.
They came separately to me,
  Then I came to see you."
"What's that, son!
  If it is here on your back
3875 Go gather for me the stones of the
clearings,
  And with them then come near.
He squeezes them to his breast
  As he comes.
Either you are governors
3880 Or you are of the lord's lineage
Here
  On the road of the land."
Zuyua
  Language.
3885 And so the night flower
  That he is asked for then
Is a star
  In the sky.

He x u kaz akab e	And so the evil of night—
Lay u e	3890 That is the moon then.
He x yax ix tz'oy e	And the tender wasting vine
Y etel noh copo e	And the large fig branch,
Lay ah cuch cab e	That is the bearer of the earth,
Otlom cabal u kaba e	The filling of the earth, as it is
	called then.
He x hun tul noh xib	3895 And so the big man
Lic u katabal ti e	That he is asked for
Lay bolon tul u mehen e	Who has nine sons then—
Lay u naa y occ e	That is the big toe there.
He ix hun tul yx nuc	And so the fat woman
Lic u katabal ti e	3900 That he is asked for,
Lay u naa u kab e	That is the thumb.
He x u tunchil chakan	And so the stones of the clearings
Lic u katabal ti e	As he is asked
Y etel u lotma u mehe	With children squeezed together—
Lay u beche e	3905 That is quail.
Bay xan mehen e*	(9.) "So then too, sons,
C ex a yax haan alab i t ech	Hold out your first food to be born
	to you.
Ma alan a pac te u u ich e	Unborn you see its face."
Ua y an	"It is here
T in pach e	3910 On my back,
Yum e	Father."
Ba la mehen e	"What's that, son!
Xen ch'a t en	Go bring me
Y ibnel caan uay e	Here the placenta of heaven.
Ti a talel ti lakin	3915 When you come to the east,
Ca bin tac ech e	When you are nearly there,
Cuch pach	Put it behind you
U tal t ech	And bring it."
Cay baac be yum e	"Wherefore even so, father,"
Cij u than	3920 So he says.
He x u yax haan	And so the first food
Ti y an t u pach	Which is on his back
Ca ti kuchi e	When he arrives there—
Lay u pach caa e	That is squash rind.
He x u y ibnel caan e	3925 And so the placenta of heaven then
Lic u katabal ti e	Which is asked of him,
Lay patbil pom e	That is shaped incense,
Oxlahun ual u patal	Thirteen pieces to the pack.
He ix licil y alabal ti e	And then as he is told
Cuch pachil u talel ti e	3930 To put it behind him and bring it:

3906. Riddle. First food? Squash rind. Placenta of heaven? Incense. Bring it behind you, close behind the sun? Shadow at noon.

Te y an u boy t u pach e
   Tzelep kin cochom
Mahen e hal ach uinic ech*
   Ah tepal ech i xan
Xen tun
   Ch'a t en
A yax *cuentex* e
   Licil a pa(36)yal chi e
He x u yax *cuentex* e
   Lic u katabal ti e
Lay kan e
   Ca tun katabac
Ti tun ua ba hun kin c u payal chi
   Yum e c u than
T u hun te kin c in payal chij
   Y etel t u lahun kin c in payal
chij
Bal x kinil
   Licil a nacsic a payal chij
Yum e t u bolon kin
   Y etel t u y oxlahun kin
Bolon ti ku
   Y etel oxlahun ti citbil
Lay licil yn xocic
   Yn *cuentex* e lo e
Mehen e*
   Xen ch'a t en a u ex
Yn uui u booc uay e
   Y etel nach u boocc e
U booc yn u ex e
   U booc yn nok e
U booc yn y ub ak e
   Pay num u boc
T u tz'u caan e
   Y etel t u tz'u muyall e
Y etel yn yax pakab che e
   Y an ti çac hoth e
Ua hal ach uinic ech i
   Be
Yum e bin yn tales
   Cij u than
He x u boc y ex
   Lic u katic e

There is his shadow behind him,
   To be clearly close beside the sun.
(10.) "Son, you are a governor
   And you are a ruler as well.
3935 Go then
   And bring me
Your green beads,
   As you are praying."
And so the green beads
3940   Asked of him,
That is a hammock.
   So then he is to be asked
How many days he prays.
   "Father," he says,
3945 "I pray for one day
   And I pray for ten days."

"What then are the days
   When you raise your prayer?"
"Father, the ninth day
3950   And the thirteenth day,
To the nine gods
   And the thirteen spirits.
That is when I count
   My beads perhaps."
3955 (11.) "Son,
   Go bring me your pants
That I might smell their scent here,
   And the burning of their scent,
The scent of my pants,
3960   The scent of my clothes,
The scent of my incense vine,
   The great scent
At the center of heaven,
   At the center of the clouds.
3965 And my green nance plants
   Which have white seeds.
If you are a governor
   So be it."
"Father, I shall bring it,"
3970   So he says.
And so the scent of pants
   That he is asked for,

3933. Riddle. Green beads? Hammock. Days of prayer? 9 and 13.
   3955. Riddle. Scent of pants? Incense. (Incense was kept burning by fanning it with the flap of one's kilt.) Green nance seeds? Ground cacao.

Lay pay num   That is the great scent
 T u tz'u caan e   At the center of heaven:
Lay pom e thabbil   3975 It is incense there in the fire
 Elel u cah   Beginning to burn.
He x yax pakab chi   And so the green nance plants
 Lic u katic e   Requested:
Lay muxbil cacau   That is ground cacao
 Cho u ua e   3980   In cocoa then.
Ba la mehen e*   (12.) "What's this, son!
 Xen tales t en   Go bring me
U yax kikel yn u ix mehen e   The fresh blood of my daughter,
 Y etel u pol e   And her head,
Y etel u hom tanil e   3985 And her entrails,
 Y etel u chac bacel e   And her thigh,
Y etel u kab e   And her arm,
 Y etel lay ualah a ma cab   And there lay out your persons
Ti suhuy cat e   Who are virgin descendants.
 Y etel u yax kan che e u ix   3990   And the new throne of my
 mehen e   daughter—
Et es t en   Show them to me together:
 Y an u ol u ilab   I want to see them.
Uch yn tz'ab   As I have been given it
 T ech   By you
Lic i uil y acal t in tan e   3995 While you stood before me
 Lic i uil u u akal u okol e   As I cursed and wept."
Cay bacac be yum e   "Wherefore even so, father."
 Y et tal u tz'iic u xicin ah bol   "And bring with it the left ear of a
                                              wild bee,
Ca beh y etel ca tun xic tun   The next day, and when it is clear."
 He x u yax kikel y ix mehen   4000   And so the fresh blood of his
                                              daughter,
Lic u katic lo e   Which he may ask for—
 Lay maya cij e   That is Mayan wine.
He x u hom tanil (37) y ix mehen e   And so his daughter's entrails,
 Lay u hobonil cab e   That is the honeycomb.
He x u pol y ix mehen e   4005 And so the head of his daughter,
 Lay u suhuy cat e tz'amlic cij e   That is a virgin jar to steep the wine.
He yx u yax kan che y ix mehen e   And his daughter's new throne,
 Lay u co uoh tun cab e   That is the contained glyph stone of
                                              the land.
He x u tz'ic u xicin ah bol e   And the left ear of the wild bee
 Lay u sulil cij e   4010   Is the dregs of the wine.

3981. Riddle. Daughter's blood? Balche. Daughter's entrails? Honeycomb.
Daughter's head? Wine jar. Daughter's throne? Glyph stone. Left ear of the wild
bee? Dregs of the wine. Daughter's bone? Last of the mead. Daughter's thigh?
Balche tree. Daughter's arm? Balche branch. Cry? Speak hoarsely.

He x u bacel y ix mehen e
    Lay u holil bal che e
He x u chac bacel lic y alic e
    Lay u cheel bal che e
He x u kab y ix mehen e
    Lay u kab bal che e
He yx licil y alic y okol e
    Calhal u than
Ca tun xic u tz'ab ti

    T en cul u ba
Ch'u u than
    Tescun u than ca bin kuchuc

Yum e he lay a u ix mehen a
    A tz'ah yn canante lic a u alic
C ech yum e
    C ech ah tepal e
Cij tun u than u mehen ti e
    Bee mehen e
U et hal ach uinicil e
    U et ah tepalil e
Kahaan baca t ech
    A u ohel baca
Cij u than
    Lay tun u kikel u ix mehen
Lic yn katic t ech lae
    Oxlahun num tun
U manel u kikel y ix mehen u
tan tun
    Y okol y ix mehen ti che lic t u
    tan cabal
Hijj ci
    Tun y okol
Ta muk y ilic t ichin
    Lic ta muk u than
Bee mehen e
    Cij tun u than ta muk y okol
Hal ach uinic ech e
    Bee mehen e ah tepal chi xan
Bee u et hal ach uinicil e
    Bin tun yn kub a pop
Y etel a tz'am
    Y etel a u ahaulil c ech mehen e
A ti al tepal
    A ti al ix ahaulil xan c ech
    mehen e

And the bone of his daughter,
    That is the last of the mead.
And the thigh that is mentioned
    Is the balche tree.
4015 And the arm of his daughter,
    That is a branch of balche.
And as he is told to cry,
    His speech is hoarse.
Then when it is going to be given to
him
4020 He has seated himself.
Sweet is his speech.
    Welcomed is his speech when it
    comes.
"Father, here indeed is that daughter
    You gave me to protect, as you said,
4025 O father,
    O ruler."
So speaks the son to him.
    "Yes, son,
Fellow governor,
4030 Fellow ruler,
Remember you are a child.
    You know the child."
So he says,
    "Here then is my daughter's blood
4035 As I asked you."
    Thirteen minutes then
The daughter's blood is passed before
the stone,
    Over the daughter in the log as
    before the earth,
The jar of wine
4040 With the stone over it.
While he looks inside it
    As he speaks.
"Yes, son."
    So he says then while he is over it,
4045 "You are a governor then.
    Yes, son, you are a ruler now also.
So we are fellow governors.
    Then I shall confer your mat
And your throne
4050 And your lordship upon you, son.
Yours is the rule;
    Yours is the lordship also, son."

Bay tun bin tz'ocebal
  U thanal u ba tabil cahob

Ca bin lukucc ob
  Y icnal yax hal ach (38) uinic
Te
  T u pol peten e
Ca tun xic ob ti y otoch
  Tij tun y an ti y otoch ob
T an u tz'aic u hanal ob hal ach
uinic
  T an ix u katic u hanal ti ob xan

Bay binebal
  U tzolic lae
Mehen e ca a tales t en*
  Can cot
Chac tz'itz'ib
  Y an tu hol ac tun e

T in uatal
  Y okol yn yax pakab chi
Chacnicen i uil
  Ualic u p'ut
Y okol yn yax pakab chi e
  Ca bin kuchuc
T in tan e
  Cay bacac be yum e
He ix lic u katic e
  Lay ciui e
He x u put lic u y alic e
  Lay y om chuc u ua e
He x u yax pakab chi e
  Cacau tz'ocan u huch'ul
Suyua
  Mehen e ca a tales t en*
U ch'ich'il akab
  Y etel u hoch'il akab
Y et tal
  U tz'omel caan
Hach y an u ol
  U ilab uay e

Thus then will be the completion
  Of the speech of the officials of the
  villages,
4055 When they are to be removed
  Together with the new governor
There
  At the head of the land.
So then they go home.
4060 Then when they are in their homes
There is the giving of their food to the
governors,
  And there is the request of food
  from them also.
Thus is the progression
  Of the count.
4065 (13.) "Son, go bring me
  The four eagles
And the red cardinal
  That are in the bottom of the
  spring.
I shall put them
4070 Over my green tonsils.
Boil up the moon
  And stand a pile of it
Over my green tonsils.
  It is to be brought
4075 Before me."
  "Then it will be so served, father."
And what it is he is asking for
  Is red food coloring.
And the pile that he mentions
4080 Is chocolate foam.
And his green tonsils
  Are cacao that has been ground.
Zuyua.
  (14.) "Son, go bring me
4085 The birds of night
  And spoons of night
And let there come with it
  The brains of heaven.
I have a great desire
4090 That they be seen here."

4065. Riddle. Four eagles? (Unclear.) Cardinal? Red food coloring. Pile of boiled
moon? Chocolate foam. Green tonsils? Ground cacao.
    4084. Riddle. Night birds? Burning incense. Night spoons? Cordage. Brains of
heaven? Incense.

Cay bacac yum e
    He x lic u katic e
Lay hoyob e
    Licil u tocabal pom e
He x u hoch'il akab lic u katic e
    Lay kan e
He x u tz'omel caan e
    Lay pom e
Suyua
    Than
Mehen e ca a tales t en*
    U bacel a yum
Lay a mucah ox p'el hab hi e
    Hach y an u ol
U ilab
    Cay bacac yum e
He x lic u katic e
    Lay tz'ijn e pibbil
Ca xic tz'abil
    Ti hal ach uinic
Mehen e ca a tales t en*
    Hun tul noh xib
Lay ma kalan u bo tonil
    U ha bon e
Hom
    Tochac u kaba e
Cay bacac be yum e
    He x lic u katic e
Lay ybach e
    Yx uech e
Mehen e ca a tales t en*
    Ox buh caan
Y an u ol yn hantante
    Cay bacac be yum e
(39) He x
    Lic u katic e
Thohob çac a e
    Lay om çac a e
Suyua thanil
    Bin katabal t u lacal
Mehen e ca a tales t en u chun cij*
    U cucutil cij

"Then it will be so served, father."
    And what it is that he requests
Is sprinkling
    And burning incense.
4095 And the spoons of night he asks for
    Is cordage.
And the brains of heaven
    Is incense.
Zuyua
4100   Language.
(15.) "Son, go bring me
    The bones of your father
That you buried three years ago.
    I have a great desire
4105 That they be seen."
    "Then it will be so served, father."
And what he is asking for
    Is manioc, baked.
Then it will be served
4110   To the governor.
(16.) "Son, go bring me
    A grown man
Without grabbing his high balls,
    His water sac;
4115 Sunk
    And impotent is his name."
"Then it will be so served, father."
    And what he is asking for
Is armadillo
4120   And armadillo meat.
(17.) "Son, go bring me
    Three slices of heaven.
I have a desire to eat it."
    "Then it will be so served, father."
4125 And what it is
    That he is asking for
Is bowls of corn gruel—
    That is corn gruel foam.
In Zuyua language
4130   Everything is requested.
(18.) "Son, go bring me maguey root,
    The bottom of the maguey

4101. Riddle. Father's bones? Manioc. Buried? Baked.
4111. Riddle. Grown man? Armadillo. High balls? Scent glands. Water sac?
Scent glands. Sunk and impotent? Converted into cooked meat.
4121. Riddle. Slice of heaven? Bowl of corn gruel.
4131. Riddle. Maguey root? Boar's head. Heart? Tongue.

Minan u kab i
  Ma a luksic y oll i
Y et tal ox thothol
  Y oc tzitzil
Cay bacac yum e
  He ix lic u katic e
U pol keken
  Pibbil
Ca bin xic tz'abil ti e
  He x y ol lic y alic e
Lay y ak e
  T u men he y akbal e u y ol

Suyua
  Mehen e ca a tales t en*
U cosil akab
  Yn hantante
Cay ba ac yum e
  He ix lic u katic e
Pollos
  Ah thel
Suyua
  Mehen e ca a u al*
Ti yax yx tz'oi
  Otlom cabal u kaba e
Ca u tales t en
  Hun xuxac pich'um
Ti u chucul y alan noh copo e
  Ti banan t u boy copo e

Cay bacac yum e
  He x lic u katic e
Eek buul
  Ti y an ti y otoch ah cuch cab e

Lay yax tz'oy e
  Y etel otlom cabal e
Lic y alic e
  Suy.
Mehen e ca xic chucbil*
  U balamil ac tun
T a menel u ciillte yn hanal
  Y an u ol yn hantante balam

That has no hands.
  Don't remove its heart.
4135 And also bring line-paw,
  Sliced-foot."
  "Then it shall be so served, father."
  And what it is that he is asking for
Is a boar's head,
4140 Baked.
Then he will go and bring it to him.
  And the heart, as he calls it,
That is the tongue,
  Because that is a symbol for his
  heart.
4145 Zuyua.
  (19.) "Son, go bring me
Hawks of the night
  For me to eat."
  "Then it will be served, father."
4150 And what it is that he is asking for
Is chickens,
  Cocks.
Zuyua.
  (20.) "Son, go speak
4155 To the first little old lady
  Named Fallen to the Ground
That she might bring me
  A large basket of blackbirds
Which are all under the big fig tree,
4160 Which are piled up in the shadow of
  the fig tree."
  "It will be served, father."
  And what it is that he is asking for
Is black beans
  That are in the house of the owner
  of the lands:
4165 That is the first little old lady,
  And Fallen to the Ground
That he mentions—
  Zuyua language.
  (21.) "Son, go and get
4170 The jaguars of the spring
So that you can sweeten my food.
  I have a desire to eat jaguar."

4146. Riddle. Night hawks? Roosters.
4154. Riddle. First little old lady? The landowner's wife. Large basket of black-birds? Black beans. Fig tree? (Perhaps ceiba tree.)
4169. Riddle. Jaguar of the spring? Agouti.

Cay bacac be yum e
  He x balam
Lic u katic e
  Lay haleuu e
Suyua than
  Mehen e ca a tales t en*
Uuc y al u pix
  Yx ma yum
Y an u ol
  Yn hantante
T u kin i
  Uil u hantabal e
Cay bacac yum e
  He x lic u katic e
Lay tz'otob
  Chay e
Mehen e ca a tales t en*
  Yax tzublalob uay e
Ca tac ob ti okot
  Yn chaante
Y et tal ob u pax
  Y etel çoot
Y etel u ual
  Y etel u kab u pax
Lay yn pakob
  Cay bacac yum e
He x lic u katic e
  Ah tzo
He x u pax e
  U koo
He x u çoot e
  U pol
He x u ual e
  U ne
He x u kab u pax e
  U chac bacel
Suyua than
  Mehen e ca a tales t en*
U caz peten
  Y an u ol yn han(40)tante
Cay bacac yum e
  He x lic u katic e

"It shall be so served, father."
  And the jaguar
4175 That he asks for,
  That is agouti.
Zuyua language.
  (22.) "Son, go bring me
Seven knee babies
4180   And orphans.
I have a desire
  To eat them
At the beginning
  And end of my dinner."
4185 "It shall be served, father."
  And what it is that he is asking for
Is stuffed leaves
  Of cabbage.
(23.) "Son, go bring me
4190   Green dandies here.
Let them come dancing
  So I can watch it.
And bring with them drums
  And rattles
4195 And fans
  And drumsticks.
These are my expectations."
  "It shall be served, father."
And what it is that he is asking for
4200   Is turkeys,
And their drums
  Are their pouches,
And their rattles
  Are their crests,
4205 And their fans
  Are their tails,
And their drumsticks
  Are their thighs.
Zuyua language.
4210   (24.) "Son, go bring me
The stink of the country.
  I want to eat it."
"It shall be served, father."
  And what it is that he is asking for

4178. Riddle. Knee babies and orphans? Stuffed cabbage leaves.

4189. Riddle. Green dandies? Turkeys. Dancing? Turkey strutting. Drum? Turkey craw. Rattles? Turkey crests. Fans? Turkey tails. Drumsticks? Turkey thighs.

4210. Riddle. Stink of the country? Honey. Possibly a pun on *cab* 'honey, land' is implied and there is also a pun with *kab* 'juice'.

U kabil
  Cab
Suyua
  Mehen e ca a tales t en*
U tun chil chuh cab
  Lay elel e
Y et talel y alil i
  U chebal
Yn tupic uay
  Ix u xicil t in tan e
He x
  Lic u katic e
Pibil
  Maçal
He x y alil e
  U ti al u tupic e
Lay u kabil
  Cab e
Suyua than
  Mehen e ca a tales t en*
Akab coc ay lay hun xaman

  Hun chikin u man u booc
Y et talel u letz
  Ak balam
Cay bacac yum e
  He x lic u katic e
Chamal
  He x u letz
Ak balam lic u katic e

  Lay kak e
Mehen e ca a tales t en*
  A u ix mehen yn u ilab
Lay hach çac hatz'en u u ich e
  Hach cich pam e
Çaçac u booch'
  Y etel u kax i
Hach y an u ol ti
  Cay bacac yum e
He x lic u katic e
  Sac luch y etel tzun e
Çac a e
  Suyua

4215 Is the juice
  Of honey:
  Zuyua.
    (25.) "Son, go bring me
  The stone in burning hot honey.
4220   It is to be burning.
  And bring with it the juice
    Of its tree
  So I can extinguish it here,
    And take it apart before me."
4225 And what it is
    That he is asking for
  Is oven-baked
    Yams.
  And the juice
4230   To put it out
  Is the juice
    Of honey.
  Zuyua language.
    (26.) "Son, go bring me
4235 The night firefly that is far to the north.
    Far to the west passes its odor.
  And bring with it the signal
    Of the tongue of the jaguar."
  "It shall be served, father."
4240   And what it is that he is asking for
  Is tobacco,
    And the signal
  Of the tongue of the jaguar that he asks for
    Is fire.
4245 (27.) "Son, go bring me
    Your daughter for me to see.
  Have her face wrapped all in white.
    She is very beautiful.
  Brilliant white is her shawl
4250   And her sash.
  I very much want some."
    "It shall be served, father."
  And what it is that he is asking for
    Is a white bowl with chicken
4255 In corn gruel.
    Zuyua.

4218. Riddle. Stone? Yam. Burning? Baked. Juice (to put it out)? Honey.
4234. Riddle. Night firefly? Cigar. Jaguar tongue? Fire.
4245. Riddle. Daughter? Chicken. White dress? Corn gruel.

Mehen e ca a tales t en*
   Sa bel u kaba e
Lay samacnac u booc e
   Cay bacac be yum e
He x lic u katic e
   Lay *milon* e
Mehen e ca a tales t en*
   Yax yx lochen cal
Yayax u pach
   Y an u ol yn hantante
Cay bacac yum e
   He x lic u katic e
U cal ah tzoo
   Suyua
Mehen e ca a tales t en*
   Hun tul ch'uplal hach çac
Uouol u p'ul y oc
   Uay yn silic u pic
T u p'ul y oc e
   Cay bacac be yum e
He x lic u katic e
   Chicam
He x u silic u pic e
   U tz'ilic u pach
Mehen e ca a tales t en*
   Hun tul ch'uplal hach cich pam
Hach çac u u ich
   Hach y an u ol tij
Uay yn pulic u pic
   Y etel y ipil t in tan e
Cay bacac be yum e
   He x lic u katic e
Hun cot
   Yx tux ulum u hantante
He x u pulic u pic o
   (41) Y etel y ipil e
Lay u thocol
   U kuk mel e
Ca tun kaktabac
   U ti al hanal
Suyua than
   Mehen e ca a tales t en*

(28.) "Son, go bring me
   A swollen bald, as it is called,
And it should be redolent in odor."
4260   "It shall be served, father."
And what it is that he is asking for
   Is a melon.
(29.) "Son, go bring me
   A green and curve its neck—
4265 Very green on the back.
   I want to eat it."
"It shall be served, father."
   And what it is that he is asking for
Is the neck of a turkey.
4270   Zuyua.
(30.) "Son, go bring me
   A woman with very white
Well-rounded knees.
   Here I'll roll up her petticoat
4275 To her knees."
   "It shall be served thus, father."
And what it is that he is asking for
   Is gourdroot.
And what it is to roll up her petticoat
4280   Is to peel its rind.
(31.) "Son, go bring me
   A woman who is very pretty
With a very white face.
   I very much want one.
4285 Here I'll throw down her petticoat
   And blouse in front of me."
"It shall be served so, father."
   And what it is that he is asking for
Is a hen
4290   And a hen turkey to eat.
What it is to throw down her petticoat
   And blouse—
That is the plucking
   Of its pin feathers,
4295 And then the meat is cooked
   For eating.
Zuyua language.
   (32.) "Son, go bring me

4257. Riddle. Swollen bald? Melon.
4263. Riddle. A green? Turkey neck.
4271. Riddle. Plump woman? Gourdroot. Roll up her petticoat? Peel it.
4281. Riddle. Pretty woman? Turkey hen. Undress her? Pluck her.
4298. Riddle. Guardian of fields? Yam.

Hun tul ah canan col
  Noh xib uay e
Y an u ol u ilab u u ich
  Cay bacac be yum e
He x lic u katic e
  U cucutil macal u hantante
Tz'a nat
  Mehen e ca a tales t en*
Yx canan col
  Yx nuc ek
Tun lah u uinicil e
  Uuc nab u tan y it te
Y an u ol u ilab
  He x lic u katic e
Lay u yax ych
  Tz'ol e
Suyua
  Than
Bin kuchuc u kin
  Hele ti kin
T u pochektah ca yum
  Yax hal ach uinic lae
Lic i tac y ulel uay
  Ti luum
T u lumil
  Yucal peten lae
C u payic ba tabob
  Ca bin tac ba tabob
Payal u cahob t u men ca yum
  Hal ach uinic
T ex*
  Ua ba tab e
T on i be
  Yum e
Ci uil
  U than ob lae
Mehen ex e
  Ua t ex hal ach uinic
Uay
  Ti luum
Lac ci uil
  Y alabal ob lae

A guardian of the fields,
4300   A grown man here.
  I want his face to be seen."
    "It shall be served so, father."
  And what it is that he is asking for
    Is the body of a yam to eat,
4305 Giving the explanation.
    (33.) "Son, go bring me
  Also a keeper of fields,
    A black old lady—
  Then all her people,
4310   Seven palms across the bottom.
  I want it to be seen."
    And what he is asking for
  Is the green fruit
    Of the squash.
4315 Zuyua
    Language.
  The day is to arrive.
    That then is the day
  For the imposition of our father
4320   The new governor then,
  Just as he is about to arrive here
    In the land
  In the territory
    Of the Neck of the Country.
4325 And he separates the officials;
    Then he will change the officials,
  Dividing up the towns by our father
    The governor.
  (34.) "And you,
4330   Are you officials?"
  "We are,
    Yes, father."
  Right at the moon
    These are their words.
4335 "You, sons,
    Are you the governors
  Here
    In this land?"
  Right at the moon
4340   These things are said.

4306. Black old lady, guardian of fields? Green squash.
4329. Riddle. Jaguar? Horse. Jaguar's wing? Horse's chest. Jaguar's necklace?
Rattles. Piles? Saddle blanket.

Xen ex ch'a xiknal balam

    Ca tac ex a tz'ab ex yn hante
Cicij tz'a ex y u ob
    Cicij tz'a ex u p'ut oob
Ca tac ex a tz'a ex yn hante
    Y etel xen ex tac t u sebal hach
hel e
Y tac a tal ex e mehen ex e
    Hach y an yn u ol yn hante
C ex mehen ex e
    C ex hal ach uinic ex e
He ob x ma y ohel e
    Otzilhom
U tucul
    Y etel u pacat
Be ma bal bin y alab
    He yx y ohel ob e
Cil mac y ol
    Ca bin xic u ch'ab xiknal balam

Ca tun tac
    Y etel
T ech ua mehen e
    T en i be yum e
T ech ua ch'ibal e mehen e
    T en i be yum e
C ex a lak ob e mehen e
    Yum e ti y an ob ti kax e
U xachet ob balam e
    Minan balam t u than (42) ob
Ca tun u manes t u tan
    He x lic u katic e
Lay balam e
    U tzimin ah ba tabil u kat u
hante
Lay tzembil tzimin e
    He x y u e
Lay *cascabeles* e
    He x u p'ut e
Lay chachac kuch e
    Cici tz'abil
Y etel u *silla*
    Y etel u *freno*
Suyua
    Than.

"Come on and take the wingspread of
the jaguar.
    Approach and accept my food.
Kindly give the necklaces.
    Kindly give the piles.
4345 Approach and give it to me to eat.
    And go so as to hasten the great
change.
And so come, you sons,
    I have a great desire to eat.
O you sons,
4350   O you governors.
And they who know
    No poverty
Think
    And watch.
4355 Thus nothing will be said
    And indeed they will know.
Gladly
    They will go to take the jaguar's
wing,
So then they approach
4360   Together."
"Is that you, son?"
    "It is I, yes, father."
"Are you of the lineage, son?"
    "I am, yes, father."
4365 "Do you have your companions, son?"
    "Father, they are in the wild
Searching for jaguars.
    'There is no jaguar,' they said."
And then it is brought before him
4370   And what it is that he is asking for,
That jaguar
    Is a horse that the official asks
to eat.
That is the chest of a horse.
    And the necklace
4375 Is rattles,
    And the piles
Are bright red cloths,
    Sweetly given
With its saddle
4380   And bridle.
Zuyua
    Language.

31. Additional Riddles

(67) Oxlahun etz'nab uchc i*
  U hetz' cab

On 13 Etz'nab there occurred
  The seating of the land.

Oxlahun chen eb uchc i
  U chektabal *ygleçia mayor*

4385 On 13 Ch'en (13) Eb there occurred
  The pacing of the great church

Ti can akab naa
  Yglesia mayor ti caan

In the 4 Akab house,
  The great church in heaven.

Bay ca chektabi
  Uay xan e

Thus it was paced off
4390 Here also.

Oxlahun te katun
  U cuch lahun chekbij

The thirteenth *katun*
  Had the burden of ten paces.

Caan can chek lukci i
  Bolon chekeb tun u cuch c u
  binel canal e*

On high four paces had gone by,
  Nine paces were then the burden to
  come on high,

He ix ca ca put chektabi
  Likul t u u ich luum e

4395 And that is the two-by-two pacing
  Rising from the face of the earth:

Can chekeb
  Ca hek t u u ich luum i*

Four paces
  Then branch off from the face of the earth.

4383. The pattern of dates that follows does not have a definitive solution and appears to contain at least two errors. The day Eb can never fall on a day 13 Ch'en (line 4385). And I believe line 4392 should read *ox lahun* '13' rather than *lahun* '10'. Even without this second correction, however, lines 4393 and 4394 clearly place us in *katun* 3 Ahau (1618). I have searched in that *katun* for a point at which these dates might make some sense. I find it in 1620. In that year 13 Etz'nab 5 Uayeb was the day before the beginning of the Mayan year on 1 Cauac 1 Pop. The first occurrence of a day Eb would be thirteen days after that, on 1 Eb 14 Pop. The only occurrence of the day Eb in the month of Ch'en would be on 5 Eb 14 Ch'en and the next day would be 6 Ben 15 Ch'en. Perhaps this is the date intended in line 4385, but its significance is not obvious. The Julian date would be December 21, which was considered the midpoint of the Mayan year (see line 1365). Thus the dates 13 Etz'nab and 13 Ch'en may refer to the beginning and the middle of the year 1620. (Parenthetically it may be noted that if we correct this date to the Gregorian calendar we reach December 31. There is no evidence that the Maya used the Gregorian count before the nineteenth century.) A final consideration relates to the assertion that the seating of the land occurred on 13 Etz'nab. It should have occurred at the seating of the *katun* in 1618. It may be significant that Akbal is the fourth day after the beginning of the months in 1620, while Eb is nine days after that. However, the only occurrence of 4 Akbal in that Mayan year falls on 4 Akbal 5 Ceh, or January 22, 1621, the eve of Candlemas. This text is identified in line 4547 as having been composed in Mani. It may indicate that the Mani sun priests of the 1620s were not what they had been.

4394. I read this as a *katun* date: 3 Ahau was the fourth *katun* in the cycle that began with 11 Ahau, leaving nine *katuns* to go to complete the cycle.

4398. I believe the two-by-two pacing refers to the seating of the direction priests, two of the foot and two of the hand (note 3127).

*Map of Yucatan (1618). From the
Garrett Collection of Manuscripts in
Middle American Languages, The
Princeton University Library, The
gift of Robert Garrett.*

He Manii e		This is Mani,
Chun peten*	4400	The base of the country.
Campech		Campeche
U ni xik peten		Is the wingtip of the country.
Calkini		Calkini
U chun u xik peten		Is the base of the wing of the country.
Ytzmal	4405	Izamal
U chumuc u xik peten		Is the middle of the wing of the country.
Çaci		Valladolid
U ni xik peten		Is the wingtip of the country.
Conkal		Conkal
U pol peten	4410	Is the head of the country.
Chumuc cah		The middle city
Ti hoo		Of Merida
Yglesia mayor		Is the primate church,
U kakal na		The fiery house,
U uitzil na	4415	The mountain house,
Akab na		The night house,
U uil u		The moonphase of the moon
Dios yumbil		Of God Made Father,

4400. The metaphor of the geography of Yucatan as a great bird is reasonably accurately applied.

Dios mehenbil	God Made Son,
Dios espiritu santo 4420	And God the Holy Ghost.
Mac x oc t u nail *Dios* e*	(35.) "And who entered into the house of God?"
Yum e lay ix kalem u kaba e	"Father, that was the Radiant Lady by name."
Bax u kinil takc i*	(36.) "What was the time of bearing
T u nak suhui ch'uplal e	From the womb of the Virgin Girl?"
Yum e canil oc takci 4425	"Father, 4 Oc was the bearing
T u nak	Of her womb."
Mehen e bal x kinil hokc i*	(37.) "Son, and what was the time he appeared?"
Oxil oc hokc i	"3 Oc he appeared."
Bal kinil cimc i*	(38.) "Which day did he die?"
Hun cimil cimc i 4430	"1 Cimi he died.
Be ti ix oc i	And thus it was
T u mucnal ti hun cimi e	He was buried on 1 Cimi."
Bax oc t u mucnal*	(39.) "What came to the burial?"
Yum e maben tun oc t u mucnal	"Father, a stone coffer came to the burial."
Bax oc t u chac bacel* 4435	(40.) "What entered into his thigh?"
Yum e lay chac haal tun e	"Father, that was a large arrowhead
Lay oc t u tunil cab	That entered into the stone sent down
Te ti caan e	From heaven."
Cun x u kab e	"And whence is its name?"
Yum e halal tun 4440	"Father, the arrowhead.
Lay ix lic u kinbeçabal	It is like the sunrise.
Xan	Also
Lay oc ti chac cui tunil	That enters into the red hard stone;
Bin ti lakin	It went to the east.
(68) Ca tali te ti xaman e 4445	Then it went to the north;
Lay oc ti çac cui tunil	That enters into the white hard stone.
Lay ix ti oc ti ek cui tunil	And that enters into the black hard stone
Ti chikin	In the west,
Bay ix ti kan cui tunil	And thus into the yellow hard stone
Ti nohol 4450	In the south."

4421. Riddle. Who entered the church? The Virgin Mary.

4423. Riddle. When did the Virgin Mary conceive? 4 Oc. (This is the center of the first of the four Burner cycles.)

4427. Riddle. When was Christ born? 3 Oc. (This is 220 days after 4 Oc.)

4429. Riddle. When did Christ die? 1 Cimi ('death').

4433. Riddle. What came to Christ's burial? A stone coffer.

4435. Riddle. What entered Christ's thigh? An arrowhead. What was the name of the arrow? The sunrise, which pierces hard stone to the east, north, west, and south.

Mehen e hai p'el kom okop*
   Lay licil y auat chul chultah e

Mehen e tab y an tz'onot*
   Lah tz'am y alil e
Minan u chichil y it e
   Ti tacan chulul
T u hol e
   Lay ku na e
Mehen e c ex yax *casamientosob*
e*
   Lub u muk *rey* t u men ob e

Y etel ix lubci u muk
   U chi y anil hal ach uinicob e
T u menel ob e
   Y etel lay ob ix in muk
T u men ob xan
   Lay uah e
Mehen e t a u ilah ua yaxal haal
tun e*
   Ca p'ell ob e
Ti uaan *crus* chumucc e

   U u ich uinic
Mehen e tub x y an ob ah yax oc
haob e*
   Y anil hun tul yx ma na
Y an y u e
   Y an ix u tzitz moc xan
Lay peeu e
   Y etel x ma yum e
Mehen e c ex x top'lah kauil e*

   Y etel u tz'omel cootz'
Tz'oc yt peeh e
   Y etel kulim pak i

(41.) "Son, how many pits in a ditch?"
   "That is like the sounds of a flute
   being played."
(42.) "Son, where is the cenote
   Completely drenched in water;
4455 It has no stopper in the bottom
   To keep it from leaking
On one's head?"
   "That is the god's house."
(43.) "Son, and even first marriages?

4460   Rested is the strength of the king by
   them
And also rested is the strength
   Of the time of the governors
By them;
   And they are my strength too,
4465 Also because of them."
   "That is food."
(44.) "Son, have you seen whether the
waterholes are green?
   There are two of them.
There stands a cross in the middle of
them."
4470   "Men's eyes."
(45.) "Son, and where are the first
baptized?
   There is one and she has no mother.
She has a necklace
   And she has a speckled ribbon too."
4475 "That is dwarf corn,
   And she has no father either."
(46.) "Son, and even the sprout of the
deity
   With his brains rolled?
It has the bottom puckered
4480   And is a bitter plant."

4451. Riddle. How many pits in a ditch? As many as notes on a flute.
4453. Riddle. What is a cenote with no plug? The church. (Because it drips water.)
4459. Riddle. What are the first marriages that refresh everyone? Food.
4467. Riddle. What are two green waterholes with a cross between them? Eyes.
4471. Riddle. What is the first baptized orphan with a necklace and a speckled ribbon? Dwarf corn.
4477. Riddle. What is God's sprout that's bitter and has rolled brains and a puckered bottom? A turkey gizzard.

U tuchil ulum
   Mehen ex e taleç ex t en*
Hokbah caan
   Y etel hokob co e
Ceh
   Y etel ba
Mehen e cex ix nuc*
   Uuc nab u tan y it e
X ek tunlah ch'uplal e
   Lay tz'ol e
Mehen e yl ex t en çaclah ch'uplal*
   Ueuel uak u pic i
Lic u conic çac tok e

   Lay ca e
Mehen e taleç ex t en ca cot ix kan*
   Hun cot chochacbil i
Hun cot ti x bin xotoc u cal i

   Bin ix uuk ich u kikel xan
Yx kaan ceh
   Y etel yax luch
Y anil chuc ua
   Mehen ex e uleç ex t en*

Hun kal ah kochcinil tunob uay e
   Y etel ca tul *casadosob* e
Bech'
   Y etel mucui
Mehen e tales t en çum*
   Ox bal u haxal
Yn kat in u ila e
   Lay huh e
Mehen e tac (. . .)ci*
   Paac tanal
U ilab uay e
   Lay ci e

"It is a turkey gizzard."
   (47.) "You, son, bring me
The ties of heaven
   And the ties of teeth."
4485 "Deer
   And gopher."
(48.) "Son, and even a fat old lady
   With a seven-palm rear
And a dark-skinned girl?"
4490 "That is flat squash."
(49.) "Son, find me a light girl
   Dressed in a full skirt
As though she were selling white knives."
   "That is grindstone squash."
4495 (50.) "Son, bring me two eagles, yellow ones,
   And one eagle bright red;
One eagle which is to have its throat cut
   And its blood is to be drunk too."
And it is a grown deer
4500   And a fresh gourd
Of chocolate.
   (51.) "You, son, have me brought here
A score of bearers of flat stones
   And two married people."
4505 Quail
   And doves.
(52.) "Son, bring me a rope
   Three strands wide.
I want to see it."
4510   That is iguana tail.
(53.) "Son, (bring something?)
   Folded in half,
To be seen here."
   That is henequen.

4482. Riddle. Ties of heaven? Deer. Ties of (i.e., many) teeth? Gopher.
4487. Riddle. Fat old lady with a seven-palm rear? Flat squash. Dark-skinned girl? Flat squash.
4491. Riddle. Light girl in a full skirt selling white knives? Grindstone squash.
4495. Riddle. Two yellow eagles? Grown deer. Red eagle with its throat cut and we drink its blood? A fresh gourd of chocolate.
4502. Riddle. Bearers of flat stones? Quail. Two married people? Doves.
4507. Riddle. Three-strand rope? Iguana tail.
4511. Riddle. Something folded in half? Henequen.

Mehen e bin a taleç ex u mac u hol caan*

   Y etel yebal uay e

Bolon tas lah cab

   Noh uah

Mehen e t a u ilah ua*

   Ah noc xamach

Noh xib e

   Hach noh u ko e

Hoctan u tal ti luum e

   Lay ah tzo e

Mehen e tales t en ah canan colob*

   Noh xibob

Hun tuch u tal u choon e

   Y etel y atan e

T ix mumil chac

   Tal e cex uay e

Y etell ix ah canan col ch'uplalob e

   Bin çaclah ch'uplalob e

T en ix bin luksic u picob y okol e

   Ca tun in hante

Lay *chicam* e

   (69) Mehen e tales t en*

Noh tzublal yn chaante

   Ma u ill ob y okot ob

Ca bin in u ilab e

   Lay ah tzo e

Mehen e c ex yax ah mol e*

   Pul nok

Y etel pul *camissa* e

   Y etel çuyem

4515

4520

4525

4530

4535

4540

(54.) "Son, go and bring me the man who pierces the sky

   And the fog here,

And the nine layers of the whole earth."

   It is a large tamale.

(55.) "Son, have you seen

   The raiser of the griddle,

The grown man?

   He has a very large pouch

And sitting down he comes along the ground."

   That is a turkey cock.

(56.) "Son, bring me the guardians of fields,

   The grown men

Whose craws come to their crotches

   And their wives

Are cheery and big.

   Bring them here

And also the guardians of fields of girls.

   It will cheer up the girls

That I shall raise their skirts up over them

   And then I'll eat (them)."

That is gourdroot.

   (57.) "Son, bring me

A great dandy for me to look at.

   I haven't seen them dance,

And I am going to have them seen."

   That is a turkey cock.

(58.) "Son, and even the first collector?"

   Throw off your clothes

And throw off your shirt

   And cape

   4515. Riddle. Man who pierces the sky, the fog, and the underworld? Large tamale.

   4519. Riddle. Raiser of the griddle? Turkey cock. Grown man with large pouch? Turkey cock. Who walks sitting down? A strutting turkey cock.

   4525. Riddle. Guardians of fields with their craws to their crotches? Gourdroot. Men with big cheery wives? Gourdroot. Guardians of fields of girls? Gourdroot. Lift up their skirts? Peel them.

   4536. Riddle. Great dandy? Turkey cock. Great dancer? Turkey cock.

   4541. Riddle. Who was the first collector? Man. (Demonstrated by shedding clothes.)

Y etel p'oc

   Y etel xanab e

Mehen e tab ech ti mani*

   Ti ua ti man ech

Ti canal buk tun e

   Nixbebal

U hol caan e

   Y anil u hol paa e

He ca ti man e chi e

   T a u ilah ua uinicob

Tzayan ob

   U talel ob t a tan e

Ti y an bolon

   Chaan

Y etel yax

   Ah kulel e

U kulil ych

   Y etel u uabal tz'amil ich

Mehen e t a u ilah ua*

   U kaxal y aal ku e

Ti mani y alan u uitzil ku e

   Tij x ti oc y alan u uitzil ku e

Ti y an *cruz* i

   Ti chakan i

Coop nebal caan tii

   Ti mani y aal ku i

Mehen e tab x c u manel y aal ku e

   Te c u hokol cui tun e

Yum e u hool uinic

   Y etel yukul co uinic t u manel

T u u ol u cal uinic

   T u hokol t u chun e

Mehen e max t a u ilah ti be

çam e*

   (. . . . .)*

4545 And hat

   And sandals.

(59.) "Son, where are you in Mani?

   Which of you is it who passes

By the high year stone

4550   With some kind of grapes

As doorman

   And having a hole in the wall?

When it is that you have passed by it

   You may see people

4555 Looking for something

   Passing in front of you.

Who is there is great

   And small

And young

4560   And official."

The socket of the eye

   And a pair of eyeballs.

(60.) "Son, have you seen

   The dropping of the water of God?

4565 That passes under the mountain

of God

   And that is what enters under the

mountain of God

Which has a cross

   On the flat part.

Curled and pointed is the top of it,

4570   Which passes the water of God.

Son, and where will the water of God

pass

   Where the hard stone appears?"

"Father, the man's head

   And all the man's teeth will it pass

4575 To the middle of the man's throat

   And appears at the bottom."

(61.) "Son, whom did you see on the

road awhile ago?"

   (. . . . .)

4547. Pun. Mani (town name): *man* 'pass'. Riddle. What is it that is near the high stone with grapes for doormen in the hole in the wall that sees everybody? Eye sockets and eyeballs.

4563. Riddle. God's water goes under a mountain over a hard stone: what are they? Head and teeth. (The question is incomplete.)

4577. Riddle incomplete.

4578. Line missing.

Mehen e tab x t a mançah a lakob*

    Tzayan u talel ob t a pach ob e   4580
He in lakob lae
    Ma t an in patab
Lay in mucut u xot kin *Dios* e

    Ca bin cimic en e
He lay   4585
    U booi uinic e
Mehe mac x t a u ilah ti be*

    T a u ilah ua noh xibob y an palal
    t u pach ob e
Yum e he noh xibob
    T in u ilah ti be e   4590
Ti y an ob t in pach
    Ma ix t an u p'atben ob e
Heklay u naa oc
    Y etel y alob e
Mehen e tab x t a u ilah ix nucob*   4595

    Y an u mek u çacal ob
Y etel u lak palal ob e
    Yum e he x lae
Tii to y an t in pach licil yn hanal
    Ma y to uchac yn p'atic   4600

U naa yn kab
    Y etel y alob
Mehen e tab x ti man ech y anil y
oc haa e*
    Yum e he y oc haa e
Ti yx y an te u icnal e   4605
    Heklay u bel yn pach e
Mehen e tab x t a u ilah noh xib*

    Kaan y okol tzimin e
Ch'acat nebal y oc haa e
    Yum e he x noh xib lae   4610

(62.) "Son, and where did you send
your neighbors
    Who were coming right behind you?
These were my companions;
    I wasn't being waited upon.
That is my anticipation of the
judgment of God
    When I shall die."
And those
    Are a man's shadows.
(63.) "Son, and whom did you see on
the road?
    Did you see grown men with
    children on their backs?"
"Father, these were the grown men
    I saw on the road.
They are here behind me
    And they have not abandoned me."
Meaning the big toe
    And the little ones.
(64.) "Son, and where did you see
grown ladies
    Having embraced their stepchildren
With their other children?"
    "Father, that is this:
What it is I have in my grasp as I eat,
    And that is not something I could
    abandon:
My thumb
    And its little ones."
(65.) "Son, and where is it you went to
have a water ditch?"
    "Father, this is the water ditch
And it is here on me.
    It means the spine of my back."
(66.) "Son, and where did you see a
grown man
    Mounted on a horse
Across the point of a water ditch?"
    "Father, this is the grown man here.

4579. Riddle. Where did you send your neighbors? To the judgment of God.
Who are the companions behind you? Our shadows.

4587. Riddle. Grown men with children on their backs? Big toes and little ones.

4595. Riddle. Grown ladies with children? Thumb and fingers. (What I'm eating
with.)

4603. Riddle. Where is your water ditch? My spine.

4607. Riddle. Man on a horse at the head of a ditch? My back: it holds a
grown man.

Tiy to y an u icnal e

   Heklay u tzimin yn pach e

(70) Lic a u alic

   Kalic noh xib e

Mehen e he x noh xib

   Y an t a pach

Lic a u alic

   Be chican

Hahil

   Y etel tohil

Mehen e xen ch'a u pucçikal

tunich*

   Y etel u tamnel luum

Te uil

   Kin c ilic çamal e

He ix u ilah hun p'elli e hauaan

   He ix hun p'eli e nocaan

Bay u binel

   Ychil *mitnal* e

Heklay haleu e

   Y etel tzub e

Y etel yax ba tab

   Y etel yax ah kulel e

He x u ti al u pucçikal tunich e

   Heklay u ni cob

Y etel u mac u u ol

   U cal *mitnal* e

Heklay is

   Y etel *chicam* e

Mehen e ca xic ech a ch'ab ix hal is

co uay e*

   Hun cuy ual u pol e

Hach cich pam ix lok bayan

   T en i

Bin lukçic u pic

   Y etel u bucc e

Çamacnac uil u boc

   Ca bin yn lukes u bucc e

What it is I have on me.

   It means the horse is my back.

As you say,

   It holds up a grown man."

4615 "Son, and that grown man

   Who is on your back

As you say,

   Has thus manifested

Truth

4620   And right."

(67.) "Son, go get the heart of a stone

   And the liver of the earth.

There is the moon phase

   (And the) sun they will see

   tomorrow.

4625 I see one face up

   And one face down.

Thus he will go

   Into hell."

Meaning a paca

4630   And an agouti,

And a new official

   And a new assistant,

And that is because the heart of a

stone

   Means the crowns of the teeth

4635 And the man of the middle

   And the throat of hell

Means sweet potatoes

   And gourdroot.

(68.) "Son, go then and get a real sweet

potato tooth here

4640   With a soft fan on its head,

A very beautiful young girl.

   And I myself

Am going to remove her skirt

   And clothes.

4645 One should only perhaps smell her

fragrance,

   Then I'll take off her clothes.

4621. Riddle. Heart of a stone? Teeth. Liver of the earth? Paca. Moon phase?
New assistant. Tomorrow's sun? New official. One sliced and one sprinkled? (Possibly agouti.) Man of the middle? Sweet potato. Throat of hell? Gourdroot. This
riddle is garbled and incomplete.

4639. Riddle. What is a beautiful young girl with sweet potato teeth, a fan on
her head, and I'm going to take off her clothes? Baked green corn.

Hach cilmac yn u ol yn ca bin u ilab
   Çamacnacil u bocc e
Y etel hun çuyil u pol e
   Heklay pibil nal e
Mehen e ca tun xic ech a chab
noh xib*
   Y etel u xiuil tanil kaknab e
He x noh xib lae ac
   Y etel ix bau
Mehen e ca tun xic ech a ch'aab
u tunichil y it kax ek e*
   Lay ah tzatzac e
Mehen e ca tun xic ech a ch'aab u
tunichil chakan uay e*
   Lay bech' e
Y etel yax ah menob e*
   Ca tul ob t u ba
Heklay baa
   Y etel tzub
Y etel haleu
   Y etel citan e
Mehen e ca xic ech a ch'ab u
chac bacel luum*
   Lay tz'in e
Mehen e ca xic ech a ch'aab yax
tzublal uay e*
   Y etel yax kayomob e
Cutz
   Y etel h tzoo
Mehen e bin a u ules a u ix
mehen e*
   Te y an kin çamal u ilab e

Payan be bin talebal u tz'etz'il e
   Pach hebal bin talebal u nohol e

I am delighted that I shall see her
   And with the fragrance of her scent
And a tuft on her head."
4650   Meaning baked green corn.
(69.) "Son, go then and get a grown man

   And the grass of the seashore."
And that grown man is a turtle
   With a crab.
4655 (70.) "Son, go then and get the rocks of
the bottom of a dyewood tree."
   That is sardines.
(71.) "Son, go then and get the rocks of
the meadow here."
   That is quail.
(72.) "And the first shamans
4660   Who shelter themselves?"
Meaning gopher,
   Agouti,
Paca,
   And wild pig.
4665 (73.) "Son, go get the thigh of the
earth."
   It is cassava.
(74.) "Son, go get the green dandy here

   With the green singers."
Curassow
4670   And turkey cock.
(75.) "Son, you will have your daughter
brought here.
   There is time tomorrow for her to
be seen.
First off shall be brought the little one,
   After that shall be brought the
big one.

4651. Riddle. Grown man of the seashore? Turtle. Grass of the seashore? Crab.
   4655. Riddle. Rocks of the bottom of a dyewood tree? Sardines. (Presumably refers to a cenote fish.)
   4657. Riddle. Rocks of the meadow? Quail.
   4659. Riddle. First shamans who shelter themselves? Gopher, agouti, paca, and wild pig.
   4665. Riddle. Thigh of the earth? Cassava.
   4667. Riddle. Green dandy? Turkey cock. Green singers? Curassow. (See line 4536.)
   4671. Riddle. No answer given.

Ca ix cici kaxac u kax pol e	4675 And then her head should be nicely tied up
Ti kukmil kax	With a (quetzal) feather tie.
Ti y an uil u boch' e	She may perhaps have a shawl.
T en i to uil bin luksic u boch' e	It may perhaps be I who remove her shawl,
Y etel ti y an ah kulel t u pach e	And she has an official behind her."
(. . . . .)*	4680 (. . . . .)
(71) Mehen e ca tun xic ech a ch'ab*	(76.) "Son, go then and get
Un crus nicte	A cross of flowers
Kutz' ben e	All dressed up at the moon
Te uil kin çamal e	Of the sun tomorrow."
Kelbil yxim	4685 Toasted corn
Y etel cab	And honey.
Mehen e uay t in cucyah a pectzil e*	(77.) "Son, here have I rolled, you are aware,
Yan yan cootz'	Many many rolls
Ti ac tun y an a u icnal e	In the stone holder you have on you.
Ca ix a cucles c ilab uay	4690 And when you have rolled it for us to see here
T u kin tzil hanal e	It may be cooked and cracked to eat."
Tzabbil hee.	An opened egg.

4680. Line missing.

4681. Riddle. Cross of flowers all dressed up by sundown? Toasted corn and honey.

4687. Riddle. What is it that is rolled in a stone holder that you have on you and that you cook and crack to eat? An egg.

32. Astronomical Notes

(26) He ca bin kuchuc lay kin*	This is when it shall be arriving, this day:
T u buluc pis *Junio* e	On the eleventh measure of June
U cha	4695 Is exactly
Ucil kin	The longest day.

4693. As Roys 1967: 86, note 3 observes, this text is preceded by a small cross, perhaps indicating that the content is Christian, which it is. Dating the chapter is problematic: it contains no direct hints. The author had assimilated Spanish astronomy and had also played cards with a Spanish deck (line 4740), but uses few Spanish words. Placing it in 3 Ahau is frankly impressionistic. Its dating of the solstice in the Julian calendar is *post* 1600.

The course of the sun (1618). From the Garrett Collection of Manuscripts in Middle American Languages, The Princeton University Library, The gift of Robert Garrett.

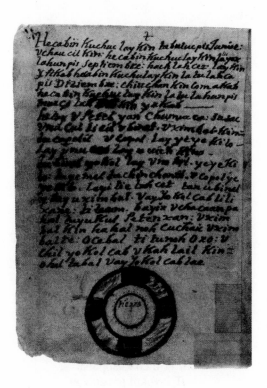

He ca bin kuchuc lay kin

    La t u y oxlahun pis *Septiembre*

Hach lah
    C et
Lay kin
    Y etel akab
He ca bin kuchu lay kin

    La t u lahca pis *Diziembre*

Chiic chan kin
    Com akab*
He ca bin kuchuc lay kin

    La t u lahun pis *Março*

Lah
    C et
Kin
    Y etel akab

This is when it shall be arriving, this day:
    On the thirteenth measure of September
Very full
4700   And equal
Are the day
    And the night.
This is when it shall be arriving, this day:
    Then on the twelfth measure of December
4705 Appears the small day
    And short night.
This is when it shall be arriving, this day:
    That is on the tenth measure of March.
Full
4710   And equal
Are the day
    And the night.

4706. Roys 1967: 87 has '(but) the night (begins to) shorten', which is correct, but that's not what the text says.

He lay u petel	There is here a circle
Y an chumuc	That is in the middle.
Ca sasac	4715 It is all white,
U nucul	Meaning
Licil u binel	That during the coming
U ximbal kin	And going of the sun
T u ca p'elil u copoi	On its second loop,
Lay y eyekil o	4720 That is its darkening.
Lay u nucul	That is the explanation.
Lay u u ich kin o	That is the nature of the sun.
T u binel y okol	It goes around
Lay u nohol y eyekil o	And the south darkens it.
T u y emel	4725 It descends.
T u chinchanil u copol y eyekil o	It appears smaller on the loop of darkness.
Layi lic lah	And this is how it gets full
C et	And equal.
T an u binel	It goes
Y etel lay u ximbal	4730 And then it comes:
Uay y okol cab li	That is just around the earth here
Li xan e ti luum	And just also the land.
Bay ix u chacaanpahal	And so it is made to appear
T u yukul peten xan	Over the whole of the country too.
U ximbal kin	4735 The path of the sun
Hahal noh*	Is really south.
C u ch'aic u ximbalte	It goes
Ocebal	And it comes
Ti	There
T u noh oro*	4740 To the Gold south,
Uchil y okol cab	Occurring around the world
U kahlail kin	As the account of the sun
Oheltabal uay	As it has been made known here
Y okol cab lae	On this earth.
(27) Eclipse del sol*	4745 Eclipse of the sun:
U chibil kin	The eating of the sun.
(Medio mundo)	Half world:
(Tan buh y okol cab)	Half division of the world.
Ti xiblalob t u xaxob	For men at the sides
Y an lay hun buh a	4750 There is this one section;

4736. Roys 1967: 87 has 'is truly great', which is possible, though from the Yucatecan perspective it moves a good deal farther south than it does north.

4740. I agree with Roys 1967: 87, note 1 that the reference is to the Gold suit in a Spanish deck of cards. But yellow is the Mayan color of the south, and I think that's the connection.

4745. Lines 4745 and 4747 are in Spanish; the alternate lines are the Mayan translation. The Spanish appears in the accompanying illustration.

Top: *Solar eclipse (1618)*. Bottom:
Solar and lunar eclipses (1618).
*From the Garrett Collection of
Manuscripts in Middle American
Languages, The Princeton University
Library, The gift of Robert Garrett.*

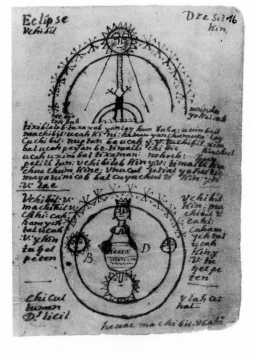

U uinbail		As in the drawing
Ma chibil u cah kin i		The place of the sun is not eaten.
He tun y an chumuc o		But when one is in the middle
Lay c u chibil		Then it is eaten.
Nup' tam ba cah	4755	Opposing each other the earth place
Y etel u t u chibil		And the moon, it is eaten.
Ximbal u cah payan be		Moving position somewhere else
Ti mai li chibic		Then it is just not eaten.
Kuchul u cah		It arrives in place
U ximbal ti xaman nohoch	4760	And goes north big
Hun p'elil i		One time
Tun		Each *tun*.
U chibil ob kin		Eclipses of the sun
Y etel u		And moon
Ti mai li kuchuc	4765	May not occur
Chum kin e		At noon.
U hucul		It is explained
U ti al y oheltic maya uinicob		So that the Mayan people may understand
Bal c u y uchul ti kin		What happens to the sun
Y etel ti u lae.	4770	And the moon.
U chibil u*		The eclipse of the moon:
Ma chibil u cah i		Its place is not eaten.

4771. The remaining text appears on the illustration.

Cah tzam ych		The earth consumes its face,
Tal u cah u		Coming to the place of the moon,
Y etel kin	4775	And the sun
T u tzel peten		Is at the (other) side of the land.
U chibil kin		The eclipse of the sun:
Ma chibil u cah i		Its place is not eaten.
Cah am ych		The earth consumes its face,
Tal u cah kin	4780	Coming to the place of the sun,
Y etel u		And the moon
T u tzel peten		Is at the (other) side of the land,
Chicul		Demonstrating
T u men Dˢ.		By God
Licil u lah	4785	When it is exactly
C et hal		Equal.
He uac		However,
Ma chibil u cah i.*		The earth is not eaten.

4788. Roys 1967: 88 translates lines 4783–4788 as 'a sign from God that they are in conjunction but are not eaten'.

I Ahau

33. Caesar Augustus and the Chan War

(93) Primero

Hun ahau katun*		*Katun* 1 Ahau
U uuc tz'it katun	4790	Was the seventh part of the *katun*.
Emal		Emal
U hetz' katun		Was the seat of the *katun*.

4789. This text is preceded by the notation *primero* and the accompanying illustration says 1640. These are late and erroneous additions. But the text itself is also wrong: this is the sixth *katun*, and it began in 1638. This was the last *katun* in which Merida attempted to claim the lordship. The Tizimin lists Puc Ha, Ol Ha, Ual Icim, Amayte Kauil, Hun Pic, and Can Ul among the claimants to power. The Chumayel gives Puc Ol, Ox Ual Ac, Hun Pic, and Caesar Augustus. How many of these actually claimed to seat the *katun* is not clear, and the guerrilla military companies were also active. Both versions mention the Chan War, centered in Tihosuco. The Mani version, much abbreviated, omits that and the names of the leaders but agrees that both Merida and Emal seated the *katun* (Craine and Reindorp 1979: 81–82). The illustration shows a crowned and bearded lord of the *katun*, a cross, a dog, a flag, and a forceps holding an extracted tooth.

Amayte Kauil, lord of Merida (1638–1658). From the Garrett Collection of Manuscripts in Middle American Languages, The Princeton University Library, The gift of Robert Garrett.

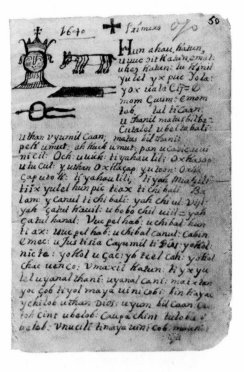

T u kinil y ulel yx puc y ol a   And at that time came Puc Ol
   Y etel ox ualacij   And the third priest Ual Ac.
Emom çuum   4795 Descended was the cord,
   Emom tab   Descended was the rope.
Tal ti caan u thanil   Come from heaven was the word
   Ma tusbil be   Of the undeviating path
C u talel u beltabal i   Which is coming to be fulfilled,
   U than u yumil caan ma tusbil   4800 The word of the Father of Heaven is
   than i   not false.
Pek u mut   Dog is its news;
   Ah kuch u mut*   Buzzard is its news.
Pan u ca tz'ic u uinicil   Flags were the second part of the people.

   Och u u ich ti y ahaulili*   A Possum was the face in the lordship.

Ox kasap u tucul   4805 Three divisions were its thought
   Y etel u than   And its word.
Ox kaçap y etel u toon   Three divisions with its secret;
   Ox kaçap u tok   Three divisions were the knives

4802. Dogs and buzzards are about equally obnoxious in the Mayan view. The former are associated with fornication and the eating of excrement and the latter with carrion.

4804. Flags and Possums were among the military companies opposing the nobility.

Ti y ahaulil i		In the lordship,
Ti y ah miatzil i	4810	In the sage's office.
Ti ix y ulel		And that was the coming
Hun pic ti ax ti chibal i*		Of Hun Pic of Ax by descent,
Balam		(As) Jaguar,
Y etel can ul ti chibal i		And Can Ul by descent,
Y ah chi ul uijl	4815	Biting spirits of the coming need,
Y ah çat ul kauil		Destroying spirits of the coming deity,
U bobochil uiil*		The Many Skunks of need,
Y ah çatul hanal		The destroying spirits of the coming food.
Uuc p'el hab u chibal hun ti ax		Seven years was the term of Hun Pic of Ax;
Uuc p'el hab u chibal can ul	4820	Seven years was the term of Can Ul.
Ca bin emec		Then will descend
U *justisia*		The justice
Ca yumil		Of our Father
Ti *Dios*		Who is God
Y okol nicte	4825	Over the flowers,
Y okol u çac yb teel cah*		Over the white lima bean town,
Y okol chac uen co		Over the red nightmare
U maxil katun*		Of the monkey *katun*.
Ti yx y ulel u y anal than i		And that will be the arrival of the existing word,
U y anal can i	4830	The existing teaching.
Ma ix tan y occ ob		But they will not half enter
Ti y ol maya uinicob i		Into the hearts of the Mayan people.
Bin kayac		There will be preached
Ychil ob		To them
U than *Dios*	4835	The Word of God
U yumbil caan		The Father of Heaven,
Ca u tohcint u bel ob		When they are made right in their ways,
Ca u pachint t u lobil u bel ob*		When they return to the evil of their ways,
U nucil i		Meaning
Ti maya uinicob	4840	That the Mayan people

4812. I am unable to locate (Ti) Ax, but it appears to be a place-name.

4817. The Many Skunks were another military company.

4826. Zac Ib Teel cah 'white lima bean trees town' is unidentified.

4828. Roys 1967: 155 reads *chac uen co* as 'lewd rogue' and *maxil katun* as 'rascal'. I think the reference is to a *katun* of bloodshed and peasant warfare. *Katun* also means 'war'.

4838. Roys 1967: 155 has 'turn their backs upon their evil ways', but *pach* 'back' is an intransitive verb in itself.

Ma u kat (94) y ub ob
  U than *Dios* e
E na yumbil ob
  Ah xot kinn ob e
Bin ix okomac y ol ob
  U hal ach uinicil bal cah
Tz'etz'ec ocan ti y ol

  Ma ix ocan ti y ol xan i e

Ba la t a than e
  Hun lukul*
Ah cici olal
  U balamil cab e*
Haxom kaak
  T u chicul maya çuhuy e
Hunnab ku
  T u çuhuyil hunab *yglesia*

Ti y auat i
  La u y ub
U than u yumil caan
  U yumil y okol cab
Bin ix okomac y ol bal cah

  Tuçinil ti tali e
Pecnom u xik cab

  Pecnom chumuc cab

Ti tali u kinil
  Ti jx y emel u tzicil ob
Ah ben tana tz'ulob i*

  U than *Dios*

Ox muc bin emebal u *justiçia*

  Ca yumil ti y okol bal cah i
Ti jx y emel noh katun

  Y okol u çac yb teel cah i*

	Did not want to listen
	To the Word of God,
	Their mothers and fathers
	And judges.
4845	And it will depart from the hearts
	Of the governors of the world.
	A little bit has entered into their hearts,
	But it hasn't entered into their hearts too.
	Whatever was said
4850	Something turned
	The believers
	Into animals.
	Fire was twisted
	Into a sign of the Mayan Virgin,
4855	The Sole God
	Into the virginity of the Sole Church.
	It was argued
	That what was heard
	Was the Word of the Father of Heaven,
4860	The Father of the World.
	And it will depart from the hearts of the world
	And falsehood will enter.
	Informed will be the wings of the land—
	Informed will be the middle of the land
4865	That coming
	Is the time.
	And that would be the descent of their reverences
	The missionary foreigners of the Word of God.
	Three times will be the descent of the justice
4870	Of our Father over the world.
	And that will be the descent of a great war
	Over the white lima bean town,

4850. Literally '(was) one separation (of)'.
4852. Or 'into jaguars of the land', i.e., partisans of the lords of the *katun*.
4867. I read *ah ben tan a* 'those who go before the water', meaning catechists who preach before baptism.
4872. See note 4826.

Oheltabal ua hal ach
  Chich y oc olalob i
Ti jx y emel ah mek tan

  U sih hoyic u u ich
U cuyil cab
  U maxil katun
U ch'uyum thulil cah*
  U ch'amacil cah
Ti ix y ulel
  U ma xul ahau i
U xot u tabil u cuch num ya lae

  Xotom ahau
Ti x y emel u koch t u lacal tal
ti caan
  U koch bal cah tusinil
Kin tun y aabil
  T u pach
Y an to t u kin
  Hunnac tzuc ti cab
Hun kal hom y ala ah canan çus

  Ah canan kaknab
Ah uaymil
  Bay ah emal
Ox much hom y ala
  T an kaknab u tz'oc katun

Bay y ili u beltabal
  T u kuchul u uutz' katun e

Ti x u cham ua pan i
  Ti jx u hitz'
U tza ciçin i
  Antacristo i*
Lom
  Tok tza
Hoc
  Mucuc tza
Tz'on
  Bacal tza

Making known whether the governors
  Were strong believers.
4875 And that will be the descent of the
tumpline chiefs,
  The birth of sprinkling the faces
Of the bewitched lands
  Of the monkey katun,
The Hanging Rabbit towns,
4880   The Fox towns.
And that will be the arrival
  Of the permanent lords,
The cutting of the ties of the burden of
suffering
  And cut lords.
4885 And that will be the descent of the tax
on everything coming from heaven,
  The tax on the lying world.
The calendar round
  Was later.
There will be one then
4890   To unite the parts in the land,
One to embrace the waters of the
guardian of sand,
  The guardian of the sea,
The Uaymil
  And the Emal alike.
4895 Three waterspouts
  Were on the sea at the end of the
katun.
Thus is seen the achievement
  Of the coming of the fold of the
katun.
And that was the deed of the Flags.
4900   And that was the end
Of the removal of the devil,
  The Antichrist.
Stabbing
  And knives were removed.
4905 Uprooting
  And burial were removed.
Shot
  And shells were removed.

4879. Hanging Rabbits and Foxes were other peasant guerrilla companies. They
were to be cured by baptism, which the lords of the Xiu found very advantageous.
It is not accidental that we move on to a mention of taxation (line 4885).
    4902. For the devil and Antichrist, read Itza.

Cum
    Tan tza
Puch'
    Tun tza
U hitz'ibte katun lae
    Tan y ol che
U kamic u matan
    Çeçar Agusto
Che
    (95) Tun
Cimil
    T u men uiih
Ocnak u chil
    Ma ya cimlal
Okom bul cum
    Y etel y ax cach
T u ho can be
    T u ho can heleb
Alan y itz'inil
    Tz'itz'i mehen
Tali
    Ti bal cah ij
Ti ix y ulel ahau
    Ti naatal nat ti
Nacom u u ich
    U mehen ku
Ti jx y ulel *obispo* i

    Santo quiçiçion u kaba
Y etel *Saul* u kat ok olal
    Y etel *christianoil*
U tz'o çitz'il
    U tz'oc numçah ya ti bal cah
He ix bin tz'occebal u thanil e

    Noh katun
Likom chan
    Y etel ho tzuc chakan*
Ti bateel
    U chan katun
Hun ahau
    Katun
Kakal
    Moçon chac u cuch katun

Darkness
4910   And ashes were removed.
Mashing
    And stoning were removed.
The *katun* was to be ended.
    And among the trees
4915 There took his request
    Caesar Augustus.
Sticks
    And stones,
Death
4920   From hunger,
Rape occurring,
    And painless death.
Departed is the bean gourd
    And the green fly
4925 From the gate of the four crossroads,
    From the gate of the four changers.
Born are the younger brothers.
    The lusting heirs
Are come
4930   Into the world,
And that will be the arrival of the lord
    Who will riddle him,
A captain person,
    A son of God.
4935 And that will be the arrival of the
bishop,
    The Holy Inquisition by name.
And Saúl, who wants religion
    And Christianity.
He ends lust
4940   And ends the suffering of pain on
earth.
And that will be the ending of words:
    The great war.
Risen will be the Chan
    And the Tihosuco plain,
4945 Who will fight
    The Chan War
Of the 1 Ahau
    Katun.
Fires
4950   And hurricane rains are the burden
    of the *katun.*

4944. Roys 1967: 157, note 9 imports five divisions from Merida for the occasion but I believe (Ti) Ho Tzuc 'in five divisions' is Tihosuco. Chakan is indeed the province of Merida, but it is also 'plain' in general.

•

Tzolen chaccil	Count the rain priests
Thul	And Rabbits.
Caan chaccil	The four rain priests
U lobil katun*	Are the evil of the *katun*.
Hun ch'ic	4955 A silence
Xulil y ocçah	Finally fell.
Ti jx y emel u cuch tza i	And that brought down the burden of removal,
Ti y emel patan i	Which was the descent of tribute.
Ti jx u katabal	And that was the demand
Prouar i	4960 For titles,
Y etel uuc çap y ibnel cab*	And the seven armspans of the navel of the earth,
Ti u hach chichtal u tanlabal	Which greatly fortified the *Dios*
Dios i	party.
U tz'oc u kamic u takin	It wound up that he got his money,
Antachristo	The Antichrist.
Ma tal i	4965 He didn't come,
Antacristo	The Antichrist:
Ma u kat ca yumil	It was not desired by our Father
Ti *Dios* i	Who is God.
Ma u satal katun lae	That war was not forgiven here
Uay tac petenil	4970 In this country,
T u men ca sihnalil*	Because we are native born
Lay peten lae	To this country.
He u chun lay *antachristoil* lae	That is the origin of this Antichristianity:
Tz'utul tz'uttil	Avarice.
He ix ma tac kul uinicob e	4975 And that is (because) people are not nearly gods:
Minan toc lukçah	They are not free to leave.
Minan çitz'il	There is no desire
Y etel pachil t u kikel u lak uinic	Or design for the blood of fellow humans
T u muk ah num ya	To force suffering,
T u muk c u hanal hun hun tul	4980 To force us to eat each other.
He c u talel e	Oh, that will happen
Ho p'el u ich che	The five maskers

4954. That is, the "orthodox" Xiu confronted the double threat of the Itza rain priests and the peasant Rabbit company. They were not so Christian that they had ceased to fear the power of the Chacs to bring down fire storms.

4961. The Spanish tribute was the mainstay of the Christianized Maya, especially when it was based on land surveys. I think the *uuc zap y ibnel cab* are 'the seven armspans of the navel of the earth': seven measures of the productive land, measured for tax purposes.

4971. Presumably the pagan Maya accused the Christianized ones of being foreign born.

Ti u hannal cab coh i*   Who ate the Earth Lions:
  Ah ben tena*   The missionaries.
Be la tun ya   4985 Wherefore it is pain
  T u y ol u yumil caan   To the heart of the Father of Heaven,
Ix pom   And incense
  Kak u tz'oc u than katun   And fire that end the word of the
                                               katun.
Likom katun *Habana*   Raised is the War of Havana,
  Oxlahun bak chem lae.*   4990   Of the thirteen-sail ships.

4983. Seemingly a reference to a specific attack on the Kinkajous or Pottos (the Earth Lions) by five masked Itza.
4984. See note 4867.
4990. So far as I can determine, ships of thirteen sails were not built before the late eighteenth-century frigates. I believe this reference, the War of Havana, Saúl (line 5063), and Antonio Martínez (line 5064) are anachronisms in this passage. See notes 6323, 6370, and Ward 1973.

34. Antonio Martínez

(103) He thanob ti utzcinnahan lae   These are the words that have been
                                             perfected
  Alabebal u xicinn ob   To be carried to the ears
Yx ma yumob   Of both the fatherless
  Yx ma nailob lae*   And the motherless.
He ix lay than lae bin tacuntabac   4995 And these are the words that will
                                             become secret.
  Bay u tacuntabal   Thus will be made secret
Ah kan thixal   Him of the yellow pectoral
  Ti tun e*   At this time.
Licil u talel   Since he is coming
  Y ocol *christianoil*   5000   To bring in Christianity
Tan cah   To the capital
  Mayapan t u chi ch'een ytza   And cycle city at Chichen Itza,
Ualac uil *suyua*   To raise perhaps the Zuyua,
  Ualac uil ytza   To raise perhaps the Itza.
Ahom cab hun lakin   5005 Wakened is the earth of one east,
  Hun xaman   One north,
Hun chikin   One west,
  Hun nohol   One south.

4994. That is, this text is addressed to the peasants.
4998. Announcing an underground lord.

Tali

  T u chi *D*ˢ. citbil

Lay c u tzolic ob

  Ho tul ah kinob

Ah kulem

  Ah kinob

Kuchi ob

  T u tan *D*ˢ.

Lay tzol ob u cuch num ya

  Ca tal y ocol *christianoil* lae

Heklay u kaba ob

  Tz'iban ob lae

Chilam Balam*

  Noh *saçerdote*

Na puc tun

  Noh *saçerdote*

N ahau pech

  Noh *saçerdote*

Ah kuil chel

  Noh *saçerdote*

Na tzin yabun chan

  Noh *saçerdote*

U chinam *Dios* cotz'lic u pach

  Tan suhuy luum

Lay tzoli ob

  U cuch num ya

T u tan ca yumil

  Ti *D*ˢ.

Talel tun u cah y ocol *christianoil*
lae

  Xe kik

Ma ya cimlal

  Kin tun y aabil

Sakil haabil

  (104) Yx pom kakil

U cuch num ya

  U tza çiçin

Sac petahom canal

  Elom ti cab

Ychil ox ahau katun

  Hun ahau katun

U lobil ox tz'it

  Katun*

Come

5010 Before the face of God the remote.

There they will be placed in order,

  The five sun priests

By the officials,

  The sun priests

5015 Who appear

  Before God.

These are their counts of the burden of
suffering

  When they came to enter
Christianity.

The account of their names

5020   That are written is:

(i) Spokesman of the Jaguar,

  The great priest,

(ii) Puc Tun,

  The great priest,

5025 (iii) Ahau Pech,

  The great priest,

(iv) Kauil Ch'el,

  The great priest,

(v) Tzin Yabun the Younger,

5030 The great priest.

The city of God will roll on its back

  Before the virgin land

That they count

  As the burden of suffering

5035 Before our Father

  Who is God.

Coming then is the beginning of
Christianization,

  Blood vomit,

Painless death,

5040   Calendar round,

Locust years,

  And incense fever,

The burden of suffering,

  The removal of the devil.

5045 White circled will be the heavens,

  Burned will be the land

In *katun* 3 Ahau,

  And *katun* 1 Ahau,

The evil third part

5050   Of the *katun*.

5021. The prophets are numbered in the MS. Xopan Nahuat is omitted.
5050. A redundant reference to 3 Ahau.

Bay tz'ibanil t u menel *euangelistas*	Thus it has been written by the Evangelists
Y etel *propeta* balam	And the prophet Jaguar,
Tali	Who has come
T u chi u yumil	Before the Father
Caan	5055 Of heaven
Y etel luum	And earth.
Ca t u kulem	Then will be the lamentation
Tz'ibtah ob ah kinob	That the sun priests have written
T u kinil	At the time
Noh kin tun y aabil	5060 Of the great calendar round
Lahun chable*	Of Lahun Chable
Ych *christianoil*	In Christianity.
Ti ca bin uluc *Saul*	Who then will be arriving is Saúl
Y etel *Dn. Ando martines*	And Don Antonio Martínez
U ch'ab u toh y al	5065 To create the rights of the born
U mehen ob	And engendered children.
Ahan	Awakened
Tun cab e	Is the *tun* of the land.
Bay tz'ibanil	Thus it is written
T u y almah thanil	5070 In the commandments
Noh ah kin	Of the great sun priest
Propeta	And prophet
Chilam Balam	Spokesman of the Jaguar,
Y etel ti cal man ben	And he is the voice that will come to pass.
Amen	5075 Amen.
Jesus.	Jesus.

5061. Chable seated 10 Ahau in 1677. The calendar round referred to here is the one beginning in 1685.

12 Ahau

---

35. Valladolid Resurgent

---

(95) Lahca ahau	**(95) 12 Ahau**
(96) *Segundo*	**(96)** *Segundo*
Lahcabil ahau katun	*Katun* 12 Ahau
U uaxac tz'it katun c u xocol*	Was the eighth part of the *katun* to be counted.

(note 5078 on following page)

*Yax Chuen, lord of Valladolid
(1658–1677). From the Garrett Col-
lection of Manuscripts in Middle
American Languages, The Princeton
University Library, The gift of
Robert Garrett.*

Sac lah tun*	Valladolid
U hetz' katun	5080 Was the seat of the *katun*.
Yaxal chuen u u ich buleu caan*	Yaxal Chuen was the face of the Great Serpent.
Chac u u ich ti y ahaulil hokon	The rain priest was the face in the lordship that appeared.
Y an t u caanil kin	There was a day on high,
Y an t u caannil akab	There was a night on high
Hunnac ah mennil	5085 To unite the shamans,
Hunnac ah ytz'atil	To unite the sorcerers.
Y ani cici hal ach uinicil	There were righteous governors,
Cici ba tabil	Righteous chiefs.
Y anni cici olal	There was righteousness
U than bal cah tuçinil i	5090 In the speech of the sinful world.
Bin ayikalac	They will be enriched,
Ah num ya uinic i	The suffering people.
Uahal uah	Food and more food
U than katun i	Is the word of the *katun*:

5078. A late note preceding the text says *segundo*. Both it and the text are wrong: this is the seventh *katun*. The illustration bears the late notations 7 and 1660. The *katun* began in 1658.

5079. Literally 'white flat stone': the Plaza or capital, but in this case I believe it does refer to Valladolid rather than to Mayapan or Merida.

5081. I read Bolon Can 'great snake' and believe it to be a synonym for Ahau Can, an alternative title of the Jaguar Priest.

Ayikal hab	5095	Rich years
Bal bahal i xan		And propertied also.
Y utzil katun		A good *katun*
Y utzil ix chaccob		And good rain priests.
Bin meyahnac ob i		They will be industrious
Y ich ti jx u hokol	5100	And fruit will appear
Ych luumil		In the lands
Tunich		And rocks
Ti *christianoil* i		In Christianity
Y et tal *Dios* i		With the coming of God.
Minan tun ch'amac	5105	There are then no Foxes
Y etel ah cab coh ti chibal i*		And Earth Lions in office.
Ti tun u katal ok olal		Then he will ask for religion
Ti y ah belnalil cahhob i		In the officials of the towns,
Y etel u *puertail* takin		And their doors will be golden,
Y etel u *cassamientoil* cah	5110	And the marriage registry of the town
		Will be in the fourfold house.
Ti can kas na		
Ti jx u katabal ca xanab		And he will ask for our sandals
Ua la licil ca *christianoil*		If that is like our Christianity.
Heklay ti ahi cab tac menel		Relating that it has dawned for us—
He lay ca ualic	5115	That is our rise
Hele lae		Today.
He ix bin tz'ocbal nicte katun lae		And that will be the end of the Flower *katun*:
Conbil bin tz'ocbal		Selling will be ended.
Ulel u than y ahaulil i		Come is the word of the lordship.
Tij ca bin uluc	5120	Who are coming then
Uuc uitzil		Are Uuc Uitzil
Chac ek*		And Chac Ek.
Y etel tupem caan e		And in the full sky
Pa hool chacc e		Appear the chief rain gods
T u uuc lahun tunn e:	5125	On the seventeenth *tun*
(. . . . .)*		(Of the *katun*) . . .

5106. This is the only *katun* in the series that is bluntly admitted to be "good." As Roys 1967: 158, note 14 observes, the end of the five-year famine of 1654 through 1658 had something to do with this, but the temporary ending of guerrilla warfare was part of it too. Christianity is reimposed and Christian and civil marriages are reinstituted, along with the sumptuary laws.

5122. Presumably these are the designated lords of the following *katun*.

5126. Line missing.

10 Ahau

36. Chable

Lahun Chan, lord of Chable (1677–1697). From the Garrett Collection of Manuscripts in Middle American Languages, The Princeton University Library, The gift of Robert Garrett.

(97) *Tercero*

Lahun ahau katun*
  Chable u hetz' katun
Ti y ulel u cahalob

  Can uat hom
U kax e cheob
  Y okol ob y ahaulil cabb ob
Elom tz'itz'
  Elom çus chi kak

Elom u ku ch'ich
  Uakom chal tun*

(97) *Tercero*

In *katun* 10 Ahau
  Chable was the seat of the *katun*.
That will be the arrival of their resident,
5130 The four priest Uat Hom,
To tie the sticks
  Over the lordships of the lands.
Burned will be the hoof,
  Burned will be the sand at the edge of the sea,
5135 Burned will be the god of birds.
  Burst will be the cistern.

5127. The text is preceded by the notation *tercero* and the illustration bears late notes 8 and 1680. This was the eighth *katun* but it began in 1677.

5136. I agree with Roys 1967: 159, note 11 that this is a reference to drought.

Kin tun y abil	The calendar round
U cuch katunn i*	Is the burden of the *katun*.
U than ca yumil	The Word of our Father
Ti *Dios* citbil	5140 Who is God the remote,
Y etel u colel caan	And the wife of heaven
U ye katun	Is the point of the *katun*.
Ma mac bin hausic u than	No one will terminate the Word
Ca yumil	Of our Father
Ti *D*ˢ.	5145 Who is God the remote,
*D*ˢ. mehenbil	God Made Son,
U yumil caan	The Father of heaven
Y etel luum lae	And earth.
Ma manom i	It will not be passed;
Bin uchuc t u cal	5150 It will be thought about
Ti bal cahil tuçinil	In the world of sin.
Bin uluc *santoil*	There will arrive
Christiano	A Christian saint
Pulic u kin	To bear his day,
Ca u uas kes u ba ob ah nunob	5155 While the stutterers return each other
T u lobil u bel ob*	To the evil of their ways.
Ma mac bin hausic	No one will end it.
Lay tun kin tun y aabil	This is the *tun* of the calendar round,
Chabil u than y okol ob maya ah kinob lae	Fulfilling its word over the Mayan sun priests.
U than *Dios*.	5160 This is the Word of God.

5138. A new calendar round began in the eighth year of this *katun*, in 1685 (1 Kan). The "word of the *katun*" is nonetheless pro-Christian.

5156. The Itza return to paganism. Roys 1967: 160 has them turning from it.

8 Ahau

---

37. The Annals of Tixkokob

(63) Lay u kaba	This is the name of the year
Ulci tz'ulob lae	When the foreigners arrived:
De mil cinnientos i dies y nuebe años	Fifteen nineteen,
Bay lae *1519*	Hence it was 1519 V (1546 M).
Lay u habil y an	5165 That was the year it was
Ca uli tz'ulob	When the foreigners arrived

Uay

Tac cahal

C oon

Ah ytza

Uay

Ti luum

Yucal peten

Yucatan

T u than maya

Ah ytzaob lae

Bay y alci yax *adelantado*

Dn. *Juan de Montejo* y oklal

Bay alabci ti

T u men Dn. *lorenso* chable

U y ube lay *concixtador* t ix

kokob e

U kaman ix tz'ulob

T u u olol

U pucçikal

He u chun u kabatic

Dn. *lorenso* chableil e

Y oklal u tz'aci kakbil bak

U hante

Tz'ulob

Y etel *capitan* ob t u lacal

Y an ix u mehen

Dn. *Martin* Chable u kaba xan

He u habil c u ximbal

Ca hop'i

U ch'aic u ba tz'ulob

U ti al u chucic ob

Uay

Yucal peten lae

U y oheltah ix ah kin

Ah bouat

Ah xupan

U kaba

Occi

Christianoil t oon *D°. 1519 a*ˢ.

Etz'lahci

Ku na ti hoo *D°. 1540 a*ˢ.*

Here

Near the towns

Of us

5170   Itza,

Here

In the land

Of the Neck Country,

Yucatan

5175 In the Mayan language

Of the Itzas.

So, it is said, the first *adelantado*,

Don Juan de Montejo, believed.

This was said of him

5180   By Don Lorenzo Chable,

Who may have heard this conqueror in

Tixkokob.

And he received the foreigners

Into his heart

Of hearts.

5185 That was the start of his being named

Don Lorenzo Chable,

Since he prepared roast meat

To serve

To the foreigners

5190   And all the captains.

And he had a son:

Don Martin Chable is his name too.

This was the year that was current

When it began.

5195 The foreigners (then) thinned

(themselves) out

Because they were through

Here

In the Neck Country.

And the sun priest was informed,

5200   The prophet

Xopan (Nahuat)

By name.

Then came

Christianity to us in 1519 V (1546

M).

5205 Founded

Was the god house in Merida in

1540 V (1563 M).

5206. The cathedral was begun in 1542–43 (Mediz Bolio 1930: 37, note 72) and was completed in 1598 (Hunt 1974: 240).

Ca tz'oc i
    Ku na ti hoo *D°. 1599 aˢ.*

Uchci
    Xe kik
Hop'ci
    Cimil t oon *D°. 1648 años*
(64) U uiihi cimil
    Ho p'el hab *D°. 1650 años*

D°. 1651 aˢ.
    D°. 1652 aˢ.
D°. 1653 aˢ.
    D°. 1654 aˢ.
Ca tz'oci
    Uiih lae
Chac ykal ti cimi
    Padre Agustin Gomes D°. 1661
    años
Uchci
    Kin tun y abil *D°. 1669 años**

Uchci
    X u san kak *D°. 1692 años.*

Completed
    Was the god house in Merida in
    1599 V (1604 M).
There occurred
5210   Blood vomit
And there began
    Death for us in 1648 V (1652 M).
Famine
    Killed for five years: 1650 V (1654
    M).
5215   1651 V (1655 M),
    1652 V (1656 M),
    1653 V (1657 M),
    1654 V (1658 M).
Then ended
5220   The famine.
It was a hurricane that killed
    Father Agustín Gómez in 1661 V
    (1665 M).
There occurred
    The calendar round in 1669 V (1677
    M).
5225 There occurred
    Fever rash in 1692 V (1709 M).

5224. As above, this should be corrected to 1677, but it was the *katun* that began on that date; the calendar round began in 1685.

6 Ahau
4 Ahau

38. The Ending of Tribute at Chichen Itza

(73) Uuc y ab nal u hetz' katun*
  Ti can ahau katun
T u chi ch'een
  Uuc y ab nal u hetz'
Ti nohol
  Ah ba cocol
Macan u u ich
  Ci man u u ich
Y okol y aal
  Y okol uaah
Chac kitan
  Na hom
U pop
  Y etel u tz'aam
Xe kik
  U cuch
T u kin y an çaçac uil u y ex

  Çacac uil u nak
Ix ma chan men uah
  U uah katun
Hulom kuk
  Hulom yaxum
Hulom kaxte
  Hulom mut e
Hulom tzimin
  Mucuc
Patan
  Ti chi ch'een lae.

Teabo was seat of the *katun*
  In *katun* 4 Ahau.
At Chichen
5230 Teabo was its seat;
In the south
  It was the lord of Bacalar.
Covered was its face;
  Death was its face,
5235 Over the water,
  Over the food.
Chac Kitan
  And Tan Hom
Were its mat,
5240 Its throne.
Blood vomit
  Was its burden.
At the time bright white moon was its pants;
  Bright white moon was its clothes.
5245 And seized work food
  Was the food of the *katun*.
Come will be the quetzal;
  Come will be the blue bird;
Come will be the tying;
5250 Come will be the news;
Come will be the horse
  To suppress
The tribute
  At Chichen.

5227. There being no text for 6 Ahau in the Chumayel, we move on to 4 Ahau, which was seated at Teabo, Bacalar, Chac Kitan, and Tan Hom, according to this text. There was a plague (line 5241); the sumptuary laws were enforced (line 5244); there was forced labor (line 5245); and the tribute of Chichen Itza was suppressed (line 5252).

39. Calendrical Notes

(21) Katun   5255 The *katun*

T u yax chun buluc ahau   First began on 11 Ahau

D°. *1513*   A.D. 1513 V (1540 M)

Aˢ.   Years.

Tz'oci   It ended

Lay lae   5260 And that was that.

Hopci   It began

Hooil   At Merida.

D°. *1519*   A.D. 1519 V (1546 M)

Aˢ.   Years:

Sn. Fran.ᶜᵒ   5265 Saint Francis

Etz'layci   Was established

Sn. *tiago*   At Saint James

Ti Hoo   In Merida

D°. *1519*   A.D. 1519 V (1546 M).

Etz'lahci   5270 There was established

Chumuc ca hoo   In the middle of the city of Merida

Yglesia mayor   The main church

T u habil   In the year

D°. *1540* *   A.D. 1540 V (1563 M).

U ychil haab *dose* *12*   5275 Months in the year: twelve (12).

U tzol kin ychil hun p'el hab D°.   The count of days in a year: 365.
365

U tzolan akab hun p'el hab D°. *365*   The count of nights in a year: 365.

U tzolan *semana* ychil hun p'el   The count of weeks in a year: 52.
haab D°. *52*

Ca tac hun p'el kin   Then follows one day.

U tzolan *Domingo* ychil hun p'el   5280 The count of Sundays in a year: 53.
haab D°. *53*

U tzolan kin ychil uac p'el u   The count of days in six months

T u yax chun D°. *181*   From the very beginning: 181.

(22) U tzolan kin ychil uac p'el u   The count of days in the six months

T u catz'ic t u tulistal hun p'el   That are left to count to return to

hab D°. *184*   one year: 184.

He yx kin c u xocic *semana* lae   5285 And these are the days counted in one

Uuc p'el kin ychil hun p'el   week:

semana   Seven days in one week.

5274. The founding of the convent of Saint Francis in Santiago, a section of Merida, may in fact date to 1546 and the corrected date of 1563 for the founding of the cathedral is probably valid.

U *cuentail* lay xoc lae

  (23) U tzol uinal ychil hun p'el hab lae

Poop—16 *julio**

  Uoo—5 *agosto*

Sip—25 *agosto*

  Çotz'—14 *septiembre*

Çec—4 *octubre*

  Xul—24 *octubre*

Ti lic y alancal cay i

  Tze' yax kin—13 *nob*[e].

Ti c u uatz'al nal i

  Mol—3 *diziembre*

Ch'een—23 *diziembre*

  Yaax—12 *henero*

U kin hoch utz

  Sac—1 *febrero*

Licil u lolancal çacob

  Ceeh—21 *febrero*

Mac—13 *marzo*

  Licil y alancal aac

Kan kin—2 *abril*

  Muan—22 *abril*

The count of one cycle is this,

  The count of *uinals* in one year is this:

Pop—16 July,

5290 Uo—5 August,

Zip—25 August,

  Zotz'—14 September,

Tzec—4 October,

  Xul—24 October,

5295 Which is when the fish are spawning.

  Little Yaxkin—13 November,

Which is the bending of the corn ears.

  Mol—3 December,

Ch'en—23 December,

5300 Yax—12 January,

The time the harvest is good.

  Zac—1 February,

Since it is the blooming of the whites.

  Ceh—21 February,

5305 Mac—13 March,

  As it is the mating of turtles.

Kankin—2 April,

  Muan—22 April,

Glyphs for the Mayan months (1737). From the Garrett Collection of Manuscripts in Middle American Languages, The Princeton University Library, The gift of Robert Garrett.

5289. The list of the *uinals* is accompanied by crudely drawn glyphs.

Lic u mumtal u nak | As it is the rainy period,
  U caanil kin i | 5310   The time of hiding the sky.
Paax—12 *mayo* | Pax—12 May,
  Kayab—1 *junio* | Kayab—1 June,
Cumku—21 *junio* | Cumku—21 June,
  U uayayab ho p'el kin.* | The month of the *Uayebs* five days.

2 Ahau

40. Valladolid

(73) May lu* | 5315 The cycle seat
  Zaci* | Was Valladolid,
Maya *patan** | And the seat of tribute
  U hetz' katun* | Was the seat of the *katun*
Ti cabil ahau | In the 2 Ahau
  Katun | 5320   *Katun.*
Oclis t u ba | They were interpenetrated,
  Katun | The *katuns.*
Emom çum | Descended will be the rope,
  Emom çaban | Descended will be poison,
Ma ya cimlal | 5325 And painless death
  Ox mul tun tzekil* | At the three stone mounds of sacrifice.
Çac pet ay uinicil | The North priest was of Pat Ay's people,
  Ca tali | When they came
Kaxan u cuch | Tied was the burden
  Buluc ch'aab tan* | 5330   Of 11 Ch'ab Tan.

5314. The following page of the MS bears the notation *Chumayel 28 zihic ayijada Micaela Castañeda* 'Chumayel, the 28th was born the goddaughter, Micaela Castañeda'. This is in a different hand and is obviously late.

5315. I read *may cu* as 'cycle seat'.

5316. Zac I 'white sparrow hawk' is Valladolid.

5317. *Maya patan* 'cycle water (of) tribute' is obviously here used as a title for Valladolid, which is now seat of the cycle by virtue of its introduction of the new calendar of twenty-four-year *katuns* in 1752.

5318. And Valladolid seated the *katun* too.

5326. Roys 1967: 134, note 2 reads this as 'three piles of skulls'. I read it as *tz'ekil* 'massacre'. It could also be *tz'ecil* 'plastering'.

5330. Buluc Ch'ab Tan '11 grabs half' appears to have been a priestly title associated with the *lahun tun* or mid-*katun* ceremonies.

Kan
   Y opol yk
Oxil uah
   U uah cabil ahau
Tan cochhom uiih i
   Tan cochhom uah i
Lay u cuch
   Ah cabil ahau katun lae.

The South priest
   Was Op Ik.
Bamboo food
   Was the food of 2 Ahau.
5335 It was halfway famine;
   It was halfway feast.
That was the burden
   Of *katun* 2 Ahau.

---

41. The Sevenfold Creation

I and II

(48) *Dominus**
   Vobiscum
U lahci u than ob
   U kail
Ti minan caan
   Y etel luum
Tij ca çih
   T an homlah cabil
Ti minan caan
   Y etel luum
Ox amay tun *grasia* uchci*

   U patc i
U kuil
   Ah tepal e
Ti minan caan c uchi e
   Ti ca çih i
Uuc te tun
   Uuc p'el katun
Ch'uyan t u y ol yk uuc te tete

   Ci bin ca pecn i
Uuc p'el ix u *grasiail* xan
   Uuc tul ix u *santoil* xan*
A max y ic lo uchc i
   U çihil

I and II

"The Lord
5340   Be with you,"
Was the ending of the words
   Of the sermon
When there was no heaven
   And earth.
5345 Then when it was born,
   The earth came down,
When there was no heaven
   And earth.
The three square stones of grace came about
5350   And there was shaped
The deity
   And ruler,
For no heaven had been made.
   Then when there was born
5355 The seventh *tun*
   Of the seventh *katun*,
It was hung on the spirit of breath, the seventh choice.
   When we shall just be aware of it.
Seven also are its graces as well.
5360   And seven are its saints also.
Then it may not be going to happen,
   His birth,

5339. See the introduction for an analysis of this chapter.
5349. Presumably the Trinity, equated with three stone pyramids.
5360. The Maya were mightily impressed with the Spanish seven-day week, which they interpreted as a set of yearbearers associated with the planets, the sun, and the moon. No real date is implied here, but rather a mystic moment in time.

Ti hun tun g°.
    Hun picib g°.
Uchc i
    U picil akab
Ti minan Dˢ.
    C uchi e
May to u kamab
    U Dˢ.sil c uchi e
Tij li y an ychil g°. t u ba
    T u hunal ychil akbil
Ti minan caan
    Y etel luum
Ca buk i*
    T u tz'oc katun
Ti ma uchuc çihil
    Ti hun te katun
Y an ij
    U t uy ij
Adeu
    *Ti para mij**
Uchci u kuil
    Ca cal u kij
Ca ix xibn i
    T u ca picib tun g°.

Ca kuch i
    T u ca p'el katun
Al *pilcon* u kaba*
    U *angelil* çihc i
Lukul t u cibah u ca p'el g°.

    T u ca p'el u picil akab
Ti ma mac
    Y anac c uchi e
Ca u kamah u kuil t u ba
    T u hunal
(49) Ca tali
    U lukul

        In one *tun* of grace
            Or a thousand graces.
5365 There were
            Thousands of nights
        That no God
            Occurred.
        For that cycle it was just canceled,
5370   The occurrence of godhood.
        There he was in grace by himself,
            Alone in the darkness,
        For there was no heaven
            And earth.
5375 Two years
            To the end of the *katun*,
        For the birth was not to occur
            In the first *katun*.
        He was there
5380   And listened.
        "Farewell to you
            From me"
        Occurred,
            And the deity then departed.
5385 And then he was made man,
            In the second thousand *tuns* of
            grace.
        Then he appeared
            In the second *katun*.
        Woman Born Baby was the name
5390   Of the angel spirit that was born.
        Departing, he wanted a second grace
        period,
            A second thousand nights,
        Because there was no one
            Who was to be there.
5395 Then he took his divinity to himself
            Alone
        When he came
            And departed.

    5375. Roys 1967: 107, note 10 saw this as *buki* but translates it as *luki*. It remains opaque.

    5382. Roys 1967: 107, note 11 reads *u tuy ij* (line 5380) as 'long locks of hair' and refers it to cornsilk. He leaves *adeu ti paramii* untranslated, for which I can't altogether blame him. I read Sp. *adiós (a) tí para mí*, though the first element could also be Lat. *a deo* 'from God'. The passage is reminiscent of the farewell of the First Fathers in the Popol Vuh (Edmonson 1971: lines 7071 ff.).

    5389. Maya *al* 'woman's child' plus Nah. *pil(li) con(etl)* 'noble child'.

*O firmar**
  Ci jx u than
Ca u kamah u kuil t u ba
  T u hunal
Ca lukij
  Ca bin i
T u y ox picib tun *gᵃ*.
  *Alba congel**
U kaba y *angelil* i
  Lay u y ox p'el *gᵃ*.
Xic en t u can picib tun *gᵃ*.

  U can p'el uil akab
*Atea Ohe**
  Lay u kaba y *angelil* i
Çihil u cibah u can p'el *gᵃ*.
  Ca hop'i
U thanic u ba
  T u hunal
Bee ku e
  Ah tepal e
Ma ba ca mac en
  T in hunal i ba ca
C u than t u balanil
  T u kuil ychil *gᵃ*.
Xic en to
  Ci u than
Ca bini t u ho picib tun *gᵃ*.

  T u ho picib akab
Çihil u cibah u ho p'el *gᵃ*.
  T u ho p'el katun
Caa ualhi
  U thanob u kuil
Ca çih i
  Y *angelil* i
Degipto
  U kaba y *angelil* i ca ualhi

Xic en it ba ca
  Mac en uil e
Ku en ba ca
  Ah tepal en i ba ca

	"Oh, agree!"
5400	Said his word too,
	When he took his divinity to himself
	Alone.
	Then he departed.
	Then he went,
5405	On the third thousand *tuns* of grace,
	Dawn of the four changers
	Was the name of the angel spirit.
	This was the third grace.
	Let me go to the fourth thousand *tuns* of grace,
5410	The fourth moonlit night.
	Child Two Knowing:
	That is the name of the angel spirit.
	Being born he wanted the fourth grace,
	So he began
5415	To speak to himself
	Alone.
	"Come then, God!
	Ruler!
	There is no one for me:
5420	I am still alone,"
	He said inwardly
	To the deity in grace.
	"Let me go to that,"
	Said his word.
5425	Then it came to the fifth thousand *tuns* of grace,
	To the fifth thousand nights.
	Being born he wanted the fifth grace
	In the fifth *katun*.
	Then there returned
5430	The words of the deity.
	Then was born
	The angel spirit.
	The Egyptian
	Was the name of the angel spirit that returned.
5435	"Let me go (?) somewhere,
	Am I someone perhaps?
	Am I a god someplace?
	Am I a ruler someplace?"

5399. Sp. *o afirmad* 'O, affirm ye'.
5406. Sp. *alba* 'dawn' plus Maya *can hel* 'four changers, yearbearers'.
5411. Maya *al ca ohel* 'child two knowing'.

Ca ix u than u kuil t u ba
    T u hunal
An inite deis in*

    C u than
Ca u kamah u kuil t u ba
    T u hunal
Ca bin i
    T u uac picib tun *g*ᵃ.
T u uac p'el u p'isil akab
    T u uac te katun
Ku ex
    Ah tepal ex e
Nuc ex
    Yn than
Ma ba ca mac
    Y an ti hunal i ba ca
Çihil u cibah uuc p'el *g*ᵃ.

    Con la mil*

U kaba y *angelil*
    T en kul u ba
Ku t ex
    Ku ex e
Nuc ex
    Yn than
Ma ba ca mac y an

    Ma mac nucic yn than
Ci uil u than
    Ti u alic
Ta muk u sihçic
    Uuc te *g*ᵃ.
Cilmac ti y ol çihic i
    Uuc te katun
Uuc p'el çaçil
    Uuc p'el ix
U p'isil akab
    Uuc picib
A *biento**
    Boca yento

And so spoke the deity to himself
5440   Alone.
"But what if you are coming from the
gods?"
    He said.
Then he took his divinity to himself
    Alone.
5445 Then he went
    In the sixth thousand *tuns* of grace,
In the sixth measure of nights,
    In the sixth *katun*.
"You are a god!
5450   You are a ruler!
Believe
    In my word!
Nowhere is there anyone
    Who is still alone!"
5455 Being born he wanted the seventh
grace.
    Child of a Thousand is the name of
the angel spirit.
"Me,
    I am the deity himself.
God to you,
5460   Your God:
Believe
    In my word.
Nowhere is there anyone,
    No one at all, to believe in my
word,"
5465 Was just the sound of the word
    That he spoke
While he was being born,
    The seventh grace.
Happy in spirit was he born,
5470   The seventh *katun*,
The seventh illumination,
    And the seventh
Of the measures of nights,
    The seven thousands,
5475 By wind
    And breath (of mouth).

5441. Maya *(u)a* 'if' and *n(a)* 'yet', Lat. *inite deis*, Maya *in* 'I'.
5456. Nah. *con(etl)* 'child', Sp. *la* 'the', *mil* 'thousand'.
5475. Sp. *a viento, boca viento, de la*.

De la çipil na*
  *Defentenote**
*Sustina g^a.**
  Trese mil i
Y no cargo bende
  Yx hun tic
Ca tic
  Ox hun tic
Ox hun bacam u katunil

  Ox uuc pic
Ca ti ah cab
  Ti D^s. citbil
T u ba
  T u hunal
(50) T u tunil
  Ox amay tun g^a.
Ah ci cab
  Ti D^s. citbil
U kaba
  U pectzil
Unidad
  Y etel D^s. citbil
Lay
  U kaba
Hen abil ex
  U katunil ex
Ox tz'acab hun y aban
  Uaan ca tal i
Uuc pis tz'acab
  Ix t u camge
Can ten hi ix
  U yax than
Hun tz'alab ti akab
  Hun tz'alab ti canal
T en i
  U chun e
T en i
  Uil bin tz'ocebal e*
He x tun u can
  Muc-hi u than e

"From the house of blame
  (I am) defending thee.
Sustain Grace
5480 For thirteen thousand
And some twenty burdens."
  And one spread,
Two spreads,
  Three and one spreads,
5485 Three and one assimilated was the
  katun period,
  Three times seven thousand,
Then he was lord of the earth.
  He was the Holy God
By himself
5490 Alone.
In the *tun* period
  Of three square stones of grace
The spokesman of the earth,
  The Holy God,
5495 Was the name
  Of his consciousness.
Unity
  And Holy God—
These
5500 Are his names.
You are the divisions of the years;
  You are the *katun* period.
Three steps of one bush
  Stood when he came.
5505 And seven measures of steps
  In the four changers.
And four times perhaps
  Were his first words.
One step at night;
5510 One step in heaven.
"I then
  Am its beginning;
I then
  May be its ending."
5515 And this then is the teaching,
  Hidden perhaps in his word.

5477. Maya *zipil na* 'house of blame'.
5478. Sp. *defendiéndote*.
5479–81. Lat. *sustina*, Sp. *gracia, trece mil y un cargo (veinte)*. The last two
words are conceptually Mayan: a load (*kal*) is twenty (*uinic*).
5514. Compare Revelation 21:6: "I am Alpha and Omega, the beginning and
the end."

Datate uay i*
  Ti kaman cah e
T en i
  Unidate
T en ix
  Unitata
T en ix u cam e
  T en ix *Unitata*
Anun i
  Talel u cah *unidad*

"Surrender here
  In the captured city.
I am here:
5520 Unite!
I am also
  United.
I am also within;
  I am also united.
5525 Hurry!
  Come to the city of unity."

III

Nil u*
  U kaba akab
Lay u yax than ku lae
  Lay u yax than citbil lae
Ti ma xix tun
  U tunil
T u ba
  T u hunal
Ychil akbillil e
  E *tomas* çipan cas*
U kaba yk
  Hun katun u yum
O tah
  O canil*
Aucangel
  U kaba yk
*Heronix**
  U kaba yk
Xic lu to t u tanil*
  U kaba yk lae
*Virtutus**
  U kaba yk
Joramis
  U kaba yk

III

Rolling Moon
  Was the name of the night.
That was the new Word of God then.
5530 That was the new holy Word then,
Which was not the dregs of the *tun*
  Of his *tun* period
By himself,
  Alone in the nighttime.
5535 And Thomas
  Doubted
Is the name of the wind.
  1 *katun* is his father.
Five relations,
5540 Five teachings,
Archangel
  Is the name of the wind.
Herodias
  Is the name of the wind.
5545 Stained Wrap in Front
  Is the name of the wind then.
Virtue
  Is the name of the wind.
Jeremiah
5550 Is the name of the wind

5517. *Datate* is probably distorted Latin for 'give (thyself)'.

5527. Roys 1967: 109, note 4 says, "Possibly a reference to 'Egyptian darkness'." I read it as Maya *nil u*.

5536. Lat. *et (Th)omas*, Maya *zipan kas* 'let (himself) be divided'.

5540. Maya *ho tah ho canil*.

5543. Because of the *r*, this has to be a foreign name. Roys 1967: 109 has 'H(i)eron'.

5545. Untranslated by Roys. I read Maya *xic(u)l* 'staining', *to* 'wrap', *t u tanil* 'at its frontside'.

5547. I read Lat. *virtus* and suppose that the author was confused by the oblique declensions.

T u ca tz'it katun
 He tun c u than
Ca t helpah tun e
 Jax yon lacal pa*
U ma cah u kaba u cilich caanil

 U alic ca cilich yum citbil

In the second part of the *katun*.
 This then he said
When he changed the *tun*,
 "However are we here all broken?"
5555 He denies the name of the blessed heaven,
 Referring to our blessed holy Father.

IV

Bol ay u kaba u canil
 U ca tz'it caan
He ix t u tos y oc
 Sustina g°. u kaba*
Ti yx
 Ti utzhi
*Lonmias**
 Lom tun
U tunil ychil akbil
 Çih on tun
U tunil
 Etz'lic lay tunob
T u y ox ten hi
 U cutal t u y oc
Sustina g°.
 Lay tun ob
Çih ob
 Y an y alan hun uil tun
Ychac ye tun
 Ocon tun
Chac ye napal tun
 Chacci ob tun t u lacal
Ti hunac
 Tzuc ti cabob
Yax ahau
 (51) *Dios* citbil lae
Hun tic katun
 Lay çihci u oclel mehen D⁵. lae

Ca tic katun
 Citbil
Ox tic katun
 Expleo u caan u kaba chih e*

IV

Bol Ay is the name of the serpent
 Of the second part of the sky,
And he was in the dust at the feet
5560 Of Sustaining Grace, as he is called.
And it was he
 Who succeeded
Jerome,
 Stabbing stone
5565 Of the *tun* period in the night.
 We were born then
In the *tun* period
 And placed these stones
For the third time perhaps,
5570 Sitting at the feet
Of Sustaining Grace.
 These are their stones,
Their birth.
 They are under one month stone
5575 And red pointed stone,
 The stolen stone,
The red-pointed biting stone.
 They redden the stone altogether,
Which united
5580 The divisions of the lands
Of the new lord,
 This Holy God.
One spread of the *katun*,
 Then was born the proper son of this God.
5585 The second spread of the *katun*
 Is holy.
The third spread of the *katun*,
 Complete the Sky was his best name,

5554. Maya *ha(a)x y (an) on (t u) lacal pa*.
5560. Lat. *sustin(eo)*, Maya *-al*, Sp. *gracia*.
5563. I follow Roys 1967: 109, note 9 on this.
5588. I follow Roys 1967: 109, note 12 in reading Lat. *expleo* 'I complete' plus
Maya *u caan* 'his sky'.

Chac *opilla* u kaba u alic u caanil*   Great Deeds was his name spoken on
                                             high.

   Enpileo caan u kaba lae*   5590 Complete the Sky was his name
                                                      then,

Expleo u kaba   Complete was his name
   Ychil yax le *Dios* lae   In the new generation of this God.
Hebones   Hebron
   U p'elel mehen D⁵.   Was the proper son of God,
Nen bin   5595 Reflected
   Ti heclic   As is fitting
T u celembal u yum   In the strength of the Father,
   T u tunil yum e   In the stoniness of the Father.
Ca bin x çihçah   Then too will be made to appear
   U coo caanil caan   5600 The dizzy heights of heaven
Heklay hun p'el *graçia*   Relating one (more) grace,
   Hun p'el tun   One (more) *tun*.
Zihan tun kak   Born is the *tun* of fire.
   Tixitate u kaba*   Medicine Water is his name,
U çasilil   5605 The Brilliance
   Caanil   Of Heaven;
Sustinal bin u çahal   Sustaining will be the lighting,
   U çaçil caanil   The shining of heaven.
Ac pa u men katun çihci*   The little fruit-offering *katun* was
                                             born,

   Çasil ych caanil   5610 The light of heaven.
Al pa u *manga* u kaba*   Child of Fruit Offering was his name
   Xulci lae   In the end.
Cangeles yk*   The yearbearer winds
   U alic   Spoke
Ta muk u ch'abtic ek   5615 While the stars were created,
   Ma çaçac cab   And the earth was not very light.
Minan caan   There was no heaven
   Y etel luum   And earth.
Chac pauh tun   "Red Giant of the *tun*,
   Çac pauah tun   5620 White Giant of the *tun*,
Ek pauah tun   Black Giant of the *tun*,
   Kan pauah tun   Yellow Giant of the *tun*,
He yax caan   This is the new heaven,"
   U alic *Dios* citbil e   Said the holy God,

5589. Maya *chac* 'great', Lat. *opera* 'deeds'.
5590. Roys 1967: 109, note 13 suggests *cielo empireo*, but I think this is a repeat of line 5588, as in the next line following.
5604. Nah. *texiutl* 'small medicinal tree', *atl* 'water'.
5609. Maya *ac* 'small', *pa* 'guayabo'.
5611. Sp. *mango* 'mango'.
5613. *C angeles* 'our angels' from Sp. *ángeles* is also possible, but the mention
of the directional giants makes this unlikely. Roys 1967: 110, note 4 cites Brinton
citing Baeza that the Pau Ah Tun are the four winds.

U machma u tunil   5625 Seizing upon the *tun* periods,
  U machma u *cangel*   Seizing upon the four changers,
U machma u kabatil*   Seizing upon the naming
  Ti ch'uyan t u *cangeles* yk   To be attached to the four changing
                                        winds.

Cerpinus u kaba*   Cerpinus by name
  He tun y alan e   5630 Is the one underneath;
*Orale**   Orale
  U p'is luum   Measures the land.
Ox tul *personaob*   There are three persons.
  Lay *Dios* citbil   They are Holy God,
Dios mehenbil   5635 God the Son,
  Dios espiritu sancto   And God the Holy Ghost.
U alic   He returns
  Planetas   The planets:
Santurnio   Saturn,
  Jupiter   5640 Jupiter,
Marte   Mars,
  Venus   Venus,
Lic y alic   As he says,
  U machma ku i   Seizing upon the gods.
Caanil uchi e   5645 In heaven
  U ch'ab   Their creation occurred.
He u kaba caan e   This is the name of heaven:
  *Christalino**   Crystalline.
He *angelob* lae   These are the angels,
  Corpinus u kaba   5650 Corpinus is their name,
(52) U lathma u cici thanbilil   Who have compiled the blessed
                                        sayings
  Yumbil   Of the fathers
Ti minan caan   When there was no heaven
  Y etel luum   And earth.

V   **V**

Inpicco u kaba uchic*   5655 Infinite were the names given
  U tzitzatabal *angelesob* t u lacal   At the baptism of all the angels.
Baloyo u kaba   Everything was named
  Ca ca uecan   When we were sprinkled.

5627. Roys 1967: 110, note 5 reads *kabalil* as 'potter's wheel'.
   5629. *Cerpinus* suggests Lat. *corporis* 'of the body' or possibly even Cerberus, the hound of hell. Neither has much to do with surveying.
   5631. Roys 1967: 110 reads *Orele*. Neither Lat. *orale* 'pope's cape' nor Sp. slang *(ah)orale* 'come on, you' seems to help much.
   5648. Roys 1967: 110, note 7 points out that the Ixil and Kaua have a diagram showing *Christalino* as one of the eleven heavens, along with the sun, moon, six planets, firmament, and *Cielo Empireo*.
   5655. Sp. *infinito*.

Seros u kaba*	Sirius was named,
*Et sepeuas**	5660 And Thou Wast Buried,
*Laus deo**	And Praise Be to God.
Cabal chac	The second rain priest
Bol ay balam	Was Bol Ay the Jaguar
Y etel cacau balam te	And Jaguar Cacao Plant.
Esperas u kaba*	5665 Exhale was the name
Uac tas caan	Of the sixth layer of heaven.
Ysperas u kaba*	Inhale was the name
Uuc tas caan	Of the seventh layer of heaven
Ca çihi	When it was born
Y okol cab	5670 Above the earth
T u men *D*.	Through God
Ah tepal e	The ruler
T u uuc te katun	In the seventh *tun*,
Çihic ychil akbil	Being born in the night.

VI   VI

Espiritu u kaba*	5675 Spirit was its name.
*Sto. Edendeus**	Saint Edendeus
*Sto. Eluçeo**	And Saint Elisha
Santoob	Were the saints
Lay ti yla u çihil u lamay tun	Who saw the birth of the descending *tun*,
U lamay akab*	5680 The descending night.
Se repite eli tun*	"Repeat the *tun* burns;
*Entri de noche**	It comes at night."
Cii u than	Sweet are the words
Ca t u thanah	He spoke
U lamay tun	5685 For the descending *tun*,
U lamay akab	The descending night.
Tronas	"Thunder,
*Aleseyo**	Elisha,

5659. Sp. *sirios*.

5660. Lat. *et sepultatis*.

5661. Lat. *laus deo*. This is the first Latinism the author has gotten right since the opening line of the text.

5665. Lat. *exspiras*.

5667. Lat. *inspiras*.

5675. Sp. *espíritu*.

5676. Sp. *santo* 'saint', Lat. *Edendeus* 'god of Eden'.

5677. Sp. *Santo Eliseo*.

5680. Roys 1967: 111, note 5 has a preference for *amay tun*. Perhaps this could be reached by reading *ul amay tun, ul amay akab*. The couplet would then read: 'who saw the birth and arrival of the square(d) stone, the arrival of the squared night'. Does that help?

5681. Sp. *se repite* 'it is repeated'.

5682. Sp. *entra de noche*.

5688. Sp. *tronas Eliseo* 'thou thunderest Elisha'.

De mundo		For the world—
*De graçia**	5690	For grace.
Ena pediate		Enos, I asked you;
*Joçi pidiate**		Joseph, I asked you
En pieted		In piety
*Graçia**		And grace.
*St. Esuleptun**	5695	Saint Aesculepius then,
*Jaam estum**		Let me be.
*Est gra.**		There is grace
*Suplilis**		In suffering,
*Et timeo**		And I fear
*Me firme**	5700	And consent.
*Ab infinitis**		From the Infinite
*Gra.**		(Comes) grace
*Y metis absolubtum**		And you give absolution,
*Ti metis de graçia**		Which you give of grace;
*Ab egintis gra.**	5705	From what must be done, grace;
*Edendeo gra.**		From the God of paradise, grace;
*Defentis de graçia**		Protected by grace;
*Fenoplis tun gra.**		Full then of a measure of grace;
*Locomdary me gra.**		Accustom me to grace;
*Tretrisumis gra.**	5710	Thrice Tripled grace;
*No çi luçi de graçia**		You don't make a show of grace;
*Inpriçio de gra.**		Or of the price of grace."
*Trese mil i uno de cargo**		Thirteen thousand and one burdens,
*Le on te**		And here we are.

5690. Lat. *de mundo de gratia* 'out of the world, out of grace'.

5692. Sp. *Enos pedía te, José pedía te.*

5694. Sp. *en piedad (y) gracia.*

5695. Sp. *santo*, Lat. *Esculep(ius)*, Maya *tun.*

5696. Lat. *jam estum* 'let me be already'.

5697. Lat. *est* '(there) is', Sp. *gracia.*

5698. Lat. *supliciis.*

5699. Lat. *et timeo.*

5700. Sp. *me afirmo.*

5701. Lat. *ab infinitis.*

5702. Sp. *gracia.*

5703. Sp. *y metes*, Lat. *absolutum* for *absolutionem.*

5704. Maya *ti* 'which', Sp. *metes de gracia* 'you throw in out of grace'.

5705. Lat. *ab agendis*, Sp. *gracia.*

5706. Lat. *Eden deo*, Sp. *gracia.*

5707. Lat. *defensis*, Sp. *de gracia.*

5708. Lat. *pleno*, Maya *p'iz tun*, Sp. *gracia.*

5709. Sp. *(a)l acomodarme (a) gracia.*

5710. Lat. *tretrisumis* 'thrice thrice summed', Sp. *gracia.*

5711. Sp. *no se luce de gracia* 'you don't dress yourself in grace'.

5712. Sp. *ni (del) precio de gracia.*

5713. Sp. *trece mil y uno de cargo* 'thirteen thousand and one of burden'. I should say so!

5714. Maya *le on te* 'that is we there'.

Hun tic*   5715 One spread,
  Ca tic   Two spreads,
Ox hun tic   Thirteen spreads,
  Hun tuuc   One division,
Oxhun bakam   5,200,
  U katunil   5720   A *katun* period,
Ox uuc   Three sevens,
  Pis   8,000
U y ahal cab   Is the dawn.
  Ca çihi   Then is born
U lamay tun   5725 The descending *tun*,
  U lamay akab   The descending night
Ti minan caan   When there was no heaven
  Y etel luum   And earth.
Ca than   Then it was spoken
  T u men Dˢ. citbil   5730   By Holy God,
(53) T u ba   By himself
  T u hunal   Alone
Ti ox coc   For three needs,
  Ox akab c uchi e   Three nights to occur.
Lay   5735 This
  U yax than ku   Was the new Word of God
Ti minan caan   When there was no heaven
  Y etel luum   And earth.
Ca ti luth t u tunil   Then he departed on the *tun* period,
  Ti lubi   5740   Which was posted
T u ca pis tun   In the second *tun*.
  Ti ix tun   And it was then
U patah u kuil   That the deity was expected.
  Ca picnahi   Then it was known:
Hun tic pic katun   5745 "One spread of eight thousand
                                             katuns,"

  C u than hun pis ti tun *de graçia*   He said, "is one measure in the *tun*
                                             of grace.

Hun pilis tun *de gra*.   One winding of *tuns* of grace."
  Op hach kintah   The macaws grew very numerous
T u pach acan tun   Behind the standing stone.
  Mac ti çihi   5750   Who was it who was born
Ca emi   When there descended
  Ca yum   Our Father?
T ech   As for you,
  A u ohel   You know.

5715. The following passage is rendered obscure by the use of some relatively
rare numeral classifiers—*tic, tuc, bak,* and *pic*—and a rather arbitrary numerology—13, 1, 2, 7, 20, and 3. These and their multiples—21, 8,000, 5,200, 13,000,
etc.—have in any case only symbolic significance rather than numerical meaning.
Three and seven appear for Christian reasons, thirteen and twenty for Mayan ones.

Çihil
  U cah u yax batan op
Hoch'
  Ch'intah t u pach acan tun

Bal ti çihi co e
  Bal ua yum e
T ech
  A u ohel
Çihil
  U cah ah mun ti caan

*Ciripacte**
  *Horca mundo**
*Nimompanpan**
  *Est noche**
*Amanena**
  *Omonena**
*Apa**
  *Opa**
Hokci yk
  Ti ca lam tun *gra.*
*Çipionested coruna**
  *Pater profeçido**
Ci bin u than
  Ca kuch i
T u uuc p'el *capa**
  U çuhuy tun *gra.*
Bal te piones *orteçipiore**
  *Çiquenta noche**
Hun *ebritate**
  Hun cut e
*Profeçiado**
  Uchc i

5755 Being born
  He began the first axed macaws,
Drilling them
  And slinging them behind the
  standing stone.
What was it that was born, madness?
5760 What was it, father?
As for you,
  You know.
Being born
  Was the beginning of slaves in
  ·heaven:
5765 Alligator,
  The gallows of the world.
My place of stone banners
  Tonight.
Look ye
5770 And you looked.
Be here
  And you were here.
There appeared
  Wind in the excessive *tun* of grace.
5775 "They received this crown
  The fathers prophecied"
Would be his word
  When he appeared
In the seventh stage
5780 Of the virgin *tun* of grace.
"What then will he expect
  On the fiftieth night?
A drunken celebration,
  And the seating
5785 Prophecied
  Occurred."

5765. Nah. *cipactli.*
5766. Sp. *horca (del) mundo.*
5767. Nah. *nimomopanpan.*
5768. Sp. *esta noche.*
5769. Nah. *amanena.*
5770. Nah. *omanena.*
5771. Nah. *apan.*
5772. Nah. *opan.*
5775. Lat. *accipient,* Sp. *esta/*(?*usted*) *corona.*
5776. Lat. *pater,* Sp. *profeciado.*
5779. Sp. *capa.*
5781. Maya *bal te,* Sp. *anticipare.*
5782. Sp. *cincuenta noche.*
5783. Maya *hun,* Sp. *ebriedad.*
5785. Sp. *profeciado.*

U thanal *angel**		The words of the angel
Gerupite*		Jupiter.
Ca tz'ab caan *corporales**		Then heaven was given bodies
Ti *ojales* t u menel yax *papa**	5790	In branches by the first pope,
U u ich katun		The face of the *katun*,
U cuch katun ti oxlahun ahau*		The burden of the *katun* which was 13 Ahau.
Ual kahom u u ich kin		Embittered enemies of the face of the sun!
Nocpahom y okol ualac y ahaulil		Bitter rivals lamenting the lordship to be set up!
Çatai uinicil	5795	Needy the people,
Çatay ahaulil		Needy the lords.
Ho p'el kin		The five days,
Chian kin		The extra days
Ca bin pacatnac		Then will be seen:
U taahte oxlahun ahau	5800	The division of 13 Ahau,
Chicul		The fulfillment
U tz'ah Dˢ.		Of the city of God,
Uchuc u cimil y ahaulil		Occasioning the death of the lordship
(54) Lay lumoob lae		Of these lands here.
Bay ix ca bin tac	5805	And thus it will ensue
Lay yax ahauoob u paah u ba ob		That these first lords break themselves.
Ca tali		Then came
Y ocol *christianoil*		The arrival of Christianity
Uay		Here
Ti peten lae	5810	In this country.
Bay ix bin u tz'aic		And thus he will give
Chicul		The manifestation
Ca yumil		Of our Father
Ti Dˢ.		Who is God.
Ca bin tac ob	5815	Then they will approach
Y oklal minan hun olal		Lamenting that there is no agreement,
Hach man u than		And his word will be everywhere
Numçah ya		And inflict pain
Ti y al		On the born
U mehenob	5820	And engendered children,
U *christianoma* on		Christianizing us
Tan tun u mansic oon bay bal cheob e		And then treating us like animals.

5787. Sp. *ángel.*
5788. Sp. *júpiter.*
5789. Maya *ca tz'ab caan,* Sp. *corporales.*
5790. Sp. *hojales, papa.*
5792. 13 Ahau is a symbolic reference to the end of a cycle, just as the Uayeb days (line 5798) symbolize the end of the year.

Lay ya t u y ol *Dios*	That is the pain in the heart of God:
Ti ah tz'utz'ob lo e	It is these "suckers."
Mil i cinientos treinta y nuebe años 5825	1,539 years,
Bay la *1539 años**	Hence the year 1539
Likin bail u hol y otoch	Was the erection of the door of the house
Dn. Juan Montejo	Of Don Juan Montejo
Oces *christianoil* uay	To bring Christianity here
Ti peten lae 5830	To this country,
Yucal peten	The plantation country
Yucatan lae.*	Of Yucatan.

VII

VII

(56) He ix u ca kaba	And this is the second name
Dios citbil	Of the Holy God
Ca tali 5835	Who came
U y anhal	To exist,
T u *personaç* e	To become a person,
Çihanil i	And to bring to birth
Bal cah	The world
Y etel luum e 5840	And the land.
Lay tun u kaba lae	This then is his name:
*Sosue**	It is Joshua,
U ca tz'ic e	His second person.
T u y ox tz'ic e	In his third person
U ca kaba e ox uch 5845	His other name, the third to occur
Ox ten hi lae	On the third time,
*Mesister latin**	Was Master in Latin,
Tun *Dei romance**	But *Dei* in Romance.
Chac pauah tun	The Red Stone Giant
*Ut corusis** 5850	Was as the numbing Northwest Wind.
Çac pauah tun	The White Stone Giant
*Coracalbo**	Was the Bald Northwest Wind.
Ek pauah tun	The Black Stone Giant
*Colrusi pro vento**	Was the numbing Northwest Wind as a wind.
Kan pauah tun 5855	The Yellow Stone Giant
*Moses**	Was Moses.
*No vis**	You don't see;
*No va**	It won't go.

5826. This dates correctly the beginning of 11 Ahau, and that is the *katun*, albeit not the year, of the building of Montejo's house.

(*notes continued on following page*)

Stole of the Trinity (1776). From the
Garrett Collection of Manuscripts in
Middle American Languages, The
Princeton University Library, The
gift of Robert Garrett.

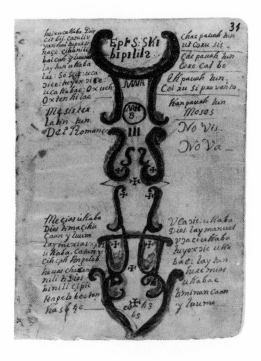

5832. In another hand on MS page (55): *chilam balam profeta* 'Spokesman of
the Jaguar, Prophet'. And on the following page, MS page (56), in yet another hand:
Bay hele lae malob kin tun ciento ycil u y . . . 'thus on the other hand this is a
good day, then a hundred in the month of . . .'. On the same MS page an illustration appears with the legend (partly in rebus) which I here transcribe and attempt
to read.

Ept S:	espíritu santo	The Holy Ghost
S k I	santo ik hun	Is holy spirit one;
bi pilil 2	bi pilil ca	As spirit two
M N R	i n i r (INRI)	Is Jesus of Nazareth, king of the Jews.
M H	manuel jeramías	The messiah Jeremiah
B III	verbum tris	Is word three,
cu h 3	cu (a)h ox	The three of them being seated
bs	ds.	As God.

The illustration looks to me like a depiction of a priestly stole. It is of interest
that this late eighteenth-century assimilation of the Trinity is still depicted as a
quadripartite design with nine crosses on it! (I am indebted to Mediz Bolio 1930:
64–65 for the courage to attack this passage.)

5842. Sp. *Josué.*
5847. Lat. *magister,* Sp. *latín.*
5848. Lat. *dei,* Sp. *romance.*
5850. Lat. *ut corus,* Maya *ziz.*
5852. Lat. *corus,* Sp. *calvo.*
5854. Lat. *corus,* Maya *ziz,* Lat. *pro vento.*
5856. Lat. *Moses.*
5857. Sp. *no viste.*
5858. Sp. *no va.*

*Meçias**	Messiah
U kaba *Dios*	5860 Is the name of God
Ti ma çihic caan	Who did not create heaven
Y etel luum	And earth.
Lay *Mexias**	That is the Messiah.
Xpto. u kaba*	His name was Christ,
Ca tun u çihçah *angelob**	5865 And then he created angels.
He uac chacannil i	However, it appeared
Ti *Dios* binil i	That God came
Çipic *angelob* e	To blame the angels,
T an has	Who suffered
Tze	5870 And wept (?).
U ca tz'ic u kaba *Dios*	The other person and name of God
Lay *Manuel**	Was Savior,
U tz'aci u kaba	The other one of his names,
T u y ox tz'ic u kaba e	The third person's name.
Lay tun *Heremias**	5875 He then was Jeremiah
U kaba	By name
Ti minan caan	When there was no heaven
Y etel luum e.	And earth.

Death (1776). From the Garrett Collection of Manuscripts in Middle American Languages, The Princeton University Library, The gift of Robert Garrett.

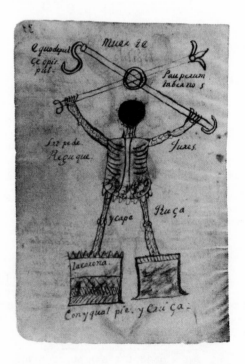

5859. Sp. *mesías.*
5863. Sp. *mesías.*
5864. Sp. *Christo,* modern *Cristo.*
5865. Sp. *ángel.*
5872. Heb. *Emanuel.*
5875. Sp. *Jeremías.*

42. The Sins of the Itza

(58) *Damaçeno**		Damascene
U kaba chakan patc i	5880	Was the name of the plain where he was shaped,
Ca yax yum ti *Adan* t u menel *D*ˢ.*		Our first father Adam by God.
He ix u kaba e		And that was his name;
Lay u yax kaba lae		That was his first name:
Adan		It was Adam.
Ca oci u pixan	5885	Then came his soul.
Ca u acunabi *parayso* e*		Then was established Paradise.
Çihanil i		That was the birth
Tun *Adan*		Then of Adam.
Ca çihi ca yax naa		Then was born our first mother
Ti *eua* e*	5890	Who was Eve,
Yax ch'uplal		The first woman,
U naa bal cah tuçinil		Mother of the world of sin.
Chun thah biin tun		The original drops will have been stones,
Hun thah bin haban		Some drops will have been bushes.
Ca çihij	5895	Then he was born,
Ti minan caan c uchi e		For there was no heaven existing.
He tun citbil e		And so the Most High
Çihij		Was born
T u ba		Of himself,
T u hunal ychil akbil	5900	Alone in the night.
He tun ob e		So there they were:
Hun pai çihci ob		The sole precursors were born.
He tun acan tun e		And then there was the covered stone
Lay luum lae		That was the earth,
Lay ix ch'ab i	5905	And it was created,
Uchci u patal *Adan* xan e		And the shaping of Adam occurred also.
Lay tac u mehen		This then was his seed;
Lay ocantac ob y icnal acan ob e		Thus were they introduced into their shapes
B la he x u kabatah ob		And so thus were they named
Ca patlah ob e	5910	When they had been shaped.

5879. The text is preceded by the word *kay* 'song', but only a slight change produces *kaay* 'preaching'. Roys 1967: 114 gives this the title "A Song of the Itza"; it is about as anti-Itza as you can get. Sp. *damaceno* 'Damascene'.

5881. Sp. *Adán.*

5886. Sp. *paraíso.*

5890. Sp. *Eva.*

Lay i tac	This then
U yax chun u uinicil	Was the first origin of the people
Dios citbil	Of the Holy God,
Dios mehenbil	God Made Son,
Y etel *Dios espiri santo*	5915 And God the Holy Ghost.
Lay molcab *D*ˢ. lae	That is the collectivity of God then.
Lay çih ob	This was their birth
T u tunil	In the time
Chac hilib tun	Of the red-striped stone
Y etel u y ub tun *graçia*	5920 And the colored stone of grace.
Lay *berbe* u kaba e*	That was the Word by name,
*Josus tin graçia**	The grace of the blessed Jesus.
He tun y ix hun y eta e	And that was the sole companion
Çihi	Who was born
T u tunil ek oyob tun	5925 In the time of the black island stone.
Lay *berbum tuorum* u kaba e*	That was Your Word by name,
T ix co al tun	And the eternal son of stone,
Ix co aal cab	And the eternal son of earth,
Ti u ch'aah	Who obtained
U colel cabil i	5930 The wife of the world.
Ca bin ti cutal ox coc ox caan	Then he will come to seat 3 Turtle and 3 Snake
U coc oxxil caan c uchi e	3 Turtle and 3 Snake will be there
Sac	To brighten
Homen	And clarify
Culic tac cabal	5935 His seat in all the earth
Ti y ol *sustinal graçia*	In the spirit of sustaining grace.
Oxlahun pic u katunil	Thirteen thousands of *katuns*
Chelan t u tunil	Are laid to this time.
Ca pecnahi	Then will be made known
U uilim hunac ceel ahau	5940 The need of the Lord Hunac Ceel.
(Kay:)	(Song:)
Ge*	Hey!
Ma et kin on	Are we not of the same sun
Ti x kan thixal	And of the yellow breastplate
Ti tun	Of stone?
E	5945 Hey!
Mac u cobol y *utztacil* uinic*	Who is the polisher of the whiteness people?
Yn nok	My clothes!
Yn uex	My loincloth!
Y alah o	For he is born,
Ua ku e	5950 Perhaps as God.

5921. Lat. *verbum*.
5922. Sp. *Jesús*, Maya *t'in*, Sp. *gracia*.
5926. Lat. *verbum tuum* or *verborum tuorum*?
5941. From here on it *is* a song.
5946. Nah. *iztac* 'white', Maya -*il*.

Ba la ca u oktic i
   Yx ci jx ma mac e
U munal en
   U chii ch'een c en
Ti uli o
   Chuc lum tz'itz'
U tah katun
   A ya
(59) T u chi ch'een ytza o
   Antan *he**
Ya o
   Y ulu
Ua yan oo
   E
Ti hun imix
   U kijnil chuccaan
Bin ahau
   T u chikin ch'een e
E
   Tab a ech y an e
Ku e
   E
Tun hun ymix
   U kin y alah
T u chi ch'een ytzao a
   Anta *here**
Ya o
   Y ulu ua yan o
Muclam
   Muclam
Ci jx
   Yaua to
Muclam
   Muclam
Ci xan y ohel ob thun
   Ci y au e
Ci xan y auat o
   T u hun te yax kin e
Chichil kin ij
   Ca te ak yabil
Ti tali o
   Ayano
Ayano
   Ayano

So then shall I also dance,
   And everyone, gladly?
I am his slave;
   I am from Chichen,
5955 Who come here
   Through the whole land
To argue the division of the *katun*.
   Ah woe! Woe!
The Itza of Chichen
5960   Are aided by heretics!
Alas!
   Alas!
O woe!
   Hey!
5965 On 1 Imix
   The time is completed,
And the Lord will be
   At Western Well.
   Hey!
5970   Where have you been then
   O gods?
   Hey!
For 1 Imix
   Is the day of birth!
5975 For those of Chichen Itza
   Are aided by heretics.
O woe!
   Alas!
Ruin!
5980   Ruin!
And again
   Woe!
Ruin!
   Ruin!
5985 And they just knew how to shed tears
   And cry.
And it was also just woe!
   On the first of that Yaxkin,
That was the hard time.
5990   Then there was the new illness
That came there.
   Alas!
Alas!
   Alas!

5960. Sp. *herejes*.
5976. Sp. *herejes*.

Y ulu	5995	Woe!
U ayano		And alas!
Y an xin mac		Could there have been someone,
Xin ahan ual e		Even a lord perhaps?
Chichil ni		A hard time (?)
Ca te ayano	6000	And then, alas!
Ox tun c acan u kin e		Three times the sun will be covered:
Ku e		The gods
C ah ualob		Of our enemies—
C ah ualob uuiyao		Our enemies: O pain!
Ma xan ulom t u chi ch'een	6005	Who else has come to Chichen Itza
ytzao a		
Anta *hereya* e*		Aided by heretics?
Y ulu		Woe!
Ua yan o		And alas!
Ox te caan		There were three heavens
U kin	6010	On their day.
He mac en ua t u than tan y ol		Indeed, who am I to speak among
uinic e		men?
C en u mac le e e ya		I am a person of lineage, hey!
Ma c en ua t u than tan y ol putun		Who am I to speak among the Chontal
Men a nate o e yan		And make you understand this, hey?
Ch'ab en	6015	I am the creation.
Akab en		I am the night.
C oon ua çihij o		Are we born here?
Eya		Hey!
Alak on mis cit ahau*		We are the serfs of the Sweeper lord.
Ho atal ux	6020	Indeed we are come in any case.
Ulu max		We have arrived in any case.
Elab in yn kacuntah		There now will I shape my song
T in kay be		And have sung thus:
Antan *hereya* o		Aided are the heretics!
Y ulu ua yan o	6025	Woe!
Eya		And alas, hey!
Cimil en y alah		I die, it says,
T u men u kin cah o eya		Because his day has begun, hey!
Ca tac en y alah e		Then hide, it says,
T u men u çat cah o	6030	Because the destruction has begun
U ti u lah ti y ol		Of the one who comes in spirit,
U tuclah t u puccikal e		Who thinks in his heart.
Men u çat cah o		Have his destruction begin.
Ualik a cun t an in kay o		If I may sing my song:

6006. Sp. *herejes*.

6019. The Sweeper and Remover (Miz Cit) officiate at the ceremonies confirming land titles at the beginning of the *katun*. Thompson 1970: 31 asserts that placing Ahau 'lord' after a name is a Chontal practice. I am not persuaded to that (see line 1149).

Antan *hereya* o	6035	Aided are the heretics!
Ayano		Alas!
Y uluu		Woe!
Ayano		And alas!
(60) Lay kay t u lacal lae		This song is all then;
U tz'oc lukanil y anumal ahau	6040	Ended is the praise of the Lord God!
Dios lae.		

43. The Sheep and the Goats

(102) Xot kin ti *D*ˢ.*		The judgment from God
T u tiblil uinicob e		On defiant men.
C on ex*		*"Let us go*
U icnal		*Together*
C ex	6045	*Ye,*
U cici than uinicil yn yum e		*Blessed People of my Father.*
Ca a nahalt ex		*Then ye shall fulfill*
Hun kul *gloria*		*A divine glory*
Mentahan		*Prepared*
T u men yn yum e c ex	6050	*By my Father for you*
Hop'c i		*When he began*
Bal cahil e		*The world.*
A tacuntah ex u almah thanil		Ye have confused the commandments.
A u utzcinah ex *penitensia*		Ye have perfected repentance
Ca sip ex	6055	When ye have sinned
T en uchi e		Against me.
Ba la c on ex		Wherefore let us go
Ti caan		To heaven."
Ca tun u sutbes		So then he turns back
U pacat	6060	His sight
Ti ah kebanob		On the sinners.
Ti lep'an y ol ti ob e		He has been angered by them:

6041. I agree with Roys 1967: 163, note 3 that this chapter, which he titles "The Last Judgment," was probably composed by a missionary priest. The biblical quotations are verbatim. The orthodoxy of the text and the limited number of Hispanicisms also argue for Spanish authorship: a Maya would have used more and different ones. Roys dates it to the seventeenth century; I date it to the eighteenth. I gather that both dates are impressionistic. The first couplet appears to be the title of the sermon, which is taken from Matthew 25.

6043. Matthew 25:34. Direct quotation italicized: "Come, ye blessed of my Father, inherit the kingdom prepared for you from the foundation of the world."

Nachhen ex*
  U icnal
C ex lolob thanbil
  T u men yn yum e
X en ex
  T u kakil *metnal*
Ma xulumte
  Lay menan
Ti ciçin
  T u men yn yum e
A poch'ah en ex
  (. . . . .)*
C en a yum ex e
  C en a u ah lohil ex e
A poch'ah ex yn than
  T u men u than ciçin e
Be
  Ba la xen ex
T u pach
  Ti hun lukul num ya
Ca tun xic ob ti *metnal*
  U lobil uinicob e
He ix y utzil uinicob e
  Bin xic ob ti caan
T u pach ca yumil
  Ti *Ds.*
Ti hun lukul *gloria*
  Y et p'isan *gloria*
*Yosapat**
  Y an ox tul uinicob
U hach palilob *Dios*
  Hach yabilob t u men *Dios*
Elias
  Y etel *matusalem*
Y etel *enoc*
  U kaba ob
Cuxan ob tac
  Hele lae
Ti c ulcinan ob
  T u men *Dios* u canant ob
U xecil
  U *sillasil*

Depart ye
  From me,
6065 *Ye who are cursed*
  By my Father.
Go ye
  Into the fire of hell.
There will not end
6070   *That which is prepared*
For the devil
  By my Father.
Ye have scorned me!
  (. . . . .)
6075 I who am your Father,
  I who am your Savior!
Ye have scorned my word
  Because of the word of the devil.
So be it!
6080   Wherefore go ye
After him
  For a period of punishment.
So then they go to hell,
  The evil people.
6085 And those who are good people
  Will go to heaven
After our Father
  Who is God,
For a period of glory
6090   Equal to the glory
Of Jehoshaphat.
  There are three men
Who are the true children of God,
  Truly beloved by God.
6095 Elisha
  And Methuselah
And Enoch
  Are their names.
And they lived
6100   Nearly till now.
They were fulfilled
  Because God had them guarded,
Their seats,
  Their chairs.

6063. Matthew 25:41. Direct quotation italicized: "Depart from me, ye cursed, into everlasting fire, prepared for the devil and his angels."
6074. Line missing.
6091. Jehoshaphat, Elisha, Methuselah, and Enoch have no obvious association with each other or with this context.

Bin u mentic *cuenta* ca yumil	6105	He will make a count, our Father
Ti D^s.		Who is God,
Ti hun p'el kom luum		In a pit of earth,
Hun p'el noh chakan		A great plain.
Tij tun u cutal*		*Then he will sit*
Y okol u xecil u tepal	6110	*In his seat of majesty*
Bin ix moloc ob		*And there will be assembled*
T u lacal bal cah tuçinil		*All the world of sin.*
Çayhom tanamob		*Winnowed will be the sheep,*
Bin y anac ob t u noh		*Who will be on his right;*
Çayhom yucob	6115	*Winnowed will be the goats,*
Bin y anac ob t u tz'ic		*Who will be on his left:*
Bin y anac t u tz'ic lae		Who will be on his left then
U lobil uinicob		Are the evil people,
Ah ma tz'ocsah ob		Those who did not fulfill
Ti y almah thanil D^s. t u lacal	6120	The commandments of God
		altogether.
Ti tun u bin ob*		*They then will go*
Ti hun lukul		*For a period*
U num yail *mitnal*		*To suffer in hell*
T u lamay cab		*Below the earth,*
Alanil	6125	Burdened
T u men ca yax yumob e		Because of our first fathers.
He tun bin y anac t u noh		Then there will be on the right
Ahau *Dios*		Of the Lord God
Lay y utzilob uinic		The good people
Ah tz'ocçahob ti y almah than	6130	Who fulfilled the commandments of
Dios		God.
C on ex*		*Let us go,*
C ex		*Ye,*
U cici than		*Blessed*
Uinicil yn yum e		*People of my Father,*
Pach ex ahaulil	6135	*Follow ye the lordship*
Menant ex		*Prepared for you*
Hopci		*At the beginning*
Bal cahil e		*Of the world.*
Bey ti tun u takal		Then there will be engendered
Noh muyal e	6140	A great storm.

6109. Matthew 25:31–33. Direct quotation italicized: "When the Son of Man shall come in his glory, and all the holy angels with him, then shall he sit upon the throne of his glory: And before him shall be gathered all nations: and he shall separate them one from another, as a shepherd divideth his sheep from the goats: And he shall set the sheep on his right hand, but the goats on the left. Then shall the King say unto them on his right hand," (the quote in note 6043 follows directly).

6121. Matthew 25:46. Direct quotation italicized: "And these shall go into everlasting punishment: but the righteous into life eternal."

6131. Repeat of the quotation in note 6043.

Ek t u nak caan   It will be black in the belly of the sky
  (103) Tac t u u ich luum   And on the face of the earth.
Bay hom iuil ci oltzil*   Like a trumpet may be the joy
  U kay *angelesob*   Of the song of the angels.
Minan y et pisan ci oltzilil   6145 It is incomparably joyful.
  Bin nacabal   There will arise
Hahal ku   The True God,
  U yumil   The Father
Caan   Of heaven
  Y etel luum lae.   6150   And earth.

6143. Revelation 11:15: "And the seventh angel sounded (his trumpet); and there were great voices in heaven, saying, The kingdoms of this world are become the kingdoms of our Lord, and of his Christ; and he shall reign for ever and ever."

---

44. Notes from Chumayel

(81) Helel *en 18 de agosto**   Today on August 18
  De *1766 años* lae   Of 1766
Ca uch i   Then there was
  Chac ykal lae   A hurricane.
U kahlayil c in tz'ibtic   6155   The account I am writing
  Ca utzac y ilic   Will make it possible to see
Ba hun hab   How many years
  Ca bin uchuc u lak lae   It will be before another like one
                                          occurs.

Helel *en 20 de henero*   Changing to January 20
  De *1782 años*   6160   Of 1782
Ca cheket-hi   Then stalked the bloated
  Chupil   Swelling
Uay   Here
  Ti cah chumayel lae   In the town of Chumayel.
T u cal uinic c u chupul   6165   In the neck people would swell up
  Ca ix emec cabal xan   And then it might go lower down
                                          too,
Tac ti chin chan   As to young
  Tac ti nohoch   And old alike

6151. The following text has usually been used to date the MS as a whole. It occurs relatively early (folio page 81) but dates itself to 1782. It is obviously late and irrelevant to the rest of the MS, but it is not the latest segment of the work. See the introduction.

P'is u mistic hun p'el na	It swept through each house
Ca bin occoc i	6170 When it entered.
He u tz'acal	This was the cure
Lae	Here:
Pah taan	Dye-tree ash
Y etel *limones*	With lemons,
Ua ix sisal xiu	6175 Or else numbing grass
Mehentac e	And seed mixed in it.
Tac t u habil *81 años* chumpah i	Around the year 1781 it got started,
Ti ix u tz'aah nohoh kin tun y	Which gave it a great cycle too.
abil xan i*	
Ol ma oc chac i	Rather there was no rain.
Ellah kax t u lacal	6180 The whole forest was being burned,
Cimlah ix	And it killed off
Kaxob xan	The forests too.
Lay u kahlay	This is the account
C in tz'ibtic	I am writing,
C en	6185 I,
Dn. Juan Josef Hoil lae. (Rubric)*	Juan Josef Hoil. (Rubric)

6178. The new calendar round began in 1789.

6186. The following two pages contain marginal notes that belong to 11 Ahau, dating to the 1830s. They are reproduced here in chronological order.

I. Justo Balam (1833)

(84) *Miercoles*	Wednesday
Helel *en 4*	Today on the 4th
De 1833	Of 1833
Abrilil	Apriltime
Uchic in chicultic	Occurred my witnessing
U kaba *Mᵃ. Ysidora*	The name of María Isidora
Hija de Andres Balam	Daughter of Andrés Balam
Y Mᵃ. Juana Xicum	And María Juana Xicum.
Domingo	Sunday,
Helel en *22 de disiembre*	Today, on the 22nd of December
De 1833	Of 1833,
Uchic in chicultic	There occurred my witnessing
U kaba *Tomas*	The name of Tomás,
Hijo de Andres Balam	Son of Andrés Balam
Maria Juana Xicum	And María Juana Xicum.
Padrinos	Godfather
Jose Mᵃ. Castañeda	José María Castañeda.
Madrina	Godmother
Manla Marin	Manuela Martin.
Cura	Curate
(Ju)an Que . . .	(Ju)an Que(vedo).
Justo Balam	Justo Balam,
Gr. cac cura	Curate's assistant.

(*note continued on following page*)

(note continued from preceding page)

II. Pedro Briceño

(83) Chumayel
Y junio 28 de 1838
Y uchic in majan
Ti Chinuh Balam
T en
Pedro Briceño (Rubric)

Chumayel
And June 28, 1838,
My loan was made
To Chinuh Balam.
I,
Pedro Briceño.

III. Pedro de Alcantara Briceño (1838)

(84) He u kinil uch i
N manic lae *libro*
1 de julio
De 1838
He u toholma ti t en e
Hun ppel *peso* ichil otzilil
He toholma ti yum *padre*
Peso
Lay u habil uch i
Manic lae . . .
C in chicultic
Y oklal u y oheltabal
He x kinil
Manic t in kab
T en
C en
Pedro de Alcantara Briceño
Cahnalal *San Antº*.

This was the time it happened
That I bought this book:
July 1st
Of 1838.
This was made good by me
For one peso in poverty.
This was made good to the lord Father
(For one) peso.
This is the year of the occurrence
Of purchasing this (book).
I am witnessing it
So that it will be known,
And that this is when
It was bought by my hand.
I
Myself,
Pedro de Alcántara Briceño,
Resident of San Antonio.

13 Ahau

45. Coba

(73) Kin chil coba*   Kin Chil of Coba
    U hetz' katun   Seated the *katun,*
Maya cu*   The cycle seat
    Oxlahun ahau katun   6190   Of *katun* 13 Ahau.
Ytzam na   Itzam Na
    Ytzam zab*   And Itzam Tzab
U u ich   Were the faces
    Ti y ahaulil   In the lordship.
Bin uiibic ox i   6195   There will be the starvation of
                            gourdroot,
    Ox te ti hab   Gourdroot tree years,
Ca kal abil   For forty years
    Lahun tz'acab*   And ten steps.
Et bom u al   Like-colored is the water,
    Et bom u tz'ub   6200   And like-colored is the odor.
Yaxal chac*   Yaxal Chac
    U cuch t u caanil   Bore it on high,
Ix ma chac bin uah   And unboiled food
    U uah   Will be the food
Katun   6205   Of the *katun,*
    Ti oxlahun ahau   Which is 13 Ahau.

6187. The association of this *katun* with Kin Chil and with Coba is pure convention (see line 631).

6189. Identifying Coba as the seat of the cycle as well as of the *katun* implies the collapse of the whole cycle system, an appropriate event for this final *katun* of the cycle and of Mayan history. While the Maya continued to count *katuns* and to write history, they wrote no more *katun* prophecies.

6192. Roys 1967: 134, note 7 implies that these are god names. I believe the Jaguar and his Spokesman either had or took on high prestige names to bolster their faltering claims to authority.

6198. The implication is a fifty-year famine.

6201. I believe the assertion is that Yax Chac was to seat the following *katun.* This, too, is pure convention: Yax Chac seated *katun* 11 Ahau at Merida in 1539 (line 1597).

Chiban kin i
   (74) Ca pic u cuch katun

Çatay uinicil
   Çatay ahaulil
Ho p'el kin uil
   Chian kin
Ca bin pacatnac*
   Lay u cuch
Ah oxlahun ahau
   Katun lae.

Eaten is the sun.
   Two thousand are the burdens of the
   katun.
Needy people,
6210   Needy lords.
Five days perhaps
   The sun has been eaten;
Then it will have been seen.
   That is the burden
6215 Of 13 Ahau
   Katun.

6213. A solar eclipse of exactly five days is a suitably apocalyptic image for the final termination of the *katun* cycle.

11 Ahau

46. Tizimin

Act 9

(64) (. . . . . .) ti culhi
   Lahun pis katun*
Ti culhi
   Nicte katun*

Act 9

(That was) the seating
   Of the tenth part of the *katun.*
It was the seating
6220   Of the Flower *katun.*

Act 12

Ox te uu
   Culan
Yum a
   Unetziuit
Kuk
   Yaxun
Ti pual y anac may chiich*

Act 12

The third moon
   Was the seating
Of a certain father
   Onetzihuit,
6225 The quetzal,
   Blue bird.
In that month was the cycle of birds.

6218. The reference may be to *katun* 10 Ahau. See note 6323.

6220. This dates the chapter as belonging to 11 Ahau (the Flower *katun*) even if it is erroneously identified as the tenth *katun.*

6224. Onetzihuitl is clearly Nahuatl, probably *ome itzihuitl* 'two flint', a curious anachronism in this context.

6227. Craine and Reindorp 1979: 67, note 9 give *ti ual yan u may dchidch* 'which would have been the cycle of birds' from the Mani.

Act 13

Ti ual y an bolon *teuitz**

Yum a
Unetziuit
Kuk
Yaxun*

Act 14

Mac bin naatic ob ch'abtan*

Kintan ob ti y ahaulil i
T u lahca pis tun
Ti y alah u kaba

Act 15

Lay uil e
Balam
U pol
Uaan u coo*
Tz'utz'ul uinicil
Pek u uincil
Man ch'acat han

Act 16

Ya t u pucçikal
Ci jx u hanal
Ci jx y ukul
(. . . . .)*
Ma la bin y ub e*
Bin ix u tus
Coil u than*

Act 13

In that month was the great sharp
stone
Of this father
6230 Onetzihuit,
The quetzal,
Blue bird.

Act 14

Which of them will understand the
"halfway seizure,"
The time of the half in the lordship
6235 On the twelfth measured *tun*
That speaks its name?

Act 15

There is seen
A jaguar,
His head
6240 Standing on his snout
Sucking people.
Dogs are the people,
Going across to eat.

Act 16

Pain is in his heart.
6245 Thorns are his food,
Thorns his drink.
(. . . . .)
He will hear nothing,
And lies
6250 And madness will be his word,

6228. I read Nah. *tehuitz(tli)* 'sharp stone'.

6232. Another allusion to the confrontation of the Xiu and the Itza in 1539.

6233. See note 5330. Formerly in the eleventh *tun*, the mid-*katun* ceremony is now placed in the twelfth year. The date would be 1836.

6240. The Tizimin presents this colorful imagery as part of a vision of the prophet. The various scribes did not understand this the same way (Roys 1967: 121, note 9).

6247. Line missing.

6248. The Tizimin makes it clear that the prophet went into a trance to produce this vision. Apparently it involved fasting and penance.

6250. That is, the nobility continued to claim title to the land of the peasants.

Ma tub u tz'aic u ba   And nowhere does he surrender
   Yx cuch luum ytz'inil   The burden of the land of the
          younger brothers.

Bin li u kebal uay   He will be removed here
   Ti peten e   In this country.
Bin bayac ob   6255 They will capture him
   X cuch lum ytz'inil   And the burden of the land of the
          younger brothers,

Ti y al ob y ix mehenob   Who are the sons and daughters
   Yx lolok bayan palalob   And captive adolescent children
Samal   Of tomorrow
   Cabeh e   6260   And the day after.
Tz'a ex a ba   Surrender yourselves,
   C ex   O ye
U itz'in   Younger brothers
   Çucun ex e   And older brothers,
Maneç ex u cuch katun   6265 And pass the burden of the *katun*
   Lic u talel e*   As it came,
Ua matan a maneç ex e   If you have not already passed it.
   Ti u motzhal t a u oc ex e   That will be taking root at your
          feet,
          And you

T e x i
   Bin u helinte   6270   Will be changed.
Ua ma a mançic ex e   But if you don't pass it,
   Te x i   It is you
Bin kuxic u chun che   Who will be gnawing at the trunks of
          trees
   Y etel xiu   And grasses.
Ua ma a mançic ex e   6275 But if you don't pass it
   Bay çinic cehil bin uchebal*   Thus Ants and Deer will come
          about
U hokol t a cahal ex   And appear in your towns.

Act 17   ## Act 17

   Ti jx u hokol ahau   And that will be the appearance of
          the lord.
Bin manac   He will pass
   U sut ychil a cahal ex e   6280   And return to your towns,
Ti ma u cuchil i e   Which is not his burden;
   Y etel oc na kuchil e*   He arrives at Entering the House,

---

6266. A plea for general acceptance of the ceremonies renewing the *katun* cycle.
   6276. The Tizimin and Mani have *cim cehil* 'death of the Deer'. The Chumayel is threatening military action.
   6282. Sound play: *cuch* 'burden', *kuch* 'arrive'.

U kin u ma ya cimlal
 Baal cheob*
Tij culhi
 T u pop
Hun çip u than
 Hun çip u can
Lay u çip katun
 Ox tzuc u uah nicte katun

Lay ti culhij
 Oxlahun y al u pop

Ah calam chuuch
 Ah cal pach keban
Ti jx u talel *Bula*
 Uac tzuc t u ba
Ox ten bin manbal *Bula*
 Ca bin uluc u *jueçil Bula* lae*
Ua ah xolte t u kin bin u *juesilte*

 Ua ix çac cib bin u kexinte
 xan (65) e
He çac cib lae
 Ti y emel *justiçia**
Likul ti caan
 Nacebal *christianoil* uinic
T u u ich u *justiçiail*
 Ti tun u mentic u pec

Caan
 Y etel luum
Ya ix bin tz'ocebal
 Nicte katun
Ma uil mac
 Bin kuchuc u thani e
Ca bin chin chin
 Polcintabac
U teel
 Chacil che e

A time of the painless death
 Of animals.
6285 He who is seated
 On the mat,
1 Spite is his word;
 1 Spite is his teaching.
That is the Spite *katun.*
6290 Three divisions are the food of the
 Flower *katun.*
He who is seated
 Has thirteen bastard children of his
 mat—
Mad coral snakes
 And asshole sinners.
6295 And that is the coming of the bull
 With six parts to it.
Three times the bull will be brought.
 Then will arrive the judge's bull.
Either the collector of money will be
judged
6300 Or else white candles will also be
 exchanged.
Those are the white candles
 That bring down justice,
Rising to heaven
 To glorify the people of Christianity
6305 Before the face of his justice,
 Who will then bring about
 understanding
In heaven
 And earth.
And the pain will be ended
6310 Of the Flower *katun.*
There may be no one
 Whose word will arrive.
We shall load up
 And shall have carved
6315 The tree,
 The very red tree

6284. From the following lines it would appear that there was a lowborn claimant to the throne of the *katun.* This text presents the pro-Christian claim, specifying animal sacrifices and Christian ideology.

6298. The six-part bull (Sp. *bula*) apparently refers to the proclamation abolishing tribute, possibly with the success of the Revolution for Independence in 1824, possibly as early as the Cortes of Cadiz in 1806. See the Tizimin, notes 5155, 5281.

6302. Tribute was collected in money and in beeswax candles. The Mayan expectation was that it would be paid back the same way.

Ti tun u y uk ba peten	That then will be spread
T u lacal e	Throughout the country.
Conbil bin tz'ocbal u than	Selling will be the end of the word
Nicte katun e 6320	Of the Flower *katun*.
Minan i uil	There is no need
Ua u ilal a tz'aic a pol ex	For you to have to surrender your heads
Ti *Arzo Obispo* e*	To the archbishop.
Ca bin emec e	When he comes down
Bin xic ex 6325	You will go
A bal a ba ex ti kax	With your property into the wild.
Ua bin a tz'a a ba ex i e	But if you are going to surrender,
Ti binan ex	Then go,
Iuil t u pach *Xpo.*	But follow Christ.
Ti y an ob cochomi e 6330	They have been cleared.
Tij tun ca bin tz'ococ	That then will be the end
U *uiçita* e	Of his visitation.
Talel bin u cib	Coming will be the candle
U lilib nicte	Of the trembling flower,
Tijx ca bin a nat ex e 6335	And that then will be your understanding.
Ca bin ticin pecnac caan e	Then will be spread the awareness of heaven.
Tij to ca bin thanac	That is what will then be said.
U tz'ibte u nak pak e	It will be written to expect it soon,
Ti yx a u alic ex kuil xan i e	And that is also what the gods have told you.
Lay bin a u ocçic t a u ol 6340	That will be the entry of the gods
ex kuil	into your hearts.
Hii u il to mac ah miatz y an a u ichil ex	Perhaps that will be someone who is a sage among you,
Bin nattic e	Who will understand.
Tij tun u binel ti kax	He will then go into the wild
U tan le u *christianoil* e	To lead Christianity.

6323. Much of the structure of this text appears to repeat the prophecy not only of 11 Ahau, thirteen *katuns* earlier, but also of 1 Ahau, eight *katuns* earlier. The reason may be that the author may have been reckoning as much in calendar rounds or Christian centuries as in *katuns*. There was a calendar round beginning in 10 Ahau in 1685, which is referred to in the 1 Ahau prophecy (line 5060). Three calendar rounds later we come to another in 11 Ahau in 1841, which may be alluded to in the present text (line 6483). Whatever the reason, the 1 Ahau prophecy refers (1) to a certain Saúl (2) who aided the bishop in imposing the Inquisition (line 4937) and who was joined by (3) Don Antonio Martínez (line 5064) to support the rights of the Christianized nobility in 1 Ahau (1638). This was the *katun* of the Chan War of Tihosuco (line 4944), but there is also mention of (4) the War of Havana and (5) thirteen-sail ships (line 4990). All of the numbered details are repeated in the present text, except that here the bishop becomes the archbishop. It is asserted that the rigors of the Inquisition are not to be repeated. People are advised to retreat to the woods to avoid the archbishop but to remain Christian.

Mac bin natic lae
  Ha li li lo
Lahu can p'el haab*
  U ba tabil
Ca bin hun kul
  Uluc mehenbil
Lay D". *Antonio Martines*
  Y etel *Saul**
Lay u kaba ob

  Ca luki ti caan
Ti jx
  Ti bin i
Tzimentan e*
  Ti y an *tzimentan*
Ti ix
  Ti y alah hun tul yx ahau u y
ichamte*
Uuc te ix
  Ti haab
U kamic u *casamintoil*
  Ca ti heb i
U *puertail* takin
  Ti can kas na
Et sabi ti
  Ca ix u tus çihçah
Chem
  Oxlahun baak*
Ca ix t u likçah katun
  Hauana u lumil*

6345 Who will understand that?
  Truly!
After fourteen years
  Of his office,
There will be a god
6350   To arrive as Son.
That is Don Antonio Martínez
  And Saúl.
These were his names when he
departed
  From heaven.
6355 And it was he
  Who came
To Tizimin.
  He was in Tizimin,
And it was he
6360   Who asked a queen to marry him.

And it was the seventh:
  That was the year
That he seized the marriage registry.
  Then he opened
6365 The money doors
  In the four-room house.
It was shown to him,
  And then he set out to build
Ships
6370   Of thirteen sails.
And then he raised a war
  With the land of Havana.

6347. The date implied is 1838. Martínez' story is strongly reminiscent of that of Santiago Iman, who was imprisoned in Tizimin in 1838 (Reed 1964).

6352. Nothing is known of Antonio Martínez or Saúl from Spanish sources.

6357. As with all other Nahuatlisms in these *Books*, it is the southern dialect, Nahuat, that is employed, hence *-tan* for *-tlan*. Now the second largest city of Yucatan, Tizimin is not mentioned in the *Books* before the nineteenth century, when it became important as a livestock center. I derive the name from *ti* 'at' *tzimin* 'horse' and Nahuat *-tan* 'place'.

6360. I believe the date 1831 is implied. The queen is a picturesque and totally obscure touch.

6370. Ships have slowly added sails throughout history, but it is not until the frigates of the late eighteenth century that they attain thirteen or more. The clippers of the early nineteenth century had three times that number or more. Even British ships-of-the-line in the Napoleonic Wars had fewer than thirteen sails (Ward 1973).

6372. The Havana connection and the French connection (line 6426) are difficult to explain, the more so since the former is explicitly mentioned in a text of two centuries earlier (note 6323). Roys 1967: 123, note 12 may be right in suggest-

(*note continued on following page*)

Ti jx y an u nup u than	And he opposed the word
Rey hauana	Of the king of Havana.
Ca alab u xicin Rey	6375 Then it was borne to the ears of the king
	That he opposed his word.
T u men u nup u than	
Ti ix y an y ah tocul u hool t u pach	And he had the commandant of the port after him.
Ca ti bin i	So he left,
Ti y ubah ix	And he heard
U chucul xan i	6380 That he was to be seized too.
Ti tun likul ca bin i	He then arose and went there,
Te tzimentan	There to Tizimin.
Ti ix tun ti chuc i	And then he was seized.
Ox p'el u lukuc y ah chucil	Three months ago his captors left.
Ca kuchi tzimetann e	6385 When he reached
Ti tun chuc i	Tizimin,
Ti jx tun (66) ti ix u xotah u than ti chucil	Then he was seized.
Ka kuch i .	He was ordered seized,
Tzimentan e	Just as he arrived
Ca ix y alah	6390 At Tizimin.
Xen uinic e*	And (Martínez) said, "Go on, man,"
C u than ti	He said to him.
O u yn kuchul i	"It is three months since I arrived,"
C u than	(Martínez) said.
Ox p'el u lukc ech hele lae	6395 "It is three months since you left, on the other hand."
Ox u ech a kuchul i	(Captain:) "It is three months since you came.
Lic tun a kuchul e	As soon as you came
Lic tun a kalal ti mascab	You were clapped in irons.

(note continued from preceding page)

ing that piracy was involved. War with the French may echo the Napoleonic Wars of the previous katun (ca. 1806). Cuba was a hotbed of Yucatecan politics during and after the Revolution for Independence (1821) and at least one episode involved Tizimin at about the right date (ending in 1838; see note 6347). In an uncanny way, Martínez' prophecy (below) also foreshadows the outbreak of the War of the Castes at the end of this katun (1848) and that, too, involved Tizimin (Reed 1964).

6391. The rest of the text is hard to follow because it starts out in third-person narrative quoting a conversation between Martínez and his jailors—two captains—whom he enlists in his cause. At line 6425, however, it shifts to first person and Martínez himself is speaking, quoting a conversation between himself and the "king" and giving his prophecy for the coming battle and for the katun. To clarify the matter I have added indications of who is speaking. The king is identified as rey in the Chumayel but as nacom 'captain' in the Tizimin. The latter makes more sense. No doubt he was a "king's man," since he was Martínez' jailor at the outset, but he underwent a change of heart and turned over the town to Martínez. Direct discourse ends at line 6466, and Martínez continues with his sermon, addressing the reader and the general public.

Ta muk tun in talel
   T in i
Bin lukçic ech ti mascab
   T ex
C ex *capitan* e
   Cabilil i
Bin y anac t in pach i
   C u than
Nacçahac bolon *çian*
   Y etel titz' u illan tz'on e
Bin ix elec kaknab
   Bin in likebal i
Ti culan
   Kak u pacat ti
Bin ix likic ex
   Y etel yom haay
Bin ix tupuc u u ich kin
   T u men chac lubuc y ikal e
Ti tun u cenic u ba *capitan* e
   Bin ix hu tuc t u u ich luum
T u men ykal xan

   Lic tun yn cumtal
T in kan che tunn e

   Lic tun u talel ox bak chem e

B ix tun u cenic u ba
   Rey xan i
Ch'aa ba yumil e
   Te u talel *françes*
Ci jx u than
   T en
Bin cimic oon
   T u men uinic e
Bal x a u il u lubul a muk e

   T u men a u et unicil e lic ech i

To ex ican t in tz'ab u tohol chem
   Tan chumuc
U et lik
   Ci jx in u ikal xan
El ix
   El ix kaknab
In bin ci jx noo
   Ci jx u u ich caan

Meanwhile I was coming.
6400   As for me,
I shall remove you from irons."
   "As for you,
You captains,
   Both of you,
6405 You must follow me,"
   (Martínez) said.
"Have nine chairs brought up
   And let us sit down,
And the sea will burn
6410   And I shall be exalted."
(Martínez) sat down
   With fire in his glance:
"And it will raise sand
   And foam on the water,
6415 And it will put out the eye of the sun
   Because of the rain-filled winds."
Then he dressed himself,
   The captain (Martínez, and said,)
"And it will be leveled to the face of
the earth
6420   Because of the wind too.
As soon as I am settled on my stone
bench
   The thirteen-sail ships will be
coming."
And then he dressed himself,
   The king('s man) too, (and said,)
6425 "Get ahold of yourself, sir!
   There come the French!"
So spoke
   His word to me.
(Martínez:) "We are going to die
6430   Because we are men!
And what do you see to rest your
strength?
   Because your fellow men are like
you!
I am going to be given the guide ship
   In the middle,
6435 And I will help propel it
   With my breath too,
And burn,
   And burn up the sea,
And I am going to tie on
6440   The face of heaven too,

He tun ca em en e
  Tak licil u u ich ca cat chem*

Mac uinicil a
  C u than t en
T en ix ix ma ok olal e
  T en ix a chaalte e
T en i bin a ca put çiheç e
  Bin ix in tumte in kaba
Lay *martines*
  Dios citbil
Dios mehenbil
  Dios espiritu santo in kaba

Ca ix in hoksah uuc tz'acab *liblo*

  In xoc ob
Ca ix ti tz'oc i
  Ti ox p'el u
Hi x u mançic u ba ob
  Ah belnalob e
Ti tun i alah u tz'ab u cahal t en

  Tan coch uinic e
Tab i an a cahal
  In cahal t u lacal

Ti a botic in cahal
  C en yax ul e
Lic tun in u alic
  Ti emi*

Act 20

Justiçia uchebal
  U nacal *christianoil*
Bolon pixanil
  Bin tz'ocebal
Ti jx u katabal
  U *probail* ti ob
Ti y ahaulil cah e
  Ua ma y ohelob e

And then I shall descend
  And be stuck up as the face that
  destroys ships."
"Who is this man?"
  (The captain) says to me.
6445 (Martínez:) "And I am an infidel.
  And I am your purifier,
And I shall be your twice-bearer
  And I shall renew my name,
Which is Martínez.
6450   God the remote,
God Made Son,
  And God the Holy Ghost is my
  name.
And then I shall manifest the seven-step books
  And read them,
6455 And then it will end
  In three months,
And they will buy each other,
  The officials."
Then (the captain) said his town would
be surrendered to me
6460   And half the people:
"Where is your town?"
  (Martínez:) "My town is the whole
  thing.
So you will pay for my town:
  I was the first to arrive."
6465 As soon as I spoke to him
  He came down.

Act 20

Justice will be achieved,
  The elevation of Christianity.
The nine spirits
6470   Will be ended,
And that will be the demand
  For titles from them,
From the lordship towns
  Or the ignorant.

6442. The sense of this is that Martínez is going to put on the mask of God to destroy the enemy. This is made explicit in line 6452, where he claims to be God.

6466. Having persuaded the captain that he understood the prophetic books, Martínez claims title to the whole town for purposes of tribute, and the captain "came down," i.e., acceded.

Ti ix u hokol ich luumil tunich

    Y etel ich luumil che

Ti uinic chahal

    Ti tun i etz'tal cah i

Minan tun ch'amac

    Bin chibalnac i*

Lay to ah bolon ahau

    Katun

Ho p'el haabil u binel

    Lay t u lah pach in than lae*

Ti kuch i

    T u kinil y emel patan

Ti tz'oc i

    U botic ob u likçah katunob ca
    yumoob

Ma ix a u alic a uah

    U alilil ex katun c u talel k
    icnal lae

(67) C ah lohil ti *jesuchristo*

    Y ah canul ca pixan

Bay uay

    Y okol cab e

Bay ca bin u ch'a ca pixan

    T u cilich caanil xan

Mehen ex e hahal *Dios*

    Amen.

6475 And that will be the demand in the
    lands of stone
    And in the lands of wood,
From wounded men,
    From thus established towns.
Then there will be no Foxes
6480   Who will bite.
That then will be the 9 Ahau
    Katun.
Five years will go by
    When they completely follow my
    word,
6485 Which will come
    To the time of the lowering of
    tribute.
It will end,
    The payments for the raising of the
    wars of our fathers,
And you will not say that your food
6490   And water of the *katun* is to come
    from us
(But from) our savior who is Jesus
    Christ,
    The guardian of our souls.
As it is here
    On earth,
6495 So our souls will be taken
    To the holy heaven also,
O sons of the True God.
    Amen.

6480. Martínez predicts the end of paganism ("the nine spirits") and the military companies by 9 Ahau (1848), when tribute (the indemnity for the War of the Conquest) will end.

6484. Either this refers to five years after his captivity in 1838 or five years before the end of the *katun* in 1848. In either case the date reached would be 1843.

Appendix A. Concordance

The following table lists the order of the chapters (C) in the present translation and the line numbers (L) at which they begin. This is followed by the numbers of the folio pages at which the same passages begin in the original manuscript (MS) and in George Gordon's (1913) facsimile edition (GG), the corresponding pages in Ralph Roys' (1967) translation (RR), Barrera Vásquez' (1948) combined translation of cognate passages from all the *Books* (BV), and Mediz Bolio's (1930) translation (MB). After that I have listed initial line numbers of corresponding passages in my translation of the Tizimin (ME) and page numbers in Craine and Reindorp's (1979) translation of the Mani (according to Pío Pérez and Solís Alcalá in Spanish), listed as (CR). Additional references to the Kaua, Oxkutzcab, and Tusik and to other published versions will be found in the notes.

C	L	MS[1]	GG	RR	BV	MB	ME[2]	CR
1.[3]	1	40	74	135	57	87	1	138
2.[4]	153	42	77	139	68	91		
3.[5]	251	42	78	140	71	93		
4.	381	53	98	160	140	110	347	
5.	399	53	98	161	140	110	367	
6.	421	54	99	161	140	111	387	
7.[6]	433	57	105	166	196	116	401	73
8.	467	54	99	161	141	111		
9.[6]	479	57	104	164	195	115		72
10.[6]	495	57	105	167	197	117	3951	74
11.	629	53	100	162	141	111	433	
12.	691	3	3	66		19		
13.[6,7]	1327	57	105	167	196	116	1207	73
14.	1361	9	15	79		32		
15.	1421	2	1	63		17		
16.	1581	8	13	77	96	29	777	77
17.	1701	38	71	131		30		
18.	1819	40	73	133	95	85		
19.	1837	47	87	147	124	100	1165	
20.[8]	1991	33	60	116		70		
21.[6]	2215	57	104	165	196	115	1239	73
22.	2243	48	89	149	126	102	1307	
23.	2299	14	25	86				
24.	2313	46	85	145		97		
25.	2505	48	90	151	128	103	1435	

C	L	MS[1]	GG	RR	BV	MB	ME[2]	CR
26.	2571	49	91	152	129	104	1475	
27.	2665	9	16	80		33		
28.	2915	49	92	153	131	105	2981	
29.[9]	2961	24	42	98	153	53		
30.[10]	3501	17	28	88	204	40		
31.	4383	36	67	125		80		
32.	4693	15	26	86		38		
33.	4789	51	93	155	133	106	3875	
34.	4991	56	103	164		114		
35.	5077	52	96	158	137	109	4117	
36.	5127	53	97	159	139	109	4263	
37.	5161	34	63	120		73		
38.[8]	5227	40	73	133	118	86	4603	85
39.	5255	12	21	84		37		
40.	5315	40	73	134	119	86	4817	86
41.	5339	27	48	107		61		
42.	5879	32	58	114		67		
43.[9]	6041	56	102	163				
44.	6151	44	81	143		95		
45.	6187	40	73	134	121	86	5061	86
46.	6217	35	64	120	158, 220	74	5155	65

1. The original of the Chumayel is in the Princeton University Library. An early copy by Carl Hermann Berendt (1868) is in the Berendt Linguistic Collection of the University of Pennsylvania Museum. A photographic copy made by Theobert Maler in 1887 was once in the William Gates Collection. Its present whereabouts are unknown to me. The entire Chumayel has been published in Spanish by Mediz Bolio 1930, 1935 in a loose poetic translation.

2. The Tizimin has also been published in a rather experimental English translation by Makemson 1951; my citations are to Edmonson 1982.

3. This chapter of the Chumayel has been published by Brinton 1882; Martínez 1927, 1940. The corresponding part of the Mani has been published by Stephens 1843; Valentini 1880; Brasseur 1864; Charencey 1874; Thomas 1882; Brinton 1882; Palma y Palma 1901; Martínez 1909, 1926, 1927, 1940; Escalona 1933; Jakeman 1945. The Tizimin version has been published by Brinton 1882; Martínez 1927, 1940.

4. See Brinton 1882; Lizana 1893; Martínez 1910; Tozzer 1921; Mediz Bolio 1935.

5. See Brinton 1882; Martínez 1927, 1940.

6. Chapters 7, 9, 10, 13, and 21 have been published by Lizana 1633, 1893; López de Cogolludo 1688; Brasseur 1857–59, 1869–70; Castillo 1866; Carrillo 1870, 1872, 1883; Brinton 1868, 1882; Charencey 1873; De Rosny 1875, 1904; Orozco 1880; Paso y Troncoso 1883; Tozzer 1921.

7. See Tozzer 1921.

8. Brotherston 1979.

9. See Martínez 1912, 1913, 1927, 1928.

10. This chapter appears in the Kaua and the Tusik.

Appendix B. A Ceremonial Circuit

Lines 771 through 1080 in chapter 12 (one of the longest texts in the Chumayel) record a ceremonial circuit of *katun* 11 Ahau (1539). The circuit is generally counterclockwise and except for its starting point at P'ool on the east coast it is confined to the area of the modern state of Yucatan, moving along the north coast past Merida, then making a southern sweep through Uxmal to Valladolid. The circuit then ceases to be a ritual counterclockwise definition of boundaries. It wanders through Izamal and vicinity, then heads south to Mani, north to Merida, south again to Mayapan, and back to Merida. Of the 171 place-names mentioned, about half can be located (see figure 44). The remainder, being named in approximate geographical order, may be located more or less accurately by the use of the accompanying map and the index. The reference numbers give the order of appearance of each place in the text. It is reasonable to suppose, for example, that Tah Aac (number 19) was located someplace between Tz'ul A (number 17) and Cooh (number 20), perhaps closer to the latter, while Pib Haal Tz'onot (number 18) may be closer to the former (see lines 822–825).

Approximately forty-one of the places named lie within twenty miles of Merida and about thirty within an equal distance of Mayapan, whereas only eighteen are that close to Izamal and only fifteen to Valladolid. The western bias of the text (which almost certainly comes from Merida) seems obvious. A confirming datum is the surprising omission of Chichen Itza from the list, since Mayapan and Uxmal are included and Chichen Itza is mentioned elsewhere in the text.

It is significant that the Xiu identify themselves with an eastern origin point when the Itza don't. The Xiu allied themselves with the Spaniards (who came from the east), something the Itza refused to do.

Acan Ceh, 162
Ake, 2, 116. *See also* Hol Tun Ake
Al A, 3
Bac A, 31
Bal Che. *See* Ix Bal Che
Balam Kin, 137
Bitun Ch'een, 129
Bohe, 119

Bon Kauil, 88
Buc Tzotz, 23
Cah Chac, 27
Can, 83. *See also* Ix Can
Can Zahcab, 106
Cau Cel, 40
Cetelac, 71
Chable. *See* Hol Tun Chable

Chac, 165
Chac Akal, 53
Ch'ahil, 164
Chalam Te, 101, 123
Che Choc Tz'iitz', 108
Che Mi Uan, 68
Ch'een Ch'omac, 138
Ch'el. *See* Ix Ch'el
Chi Can, 61

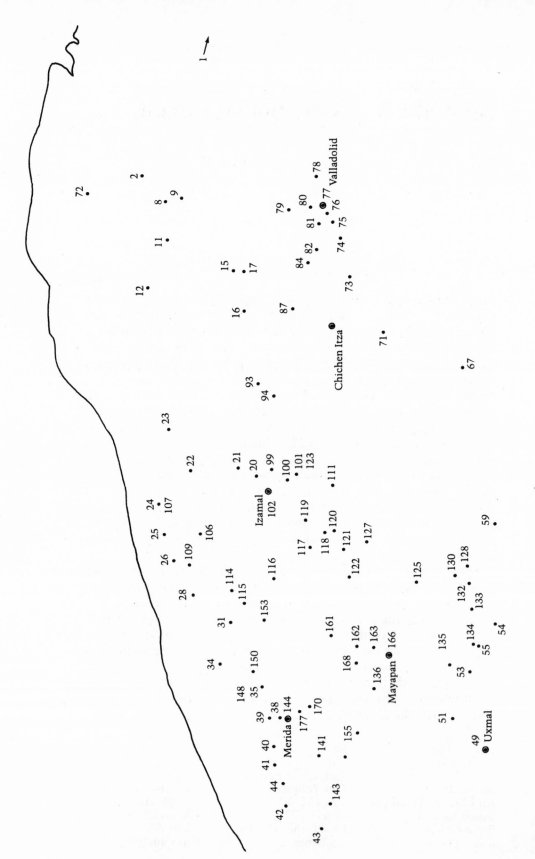

The ceremonial circuit. After Roys 1933. (1 in. = 18.6 mi.)

Appendix C. The Mayan Calendar

Yearbearer Type	Days (*Kin*)			
I	Imix	Cimi	Chuen	Cib
II	Ik	Manik	Eb	Caban
III	Akbal	Lamat	Ben	Etz'nab
IV	Kan	Muluc	Ix	Cauac
V	Chicchan	Oc	Men	Ahau

Note: These are counted permutatively from 1 to 13: 12 Imix, 13 Ik, 1 Akbal, 2 Kan, etc.

Months (*Uinals*)			
Pop	Xul	Zac	Pax
Uo	Yaxkin	Ceh	Kayab
Zip	Mol	Mac	Cumku
Zotz'	Ch'en	Kankin	Uayeb
Tzec	Yax	Muan	

Note: These are counted serially from 1 to 20: 19 Pop, 20 Pop, 1 Uo, 2 Uo, etc.

Sequence of *Uinals* (For a year 1 Kan)	Sequence of *Katuns*	Calendar Round (1 Kan equals:)
1 Kan	13 Ahau	1529
8 Kan	11 Ahau	1581
2 Kan	9 Ahau	1633
9 Kan	7 Ahau	1685
3 Kan	5 Ahau	1737
10 Kan	3 Ahau	1789
4 Kan	1 Ahau	1841
11 Kan	12 Ahau	
5 Kan	10 Ahau	
12 Kan	8 Ahau	
6 Kan	6 Ahau	
13 Kan	4 Ahau	
7 Kan	2 Ahau	

Katun Ending Dates

	Tikal				*Katun* Initial Dates Mayapan	Valladolid
8 Ahau	692	948	1204	1461	1697	
6 Ahau	711	968	1224	1480	1717	
4 Ahau	731	987	1244	1500	1737	
2 Ahau	751	1007	1263	1520		1776
13 Ahau	771	1027	1283	1539		1800
11 Ahau	790	1047	1303		1539	1824
9 Ahau	810	1066	1323		1559	1848
7 Ahau	830	1086	1342		1579	
5 Ahau	849	1106	1362		1599	
3 Ahau	869	1125	1382		1618	
1 Ahau	889	1145	1401		1638	
12 Ahau	909	1165	1421		1658	
10 Ahau	928	1185	1441		1677	

May Ending Dates

Xiu			Itza		
8 Ahau	9.13.0.0.0	692	13 Ahau	9.17.0.0.0	771
8 Ahau	10. 6.0.0.0	948	13 Ahau	10.10.0.0.0	1027
8 Ahau	10.19.0.0.0	1204	13 Ahau	11. 3.0.0.0	1283
8 Ahau	11.12.0.0.0	1461	13 Ahau	11.16.0.0.0	1539
8 Ahau	12. 5.0.0.0	1717			

(The last *katun*:   6 *Ahau*   12.6.0.0.0   1737)

Baktun Ending Dates

10 Ahau	7.0.0.0.0	347 B.C.
9 Ahau	8.0.0.0.0	46
8 Ahau	9.0.0.0.0	440
7 Ahau	10.0.0.0.0	832
6 Ahau	11.0.0.0.0	1224
5 Ahau	12.0.0.0.0	1618

Numerals

Written	Value	Maya	Nahuatl
	zero	mix baal	
	one	hun	ce
	two	ca	ome
	three	ox	yey
	four	can	naui
	five	ho	macuilli
	six	uac	chicuace
	seven	uuc	chicome
	eight	uaxac	chicuey
	nine	bolon	chicunaui
	ten	lahun	matlactli
	eleven	buluc	matlactlionce
	twenty	uinic	cempoualli

Appendix D. Seats and Lords of the *Katun*

There is considerable agreement among the *Books* on the seating and lordship of the *katun*. In this list Chumayel is coded as C, Mani as M, Kaua as K, and Tizimin as T.

Date	Seat	Lord	Spokesman
12 Ahau (1421)	Otzmal (CT)		
10 Ahau (1441)	Coba (C) Tan Xuluc Mul (C) Zizal (C)		
8 Ahau (1461)	Chichen Itza (CT) Izamal (CMT) Kan Cab A (C) Tan Xuluc Mul (CT)	Xib Chac (CMT) Kuk Can (CMT) Ul Ahau (MT) Hapay Can (CT) Can Ul (CT)	
6 Ahau (1480)	Hunac Thi (C) Merida (C) Teabo (C) Uxmal (CKMT)	Tzim Thul (C) Kak Mo (M) Kak Mo (KMT) Uxmal Chac (C)	Uayom Ch'ich' (C) Cab Xiu (C)
4 Ahau (1500)	Atikuhe (C) Bolon Te Uitz (C) Chichen Itza (CT) Hol Tun Zuyua (C) Kin Colah Peten (C) Na Cocob (C) Teabo (CK)	Kuk Can (CT)	Ahau Pech (CKMT)
2 Ahau (1520)	Chacal Na (C) Cozumel (C) Tihosuco (T)		Puc Tun (CKMT)
13 Ahau (1539)	Coba (CT) Cozumel (C) Kin Colah Peten (C) Mayapan (C) Merida (C)	Kin Chil (CT) Mutecpul (C)	Xopan Nahuat (CKMT)

Date	Seat	Lord	Spokesman
Mayapan Calendar			
11 Ahau (1539)	Colox Peten (C) Emal (CT) Merida (CKMT)	Zulim Chan (T) Yax Chac (CKMT)	Tzin Yabun (CKMT)
9 Ahau (1559)	Merida (CT) Teabo (CKMT)	Ul Uac Chan (K) Uac Nal (T)	Kauil Ch'el (CKMT)
7 Ahau (1579)	Mayapan (CKMT) Merida (CT)	Chu Uah (KMT) Yax Chac (CT) Amayte Kauil (T)	
5 Ahau (1598)	Mayapan (M) Merida (T) Zotz'il (CKMT)	Ahau Can (T) Amayte Kauil (T) Puz Hom (KT)	Hol Och (T)
3 Ahau (1618)	Merida (CT) Zuyua (CMT)	Coc Ay (CT) Coc Ay (CMT)	Antichrist (C)
1 Ahau (1638)	Emal (CMT) Merida (CT)	Puc Ol (C) Ol Zip (T) Hun Pic (CT) Amayte Kauil (M) Caesar Augustus (C)	Ual Ac (C) Ual Icim (T) Ol Ha (T) Can Ul (CT)
12 Ahau (1658)	Valladolid (CKMT)	Yax Chuen (CKMT) Pat Ay (T)	
10 Ahau (1677)	Chable (CKMT) Valladolid (T)	Lahun Chan (KMT) Pat Ay (T)	
8 Ahau (1697)	Chable (CKMT)	Amayte Kauil (KMT)	
6 Ahau (1717)	Teabo (CMT)	Kak Mo (MT)	
4 Ahau (1737)	Bacalar (C) Tan Hom (C) Teabo (CMT)	Mac Chahom (T)	
Valladolid Calendar			
2 Ahau (1776)	Valladolid (CKMT)	Pat Ay (C) Op Ik (CT)	
13 Ahau (1800)	Coba (CKMT)	Kin Chil (CMT)	
11 Ahau (1824)		Onetzihuit (C)	Antonio Martínez (CMT)

Bibliography

ANDREWS, E. WYLLYS IV
1961 Excavations at the Gruta de Balankanche, 1959. *Middle American Research Institute Miscellaneous Series* 11. New Orleans.

ANDREWS, E. WYLLYS IV, AND ANTHONY P. ANDREWS
1975 A Preliminary Study of the Ruins of Xcaret, Quintana Roo, Mexico. *Middle American Research Institute Publication* 40. New Orleans.

BARRERA VÁSQUEZ, ALFREDO
1948 (with Silvia Rendón) *El libro de los libros de Chilam Balam.* Mexico City: Fondo de Cultura Económica.
1961 Contrata de un maya de Yucatán, escrita en su lengua materna, para servir en Cuba, en 1849. *Estudios de Cultura Maya* 1:199–210.
1980 (ed.) *Diccionario Maya Cordemex.* Merida: Ediciones Cordemex.

BERENDT, CARL HERMANN
1868 Book of Chilam Balam of Chumayel. *Berendt Linguistic Collection* 50. Philadelphia: University of Pennsylvania Museum.

BLAIR, ROBERT, AND REFUGIO VERMONT-SALAS
1965–67 Spoken (Yucatec) Maya. Mimeographed. University of Chicago, Department of Anthropology.

BRASSEUR DE BOURBOURG, CHARLES ÉTIENNE
1857–59 *Histoire des nations civilisées du Mexique et de l'Amérique Centrale.* Paris.
1864 *Relation des choses de Yucatan de Diego de Landa.* Paris.
1869–70 *Manuscrit Troano. Etude sur le système graphique des Mayas.* 2 vols. Paris.
1872 *Dictionnaire, grammaire et chrestomathie de la langue maya.* Paris.

BRINTON, DANIEL GARRISON
1868 *The Myths of the New World.* New York.
1882 The Maya Chronicles. *Library of Aboriginal American Literature* 1. Philadelphia.

BROTHERSTON, GORDON
1979   Continuity in Maya Writing: New Readings of Two Passages in
       the Book of Chilam Balam of Chumayel. In Norman Hammond
       and Gordon R. Wiley, eds., *Maya Archaeology and Ethnohistory*,
       pp. 241–258. Austin: University of Texas Press.
BURNS, ALLAN F.
1980   Yucatec Mayan Ethnopoetics: The Translation of a Narrative
       View of Life. *Journal of Mayan Linguistics* 2:3–12. Iowa City.
CARRILLO Y ANCONA, CRESCENCIO
1870   Chilam Balam, "Códice de Tizimín." Manuscript. Copy in the
       Tozzer Library, Harvard University, Cambridge. (Given to Carrillo
       y Ancona by Manuel Luciano Pérez, March 23, 1870.)
1872   Disertación sobre la historia de la lengua Maya ó Yucateca.
       *Boletín de la Sociedad de Geografía y Estadística de la Re-
       pública Mexicana* (second series) 4:135–195. Mexico City.
1883   *Historia antigua de Yucatán.* Merida.
CASARRUBIAS, VICENTE
       Rebeliones indígenas en la Nueva España. Mexico City: Secre-
       taria de Educación Pública.
CASTILLO, GERÓNIMO
1866   *Diccionario histórico, biográfico y monumental de Yucatán.*
       Merida.
Chan Kan, Book of Chilam Balam of
n.d.   Copy in the Latin American Library, Tulane University, New
       Orleans.
CHARENCEY, CHARLES FÉLIX HYACINTHE GOUHIER, COMTE DE
1873   Recherches sur une ancienne prophétie en la langue maya
       (Napuc-tun). *Revue de Linguistique et de Philologie Comparée*
       6:42–61.
1874   Essai d'analyse grammaticale d'un texte en la langue maya.
       *Memoires de l'Académie Nationale des Sciences, Arts et Belles-
       Lettres de Caen.* Caen. (Reprinted by Le Havre, 1875.)
1875   *Fragment de chrestomathie de la langue maya antique.* Paris:
       Leroux.
1876   *Etude sur la prophétie en la langue maya d'Ahkuilchel.* Paris:
       Maisonneuve.
Chumayel, Book of Chilam Balam of
n.d.   Original MS in the Princeton University Library. *See also* Gordon
       1913.
CIUDAD REAL, ANTONIO DE
1600   *Diccionario de motul.* Original lost. Very early copy in the John
       Carter Brown Library, Providence.
CRAINE, EUGENE R., AND REGINALD C. REINDORP
1979   *The Codex Pérez and the Book of Chilam Balam of Maní.* Nor-
       man: University of Oklahoma Press.
Crónica de Calkiní
n.d.   Original MS lost. Copy in the Latin American Library, Tulane
       University, New Orleans.

Crónica de Oxkutzcab (Crónica de los Xiu)
    n.d.   Original MS in the Peabody Museum, Harvard University,
            Cambridge.
DE ROSNY, LEON
    1875   *L'Interpretation des anciens textes mayas.* Paris.
    1904   *L'Amerique pre-colombienne.* Paris.
EDMONSON, MUNRO S.
    1970   The Princeton Codex of the Book of Chilam Balam of Chumayel.
            Princeton University Library Chronicle 32:137–142.
    1971   The Book of Counsel: The Popol Vuh of the Guatemalan Quiche.
            Middle American Research Institute Publication 35. New
            Orleans.
    1976   The Mayan Calendar Reform of 11.16.0.0.0. *Current Anthropol-
            ogy* 17:713–717.
    1979   Some Postclassic Questions about the Classic Maya. *Papers of
            the Tercera Mesa Redonda de Palenque*, pp. 9–18. Palenque.
    1980   The *Baktun* Ceremonial of 1618. *Papers of the Cuarta Mesa
            Redonda de Palenque.* Austin: University of Texas Press.
    1982   *The Ancient Future of the Itza: The Book of Chilam Balam of
            Tizimin.* Austin: University of Texas Press.
ESCALONA RAMOS, ALBERTO
    1933   *Historia de los mayas por sus crónicas.* Merida.
ESPINOSA Y ESPINOSA, MANUEL, AND LUIS H. ESPINOSA S.
    1928   *Calendario de Espinosa para el año bisiesto 1928.* Merida.
GATES, WILLIAM
    1932   Eras of the Thirteen Gods and the Nine Gods. *Maya Society
            Quarterly* 1(2). Baltimore.
GORDON, GEORGE B.
    1913   The Book of Chilam Balam of Chumayel. *University of Pennsyl-
            vania Museum Anthropological Publications* 5. Philadelphia.
GRAULICH, MICHEL
    1981   The Metaphor of the Day in Ancient Mexican Myth and Ritual.
            Current Anthropology 2(1).
Hocaba, Book of Chilam Balam of
    n.d.   MS lost.
HUNT, MARTA ESPEJO-PONCE
    1974   Colonial Yucatan: Town and Region in the Seventeenth Century.
            Ph.D. dissertation, University of California at Los Angeles.
Ixil, Book of Chilam Balam of
    n.d.   Original MS in the Museo Nacional de Antropología, Mexico
            City. *See also* Roys 1946.
JAKEMAN, M. WELLS
    1945   *The Origins and History of the Mayas. Part I, Introductory In-
            vestigations.* Los Angeles: Research Publishing Company.
Kaua, Book of Chilam Balam of
    n.d.   Original MS lost. Copy in the Latin American Library, Tulane
            University, New Orleans.

LANDA, DIEGO DE. *See* Tozzer 1941.

LIZANA, BERNARDO DE
1633 *Historia de Yucatán.* First edition. Merida.
1893 *Historia de Yucatán.* Mexico.

LÓPEZ DE COGOLLUDO, DIEGO
1688 *Historia de Yucatán.* Madrid.

MCQUOWN, NORMAN A.
1967 Classical Quiche. In *Handbook of Middle American Indians,* vol. 5. Austin: University of Texas Press.

MAKEMSON, MAUDE WORCESTER
1951 *The Book of the Jaguar Priest: A Translation of the Book of Chilam Balam of Tizimin with Commentary.* New York: Henry Schuman.

MALER, THEOBERT
1887 Copy of Chilam Balam of Chumayel. Whereabouts unknown.

Mani, Book of Chilam Balam of
n.d. Original MS lost. *See also* Craine and Reindorp 1979.

MARTÍNEZ HERNÁNDEZ, JUAN
1909 *Chilam Balam de Maní ó Códice Pérez.* Merida: Colegio San José de Artes y Oficios.
1910 Los grandes ciclos de la historia maya según el Manuscrito de Chumayel. *Compte-rendu del XVII Congreso Internacional de Americanistas.* Mexico City.
1913 La creación del mundo según los mayas. *Proceedings, 18th International Congress of Americanists (1912),* pp. 164–171. London.
1926 *Crónicas mayas. Crónica de Yaxkukul.* Ed. Carlos R. Menéndez. Merida.
1927 *Crónicas mayas.* Ed. Carlos R. Menéndez. Merida.
1928 El juicio final. Página 102 del MS de Chumayel. *See also* Espinosa y Espinosa 1928:137–138.
1940 *Crónicas mayas.* Second edition of Carlos R. Menéndez. Merida.

MEDIZ BOLIO, ANTONIO
1930 *Libro de Chilam Balam de Chumayel.* San Jose.
1935 *Síntesis mística de la historia maya.* Mexico City.

MORLEY, SYLVANUS G.
1946 *The Ancient Maya.* Stanford, Calif.: Stanford University Press.

Nabula, Book of Chilam Balam of
n.d. MS lost.

Nah, Book of Chilam Balam of
n.d. Original MS in Gates Collection.

OPPOLZER, THEODOR
1887 Canon der Finsternisse. *Denkschriften der Kaiserliche Akademie der Wissenschaften, Mathematisch-Naturwissenschaftliche Classe 52.*

OROZCO Y BERRA, MANUEL
1880 *Historia antigua de la conquista de México.* 4 vols. Mexico City.

OWEN, MICHAEL
  Concordance of the Book of Chilam Balam of Chumayel.
  Seattle.

PALMA Y PALMA, EULOGIO
  1901 *Los mayas.* Motul.

PASO Y TRONCOSO, FRANCISCO DEL
  1883 Los libros de Chilam Balam. *Anales del Museo Nacional*
    3:92–109. Mexico City. [Spanish translation of Brinton 1882.]

PÍO PÉREZ, JUAN
  1866–67 *Diccionario de la lengua maya.* Merida: Imprenta Literaria.

PROSKOURIAKOFF, TATIANA
  1963 *An Album of Maya Architecture.* Norman: University of Okla-
    homa Press.

REDFIELD, ROBERT, AND ALFONSO VILLA ROJAS
  1934 Chan Kom, a Maya Village. *Carnegie Institution of Washington
    Publication* 448. Washington.

REED, NELSON
  1964 *The Caste War of Yucatan.* Stanford: Stanford University Press.
Ritual of the Bacabs. See Roys 1965.

ROYS, RALPH L.
  1931 Ethno-Botany of the Maya. *Middle American Research Institute
    Publication* 2. New Orleans.
  1933 *The Book of Chilam Balam of Chumayel.* First edition. Norman:
    University of Oklahoma Press.
  1939 The Titles of Ebtun. *Carnegie Institution of Washington Pub-
    lication* 505. Washington, D.C.
  1943 The Indian Background of Colonial Yucatan. *Carnegie Institu-
    tion of Washington Publication* 548. Washington, D.C.
  1946 The Book of Chilam Balam of Ixil. *Carnegie Institution of Wash-
    ington Publication* 75:90–103. Washington, D.C.
  1965 *The Ritual of the Bacabs.* Norman: University of Oklahoma
    Press.
  1967 *The Book of Chilam Balam of Chumayel.* Second edition. Nor-
    man: University of Oklahoma Press.

SOLÍS ALCALÁ, ERMILO
  1949 *Diccionario español-maya.* Merida: Editorial Yikal Maya Than.

STEPHENS, JOHN L.
  1843 *Incidents of Travel in Yucatan.* New York.

SWADESH, MORRIS, MARÍA CHRISTINA ALVAREZ, AND JUAN BASTARRACHEA
  1970 *Diccionario de elementos del maya yucateco colonial.* Mexico
    City: Universidad Nacional Autónoma de México.

Tekax, Book of Chilam Balam of
  n.d. Original in Gates Collection (1924, no. 956). Photograph in the
    Latin American Library, Tulane University, New Orleans.

Telchac, Book of Chilam Balam of
  n.d. MS lost.

THOMAS, CYRUS

1882   *A Study of the Manuscript Troano.* Washington, D.C.: Government Printing Office.

THOMPSON, JON ERIC SIMPSON

1970   *Maya History and Religion.* Norman: University of Oklahoma Press.

Tihosuco, Book of Chilam Balam of

n.d.   MS lost.

Títulos de Ebtun. See Roys 1939.

Tixcocob, Book of Chilam Balam of

n.d.   MS lost.

Tizimin, Book of Chilam Balam of

1824–37   Original MS in the Museo Nacional de Antropología, Mexico City. *See also* Edmonson 1982; Makemson 1951.

TOZZER, ALFRED MARSDEN

1907   *A Comparative Study of the Mayas and the Lacandones.* New York.

1921   A Maya Grammar. *Papers of the Peabody Museum of American Archaeology and Ethnology, Harvard University* 9. Cambridge.

1941   Landa's Relación de las Cosas de Yucatan. *Papers of the Peabody Museum of American Archaeology and Ethnology, Harvard University* 18. Cambridge.

Tusik, Book of Chilam Balam of

n.d.   Original MS in Tusik, Quintana Roo. Photograph in the Carnegie Institution of Washington, Washington, D.C.

VALENTINI, PHILIPP J. J.

1880   The Katunes of Maya History. *Proceedings of the American Antiquarian Society* 74:69–117. Worcester.

VILLA ROJAS, ALFONSO

1945   The Maya of East Central Quintana Roo. *Carnegie Institution of Washington Publication* 559. Washington, D.C.

WARD, RALPH T.

1973   *Ships through History.* New York: Bobbs-Merrill.

Index

capital, 502, 528, 1895, 1926, 2240, 2894, 5001
capitán (Sp. 'captain'), 2691, 5190, 6403, 6417
capitanil, 2727
capítulo (Sp. 'chapter'), 1837
captain, 2687, 2691, 2739, 4933, 5190, 6402, 6418;
   of land, 320, 326; village, 2727
captor, 6384, 6388
cargo (Sp. 'burden'), 5481, 5713; holder, 4875
Carnival, DRAMA
Carrillo y Ancona, Crescencio, MANUSCRIPTS
Carrying Baby Monkey, MANUSCRIPTS. See also 13
   Gods
Cartabona (?'Constantinople'), 1374
casadosob (Sp. casados 'married people'), 4503
casamentoil (Sp. casamiento 'marriage'), 6363
casamientosob, 4459
cascabeles (Sp. 'rattles'), 4375
cassamientoil, 5110
cassava (Manihot), 4666
Caste War (1848), HISTORY
cathedral, building of (1563–1604), HISTORY
Caucel ('plant cold'), village, 881, 883
Cau Ich ('plant eye'), person, DRAMA, 755, 1179,
   1181, 1428, 1539
Cauac ('storm'), day name, 2091
cave, 2135
Ceçar (Sp. César 'Caesar'), 2957, 4916
Ceel, Hunac. See Hunac Ceel
Ceh ('deer'), twelfth month, 5304
Ceh Il ('deer see'), 2938
ceiba (Ceiba), alligator, 1439, 1453, 1465, 1481;
   branch, 3683; root, as chuckawalla, 3692
Ceiba Land, 559, 3184
Cen, Ni. See Ni Cen
cenote, as black forest, 4655; as church, 4458
Center priest, DRAMA, 1769
Centipedes (Scolopendra), military company, 1277,
   1293; and Gnats, DRAMA
ceremonial, DRAMA, HISTORY, MYTH
ceremony, DRAMA; balche, 2968
Cerpinus. See Corpinus
Cetelac ('even grass'), village, 919, 1162, 1167
Ch'ab Tan, 5330
Chab, Ah. See Ah Chab
Chabi Tok ('digging knife'). See 9 Gods
Chable ('zapote leaf'), town, DRAMA, 701, 1095,
   1789, 1793, 2310, 5128; Lahun, 1789, 1793,
   5061
Chable, Lorenzo, 5180, 5186
Chable, Martin, 5192
Chac ('red, rain, great'), rain god, DRAMA, LAN-
   GUAGE, MYTH; village, 1071
Chac Akal ('red vines'), village, 900
Chac Ek ('red star'), person, 5122
Chac Kitan, town, 5237
Chac Te ('red tree'), village, DRAMA, 1502; person,
   1135, 1136
Chac Uil Tok ('red moon knife'), Flower lord, 3319
Chac, Uxmal. See Uxmal Chac
Chac, Xib. See Xib Chac
Chac, Yaxal. See Yaxal Chac
Chac, Yuuan. See Yuuan Chac
Chacal Na ('red house'), town, 342
Ch'achac ('rainstorm'), ceremony, DRAMA

chacnabiton (?Nah. chiconahuitan 'nine country'),
   place, MYTH
Ch'ahil ('dripping'), village, 1070
chair, 6406
Chakan, province, 892, 1100
Chalam Te ('flattened tree'), village, 977, 1010
Champoton (chakan putun 'Chontal plain'), city,
   30, 36, 38, 228, 387, 389, 1830; death of, 297;
   destroyed, 48; fulfillment of, 228
Chan Cah, Book of, MANUSCRIPTS
Chan, Lahun. See Lahun Chan
Chan Motul ('small macaw shelter'), person, 2401
Chan Uc ('small Bassaricus'), person, 2395
Chan War, 4943, 4946
Chan Xiu ('little grass'), person, 2386
Chan, Zulim. See Zulim Chan
Chan, Zulun. See Zulim Chan
changers, 558; four, 3055, 3090
Charles V, king of Spain, 250
Che Choc Tz'iitz' ('tree broken hoof'), village, 986
Che Mi Uan ('tree not standing'), village, 916
Che, Pot. See Pot Che
Ch'een Balam ('well of the jaguar'), village, 1055
Ch'een Ch'omac ('well of foxes'), village, 1037
Ch'el, Kauil. See Kauil Ch'el
Ch'el Na, person, 872
Chem Chan ('boat resin'), village, 710
chemistry, SCIENCE
Ch'en ('well'), ninth month, 5299
chest, 4373; weakness, 2853
Chetumal (chac temal 'red steps'), port city, LAN-
   GUAGE, 2436
chewing, 3690
Chi Can ('mouth of snake'), village, 909
Chi Chicaan ('mouth of jicama'), village, 877
Chi Chimila ('mouth of loading water'), village,
   2440
Chi Cocom ('mouth very short'), person, HISTORY
Chi Nab ('mouth swarm'), person, 1579; village,
   2389
Chi Uc ('mouth of Bassarica'), village, 2399
Chiapas, LANGUAGE
chiasmus, POETRY
chicam (Nah. xicamatl, Sp. jícama; Cal-
   opogonium, 'gourdroot'), plant, 3709, 4278,
   4535, 4638
Chicchan ('snake'), day name, MYTH, 2117
Chich, Uayom. See Uayom Ch'ich'
Chichen Itza (chi ch'een itz a 'mouth of the well of
   the water magicians'), city, 199, 274, 1156,
   1221, 1229, 1807, 5229, 5954, 5959, 5975, 6005;
   capital, 1896, 5002; cycle city, 5002; destroyed,
   28, 176, 277, 2364, 2753; seat, 423; tribute,
   1896, 5254
chicken, 4151; in atole, 4255
chief, 738, 1629, 1668, 2313–16, 2641, 3451; head,
   756; town, 2661; tumpline, 4875; word of, 3513
chiefs and justices, 2536
Chikin Ch'een, 5968
Chikin Tz'onot ('west well'), village, 792, 794
Chilam Balam ('Spokesman of the Jaguar'), LAN-
   GUAGE, MANUSCRIPTS
child, 3823–24, 4031–32, 6258; of Fruit Offering,
   5611; of god, 6093; of mat, 6292; of a Thou-

4986; of heaven and earth, 2984, 5056, 5148, 6150; of the Land, 450 (*see also* Ba Cabs); and mother, 3398, 3410; mother of, 2005, 2039; of our souls, 2249; professed, 5776; of rain priests, 724; remote, 2966; as Spanish, 525; of the world, 2595, 4860, 4870

fatherhood of country, 3430

fatherless, 3503; and motherless, 4994

feast, CUISINE, DRAMA, 5336. *See also* examination

feather, 4285–86, 4294; tie, 4676

Feathered Serpent, MYTH

febrero (Sp. 'February'), 5302, 5304

feet, 1988, 2031, 5559, 5570, 6268

fenoplis (Lat. *pleno* 'full', *plus* 'more'), 5708

fever, incense, 5042; groaning, 2849; rash, 5226

fiber, 3624

field, 938

fiery house, 2258, 4414

fifteen, 1386; Zip, 123

fifty-three, 5280

fifty-two, 5278; hundred, 5719

fig tree, 4160

fingers, 4602

finis (Lat. 'end'), 628

fire, 2924, 4244, 4853, 4988, 6412; god, MYTH; great, 116; of hell, 6068; and hurricane, 4950; as noon, 3642; and rope, 3044; *tun* of, 5603

firefly, 4235

firmar (Sp. *afirmar* 'agree'), 5399

firme (Sp. *afirmo* 'I agree'), 5700

first, *Chronicle*, POETRY; food, as squash rind, 3908, 3924; little old lady, as official of lands, 4155, 4164; shamans, 4659

fiscalob (Sp. *fiscal* 'treasurer'), 1670

fish, 5295

fists and shoulders, 3242

five, 1364, 5290; August, 5290; Cauac, 2179; days, 5314; fast days, 5314; Flower (*see* 9 Gods); Lamat, 2129; Men, 2075; relations, 5539; sun priests, 5012; teachings, 5540; years, 6483

Flags, military company, 4803, 4899

flesh, 3070; rending of, 2848

flint, 1435, 1451, 1463, 1479, 6224; colored, 1595; fresh, 1595

flood, second, 3470; seven floods, 2130

flower, 1549, 1856, 1859, 2631, 2864, 4825; eighteen Flowers, DRAMA; food, 2513; goddess, MYTH; heart of, 598, 2861; *katun* (11 Ahau), 5117, 6220, 6310, 6320; lands of Flowers, 3308; lord, 3332; of night, as star, 3843, 3849, 3888; origin of Flowers, 3347; and red, 1702; sacrifice, 3339; as sex, 666; trembling, 6334; as war, 2518, 2523–28

flowering plant, 1554, 1560, 1568

flute, 4452

fly, 4924

fold, covered, as bean burros, 3668, 3676; in half, as henequen, 4514; three folds, 3259, 3262

food, 3337, 3567, 3753, 4061–62, 4342, 4345, 4466, 4818, 5093, 5333–34; and drink, 6246; flower, 2513; of the *katun*, 5246, 6205; sweeten, 4171; time of, 453; unboiled, 6203; and water, 472, 2514, 3220, 3267–70, 6490. *See also* animals; atole; baked green corn; balche; cooking;

drinking blood; drooling; drought and famine; eat and drink; egg; feast; honey; meat; nectar; oven-baked yams; plants; roast meat; sauce; sliced; stuffed cabbage; tamale; tortilla; wine

foot, 2021; of corn, 2804; leader of, DRAMA; sole of, 734

forced labor, 5245

foreigners, 390, 620, 1363, 1604, 1840, 2248, 2316, 2341, 2382, 2417–18, 2671, 2783–84, 2709, 2723–24, 2750, 2810, 2857, 2888, 2898, 2900, 4868, 5182, 5189, 5195; arrival of, 1848, 1852, 2352, 2420, 2733, 5162, 5166; seized, 2383, 2405; without Skirts, 309

forest, burned, 6180

forgiveness, 2544, 2547, 2875

formula (Lat. *adeu*, 'farewell'), 5381

fornication, 3233

fort, 746, 750, 752

founding, of land, 2457; of people, 2458

four, 5293; Akab, 4387; ancestors, 2467; branches, 3359; Burners, 2161; changers, 5506, 5626; changes, 2583; changing winds, 5628; Chicchan, 2163; crossroads, as four changers, 2946, 3252; divisions, 180, 321; eagles, 4066; Etz'nab, 2178; Fathers of the Land, 3094; fourfold house, 5111; four-room house, 6366; fourth moonlit night, 5410; gods, 3093; Ix, 2071; Kan, 120; Leg, 2863; lords, 2167; Manik, 2127; men, 1158; Men, 2165; Oc, 2164, 4425; October, 5293; rain gods, 3305

Four-Part Country, MYTH, TOPONYMY, 180

fourteen, September, 5292; years, 6347

Foxes, military company, 1682, 2614, 4880, 5105, 6479

francés (Sp. 'French'), 6426

Fran^{co}. (Sp. *Francisco* 'Francis'), 367, 2338, 5265

French, 6426

freno (Sp. 'bridle'), 4380

fruit, 3223, 5100

full skirt, 4492

full sky, 5123

g^{a}. (Sp. *gracia* 'grace'), 4579, 4592, 5363, 5371, 5386, 5391, 5405, 5408, 5409, 5413, 5446, 5455, 5560, 5571, 5654

gait, 2528

gallows, 5766

game, CUISINE

garden, 3509

gate, 4925–26; of city, 2949

geography. *See* cave; ceiba; cenote; city, country; direction symbolism; ditch; earth; edge of the sea; forest; geology; hill; land; meadow; meteorology; port; sand; sea; town; village; well

geology, SCIENCE. *See also* flint; gold

gerupite (Sp. *Jupiter* 'Jupiter'), 5788

giant, 5619–22, 5849–55; birth of, 156; sun, 1573

girl, 2805; dark-skinned, as flat squash, 4490; light, 4491

Giver of Love, 2780

gloria (Sp. 'glory'), 6048, 6089, 6090

glory, 6090

glyph, 628, 730, 732, 2233; end of (1752), HISTORY; living, 1976

irony, 4156
irrigation, 2254
Island Flowers. *See* 9 Gods
Israel, 1413
Itza ('water magician'), HISTORY, SCIENCE, 3, 14, 28, 49, 58, 84, 89, 176, 200, 224, 251, 449, 526, 562, 571, 687, 774, 803, 1014, 1222, 1223, 1226, 1344, 1356, 1623, 1861, 1881, 2242, 2293, 2556, 2648, 2899, 2906, 5170, 5176, 5959; base, 2950; of Chichen, HISTORY, LANGUAGE, 274, 424; coming of, 432; destruction of, 273, 2747; 11,200, 2794; end of, 501; great, 2790, 2796; of Peten, HISTORY, LANGUAGE, 210, 284, 1643–44; remainder of, 274, 284; settlement, 424; stupid, 3436, 3441; wandering, 59. *See also* Batun Itza
Itzam ('lizard'), village, 979
Itzam Cab Ain ('magic earth alligator'), alligator god, MYTH, 3150
Itzam Na ('magic house'), lord God, MYTH, 523, 879, 6191
Itzam Pech ('lizard tick'), village, 860, 863
Itzam Tzab ('lizard rattle'), lord God, 6192
ix ('female, small, and'), LANGUAGE, TOPONYMY
Ix ('jaguar'), day name, MYTH, 2072; years, SCIENCE
Ix Bal Che ('little mead'), village, 893
Ix Can ('little snake'), village, 914
Ix Chel ('female magpie'), rainbow goddess, MYTH, 784
Ix Kalem ('brilliant lady'), rainbow goddess, MYTH, 4422
Ix Kani Macal ('little yellow yam'), village, 1063
Ix Kokob ('little rattles'), village, 1053
Ix Mac Ulum ('little covered turkey hen'), village, 961
Ix Meuac ('little standing agave'), village, 910
Ix Mex ('little whisker'), village, 966
Ix Mucuy ('little dove'), village, 1076
Ix Peton Cah ('little round village'), village, 890
Ix P'itah ('little jump'), village, 819
Ix Q'anil (Quiche 'she of the blood'), blood goddess, MYTH
Ix Tab ('she of the rope'), rope goddess, MYTH
Ix Tohil Ch'een ('little straight well'), village, 1033
Ix Ueue ('little old man'), village, 1059, 1060
Ix Yubak ('little mantle vine'), village, 895
Ix Xocen (?'little shark'), village, 967
Ixil ('scales'), *Book of*, MANUSCRIPTS; calendar, SCIENCE; village, 875
Iz, Bel. *See* Bel Iz
Izamal ('lizard burden'), city, 80, 91, 1624, 2304, 4405; destruction of, 265, 2764; seating of, 383

jaam (Lat. *iam* 'already'), 5696
Jaguar, Nacom, person, 2688
jaguar, 688, 700, 1124, 2639, 2653, 2688, 2740, 2941, 4170, 4172, 4174, 5663–64, 6238; as chile, 3591; god, MYTH; green, 3579, 3589, 3592; as horse, 4367, 4368, 4373; priest, DRAMA; prophet, 5052; skin, 1768; of the spring, as agouti, 4170, 4176; tongue, as fire, 4244; wing, as horse's chest, 4341, 4358, 4373
jar, atole, 4127; wine, 4002, 4039
jaramis (Sp. Jeremías 'Jeremiah'), 5549
Jehoshaphat, 3476, 6091

Jeremiah, 5549, 5875
Jerome, 5563
jerusalén (Sp. 'Jerusalem'), 3478
jesuchristo (Sp. 'Jesus Christ'), 3474, 6491
Jesús (Sp. 'Jesus'), 5076
Jesus Christ, 3474, 5076, 5922, 6491; arrival of, 1977
joçi (Sp. José 'Joseph'), 5692
josapat (Sp. 'Jehoshaphat'), 3476
Joseph, 5692
Joshua, 5842
josustin (Sp. Jesús 'Jesus'), 5922
Juan (Sp. 'John'), 1528, 2692, 5178
judge, 4844; bull of, 6298
judgment, 412, 629, 636, 3238, 6299; of god, 645, 4583, 6041; of heaven, 1255; strong, 3515
juesilte (Sp. *juez* 'judge'), 6299
juice and perfume, 1824
juiçio (Sp. *juicio* 'judgment'), 629, 646
Julian calendar, SCIENCE, 4696
julio (Sp. 'July'), 5289
junio (Sp. 'June'), 5212–13; eleventh, 4694
Júpiter (Sp. 'Jupiter'), 5640, 5788
justice, 1693, 4822, 4869, 6302, 6305, 6467
justiçia (Sp. *justicia* 'justice'), 4869, 6302, 6467
justiçiail, 6305
justisia, 1691, 4822
justisiail, 1979

Kab, Bech'. *See* Bech' Kab
Kabah ('branch cane'), town, 2756
kahlay katunob ('account of the *katuns*'), LANGUAGE
Kak Mo ('fire macaw'), fire god, MYTH; person, 268, 384, 1580, 2776
Kak u Pacal ('fire his glance'), person, 298
Kal ('roll'), village, 831
Kan ('yellow'), day name, 2113; years, SCIENCE
Kan A ('yellow water'), village, 889
Kan Cab A ('yellow earth water'), town, 332
Kan Cab Tz'onot ('yellow earth well'), village, 821
Kan Hol A ('yellow waterhole'), village, 783
Kan Hub ('yellow snail'), village, 1077
Kan Tacay ('yellow *Myozetes*'), person, 1431
Kan Tenal ('yellow death'), disease, 1697
Kankin ('yellow sun'), fourteenth month, 5307
katun ('pile of stones'), DRAMA, MYTH, SCIENCE, 5485, 5502, 5551, 5582, 5584, 5586, 5720; aspirations of, 1641; burden of, 2570, 2660, 3280, 3288, 4950, 5338, 6216, 6265; change of, 1235, 3530, 3552; Chuclum Tz'itz', 2442; commemoration of, 993; count of, 2, 12, 251, 294–95, 630, 1415, 1496, 1638, 2431, 2433, 2443, 2630, 2665; curse of, 1283; cycle, 32, 54, 252; divination, 2446; division, 5800, 5957; end of, 1291, 2217, 2560, 2630, 2655, 3744, 3746, 4896, 4914; evil of, 4954; fifth, 5428; first, 5378; Flower, 5117, 6220, 6310, 7320; fold of, 29, 54, 81, 4898; food of, 454, 5246; fruit-offering, 5609; full swollen, 2649; good, 5097; histories, DRAMA, HISTORY, MANUSCRIPTS; hoof, 488; house of, 3541; interpenetrated, 5322; keeper, 1576; lord of, HISTORY, 1594; nature of, 1290, 3266; not seated, 366, 374; roll mat of, 2222;